# INDIA TODAY

## Issues Before the Nation

# INDIA TODAY

## Issues Before the Nation

***A Festschrift in Honour of***
***Prof. (Dr) K. Raman Pillai***

*Editors*

**B. Vivekanandan**
*M.A. Ph.D, D.S.Sc (h.c)*

**R. K. Suresh Kumar**
*M.A. Ph.D*

**and**

**P. Sukumaran Nair**
*M.A. Ph.D*

GYAN

ISBN: 978-81-212-1231-1

Price: ₹ 1150

First Published 2014

*Published by*

Gyan Publishing House
23, Main Ansari Road
Daryaganj, New Delhi-110002
Phones: 23282060, 23261060
Fax: 91-11-23285914
E-mail: books@gyanbooks.com

*Laser Typesetting:* Gyan Publishing House, Delhi
*Printed at:* Chawla Offset Printers, Delhi

**Cataloging in Publication Data--DK**
Courtesy: D.K. Agencies (P) Ltd. <docinfo@dkagencies.com>

**India today :** issues before the nation : a festschrift in honour of Prof. (Dr) K. Raman Pillai / edited by B. Vivekanandan, R.K. Suresh Kumar and P. Sukumaran Nair.

p. cm.

Includes bibliographical references and index.

ISBN 9788121212311

1. India--Politics and government. 2. India--History. I. Pillai, K. Raman (Kesavakurup Raman), 1929- II. Vivekanandan, B. III. Suresh Kumar, 1957- IV. Sukumaran Nair, P., 1955-

DDC 320.954 23

Prof. (Dr) K. Raman Pillai

# Contents

# Acknowledgements

In the publication of this volume, we have accumulated considerable indebtedness.

We are extremely grateful to all distinguished contributors to this volume for their generous cooperation with our schedule to publish this festschrift in honour of Prof. K. Raman Pillai on his 85th birth anniversary by sending their papers to us containing their expert opinion on the themes they have focused on in the volume.

Similarly, we are very grateful to the C. Achutha Menon Foundation for the infrastructural support given to us during the course of preparing this volume. We are also grateful to N. Bindu for the assistance given to us in typing out the manuscript.

And, finally, we are grateful to our publishers, Gyan Publishing House Pvt. Ltd., New Delhi, for Publishing the book in stipulated time in an elegant manner.

**Editors**

# List of Contributors

**Prof. (Dr) P.J. Alexander, IPS,** Former Director General of Police, Kerala State, Former Professor and Director of the Institute of Management in Government, Kerala, Trivandrum.

**Prof. (Dr) Arun Kumar,** Professor and Former Chairman, Centre for Economic Studies and Planning, School of Social Sciences, Jawaharlal Nehru University, New Delhi.

**Prof. (Dr) C.P. Chandrasekhar,** Professor and Former Chairman, Centre for Economic Studies and Planning, School of Social Sciences, Jawaharlal Nehru University, New Delhi.

**Mr. K. Govindan Kutty,** Senior Journalist, Formerly attached to the Indian Express, New Delhi.

**Dr. R. Hali,** Former Director of Agriculture, Kerala State and a Former Special Consultant of the Dr. M.S. Swaminathan Foundation, Chennai.

**Mr. Jacob Punnoose, IPS,** Former Director General of Police, Kerala State.

**Dr. Jayaprakash Narayan,** Formerly in IAS, PUCL Activist, a leading Psephologist and the Founder President, Lok Satta Party in Andhra Pradesh, Hyderabad.

**Prof. (Dr) N.A. Karim,** Former Professor of English and former Pro-Vice Chancellor of the University of Kerala, Trivandrum.

**Prof. (Dr) N.R. Madhava Menon,** Former Director, National Judicial. Academy, Bhopal, Member, Advisory Committee, National Mission on Justice Delivery and Legal Reforms, Government of India, New Delhi.

**Dr. Manendra Kumar Sahu,** Member of the Faculty, Centre for African Studies, University of Bombay, Mumbai.

**Prof. (Dr) R.V.G. Menon,** Former Principal, Government Engineering College, Trivandrum, Former Director, Association of Non-Conventional Energy and Technology (ANERT).

**Mr. C.P. Nair, IAS,** Former Chief Secretary, Government of Kerala, Trivandrum.

**Mr. Justice K. Narayana Kurup,** Former Judge of the Kerala High Court.

**Mr. C.P. Narayanan,** Member of Parliament, Rajya Sabha and Educationist.

**Prof. M.A. Oommen,** Emeritus Professor, Economics, Formerly Professor. of Economics, University College, Trivandrum, Honorary Director, K.M. Mani Centre for Budget Studies, Cochin University, Cochin.

**Prof. (Dr) T.K. Oommen,** Renowned Sociologist, Emeritus Professor, School of Social Sciences, Jawaharlal Nehru University, New Delhi, Former President, International Sociological Association and a recipient of Padma Bhushan.

**Prof. (Dr) R.L.M. Patil,** Former Professor and Head, Department of Political Science, University of Bangalore, Former Vice-Chairman, Karnataka State Higher Education Council, Bangalore.

**Prof. (Dr) J. Prabhash,** Professor of Political Science and Director, School of Social Sciences, Kerala University and former Pro-Vice Chancellor of the Kerala University, Trivandrum.

**Prof. (Dr) V.N. Rajasekharan Pillai,** Former Vice-Chancellor, Indira Gandhi National Open University (IGNOU), New Delhi and Mahatma Gandhi University, Kottayam, Executive Vice-President, Kerala State Council of Science and Technology, Trivandrum.

**Dr. P. Sukumaran Nair,** Former Associate Professor and Head of the Department of Political Science, N.S.S. College, Pandalam, Executive Editor of the Quarterly Journal, Social Science in Perspective, Trivandrum.

**Dr. P. Suresh Kumar,** Head, Research Centre and Post-Graduate Department of Economics, Government College, Attingal, Trivandrum.

**Dr. R.K. Suresh Kumar,** Former Associate Professor and Head, Department of Political Science, University College, Trivandrum, Editor of the Quarterly Journal, Social Science in Perspective, Trivandrum.

**Prof. (Dr) V. Suryanarayan,** Former Director, Centre for South and South-East Asian Studies, University of Madras, Chennai and a former Member of the National Security Advisory Council, Government of India, New Delhi.

**Dr. K.G. Thara,** Director, Disaster Management Centre, Trivandrum, Member State Disaster Management Authority, Trivandrum.

**Dr. Uttam Kumar Sinha,** Fellow, Institute for Defence Studies and Analysis, New Delhi, former Member of the CSCAP – India Study Group on Water Resources Security, Chair of Water Dispute Resolution Mechanism of the Near East and South-East Asia Regional Strategic Network of National Defence University, Washington D.C.

**Prof. (Dr) B. Vivekanandan,** Former Professor and Chairman, Centre for American and West European Studies, School of International Studies, Jawaharlal Nehru University, New Delhi, Recipient of the prestigious Honorary Doctorate, the highest honour, of the University of Helsinki – the first Indian chosen for it in the 350 years history of the University's Award Conferment.

# Academic Profile of Prof. (Dr) K. Raman Pillai

**Academic Qualifications**

B.Sc. Madras University

B.Ed Travancore University

M.A. (Political Science) Kerala University I Class, 2nd rank

Ph.D. Indian School of International Studies, New Delhi

Topic: Attitude of Opposition Parties in India Towards Foreign Policy

**Academic Positions Held**

Graduate Teacher, Dept. of Education, Government of Kerala

Research Fellow, Indian School of International Studies, New Delhi

Research Officer, Nehru Memorial Museum and Library, New Delhi

Senior Lecturer in Political Science, Ramjas College, University of Delhi

Professor and Head, Dept. of Political Science, University of Kerala

Director, Academic Staff College, University of Kerala

U.G.C. Visiting Professor, School of International Relations, Mahatma Gandhi University, Kottayam

**Membership of Academic and Professional Bodies**

Chairman, P.G. Board of Studies in Political Science, University of Kerala

Member, Board of Studies in Social Science, M.G. University, Kottayam

Member, Board of Studies in Political Science, S.V. University, Tirupati

Member, Board of Studies in Political Science, Madurai Kamaraj University, Madurai

Member, U.G.C. Special Assistance Programme, Dept. of Political Science, University of Madras

Member, U.G.C. Expert Committee for University of Mangalore and Alagappa University

Member, U.G.C. Expert Panel in Political Science

Member, NCERT Expert Committee

Member, Senate, University of Kerala and CUSAT
Member, U.G.C. Committee on Human Rights in India
Life Member, Indian Political Science Association (IPSA)
Vice-President, IPSA
Life Member, Indian Institute of Public Administration (IIPA)
National Ex. Committee Member, IIPA, New Delhi, President, IIPA Kerala Regional Branch
Life Member, International Association of World Educators for Peace
Director, Centre for Policy Research, University of Kerala
Convenor, Gandhi Bhavan, University of Kerala
Director, V.K. Krishna Menon Centre for International Relations, University of Kerala
Member, U.G.C. Curriculum Committee in Political Science and International Relations
Life Member, Institute for the study of Developing Areas (ISDA)
Working Chairman, Kerala Election Watch

## Research Work

Research Scholar, Indian School of International Studies, New Delhi
Research Fellow, Indian School of International Studies, New Delhi

Successfully guided 15 Research Scholars for Ph.D and 18 scholars for M.Phil. Completed a U.G.C. Research Project on Coalition Politics in Kerala and another on 'Agricultural Development in Kerala'. Published a large number Research papers in various Research Journals. Editor-in-Chief of various Research Journals such as ISDA, Journal of Political Science, Kerala and Quarterly Research Journal, 'Social Science in Perspective', Member of the Editorial Advisory Board of several Research Journals.

## Publication

Books - 10

1. India's Foreign Policy : Basic Issues and Political Attitudes (Meenakshi Prakashan, Meerut, 1969)
2. Political Triangle: Pakistan, India and Britain (Y.I.P. New Delhi, 1970)
3. Comparative Government and Politics: A Study of the Government and Politics of U.K., U.S.A., USSR and P.R.C. (Datta, Delhi, 1976)
4. Indian Foreign Policy in the 90s (Radiant Publishers, New Delhi, 1995)
5. Kerala Rashtriyathinte Anthardharakal (Mal) ed., State Language Institute (Trivandrum, 2000)
6. Democratic Decentralisation in Kerala - The Role of Gramasabha: A Study (ed.) IIPA Kerala Regional Branch, Trivandrum 2006
7. Facets of Indian Politics, APH Publishing Corporation (New Delhi. 2010)
8. Land Reforms (ed.) APH Publishing Corporation (New Delhi, 2010)

9. Loka Rashtriyam Chila Nerkazhchkal (Mal) State Language Institute, (Thiruvananthapuram - 2011)
10. Electoral Reforms (ed.) Kalpaz (New Delhi, 2012)

## Contribution to compendiums (21)

1. 'The Pith of Kerala History' in Kelappan Smaraka Grandham (Calicut, 1982)
2. 'Totalitarianism in 1984 - A Critique' in George Orwell and 1984 (Trivandrum, 1985)
3. 'Nehru and the Hindu - Muslim Question' in Studies on Nehru, ed., V.T. Patel (Sterling, New Delhi, 1987)
4. 'The Democratic Process in India: Some Refletions', in T.P. Sankarankutty Nair ed., Modern India: Society and Politics in Transition (Inter-India Publications, New Delhi, 1988)
5. 'Three decades of Kerala Politics' in Three decades of Kerala (M) (State Language Institute, Trivandrum, 1988)
6. 'The Star Wars' in Youth for Peace (Trivandrum, 1988)
7. 'Electoral Reforms in India' in K.C. George Memorial Volume (Trivandrum, 1988)
8. 'Tensions within Regional Organisations: A Study of SAARC' in Rama S. Melkote, ed., Regional Organisations - A Third World Perspective (Sterling, New Delhi, 1989)
9. 'Ambedkar and the Constitution Making' in Dr. B. Gopal, ed., Dr. B.R. Ambedkar the Visionary (Sterling Publishers, New Delhi, 1993)
10. 'Coalition Government in Retrospect' in For An Indian Model (Achutha Menon Foundation, Trivandrum, 1993)
11. 'Human Rights in India: An Overview' in T.P.S. Nair, ed., Society and Politics: Issues and Perspectives (Trivandrum, 1998)
12. 'Politics in Post Independent Kerala' in Fifty Years of Independence (P.R.D., Kerala, 1998)
13. 'Society and Politics: Issues and Perspectives' T.P. Sankarankutty Nair, ed., (IIPS Trivandrum, 1998)
14. 'Gandhi's Legacy and New Human Civilisation', B. Mohanan ed., (New Delhi, Gyan Publishing House, 1998)
15. 'Coalition Politics: The Kerala Experience' in M.A. Oommen, ed., Kerala's Development Experience I, ISS (New Delhi, 1999)
16. 'Administration and Politics in Kerala' in T.N. Jayachandran, ed., Keralam 2000 (Mal) (Trivandrum, 2000)
17. 'Sardar K.M. Panicker Remembrance' (Mal) Kerala Language Institute (2000)
18. Engaging with the world: Critical Reflection on India's Foreign Policy, Rajen Harshe, ed., (Orient Longman, 2005)

19. 'K. Damodaran Smrithichitrangal' (Mal) Viswamangalam Sundaresan, ed., Gautha Books, (Trivandrum 2007)
20. Future of Parliamentary Democracy in India, G. Gopakumar, ed., (ICON Publishers, New Delhi, 2007)

## Articles

More than 120 articles in various Indian and Foreign Journals.

## AIR / D.D. Talks/Discussion

Participated in more than thirty talks/discussions on AIR and more than twenty discussions in D.D. and other T.V. channels on contemporary social issues and election analysis.

## Visits Abroad

Visited France under the Cultural Exchange Programme of the Government of India. Visited West Germany, Switzerland, Belgium, Netherlands and United Kingdom.

## Extension Work

As head of the Department of Political Science, he was instrumental in celebrating the silver jubilee of the Dept. with a variety of academic programmes such as extension lectures and seminars on Kerala Politics, State of Political Science, Publication of a journal in Political Science, an exhibition on Kerala Politics, Organisation of two Refresher Programmes for college Teachers and publication of a worthwhile souvenir. Eminent social scientists from India and abroad participated in the lecture series. The exhibition organised by the Department was aclaimed as a window on Kerala Politics by newspapers in Kerala. The extension lectures in connection with the silver jubilee were held in different colleges in Kerala.

Besides teaching and research Dr. Pillai was actively engaged in extension work throughout Kerala. He was a member of Kerala Grandasala Sangham and established two Libraries in his native place. He was secretary, Delhi Malayalee Association and President, Kerala Kalavedi. In these capacities he has organised a number of cultural programmes in Delhi. He had a stint as Director, State Research Centre, and as such got involved in literacy movement and preparation of books for neo-literates. For twelve years, he held the position of President, Indian Institute of Public Administration, Kerala Regional Branch. In that capacity he organised a series of lectures, conferences and seminars across Kerala. He was member of the state level Advisory Committee on People's Planning.

Dr. Pillai has delivered Memorial Lectures in the Universities of Madras, Mysore, S.V. University Tirupati, Madurai and Kakatiya University. Besides he has delivered extension lectures in the Academic staff colleges in the Universities of Madras, Mysore, Bangalore, Mangalore, Aligarh Muslim

University and Jamia Millia, Delhi. He has served as examiner for IAS examination for more than five years.

As a public speaker, Dr. Pillai has delivered a large number of public lectures under the auspices of various academic and cultural organisations such as the State Resource Centre, Center for Inter-disciplinary studies, Centre for Development Studies, Indian Institute of Social Science, Kerala Hindi Prachar Sabha, Kerala Law Academy, Law College, Trivandrum, Russian Cultural Centre, Kamaraj Foundation, Institute of Management in Government, Indian Institute of Public Administration, A.K.G. Study Centre, Charchavedi. He has also addressed seminars organised by political parties such as the Indian National Congress, Communist Party of India (Marxist) Communist Party of India, Bharatiya Janata Party and Socialist Party.

He has organised more than eighty seminars and conferences and actively participated in more than 100 seminars at Regional, National and International levels. Currently he is Secretary, C. Achutha Menon Study Centre and Library, Thiruvananthapuram. In this capacity he has organised a series of memorial lectures, conferences and national seminars on contemporary issues and published as many as ten books on socially relevant themes.

# Introduction

This Festschrift, India Today: Issues Before the Nation, is being published in honour of Prof. (Dr) K. Raman Pillai, doyen of Political Science in Kerala and, presently, the Secretary of the Achutha Menon Foundation, Trivandrum, on the occasion of his 85th birthday. Through his dedication and hard work over the years, Prof. Raman Pillai has distinguished himself as an outstanding, and socially conscious, academic of highest integrity, a social activist, an ideal teacher who has also been a tower of strength for his students who could turn to him any time for solace and succour, an accomplished administrator, an author noted for clarity and precision, a humanist and a superb organiser. Those who met him even once will never forget him.

Though Prof. Raman Pillai took his Ph.D on India's Foreign Policy from the prestigious Indian School of International Studies, New Delhi, and did his post-doctoral research also in the same institution on India's relations with Britain and Pakistan, in subsequent years the spectrum of his academic domain got widened to India's domestic policies, and social and political issues. After his return to Trivandrum as Professor of Political Science, and soon became the Head of the Department of Politics of the Kerala University, his study and research activities got further steeped into socio-political issues of Kerala, and assigned many of his Ph.D students to the task of studying them. He took the initiative to establish the V.K. Krishna Menon Study Centre in the Kerala University, to commemorate the great patriot who led India's freedom struggle in London, the heart of the mighty British Empire. As its Director, he organised many special lectures, national seminars and conferences on International Affairs and India's Foreign and Security policies. In addition, as the Director of the Centre for policy Studies of the Kerala University, he has organised lectures and seminars on public policies and their implementation. Apart from organizing these stimulating academic events in the Kerala University, Prof. Pillai delivered many lectures in other Universities in India and abroad. His research visits abroad included countries like France, Britain, Federal Republic of Germany, Switzerland, Belgium and The Netherlands.

Prof. Raman Pillai is a staunch supporter of value-based politics pursued by men of unimpeachable integrity. He considers that incorruptibility, anchored in simple living and un-ostentatious habits, is imperative for a person in public life. For him, Chelat Achutha Menon epitomised the qualities which he looked for in an honest politician. That admiration led him to assume the responsibility of the Secretaryship of the C. Achutha Menon Foundation in Trivandrum and to devote all his time and energy to make it a more vibrant institution, brimming with a lot of educational activities, and made it a hub of interaction between political leaders, policy makers and the intelligentsia in Trivandrum. A few years ago, the Indira Gandhi National Open University (IGNOU) has made the Foundation's Achutha Menon Study Centre as its study centre in Trivandrum. The grand and spectacular way in which Prof. Raman Pillai has organised an year-long C. Achutha Menon Birth Centenary Celebrations in 2012-13, with a string of special programmes, including lectures, national seminars, photo exhibitions, elocution competitions, literary awards, etc. which pinnacled with the release of a commemorative postal stamp of C. Achutha Menon, bears testimony to his superb abilities. The event received acclaim from everybody.

It is said that behind the success of every man there is a woman. This aphorism is most appropriate in the case of Dr. Pillai. His beloved wife Smt. Subhadramma was an embodiment of love and affection. She had stood by him in thick and thin and gave solid moral support to Dr. Pillai throughout his career as a teacher, researcher and social activist. She was his alter ego and followed him like a shadow. She was a very warm and hospitable hostess to hundreds of Dr. Pillai's friends and students. Most of them still cherish her cordial behaviour, ever smiling face and warm hospitality. Her unexpected demise a decade ago was a rude shock to Dr. Pillai who took several months to recover from that shock. The Pillais are blessed with a daughter Sree Rekha, a Senior Journalist, and a son Rajesh Pillai, an outstanding film maker.

Keeping in view his valuable services to society in various capacities, friends and well-wishers of Prof. Raman Pillai have resolved to honour him with this Festschrift, titled India Today: Issues Before The Nation, on the occasion of his 85th birthday. The objective of the Festschrift is to focus, and stimulate a nation-wide debate, on the major challenges India is faced with, through their dissection by a galaxy of well-known experts, and to explore appropriate remedial measures to steer the country to become a genuine 'People's Home'.

Issues chosen for analyses in this Festschrift are: the Challenge of Reconciling Tradition and Modernity; India's Black Economy; Pampering of Business Houses at the Cost of the Nation; Access to Justice — A Case for Judicial Reforms; Top Heavy Administration; Environmental Issues and People's Concerns; Challenges Before India's Relations With its Neighborus; Revamping Police Administration; the Alchemy of Parasitical Politics; Internal Security; Electoral Reforms; Research and Development Investment in Science and Technology; Misuse of Rajya Sabha; Deepening Democracy Through

Local Governance; The Issue of Water; India's Energy Scenario; Perils of Nuclear Power and Options of Alternative Energy; Erosion of Ethics in the News Media; Commercialisation of Education and Professions; MNCs and FDIs in Indian Market; Food Security and Farmers' Welfare; Death of Discipline, Dignity and Decorum in Elected Bodies; Corruption; Criminalisation of Politics; and A Welfare State Solution. Needless to underline that these are core issues of national concern today which demand effective solutions for taking the country forward.

Eminent experts who have examined these issues, in depth, in this Festschrift are: Prof. T.K. Oommen, Prof. Arun Kumar, Prof. C.P. Chandrasekhar, Prof. V. Suryanarayan, Prof. V.N. Rajasekharan Pillai, Prof. N.R. Madhava Menon, Prof. R.V.G. Menon, Prof. P.J. Alexander, Mr. C.P. Nair, Prof. R.L.M. Patil, Prof. M.A. Oommen, Prof. N.A. Karim, Prof. J. Prabhash, Mr. Jacob Punnoose IPS, Mr. C.P. Narayanan M.P., Mr. K. Govindan Kutty, Mr. J ustice Narayana Kurup, Dr. K.G. Thara, Dr. R. Hali, Dr. Uttam Kumar Sinha, Dr. Manendra Kumar Sahu, Dr. Jayaprakash Narayan, Dr. R.K. Suresh Kumar, Dr. P. Sukumaran Nair, Dr. P. Suresh Kumar and Prof. B. Vivekanandan.

How to reconcile tradition and modernity has been a persistent challenge of contemporary India. In his scholarly article Prof. T.K. Oommen, eminent sociologist, examines the experiment of reconciling tradition and modernity. He begins by stating that tradition is both an asset and a liability. Hence, in the process of transforming a system, there can be selective retention and replacement of its traditional aspects. Based on pragmatic considerations and historical experience, the author evaluates the assets and liabilities of our tradition. He notes that the fundamental values that the Indian polity pursues today are embodied in our constitution, and that these values are embedded in the basic goals of Equality, Secularism and Democracy. How far these goals are accepted by the different sections naturally vary in a parliamentary democracy. In the case of 'equality' the birth pangs of an egalitarian society are constantly felt inspite of the long history of a feudal hierarchical system in vogue in India. This is the case with 'secularism' also if we take tolerance of diversity is a basic value in secularism, even though its institutionalisation remains far from achieved. As far as 'Democracy' is concerned it is yet to be based on universalistic values and a trans-local orientation. The author then proceeds to examine the possibilities of reconciliation of traditional and modern thinking in these areas and suggest that India should aim at a judicious combination of assets both in the traditional and modern values. What that appropriate mix will consist of, will be decided by the historicity of a society, and its present existential conditions.

Prof. Arun Kumar draws our attention to the crucial issue of 'India's Black Economy' through his penetrating analysis of its causes, implications and remedies. We are cautioned that our black economy is roughly estimated to be 50 per cent of GDP - generating, at current prices in 2012-13, about Rs. 50 lakh crore or 1 trillion. Unearthing of more and more big scams indicate the extensiveness of its depth and reach. The people have no choice since nobody seems to be above corruption. The worst implications of this syndrome are the spread of illegality and weakening of democracy, falling literacy rates, and inaccessible health facilities, loss of work ethics, increasing inefficiency, inequality and policy failures. The cause of the growing illegality lies in the political economy of conflict in our society, with the elite making incomes over and above what they can make legally. Electoral reforms, democratisation of political parties and the Right to Information, if provided with the right kind of teeth, can go a long way on tackling the black economy. The author advocates raising direct taxes on wealth and profit in this regard.

The neo-liberal reforms pursued in India from 1991 has ensured that while the economic gains of it went to the business sections, the sufferers were the common people. The state was an active player in this disproportionate sharing, by favouring the business, profit earned through a host of tax concessions. How this was meticulously done by the government, and at what cost, forms the theme of Prof. C.P. Chandrasekhar's brilliant article titled 'Pampering Business Houses at the Cost of the Nation'. A feature of the neo-liberal era in India, as elsewhere in the world, is the role played by the state in redistributing assets and incomes in favour of the small elite, including specially chosen business groups. One way in which this redistribution is done is through disinvestment as in the case of BALCO, IPCL etc. and that too at prices that have been found to be way below the true value of the assets involved. He wants us to understand that corruption tends to be greater in periods when there is a state engineered redistribution of wealth in favour of a few at the explicit expense of the many. The author rightly notes that it reflects an aggravation of the tendency towards primitive accumulation of capital, characteristic of capitalism throughout its history. He also makes it aware of the fact that the transition to a neo-liberal order also debases our electoral democracy by making our elected representatives increasingly corrupt. The author, supported by facts, unbares the neo-liberal project in India as a class project intended to divert wealth to business with the result that the fiscal room needed to combat hunger, create employment, reduce poverty and advance human development, is lost.

Prof. N.R. Madhava Menon, eminent jurist, honestly admits that so long as human beings are imperfect, the Justice they administer will also remain imperfect. Justice delayed is justice denied. The inadequacies of the laws are to be overcome in order to advance the cause of equal justice particularly to the weaker sections of society. He asserts that it is the obligation of every democratic state to ensure that barriers to justice are removed and access improved to ensure equal justice under law, a reality to every section of the citizenry. As most of the existing remedial mechanisms and innovations in effect work to the advantage of the wealthy and mighty, the author with all his practical wisdom on the justice delivery system takes a close look at the challenge of access to justice and builds up a case for judicial reforms. He rightly notes that the bulk of the country's poor are not aware of their legal rights and entitlements. Many of those who are aware do not have the economic capacity or the technical know -how to process their grievances through the formal judicial system. It is in this context that he places hopes on the initiative of the Government of India launching a 'National Mission for Justice Delivery and Legal Reforms' with a view to strengthen access to justice.

The veteran civil servant Mr. C.P. Nair takes a pot shot at the top-heavy administrative structure of the state. To him, the number of 'high level' 'expert' committees that have enquired into, and reported upon, administrative reforms since independence is large, but, far from implementing their well-meaning recommendations even on a selective basis, no serious effort has been made to even make an in-depth appraisal of these proposals. The Government of India today has eighty five Secretaries and eighty seven departments which show a six fold increase from the Nehru days! It is interesting to note that the ever increasing number of bureaucrats, and even the inflated kitty to sustain them, is taking place in the backdrop of the global trend of down-sizing bureaucracy. The 5th Pay Commission had recommended that the number of employees should be reduced by three per cent annually. In the case of Kerala, reducing the number of employees does not form an important agenda in any of the departments. The author observes that the inevitability of reducing the size of the 6 lakh strong privileged class, that gobbles up the vast bulk of the income of government without providing corresponding benefits, becomes all the more important if we consider the crisis-ridden financial landscape of this "debt stressed state". The article examines the strong correlation between the continuing fiscal crisis of government and the exponential growth of the bureaucracy in terms of sheer numbers. Based on his vast experience, he warns that the time has come to comprehensively revamp and redesign the administrative machinery of the state government.

In his scholarly article on 'Challenges before India's Relations with Neighbours' Prof. V. Suryanarayan reminds us that, accustomed as we were to cold war conflict, ideological rhetoric and peculiar mindsets, we fail to understand the meaning and significance of the paradigm shift that has taken place around us. Basing the yardstick for measuring the success of foreign policy on the ability of a leadership to correctly anticipate the turn of events and adjust the country's policy accordingly, the scholar examines the success and failures of India's foreign policy right from the days of Jawaharlal Nehru and the policy of non-alignment. Paying rich tributes to Nehru for having been able to understand the cross currents of history, and fashion the foreign policy accordingly, he observes that we did not have the courage of conviction to explain the nuances of Indian foreign policy cogently and boldly on many issues. We have also not fully grasped the concept of Ocean as a unifying force and focus of regional cooperation. He advocates initiatives from our part in exploiting the northeast connection to strengthen our relations with Southeast Asian Countries. Regarding the Palk Bay issue between India and Sri Lanka, the author wants India to project the vision that Palk Bay constitutes the common heritage of fishermen of both countries and the constitution of a Palk Bay Authority to co-ordinate and implement the policies of the two governments. The article also focuses on the role of federal units in the making of Indian foreign policy and the issue of bringing about harmony on the thinking of the central and state governments with reference to neighbourhood policy. After a brilliant analysis of the rise of a globalised China and its implications for India, he advises that India must step up its diplomacy in Southeast Asia and enter into dialogue with governments and leading think tanks.

Prof. R.V.G. Menon is dismayed at the growing tendency among certain affluent and greedy sections of Kerala society to stamp the environmentalists as enemies of development. They consider activists taking up the issues of destruction of paddy fields, and large scale cutting down of trees, as 'environmental extremists' who carry things too far. This vituperous campaign has provoked the author to have a serious look at the "environmental issues and peoples' concerns". He opines that all the laws enacted so far meant to safeguard the environment are being flagrantly flouted in the name of 'development'. The destruction of environment in the name of 'development' results in an impoverishment of the basic ecosystems on which the poorer sections depend directly for livelihood. It is one of the fallacies of Economics to argue that those who find themselves displaced from one sector, can be easily accommodated in another growing sector because of various human factors. By taking a leaf out of Prof. Wilkinson's book "The Spirit Level: Why Equal Societies Almost Always Do Better", the author cautions us that the rich also need to be concerned with environmental issues as it is "Our Common Future".

Prof. V.N. Rajasekharan Pillai not only addresses the challenges that we face in increasing our investment in science and technology but also comes up with innovative suggestions for a thorough transformation in the performance and outcome of science education and research in India. He reminds us that the relative investment in scientific research and development as a fraction of the Gross Domestic Product has remained stagnant in India for the last five successive five year plans even though we could have invested much more in Science and Technology in the last one and a half decades of rapid economic growth. Looking into the resource needs for a strong Research and Development system he argues for substantial public and private investments. Presenting facts and figures he draws our attention to the fact that almost 80 per cent of the Research and Development expenditure in India comes from the public sector. It is necessary that the public and private industries need to be incentivised to invest atleast two per cent of their sales turnover in research and development. While demanding an enhancement from 0.9 per cent to two per cent of the GDP for science and technology, it is also necessary to ensure quality and out-come based allocation, distribution and utilisation of funds.

The abdication by the state in India of its responsibility to ensure Rule of Law through Police reforms is unfortunate and hence condemnable. Naturally, the academic brilliance, practical experience and wisdom as a top police functionary has motivated the scholar in Prof. P.J. Alexander to examine this urgent issue under the rubric "Revamping Police Administration: All Eyes on the Apex Court". Inspite of public outcry on police ineptitude in the past and present, the response from the state is disheartening. The author reminds us that with 'police and law and order' in the State list, the Centre could go their way and States their own route on 'police reforms'. This has sealed all the attempts at reviving interest in the recommendations by different Commissions for police reforms. The author rightly observes that as of now "all eyes are not on the Committee of Ministers attempting to design a system to insulate the country's premier investigating agency from being interfered with, but on the Apex Court. His first-hand knowledge of the totality of the issue enables him to conclude that it would not be easy to bring about the required transformation easily. It requires careful planning and introduction of structural changes and infusion of ethical and legal concerns that govern our society. The objective should be to transform the police in to a service providing force and made accountable to the law, and not to the political executive. As an unfinished national agenda 'police reforms' have to be treated as a national priority.

It is well known that wise men speak because they have something wise to say, and not because they have to say something. In a situation in which India is facing all kinds of threats to its internal security Mr. Jacob Punnoose, former police chief of Kerala, notes with conviction that the paradox of India has been its unitary multiplicity, which provides us with strength as well as sorrows. It is the manipulation of our diversity that results in discords, conflicts, militancy, insurgency and terrorism. Inspite of more than six decades of impressive performance of our democratic system of governance, sacrifices of police force, military and of the civil service, the country is still facing threat to its internal security, which arise from insurgency, militancy, terrorism, organised crime, and external forces. If we are not to succumb to such acts, we should root our strategies on past experiences and take into account the special features of the existing insurgencies and the global security scenario. The author displays thorough knowledge of the concerns of internal security in major problem areas. Through his comprehensive approach to the problem he reminds us sharply that inaccessibility and remoteness are by themselves reason for insurgency when it combines with relative sense of deprivation and under development. The police force engaged in addressing the internal security concerns of the nation should view security in the democratic context, keeping in mind the human rights perspective.

Prof. J. Prabhash, in his article titled 'The Alchemy of Parasitical Politics', reiterates that political parties are the ones who can make or unmake the country. Applying his analytical skills he notes that they have to act as conveyor belts between the state and society so much so that social issues get political attention they deserve, and eventually even get settled in a democratic manner. The political parties today suffer from a chronic deficit of popular trust. According to the author, any analysis on this has to begin with the metamorphosis in the nature of the Indian National Congress, from a loose coalition of social groups to one which has lost its federal — coalitional character, mass appeal and openness, and became dynastic and leader centric. The opportunities provided by this metamorphosis has resulted in the degeneration of politics and erosion of democratic values and institutions. This degeneration is to be addressed, through the strengthening of democratic inputs into the political process while restoring a sense of collective good and shared future and a strong political leadership that is capable of assimilation and corrective measures.

Dr. Jayaprakash Narayan in his paper addresses the pressing issue of the urgency of electoral reforms for democratic revival in India. While admitting that the record of the post-colonial India as a country having a stable democratic regime is commendable, one need to also look at the distortions and growing crisis of democracy which undermine our accomplishments. The distortions relates to the use money power in elections and reckless distribution of freebies instead of providing quality education, health care, skilled jobs and incomes, the criminalisation of politics, the exploitation of primordial loyalties and the dwindling support base of national parties. The author examines the concerted attempts over the years to bring in democratic reforms and the role of civil society groups and the judiciary in this. To him these reform initiatives indicate that our political and governance system is alive to the challenges and capable of addressing them. But these responses are insufficient to address the structural problems deepening the political crisis like the asymmetry of power between the ordinary man and the powerful bureaucrat, the humiliating submission to the ruling class and the party bureaucracy and the centralisation of power. The existing system of election in the country, i.e., the first-past the post system, further worsened matters. It is in this context that the author wants us to have a look at the alternative methods of election focusing on the proportional system of representation. The author feels that a few sensible changes, with adequate safeguards and checks and balance, will do wonders for Indian democracy to stabilise.

Prof. N.A. Karim finds a steady decline in the conduct of India's elected democratic bodies, from Parliament to Panchayats. He opines that all these undesirable trends set in with the neo-liberal market centred economy and development mode. The fiber of morality of the nation is all gone with a new generation of rich middle class, who know the price of everything, and value of nothing. It is this change that is reflected in the working of our democratic institutions including elected bodies from parliament to gram sabhas. The author is critical of the government efforts at thwarting the demand of opposition parties to discuss government misdeeds, as it invariably leads to confrontations and disruption of the House. The people can expect only unruly behavior in the legislatures, as the representatives have come to the House through the present process of elections, vitiated right from the beginning with influence of money, and caste-religious interests. In this context he argues for radical electoral reforms.

The well-known economist Prof. M.A. Oommen holds the view that the recent experiences like the pioneering initiative of India's decentralised democracy, Brazil's participatory budgeting and South Africa's developmental local government hold great lessons in building a responsive and participatory local governance system in India, in future. His paper builds up a conceptual framework for deepening democracy. The UNDP's Human Development Report, 2002, after evaluating human development in various countries, observed that "if global progress continues at such a snail pace, it will take more than 130 years to rid the world of poverty". If we want to deepen and widen democracy to remove poverty, the working of representative democracy should be reformed. The author convincingly argues that local democracy, as a policy variable, has not received the attention that it deserves in the Report. To him, the building up of a public sphere, direct participation of citizens, and working towards an inclusive society, are all fundamental democratic values which are missing in the conventional type of representative democracy. Hence, the scholar asserts that deepening democracy cannot be conceptualised without reference to those foundational values. Decentralisation does not mean delegation or de-concentration, but larger devolution of powers, responsibilities and authority to the lower tiers of government. It is the empowerment of the people through the empowerment of local governments. Local governance is thus inclusive, participatory and widens the public sphere and centers around the theme of improving the quality of citizen well-being in an environmentally sustainable manner. Comparing the progress of local governance in different countries, the scholar feels that the real task ahead for India is to hasten and deepen the process of democratic decentralisation and participatory democracy.

Prof. R.L.M. Patil shares with us information about the sketchy tale of the appearance of Rajya Sabha in our polity right from the British days. He does not see any glory in its functioning for the last many decades in terms of its expected role of holding dispassionate, non-partisan, learned and dignified discussions on issues of public concern. Further, the Council of States cannot also be considered as the true representative of the state units. It is also seen at present that it is not the seasoned people who become members of the Rajya

Sabha. In this regard the scholar points to the tendency at present to purchase the seats in the upper house of parliament by moneyed interests. As the constitution makers failed to spend enough time and wisdom regarding the position of Rajya Sabha during the debates in the Constituent Assembly it was natural that the House lost sight of its original purpose. The article echoes the view that the Council of States should be reoriented.

Dr. Uttam Kumar Sinha in his paper titled 'Water Issues in India: External and Internal Dynamics' explains that as global economic activity and development continues there will be increasing demand for water, which will be compounded by the decreasing availability of water resources in most major hydraulic basins because of deterioration either in quality or in quantity. Naturally, competition for ground water would become an additional factor of social and political instability, both internally and regionally. This prospect makes water a challenging issue in future. Looking at the internal dynamics of this challenge, he notes that the propellers of future water challenge would essentially be tied to development and economic growth, with the agriculture sector as the largest user of water. According to him, there is a growing need to synchronise internal water management measures with external riparian policies. The external dynamics of this issue assumes importance since most of the rivers are trans-boundary in nature, which makes riparian relations critical. He notes that this is of particular importance to South Asian countries. He wants climate change also to be taken in to account while framing a proper water policy. The risks and uncertainties over the impact of climate change on water resources are potentially high in many South Asian countries, and from a hydrological perspective China cannot be ignored from the South Asian regional configuration because of its upper riparian hydrological position. Hence it becomes fundamentally important to counter China's 'hydro aggression', with the lower riparian 'hydro-solidarity'. While the author agrees that the states need to reorient their riparian policies on a multilateral basis, a shift from merely 'sharing of waters' to 'sharing benefits' is also necessary.

Dr. K.G. Thara in her article takes a look at India's energy sector and traces the country's potential and efforts at developing alternative energy. The author notes with concern that, for propelling its development objectives, India's primary energy supply should increase at the rate of 5.8 per cent per annum. It is observed that the recent events in Japan have shown that while the likelihood of a nuclear power plant accident is low, its potential consequences are grave. Another disadvantage of nuclear energy is that it has a high cost and capital intensive nature. It also takes a long time to commission the project, and is acknowledged as highly polluting. The author has drawn attention to the fact that coal, nuclear and natural gas power plants use more fresh water than any other economic sector. India has to actively promote technologies that maximise energy efficiency, tone up demand side management and enforce effective energy standards. Along with this, a decentralised model of energy system, based on renewable energy, which provides for energy access to all is necessary.

An indepth analysis of energy crisis in India and the various options to overcome it forms the theme of Manendra Kumar Sahu's article. He argues for the adoption of a decentralised model to meet our energy needs. He cautions us that India's current account deficit has reached a record high of 6-7 per cent of GDP primarily because of surging energy imports. This is going to worsen unless there is dedicated effort to utilise more and more domestic resources. The early incorporation of local resources and decentralised energy would provide better energy security than imported energy. The author also dwells on a host of other benefits that the decentralised model of energy generation can provide.

By recalling C.P. Scott's view on journalistic ethics that "facts are sacred, comment is free", Mr. K. Govindan Kutty, veteran journalist, examines how far the present journalistic practices affect ethics of journalism. He gives various illustrations of the breaking of the basic norms of ethics by the fourth estate. To him ethics of journalism is broken by ordinary reporters and editors. It is the very casualness of the violation which makes it ever more sinister. Commenting on the plurality of truth, the author states that what comes a journalist's will necessarily be a fragmented fact. Journalists are only channels, not sources and they will be true only to the extent to which their sources are true. When ones' own version becomes incorrigible, leaving no scope for amendment, fascism sets in, resulting in the negation of ethics. But the problem, as the author sees it, is the difficulty in determining the ethicality of an act. But the solace is that one reporter, or editor, or a team of them, will not be able to sell a lie, with success, on a regular basis. Though he asserts that the breach of ethics, including sale of lies and reckless probe into privacies, happens as a matter of professional incompetence or gullibility, he concedes that it may also be because of professional conceit as journalism revolves around power. The article also discusses unethical practices like 'paid news', 'praise as news', and the precarious proportion between news and ads in today's news papers.

It is not just the governors ruling the country who have made education inaccessible to poor sections by championing the case of neo-liberalism but also the judiciary through its verdicts. Mr. C.P. Narayanan, educationist and Member of Parliament, in his article on 'Commercialisation of Education and Professions' rolls up his sleeves to expose the tall claims, of neo-liberalisation in the field of education. It is the absence of critical thinking and people's participation which helped private interests to gain control over education. The current perspective of education is one which passes the onus of educating people from the society to each individual or his family. The basic fact about education, at all levels, in India is that there exists a chasm between the few who can afford it, and the majority who cannot afford it. In India today the initiative to universalise education has been transformed into a big enterprise worth hundreds of billions of dollars. Naturally, we see overseas education entrepreneurs making a bee-line to India to reap huge profit.

Dr. R.K. Suresh Kumar emphasises the fact that criminalisation of politics cannot be singled out for a debate independently of the ongoing discourse on the quality of democracy. Every type of representative government in due course creates oppressive political, social and economic systems that damage people living under it. Criminalisation of politics is unfortunate but often a necessary means to secure political ends in India. In India of today, politics has become coterminous with crime and unlawful activity in general. The last few decades have seen the emergences of "corporate led growth" in India. The state power is misused to illegally allocate natural resources like land, minerals, water and airways to private players. Such a context offers enough space for criminalisation of our political system. The parliament finds itself disabled on the discharge of its essential functions as criminals enter the legislatures. Thus criminalisation of politics creates an inhospitable climate for democracy to sustain. The author observes that Indian democracy is yet to comprehend the dynamics of a democratic polity based on universal adult suffrage.

Applying his analytical skills Dr. P. Suresh Kumar addresses India's major concern for economic development, under the caption 'A Bull in the China Shop: MNCs and FDIs in the Indian Market'. The article asserts that the traditional economic theorisation that more inflow of capital will fill the resource gap, and lead to higher growth and welfare of the people, remains as an illusion in the Indian context. The argument that it fills the current account deficit, enabling the economy to sustain its economic development, also remains as a questionable proposition. Our experiences shows that the inflow of foreign capital need not lead to the structural transformation of the economy benefiting our farmers, petty producers, unorganised workers and the common man. We cannot expect wonders from FDI inflows as it invariably succumbs to monopoly practices. He points out that the capital inflow in different forms, like Special Economic Zones, setting up of MNCs and other forms have not produced the desired results. Against this backdrop, the author feels that what we require is an indigenous model of development, based on democracy, decentralisation and humanism. The FDI should only be allowed within these parameters.

Dr. P. Sukumaran Nair in his article titled 'Mounting Corruption and Political Indecisiveness' observes with serious concern that 'corruption in a civilised society is like cancer, which if not detected in time is sure to malign our polity leading to disastrous consequences'. The author discusses the nature, history, depth and reach of corruption in India in an empirical manner. Though the issue of corruption is an all pervasive one, he specifically gives attention to legislator's and corruption, judicial system and corruption, and corruption in police force. An examination of the important scams and scandals in the country has convinced him that the existing legal frame work and institutional devices to check corruption is not strong enough to restrain corruption. Our pathetic apathy has led to the phenomenal growth of corruption, which is mainly due to lack of political will, institutional failures, incapability of political parties, the unholy nexus between politician, civil servant and criminals and poll related malpractices. In order to restrain corruption; bridling the politico-bureaucratic nexus, modification of obsolete laws, revamping of institutional frame work, election of honest legislators and electoral reforms are essential. Curbing black money and reforming the police force is important. Positive intervention by the media and civil society initiatives can go a long way in making our criminal justice system effective. It is true that corruption cannot be eradicated as it is deeply immersed in the political system. It will be well and good if all concerned remember that 'war against corruption is the mother of all the wars'. What is needed is a change in the mindset of the society.

It is not enough that we bat against corruption which has become rampant in every walk of life but also to avoid the rot, out of our own hearts and minds. Justice Narayana Kurup brings to focus the chasm between our desire to eliminate this malady and the prevailing reality of our times. Corruption knows no geographical boundary, nor does it know any institutional boundary. The root cause of it is lust for money and greed. Corruption is resorted to by political parties and politicians in almost every country of the world. Though nations have adopted crafty devices to prevent corruption none of these has been successful. Commenting on the Indian scenario the author finds a growing tendency on the part of the government to spend time catching the financial sprats, while the big sharks swim freely on the ocean. He notes that the country is yet to enact a legislation that empowers confiscation of properties of public servants adjudged guilty of corruption. The article cautions us that judicial corruption damages not only the image of the individual judge involved, but the institution of the judiciary as a whole, because honour is indivisible. Our experience so far has shown that inspite of the existence of the Prevention of Corruption Act; the executive institutions in this regard have defeated the very purpose of the Act itself.

The article examining India's efforts to ensure food security in future brings out the visionary and realist in Dr. R. Hali. His narration of the achievements and potential of India as a global 'green power', to be reckoned with by other nations, is based on genuine facts and his vast experience in this field. He gives full credit for this to the farmers of the country. He warns us that assuring food to over hundred and twenty crore of people, without fail, needs a lot of preparation. But the agricultural sector faces many serious challenges due to changing crop patterns and life style. The author wants us to realise the truth that farming is not providing enough profit to the farmers to meet their needs. In order to enable the farmer to produce more, their life should be made secure with the participation of the entire community. He feels that it is high time we realise that farmer's welfare and food security are the two sides of the same coin.

Prof. B. Vivekanandan builds up a strong case for a welfare state remedy in societies plagued by hunger, violence and mal-governance. There is no doubt that the future of mankind lies in the welfare state system based on human solidarity as it has got a consistent track record of providing a life with dignity, and free from fear and want. According to the author, the welfare state system promotes basic honesty and truthful behavior in humans, and is an effective antidote to corruption, greed, illegal acquisitiveness etc., which constitute the springs of many foul thoughts and behavior in our polity and society. He sounds practical when he writes that the funds required for undertaking the responsibility of providing employment, social security, health care, education, housing, pension and so on could be raised through universal taxation. The creation of a mentality of concern for the fellow beings is a higher form of social engineering, aiming at the creation of a more civilised, a more compassionate society. The author systematically traces the ideological foundation of the welfare state system and states that the present construct of a welfare state system is a social democratic or democratic socialist construct of the 20th century, which pre-supposes the existence of a strong, democratic and benign central state. The experience of Sweden as a model welfare state is examined by the author, based on empirical knowledge, as is the case with the leap in the social budgets of the Scandinavian countries. The author then critically examines where does India's political will stand on the agenda of the country's transformation into a welfare state? The only way ahead for India is to make the construction of a welfare state system the national vision. The author is sure of its success even in a big democracy like India.

**Editors**

# 1

# *Reconciling Tradition and Modernity: The Persisting Challenge of Contemporary India*

*T.K. Oommen*

Conventional conceptualisation envisioned many traditions but one modernity; western modernity. But gradually the idea of singular modernity came to be interrogated and the notion of multiple modernities gained acceptance. Further, western modernity itself came to be recognised as being multi-dimensional seen in terms of structural differentiation (Emile Durkheim), onward march of rationality (Max Weber), the project of making history (Karl Marx) and compression of time and space (Georg Simmed), to refer only to four classical social scientists. Gradually the idea of modernity as a spatial phenomenon anchored to one or another geographical space (West, North etc.) spreading to the rest of the world was also abandoned and modernity became a temporal one. Thus conceived particular civilisations, societies and polities which can and do move from their specific traditions to particular modernities. One can then speak of not only German and Japanese but also Iranian and Indian modernities. Keeping these considerations in mind I intend to discuss the experiment of reconciling tradition and modernity in India.

## I

Tradition is both an asset and a liability. To a large extent the success of a modernising society depends on its ability to convert the assets in its tradition to contemporary advantages and to reject the liabilities which are obstacles in its social transformation. My position assumes that notwithstanding the interdependence of system components, the constituting elements have some degree of autonomy. In all social systems some aspects are relatively more autonomous while others have a greater amount of reciprocal involvement vis-a-vis other system components. This means that in the process of transforming a system we can pursue the path of selective retention and replacement of its traditional aspects.

Why not destroy the past and create a New Social Order in tune with the aspirations of the people and the spirit of the contemporary era? My preference for a selective retention approach is dictated by pragmatic considerations and historical experience rather than ideological presuppositions or national chauvinism. All systems are responsive to stimuli, although the degree and intensity of this response would vary depending upon the character of their antecedent, institutional framework and historicity. To this extent their past is gradually but surely to be replaced. But at the same time all systems tend to preserve some aspects of their past and even in those societies where revolutions have taken place, persistence of certain aspects of their past structures continues. If this is the reality, why not accept it and evolve one's strategy of change accordingly? But there is a significant difference here. Instead of fatalistically accepting the 'natural tendencies' in the system, we must opt for a conscious intervention in changing the system and hence the plea for selective retention and replacement.

In evaluating the assets and liabilities of Indian traditions we face certain specific problems and the requisite clarifications are required. India's is an ancient civilisation with a deep historicity. It is difficult to demarcate India's hoary past into clear-cut time boundaries. Besides, the Indian diversity is so stupendous that to speak in singular about this polity is extremely hazardous. This is true not only in terms of the difference in folk and elite conceptions of Man and Society, but also in terms of the variations in its little (micro) and great (macro) traditions. Yet one can conceive of a certain unity amidst this multiplicity and, when we speak of India's tradition, we refer to this unity. While India is an 'Old Society', it is also a 'New Nation', to recall the familiar cliché.

When did modernity have had its beginnings in India? Broadly speaking India's modernisation started in the 18th century. India's contacts with the West, particularly with the British colonial rule accelerated the process of modernisation in certain dimensions. However, the Indian polity as we know it today emerged only in 1947. The blue print of the society towards which India strives to become is embodied in its Constitution. Therefore, when I refer to modern India the frame of its reference is independent India.

To start with I propose to analyse the basic features of India's tradition and modernity. In undertaking this exercise we shall differentiate between the ideological and empirical components of the system. This is necessary because in all societies at all times there exists a gap between 'what ought to be' and 'what is', between theory and practice. This gap is not always and necessarily indicative of human fads and foibles alone but of the imperfections of the goal itself or the impossibility of adequately translating ideologies into praxis. Thus I recognise not only a 'praxis-lag' but also a 'theory-gap' in our attempt at an objective evaluation of any situation.

The traditional society in India was organised based on several principles but the three cardinal ones were hierarchy, diversity and holism. Hierarchy implies the ordering of the units which constitute a system in relation to the whole in a superior-inferior gradation. Hierarchy manifested itself not only in the system of caste and sub-caste (*jati*) stratification based on the notions of ritual purity and pollution acquired by birth, but also in the Hindu concept of life cycles and age-grades (*ashrams*) and moral duties (*dharma*). Marrying within one's own caste (*jati*) was superior both to hypergamy, that is the practice of a male seeking his spouse from a lower caste, and hypogamy that of a female marrying into a lower caste. Of the triple objectives of marriage, religious duty (*dharma*) had precedence over securing progeny (*praja*) or sexual pleasure (*rati*). The one who renounced the world (*sanyasin*) was morally superior to the one who still remained mundane. According to the Hindu Doctrine of Creation the Brahman who emerged from the mouth of the Creator occupied an admittedly exalted position as compared with the *Shudra*, who emerged from the feet of God. Thus the notion of hierarchy was omnipresent and all powerful in regulating human conduct in every minute aspect of life. While the ideology of hierarchy institutionalized inequality in every conceivable aspect of human life, it allocated a secure and definite place to each individual and caste group. The valuation of individuals and groups and the allocation of societal resources were based on status and the status was inscriptive, even though birth into a group was believed to be based on moral merit, gathered during the previous birth, as implied in the theory of *Karma* and Reincarnation.

Endorsing diversity implied tolerance of other styles of life while preserving one's own. Hinduism, the dominant religion of India, was essentially tolerant and instead of abruptly converting, it gradually assimilated other faiths. In fact conversion to Hinduism was almost impossible as the contingency of placing the convert in the hierarchical order could not be easily solved. Hindus believed in the existence of multiple paths leading to the same ultimate goal. Thus the faiths of the Muslim conquerors, Christian colonizers, Parsi merchants and traders, etc., not only survived but prospered for centuries in India. The differences at the level of doctrines and rituals notwithstanding, the followers of different religions lived in harmony in India till the 'modern' democratic politics made it necessary for each group to compete and vie with one another to maximise the benefit made available through state patronage.

The caste system provided an institutional basis for reinforcing the diversity of traditions in Hinduism. Each caste had its own occupation, customs, rituals, traditions, and government (caste *panchayat*). While each caste was insulated on the one hand, it was also interdependent on several other castes. Autonomy co-existed with dependence and this led to an appreciation and recognition of other's distinctiveness. Apart from this, given the linguistic diversities and cultural differences, castes operated essentially as regional entities. This resulted in a localistic orientation of castes; castes with the same name differed sometime substantially in their customs and traditions between different localities, particularly linguistic regions. This means that diversity had not only a vertical dimension but also a horizontal one. And, co-existence of culturally diverse groups became a norm. However, co-existence was not always harmonious, particularly in its political context. Some groups dominated over others and a superior-inferior relation was implied in so far as the inferior groups accepted the domination of superior groups without overt protest, which they often did due to the unequal distribution of material resources. Thus the hierarchical principle was implicit here too, reinforcing the organic link between diversity and inequality.

Holism assumed a relationship between individual and group in which the latter had primacy over the former; the individual was expected to perform his/her duties and claim his/her rights always keeping in mind the wider interests of the community. The individual subservience to traditional collectivity was manifested in a multiplicity of contexts, be it joint family collectivism, village panchayat or caste council. The families were often joint in a sense that they consisted of a large number of kin, including dependents—the aged, widowed, physically handicapped etc. Although each contributed according to one's ability, one was expected to draw from the familial pool of wealth only according to one's need. Similarly the destitute and dependents of village community were the responsibility of the rich: the latter often operated as trustees of community wealth rather than as private profiteers. This called for self-restraint of one's wants in the interests of fellow humans, the community-at-large. However, in so far as the individual was subservient to the community it implied a hierarchical relationship. Thus, in the final analysis, the hierarchical principle was all-embracing; it encompassed the phenomena of diversity and holism.

Notwithstanding the ideological prescriptions, practical aberrations were not uncommon. Thus hierarchy was clear and sharp only at the polar points of the caste system, the disputes over caste rank being almost always endemic in the middle region often facilitating mobility despite the rigid institutional framework. Further the indeterminacy over rank arose contextually, the king assuming superiority over the priest in secular matters and the priest claiming over-arching importance of the sacred over secular, thereby affirming his over-all superior status. Additionally, the problem of allocating status to the groups— Tribals, Muslims, Christians, etc. — either assimilated into the Hindu fold or obtaining outside of it was also problematic as each person or group has to be placed in relation to others in a caste society. Similarly, diversity, while it implied tolerance, had not infrequently led to bigotry and domination, creating hostility between groups. Finally, holism, while it implied collectivistic orientation, did not always impart the requisite altruism to sustain it. Individuals often felt the weight of the heavy yoke to which they were tied by group control, inhibiting their initiative, often leading to considerable tension in interpersonal and individual-group relations. All this is indicative of the dissensus that existed between theory and practice, prescription and performance, in the traditional Indian society.

## II

The fundamental values that the Indian polity pursues today are embodied in its Constitution. These values are embedded in the basic goals of Equality,

Secularism and Democracy. It is wrong to assume that everybody holds these values equally dear! Some think that equality should be the most important goal to be pursued with immediacy, for, the realisation of other goals is contingent upon the establishment of an egalitarian society. Similarly, there are others who bestow primacy on the values embodied in a democracy and argue that the pursuit of other goals in a manner endangering it, is worthless. That is to say, notwithstanding the over-all consensus about the basic values, disagreements exist over their importance or the mode and sequence of their realisation. Perhaps such a situation is unavoidable in a country where a multi-party system exists under a parliamentary democracy. We ignore this dissensus while pursuing the present analysis. Yet another clarification ought to be made here. None of the goals are completely achieved as yet and may be they will not be achieved in the near future and performance in relation to each varies substantially.

While recognising the concentration of economic resources in the upper layer, the Indian constitution did not attempt collectivisation of private property but only sought to limit it; the legitimacy of private property as an institution is not fundamentally questioned, only its cautious restriction is aimed at. Viewed against the background of the radical ideologies of socialist regimes which existed when India became politically independent this perspective is certainly less than radical but it is certainly progressive when it is matched against the backdrop of the pre-existing system of property relations. The Indian social system with its all-pervasive institutionalised inequality, allocated roles and resources and distributed rewards on the basis of caste status which in turn was based on birth. The recognition of the need for providing an opportunity structure which facilitated citizens to acquire material resources and move up in the social ladder ignoring their past background was radical only if viewed in terms of the antecedent social structure of India. Equality enunciated in the Indian Constitution is based on the principle of allocation of material resource and occupational roles, based on merit. In so far as the erstwhile social system was characterized by extreme inequalities and in so far as a sudden break from the past did not take place, considerable continuity is in evidence. In effect then, those who have "merit" today are also the ones who have had material resources and higher caste ranking in the past. The net result has been the gradual development of a society which recognises merit as the basis of distribution of resource and allocation of roles as against an egalitarian society which insists on need as the basis of distributive justice. While the shift from a feudal hierarchical system based on status to a capitalistic system hinged on merit it is not yet complete, the birth pangs of an egalitarian society are constantly felt and the process seems to be long-drawn and difficult.

Secularism in the Indian context meant in practice, tolerance for other communities—particularly religious communities. The import of introducing secularism as a value in the Indian Constitution should be seen against the backdrop of the circumstances which led to the split of the Indian sub-continent. India has a multi-religious polity in terms of its ideology and existential realities, but its birth was co-terminus with that of a Muslim polity—Pakistan, occasioned by animosity between Hindus and Muslims. India remains even to this day the second biggest Muslim country in the world with a population of 135 million Muslims. Such a situation called for the explicit recognition of the distinctiveness of other religious groups and hence the importance of secularism as a value. Secularism meant not only non-interference in the affairs of other communities but also developing a positive appreciation for their distinct style of life. After independence, the need for recognising cultural autonomy in the regional-linguistic context became compelling. The official recognition of the cultural autonomy of regional linguistic entities became explicit in the late fifties when the Indian states were re-organised on the basis of language (culture). This may be interpreted as another aspect of Indian secularism, if tolerance of diversity were the basic value in secularism. Notwithstanding the fact that secularism is fundamental to Independent India its institutionalisation is far from achieved, communal riots and linguistic squabbles are not infrequent. Most countries have one official language; India has twenty two. Similarly India does not have an official religion although 82 per cent of India's population profess Hinduism.

While Indian democracy shares its form with other democratic polities and emphasises equality of opportunity, its substance is certainly different. Democracy assumes the existence of autonomous and independent individuals capable of participation in the decision-making process. In the traditional social system of India the individual as an autonomous entity making decisions for himself/herself was non-existent. The Indian tradition did not in fact admit of the concept of individual and the Indian individual emerged only when he renounced the world by assuming the role of Sanyasin or family ascetic. This all pervasive holism was not conducive to the functioning of democracy which pre-supposed the existence of autonomous individuals. This is the reason why Indian democracy is anchored in primordial loyalty structures such as religion, caste, linguistic groups, etc., wherein ideological polarisation is nebulous and frequently mediated by traditional values and rigid institutional structures. The democratic citizen in so far as she/he wants to combine the values of equality and secularism should develop a civil collectivistic orientation. At the same time the collectivistic orientation should be qualitatively different from the traditional primordial linkages; it should be based on universalistic values and should have a trans-local orientation. One of the basic challenges in reconciling the traditional and modern values lies precisely here.

Having discussed the fundamental value-themes of traditional and modern India, I propose to examine the possibilities of their being reconciled. First, the possibility of reconciling these value-pairs and second, unfolding their internal consistency so as to understand the possibility of bringing about consensus not only between tradition and modernity but also within each of the value-packages.

It is clear (see Chart I) that there is no basic contradiction between the traditional value of diversity and the modern value of secularism since tolerance of others' style of life is basic to both. However, diversity of the past was associated with distinct ascriptive privileges of each of the groups which often provided legitimacy for inequality. This in turn rendered those with disproportionate share of privileges the dominating elite, leading to the co-existence of diversity and inequality. But secularism as it is understood in the Indian Constitution provides for equal respect for all and hence calls upon the advantaged groups to change consciously their behaviour in such a way so as not to handicap the less privileged groups. This is the critical difference between the traditional and modern values rending secularism in effect pluralism. Diversity is a fact but pluralism is a value-orientation to that fact accepting the dignified co-existence of the diverse element in the polity.

**Chart 1**

| *Traditional Values* | *Modern Values* | *Pre-requisites for Realisation* |
|---|---|---|
| I (a) Diversity | (b) Secularism (Pluralism) style of life | Tolerance and respect for others' |
| II (a) Hierarchy | (b) Equality of | Status based allocation of roles and resources for II(a) but need based allocation of resources and merit based allocation of roles for II(b) |
| III (a) Holism | (b) Individualism | Renunciation of self-interest for III(a) and assertion of self-interests for III(b) |

As pointed out earlier hierarchy was the over-arching value of the Traditional Order. The significant point in this context is the principle of distribution of resources and allocation of roles based on birth. This is in direct contravention to the principle of need-based distribution of resources and merit based allocation of roles as implied in an egalitarian modern system. Perhaps one can discover a linkage here; in the traditional system status defined the need and in the modern system need ought to be defined on the basis of contribution made by individuals and groups and the roles they play for the maintenance of the system and its change in a desirable direction. If those who occupied higher status are also taken to be the ones who contributed more to the system, the contradiction between the two principles of allocation can be resolved. But this cannot be done. The basis of status in the traditional order was by birth and that in modern society is based on merit and hence the irreconcilability of the principles of hierarchy and equality.

The traditional principle of holism required that the individuals should renounce their self-interests at the altar of collective goals, To the extent that no autonomy was bestowed on the individual and s/he remained encompassed in the current of collective life, there was no basic problem. However, with the introduction of democracy which requires individuals to be autonomous entities asserting their independence from group, the inevitable development of self-interests, often at the cost of collective orientation, is in evidence. This is complicated because of the extreme distributional imbalances in terms of wealth, power and prestige which are a legacy of the antecedent social order. Thus we find the principles of holism and individualism (democracy) as being mutually inimical. The upshot of our analysis, then, is that the possibilities of bringing about a reconciliation between India's traditional and its modern values is limited except in the case of diversity and secularism.

As of now the modern values enshrined in Indian Constitution are not fully translated into practice. Even as one recognises this praxis-lag, one should take into account the transmutation in the transitional stage during which a synthesis of the traditional and modern values is being evolved. Perhaps a couple of illustrations will clarify the situation. Traditionally castes were status bestowing entities and they emphasised the ritual dimension (purity-pollution) of status. In modern India the castes are increasingly getting secularised in that they perform instrumental functions for their members. Thus, caste associations open educational institutions, establish financial agencies-banks, co-operatives—, institute funds for housing, travel abroad and the like, field candidates in elections through political parties. And all these predominantly for the material welfare of the fellow castes members which help improve their secular status. This secularisation of castes in terms of functions, particularly in urban India, changes their substance while retaining the traditional forms. The traditional caste diversity which jealously guarded ritual purity is no more universally functional but the modern caste secularism which insists on the material improvement of the caste members is ever expanding. The recruitment to caste associations is based on membership in primordial groups and hence ascriptive but the goals these associations pursue are instrumental and achievement oriented.

Although the induction of democratic political framework assumes individual autonomy and freedom, the actual operation of the democratic process in India is infused with a high amount of traditional collectivism. For instance, decisions in the political context are rarely arrived at by individuals as independent entities; the prevalence of 'group-voting' by kin-groups, castes or territorial groups (villages) is not uncommon. The insistence on consensus in decisional process, avoiding the animosities associated with intense competition is quite frequent in political parties. Finally, given the present state of Indian economy social welfare measures to assist the unemployed, the aged, the disabled etc., are rarely fully instituted by the State and the burden of supporting the dispossessed and disadvantaged is often accepted by the kin, caste and religious groups. In fact Indians who occupy well-off positions as compared with other members of their religion, village, caste or kin would consider it to be their moral obligation to help their less fortunate brothers and sisters through educating them or finding a job or raising material resources for them. Thus, while the context in which the modern Indian operates has undergone a partial change, the fulfilment of traditional obligations which calls for a collectivistic orientation persists. In the final analysis, what we witness in India to-day is neither the unbroken continuation of traditional norms nor the complete institutionalisation of the newly introduced modern values but an intermediate situation indicative of an ongoing process of transition.

Let me now examine the theory-gap in the two value packages--traditional and modern-so as to understand whether they are internally consistent. In the context of tradition, diversity which was based on tolerance and holism founded on collectivistic orientation are not mutually inconsistent, because tolerance implies a collectivity orientation. However, hierarchy which was based on the principle of status-ascription led to a segmentation of the society leading to multiple group formation each of which was imprisoned in its narrow grooves. Additionally, diversity fostered local or group pride overlooking wider interests thereby reinforcing hierarchy. Under such a situation holism in effect meant the collectivity orientation of insulated communities. This was not conducive to the emergence and growth of modern collectivistic values. But since the over-arching value of hierarchy enveloped other values, and a all-pervasive and dominating elite acted as the custodian of societal values, the requisite stability was forged through a coercive equilibrium and the traditional society was rendered a functional entity.

The basic inconsistency that we witness in the value package of modern India is that between equality and individualism. If the basic tenet of equality is a pattern of need-based allocation of resources and distribution of rewards to role incumbents, this calls for a collectivistic orientation and altruism based on merit cutting across narrow group boundaries. One cannot insist on one's share, in such a system, based on one's status or even merit. One should be willing to contribute to the system as much as one can, that is based on one's ability, but should be prepared to accept the principle of need-based allocation. The spirit of possessive individualism, implied in democracy, rebels against this as it ceaselessly emphasises the importance of individual merit and it bestows undue importance to welfare of individuals. It is argued by some that maximisation of interests by all individuals will automatically lead to collective welfare and therefore common interests will not be endangered, the refrain of rational choice theorists. But there are two problems here. First, such a system inevitably fosters acute competition between individuals for achieving their self-defined goals; those who win the rat race nevertheless remain rats! Secondly, no system by definition can facilitate the maximisation of interests by all individuals who constitute it, at any rate viewed from the subjective perceptions of participants. And, subjective evaluations are relevant in the context of heightening or lessening psychological deprivations. The options here are two – Voluntary restraint by individuals keeping in mind the community interest or imposition of controls by an agency external to the individual, usually the state. While the latter will inescapably degenerate into totalitarianism, the former will inevitably require individuals who have internalised a high degree of altruism. If one is utopian, the other is dehumanising.

## III

The analysis I have attempted unfolds that both the traditional and modern values of India have assets and liabilities embedded in them. And one should consciously opt for a judicious combination of assets both in the traditional and modern values in a consistent fashion to secure the most appropriate mix. Once again, we are at a new set of problems. What is the most appropriate mix? I can only assert that there is no mix which is universally appropriate; appropriateness will have to be defined contextually. The context is provided by the historicity of a society, and its present existential conditions.

We have seen that while the traditional value of holism fostered primordial collectivism, with the introduction of democracy possessive individualism is gaining ground leading to the emergence of instrumental collectivism. What we need to inject into the system is ideational collectivism wherein humans are motivated to plunge into collective mobilisation with an altruistic orientation for systemic welfare rather than narrow individual and primordial group interests. While retaining the collectivistic orientation found in Indian tradition, the content of collectivism should be transformed. We must recognise that a democracy innate to India cannot admit possessive individualism. Traditional principles of allocation of roles and distribution of resources were based on hierarchy. Today it is based on merit but most of the meritorious are drawn from the traditional elite which inevitably will ensure the persistence of traditional inequality. What we should pursue is a system of need based allocation of resources and fostering those with merit from the traditionally underprivileged. The traditional value of diversity insulated individuals and groups into their narrow socio-cultural grooves, incapable of developing wider perspectives. Secularism of modern India has the potential to foster inter-group harmony but has not yet achieved it. It is necessary to harness the diversity principle of traditional India so as to utilise it in order to transform the persisting hostility, particularly to non-Indic religious communities who constitute a substantial proportion of Indian population. But in pursuing these objectives the principle of reciprocity cannot be ignored; the minority religious groups should be prepared to accept a regime of secularism. Thus viewed, Indian secularism is capable of promoting inter-group equality and harmony.

# 2

# *India's Black Economy: Causes, Implications and Remedies*

*Arun Kumar*

## Introduction

India's black economy is roughly estimated to be 50 per cent of its GDP — generating at current prices in 2012-13, about Rs. 50 lakh crore or $1 trillion. It is so extensive because it is generated in every sector and economic activity and all the elite sections of society are involved in it. It is in both the public and the private sectors and involves everyone down the line from the Prime Ministers, Chief Ministers, top industrialists, army men, judges, bureaucrats, lawyers, teachers and so on. Taxes not collected at current rates of taxes amount to about Rs. 20 lakh crore in 2012-13. Thus, the Union budget instead of showing a Fiscal Deficit could have shown a surplus of Rs. 14.5 lakh crore. If this amount could be collected, there would be enough money for employment generation, education, health and infrastructure, like, roads and power.

An indication of the growing black economy is the rapid unearthing of more and more and bigger scams. The speed with which scams are being revealed makes the public forget the scams they were exercised about just a few months back. Today, with IPL in the news and the imbroglio around the JPC on 2G and the expose of the attempt of the Law Minister to influence the CBI, the Westland Helicopter deal has receded to the background. The wrong doing in the Tatra truck deal and the Army Chief's complaint that he was sought to be bribed are forgotten. Similarly, the Adarsh Society scam, ISRO-Dewas deal, Commonwealth Games scam, and the Hasan Ali case are hardly talked of. Bigger scams have taken hold.

While the biggest scam prior to 1990 was the Bofors scam at Rs. 64 crore, in the 1990s there were many scams that were above Rs. 1,000 crore (Kumar, 1999). The largest was the Harshad Mehta led Stock Market Scam of 1991-92, estimated by the Janakiraman Committee Report at Rs. 3,128 crore (RBI, 1993). The Telgi scam regarding forged stamp papers was also initially estimated to be in thousands of crore but no firm figure emerged. In the first decade of this century, there has been a flood of revelations of major scams — almost one a week — not counting the smaller cases of corruption involving a few crore or less (Kumar, 2013). Now the scams run into tens of thousands of crores and at times in lakhs of crores. In the allotment of natural resources, like, mines and spectrum, huge scams have been unearthed.

If we cut back to the end of 2006 what was the situation? MPs had been caught accepting money for asking questions in Parliament. This is nothing new. During the debate on the nuclear issue, MPs produced wads of notes in Parliament which they said were for buying their vote in favour of the government. The government cleverly deflected the issue but this is also nothing new. In the 1990s the JMM MPs were caught with cash in their bank accounts which had been given to them for helping the government survive.

Around that time, Mayawati, Badal and Jogi were in the news on the same day for violating some law or the other. They were in the distinguished company of Laloo Yadav and Jayalalitha who already had cases against them. Daler Mehndi, Bharat Shah, four members of the elite Presidents guards, doctors in private clinics, manufacturers of spurious drugs, judges of high courts, Vice Chancellors of Universities, bureaucrats and police officers, journalists, film producers, etc., all hit headlines for having committed some illegality or the other in the mid-2000s. These are the elite sections of our society so that the implications of such widespread illegality are serious. It is gnawing at the innards of our society with influential sections of society increasingly in the grip of illegality to generate extra incomes; above what they make legally.

The list is unending, in the 1990s and 2000s, illegality in petrol pump allotments, admissions to professional courses, procurement of defense materials, allotment of licenses, disinvestment of shares of public sector, etc., have come to light. Yet, there have been few prosecutions in cases of graft and the public impression is that the system is very corrupt. The quick action against the MPs caught asking for money for questions is an exception and not the rule. People in their day to day dealings (police, telephone, electricity, petrol pumps, medical clinics, etc.) face constant harassment, whether in the public or the private sector.

For the public, illegality and corruption are a constant and they feel helpless to do anything about it. They are exercised at the time a scam is revealed and then they go back to their routine. They re-elect the corrupt time and again thus signaling to the political class that they can ride out the storm and return later without reforming themselves.

The public has little choice since almost all the political parities have been caught indulging in corruption. Thus, a change in the ruling party means that another corrupt set up comes to power. The net result is that the people vote for their own corrupt who would help them. Hence the Dalits would vote for their own and the backward castes would vote for their brethren and the Muslims vote for their community and so do the upper castes. That is why today it is said that corruption is no more an issue. The politicians have decided that they only need to wait patiently in the wings for their turn. The clever thing to do is to collect enough while in power and when out of it not unduly ruffle the feathers of the ruling group — behave like a 'responsible' opposition. This is the weakness of our democracy that people have little choice — that between Tweedledee and Tweedldum (Kumar, 1999). Be that as it may, what are the implications of a large and growing black economy in India?

## Implications of the Black Economy for the Nation

### *Spread of Illegality and Weakening of Democracy*

Illegal activities at the top echelons (political, bureaucratic and business) in the country have serious implications. National Security is being seriously compromised. Even cabinet decisions are often not a secret as Wikileaks revelations suggest. Foreign agencies and business interests may get the most sensitive information for a price (or via blackmail because they may have information on the illegality of the top people in administration). The recent attack on the top leadership of the Congress (I) in Chattisgarh or the earlier attack on Mr. Naidu's motorcade are indications of serious security lapses. There is not only leakage of information on movements of leaders but also laxity in policing since there is huge corruption in the police set up everywhere. Police is busy collecting Hafta from illegal activities rather than in controlling illegality in its jurisdiction (Kumar, 1999). Contraband (arms, drugs and so on) and suspects slip in and out of airports and ports and across borders.

There is growing criminalisation in society since almost the entire official machinery is involved in committing illegality — there are always the exceptions that prove the rule. The businessmen and politicians use the police and the bureaucracy to commit illegality. When the latter gets the license to commit illegality, they also do it for their own ends for making money from those committing illegality. The result is that the force for maintaining law and order — the police – is often a party to the illegality.

Posts of lucrative thanas are apparently auctioned for a price. The price paid (and above that for ones own use) has to be recovered by collecting hafta from the jurisdiction of the thana. Illegal activities like, theft, pick pocketing and encroachment are encouraged to enable the hafta to be collected. Traffic police turns a blind eye to violation of traffic rules or over charging by transporters since it collects a monthly payment from commercial operations. If a theft occurs in an influential person's house, the stolen items are recovered since the police know who the thieves are in that area. If the police is in league with criminal elements in society is it any surprise that criminalisation is increasing by leaps and bounds?

Illegality is committed in the thanas themselves with the police violating the rules. This is justified on grounds of extracting information from the criminals. However, it is mostly the honest who are harassed to extract money whereas the criminals with their nexus escape to continue their activities in collusion with the police. No wonder, an alternate system of justice has emerged where the public takes the law in its own hand or goes to the corrupt and the powerful to get justice. It has affected our politics which is now increasingly criminalised with those having a criminal background entering the legislatures in increasing numbers. What can be expected when in the biggest state of the country, a minister with a criminal record was recently appointed as the jail minister? There is a vicious cycle in which respect for justice is eroded, social functioning is impeded and democracy weakened.

***Economic Aspects***

All the key economic problems can be linked to the impact of the growing black economy. In an economy where billions of dollars are spirited out of the economy, where black transactions abound in the stock markets and the real estate markets, where getting admission for children requires bribes, is it surprising that the impact of the black economy is all pervasive? What is being revealed by official agencies or in the media with relentless regularity is only the tip of the iceberg.

Due to the black economy, policy fails and society is unable to achieve its goals, like literacy and health, and a vast majority live in rather uncivilised conditions which are prevalent in very few countries of the world. As the Finance Minister in his budget speech said in 2007, 'expenditures do not mean outcomes'. Rajiv Gandhi said in 1987, out of every rupee sent to the field, only 15 paise reaches the ground. He did not mean that all of it was lost due to corruption but also due to the bureaucratic costs. Now the courts feel only 5 paise reaches the ground.

The black economy has destroyed the work ethics of a vast section of society so that we do not achieve (with few exceptions) world standards whether in sports or in technology. There is waste of resources and alienation of the citizen from society making collective effort almost impossible. An economy that has the potential of growing at 10 per cent per annum is growing at an average of 5.4 per cent per annum since the 1980s (Kumar, 2005). In brief, the black economy has affected the social, political, economic and cultural life. It is in our own enlightened self interest to curb it.

***Increasing Inefficiency***

Many aspects of the black economy are like 'digging holes and filling them' (Kumar, 1999). If during the day a person is set to work digging a hole and at night another person is asked to fill it up, next morning there is zero output but two people have earned incomes for the work they have done. Thus, there is activity without productivity. Assets are not created commensurate with the expenditures. So, for instance, in road construction, sub-standard material is used so that it gets potholed when the rains come and has to be repaired. Thus the road budget is spent on repairs rather than building new roads for say, rural connectivity.

In schools, the teachers teach poorly so that the students do not learn or enjoy classes. They get put off from learning and divert their attention to other things. When they go home they are forced to take tuition so as to do well. Teachers have a vested interest in not teaching well so that they can get tuitions to make extra money. The implication for learning is that the children find it difficult and mug up the material rather than understanding it. They stop questioning and lose curiosity about various things in life. Their time is wasted first in the class and then in tuition. The time that could have been used for other activities and for learning is lost. Further, the tuition syndrome leads to leakage of question papers and other malpractices so that the tutees can do well in the exams and justify the tuition.

Because of poor teaching and learning, students attend coaching classes to pass competitive exams. Their intermediate training is not good enough to help them do well in the competitive exams. This results in massive waste of resources for the nation since the outcome with regard to learning is poor. Further, most of the students in higher education are indifferent to quality. So, in spite of the large numbers of students in higher education, we produce very few who are internationally competitive.

Such examples of waste are all around us. In the bureaucracy where work is not done and people run around in circles or in the judiciary where cases go on for years even though they are supposed to be solved in months. There are crowds milling around the offices and courts but little gets accomplished. The police do not register cases and harass the public. Cases are poorly investigated and in the end they are thrown out by the courts so that justice is not done in spite of the efforts of many people.

Another aspect of the black economy is that it makes 'the usual the unusual and the unusual the usual' (Kumar, 1999). That which should happen does not and that which should not happen does. So the citizen should get 220 volts electricity but often they get 170 or 270 volts and expensive equipment burns out. One needs additional circuits and voltage stabiliser for equipment and capital costs rise. Cost of servicing equipment rises as the breakdown rate increases. The fluctuating voltage and variable cycles of supply of electricity also leads to poor quality production since machines can malfunction. In continuous flow production like in case of chemicals, such malfunction can lead to clogged lines and so on.

One should get clean drinking water in the taps but often it is polluted. This is because the pipelines may not be properly laid and sewage seeps in. Thus, one has to incur additional expenditure for boiling water or by using purifiers of various descriptions. Further, one buys bottled water at thousand times the cost, etc. Even then, a little carelessness leads to water borne diseases and additional health costs which are unnecessary. Parents remain tense about what the children will drink in school and so on.

One does not get the service one should get from the bureaucracy so one has to approach touts and pay them extra. This is true for tax assessment, getting passport or driving license made, admission to schools, admission to professional courses, getting railway reservations and so on. Either one fights everywhere or gives in and pays the extra cost (bribe included) and in turn generates extra income where ever one gets a chance. How many places can an individual fight?

The result is that people have got alienated from the system. They have lost faith that things can work and they automatically assume that they need to pay extra. Even in a medical emergency it is often the case that one first calls up some friend/relation for advice as to where to go rather than going straight to the nearest hospital emergency room. It is often a miracle that one survives a medical emergency since so many things can go wrong. In a road accident few stop to help take the victim to hospital. In the hospital the doctors may wait for the legal formalities. They may do a slip shod job of treatment and the drip or the medicines may be spurious or sub - standard and may not have the desired effect and so on. Since all this is so much a part of life, people stop resisting corruption and extortion and that helps it grow further. People lose faith in the collective and try for individual solutions. This weakens democracy.

These various aspects of the functioning of the black economy result in growing inefficiencies of the system and wasteful use of capital and resources. It has been estimated that due to such inefficiencies, India has been losing five per cent rate of growth for the last three decades (Kumar, 2005). Thus, its rate of growth could have been 8.5 per cent in the seventies and 12 per cent now, if the black economy had not existed. The per capita income could have been about $10,000 and it would have been the second largest economy in the world. Thus, though the black economy generates output and employment far more is lost than gained. In other words, development is set aback

***Impact on Inequality***

The black economy is concentrated in the hands of at the most three per cent of the population (Kumar, 1999). Yes, there is petty corruption but this is insignificant compared to the huge earnings of the few. According to a calculation, in 1995, the ratio of incomes between the top 3 per cent and the bottom 40 per cent was 12:1 in the white economy but it became 57:1 including the black economy. By now, the disparities have become much worse. Thus, in a vast and poor population of 1.25 billion, there are 35 million well off, the size of a European nation, that can afford all the luxuries. This explains the existence of vast poverty in the midst of glitzy markets and ostentatious consumerism of the well off.

The result of this skewedness of income is that the savings propensity of the economy is higher than recorded in the white economy (Kumar, 2005). This is simply the result of the rich saving more than the poor. Due to wastage of capital and unproductive investments, the investment rate in the economy is lower than it could have been. The result of both these trends is that the level of output is lower than it can potentially be — missed development.

***Black Economy and Illicit Financial Flows***

A recent report estimates that since independence, more than $460 billion has been lost by the nation due to flight of capital (GFI, 2010). This is much larger than India's foreign debt or the Aid it received. A capital short country has been exporting capital on a large scale. In a sense, the drain of wealth during the colonial rule has continued in a different form after independence. Those resorting to flight of capital include the businessmen, corrupt politicians, bureaucrats, professionals and so on. These are the people whose interest in the country has weakened as their wealth abroad has increased and they often push the interest of foreign powers. They are also open to black mail by the foreign agencies who track the flow of illicit funds from and back into India.

This figure of illicit financial flows (flight of capital is part of this) does not take into account loss of capital due to illegal activities like havala, narcotics drugs trafficking, smuggling and so on (Kumar, 2012). If all this could be taken into account, the opportunity cost should run into a few trillions of dollars. If this amount had been invested in the country, say, in rural areas that are woefully short of basic infrastructure, like, water, sanitation or electricity, conditions of life could have been far better. Alternatively, if this capital had been invested in industry, industrialisation, technology and productivity could have been far greater/higher than at present. Thus, flight of capital associated with the black economy results in slower development than India can achieve.

Of late, there is a return flow of capital called 'round tripping'. From the late 1990s the software industry became the conduit for bringing back capital without paying taxes. Later the Mauritius route was also added to facilitate this 'round tripping'.

The flight of capital associated with the black economy is the main cause of the BOP problems that have plagued the Indian economy for much of the time since independence. It takes place through under and over invoicing of foreign trade, transfer pricing and havala (parallel banking). Much of this is managed through shell companies set up in tax havens (over 70 at current count) to launder the money siphoned out of the country.

***Black Economy and Policy Failure***

Black economy leads to policy failure. Policies on paper and as they are implemented are vastly different. Whether it is environmental regulation or industrial location or urban zoning or traffic lights, all laws are routinely violated. No wonder at a low level of per capita income, India has some of the worst air and water pollution in the world. Due to insanitary conditions and water pollution, most people suffer from poor health resulting in low labour productivity. Literacy is low because money sent for constructing schools is often siphoned off and teachers are not appointed. Children even in the fifth grade are found to have acquired few skills (ASER reports) so for the rest of their life they are condemned to work at low levels of productivity and remain poor.

The black economy results in loss of revenue of about 20 per cent of GDP, at current rates of taxes. In comparison, the fiscal deficit is currently around six per cent of GDP for the Centre. If the black economy had instead been white, there would have been a surplus in the budget and there would have been much greater investments in infrastructure and poverty removal. Also with less corruption, expenditures would have been more effective. The revenue deficit which underlies the fiscal deficit and rising debt in the budget would have been wiped out so that the fiscal health of the government would have been better.

**Growing Size of the Black Economy Since 1991**

The size of the black economy is given relative to that of the white economy — as a per cent of the declared GDP. The size of the black economy was estimated to be four per cent of GDP in 1955 (GOI, 1956), seven per cent in 1970 (GOI, 1971), 18 per cent in 1980-81 (NIPFP, 1985) and 40 per cent in 1995-96 (Kumar, 1999). The last estimate includes eight per cent contributed by illegal activities like, drugs, mafia and smuggling. 32 per cent comes from the legal activities like, manufacturing, finance, trade and construction. It is growing in spite of the reduction in tax rates and whittling down of the degree of controls and regulation in the economy over the last two decades. This is not surprising since these are not the causes of generation of the black incomes.

Since generations of black income involves illegality, the above figures suggest that illegality in the country has been growing. More and more scams are surfacing and the sums that are involved in them are increasing exponentially. If currently illegality is associated with about 50 per cent of the economic activity, it has to be 'systematic and systemic'. Systems are set up to bribe politicians and bureaucrats, for adulteration of food, for producing spurious medicines, for not declaring the full output produced so that profits are generated off the balance sheet and so on. It is not that one day one generates black income and not the next day; it is a 24×7 activity.

Some with faith in the market mechanism believed that the black economy would shrink with the implementation of the New Economic Policies (NEP) in 1991. The package consisted of the lowering of taxes and reduction of controls like, MRTP, FERA, reservations, licensing and so on. However, the black economy grew even faster as the restraint on businesses declined (Kumar, 1999). For instance, they could take their money out more easily as exchange controls were relaxed. So, they started taking out more of their capital. They could play around more easily in the financial markets and so could generate more of black incomes. The increase in the collection of direct taxes as a per cent of the GDP since 1999 is not due to a reduction of the black economy but due to the dramatic rise in the income of the corporate sector (Kumar, 2007) and the black economy has continued to grow.

Gold inflow is an example of the above argument. When its import was banned till 1992, the smuggling of gold into the country was to the extent of 160 tons (Sarma, 1992). After 1992, when gold was allowed to be imported, the amount of gold inflow increased to 900 tons by 1999 and half of it was smuggled. Thus, the legal part of imports ofcourse increased but the illegal inflow also increased. The loss of savings for the country increased by a factor of 5.5 times. For a poor country this is criminal since it aggravates poverty. Of late, this has become an important reason for the high current account deficit and the BOP crisis.

**The Underlying Cause: The Growing Triad**

To effectively tackle the black economy there is a need to identify the causes underlying its existence and growth. For illegality to be involved in 50 per cent of the economic activity, it is only possible if the people in-charge of implementation of rules are party to black income generation. They connive in the persistence of illegality and share the extra profits generated. A Triad exists between the corrupt businessmen, corrupt politicians and the corrupt executive (Kumar, 1999). The last consists of the police, the bureaucracy and the judiciary. Since the 1980s the criminal has entered the Triad. So, either the businessman or the politician has a criminal record and this has led to growing criminalisation in society as discussed earlier. This nexus is so powerful that a financially honest PM voluntarily tolerates the corruption all around to survive and he also provides credibility for a corrupt system – a mascot.

The Triad is mutually convenient to all. The businessmen are able to influence policy and protect their ill gotten profits. The other two in the Triad need the businessman to invest their funds and launder them. Most politicians have at least one businessman close to them who provides such services. The media is increasingly a party to some of these illegalities.

The reduction in tax rates and removal of controls like MRTP, FERA, licensing and easing of reservations for small scale after 1991 has not led to a reduction of the size of the black economy. It is because the Triad has grown stronger and forms of making black incomes have changed.

**Remedies**

The cause of the black economy is not just technical (high tax rates or controls) and that is why it continues to grow in spite of the hundreds of steps taken to tackle it in the last 50 years. There have been more than 40 committees that have gone into the different aspects of the black economy and they have suggested thousands of measures. So we are not short of suggestions or of measures to tackle it, like, demonetisation, voluntary disclosure, payment by cheque, anti-defection law and citizens' charter. Some of these steps have not only not helped curb the menace but have often fuelled it because they have added to the complexity of the laws or turned people into habitual law breakers (Kumar, 1999). The cause of the growing illegality lies in the political economy of conflict in our society with the elite forming the Triad and making incomes over and above what they can make legally.

To tackle the black economy, the Triad has to be dismantled. It functions in secrecy. Hence the most important step is the 'Right to Information'. This would make the politician and the executive accountable and their functioning transparent so that unlike at present, they cannot subvert the law deliberately. The present dispensation on Right to Information is entirely inadequate since it is far too complex for the common man to use. The mind set of the politicians and the bureaucracy needs to change. Unfortunately, those heading the Right to Information bureaucracy have mostly been bureaucrats.

Howsoever good bureaucrats may be, their training has been to not give information and to not push the system to reveal it. Someone from outside the system was required to head it — who would be willing to put the politicians and the bureaucrats in the dock. It is argued that a Seshan or a Kiran Bedi have done much good to the system even though they are from the executive level. However, in any absolute sense, they have done little and even that stands out compared to others. They have played the system and done well because they have made compromises with it rather than challenging it. They are used by the system to legitimize its choices so that it can continue to more or less function as it is. We need people who would challenge the system every step of the way otherwise the Right to Information will also get discredited over time.

A major reform required is that political parties function democratically. Many of today's leaders come up without serving the people and take over parties. Parties and constituencies are often passed on to relatives like property from one to the other. Such leaders are often contemptuous of people and represent the interest of society's upper crust.

Electoral reform is required so that genuine representatives of the people enter the legislature (not purchasable by vested interests). State funding of elections will not help since it only gives additional funds to the corrupt. Election expenses are 10 times the allowed limit and a bulk of the expenditures are on illegal activities and are raised from illegal sources (Kumar, 1999). For these purposes, state funding will not help or cannot be used. Citizens' groups which can present an independent record of the performance of the candidates before elections will help make the voters better informed (For a more detailed discussion on this, see Kumar, 1999).

Audit of accounts of parties, Lok Pal, etc., will hardly help. Accounts are easily manipulated. Who will prevent the Lok Pal from getting corrupted? Philippines has functioned with an Ombudsman who is unable to check corruption in high places. If Justice Ramaswamy could be in the dock and the Chief Justice of the Punjab High court had to take steps against other judges, what is the chance that the highest will not be corrupted/silenced? After initial euphoria, what have the CVC and Chief Election Commissioners achieved? Mere formalism will not work. Vote should not merely mean the duty to go to the polling booth on the Election Day. A politically alert public which votes consciously in national self interest and not on sectarian lines — caste and communal — is needed.

Reform of Judiciary is required. Cases have to be speeded up and procedures simplified. With 30 million cases pending in courts the powerful manipulate it for their own ends and faith in justice is eroded which undermines any notion of a civilised society. There is neither a shortage of judges nor of courts. The problem is that the judiciary does not act and is unaccountable to the public. Cases that should be wound up in 6 months take more than six years thus clogging courts and wasting everyone's time. The age of retirement of the executive should be raised to 70 years and after that they should not be allowed to serve in the private sector. Those taking early retirement should be disqualified from work for others for 10 years - not even consultancies for the private sector. Businesses have to be made accountable and transparent. Independent directors on the Board of the Companies are needed as public watchdogs. Such directors should be chosen from outside the Triad (who are easily corruptible in different ways). The members of the Triad belong to the same class and have sympathy with the manipulations indulged in by businesses since they are also somewhere associated with such actions (What happened in the case of Satyam). Directors should be made to pay for the wrong actions of the companies they are supposed to be associated with. Chartered Accountants have to be made accountable through fines on them if accounts are found to have been falsified.

Direct taxes need to be simplified by elimination of concessions and deductions. Taxation of business income should be based on gross profit and not net profit. Internal indirect taxes should be levied only on final luxury products. Estate duty, Gift Tax, property and wealth taxes should be revived to unearth black incomes (Kumar, 1994).

The common man is hit more by the indirect taxes (which are still 60 per cent of all taxes collected) than the direct taxes. Even though some direct tax is paid by the workers in the organised sector, most of it is paid by businessmen and managers. Low direct taxes help these rich people. High indirect taxes hurt the common man since they through their consumption are forced to pay a substantial part of their incomes as taxes. Raising direct taxes on wealth and profit would enable the state to lower the indirect taxes and this will help check the growth of the black economy (Kumar, 1999).

**Conclusion**

In brief, the black economy underlies the major macro-economic problems faced by India – fiscal crisis, inflation and BOP problems. The micro and the sectoral problems of the economy, like, education, health and infrastructure also relate to the black economy. It weakens democracy. If not checked, India's growth story can become a thing of the past. It is argued above that NEP has not been able to check the growing black economy as the pro-market thinkers hoped for. Instead, as restraint on businesses has decreased, the black economy has grown further since 1991.

No law is worth the paper it is written on if it is not implemented. Political will is required to take the tough steps and that means strengthening democracy. The politicians know/have the intelligence about the corruption of those in the Triad but who will bell the cat since when out of power they can also be caught as has happened to Badal and Amrinder Singh or to Jaylalitha and Karunanidhi. Thus, mostly there is a conspiracy of silence amongst the members of the elite.

If matters are to be resolved, the public has to act against the entire political class via alternative movements on a host of issues which will throw up an alternative leadership. In recent times, new political parties and social organisations have come up to take up the issues of the common people of India. However, the task is not easy but has the task of nation building ever been easy?

## References


- GFI, (2010): 'The Drivers and Dynamics of Illicit Financial Flows from India: 1948-2008'. *http://india.gfip.org.*
- GOI, (1956): *Direct Tax Reform: Report of a Survey,* (Chairperson: Kaldor).
- GOI, (1971) : *'Direct Taxes Enquiry Report',* (Chairperson: Wanchoo).
- Kumar, A. (1994): "Proposals for a Citizens Union Budget for the Nation for 1994 95: An Alternative to the Fund Bank Dictated Union Budget for 1994 95". Presented to the Citizens' Committee on February 12, 1994 at Gandhi Peace Foundation, New Delhi. Prepared for the Preparatory Committee for Alternative Economic Policies.
- ________, (1999): *'The Black Economy in India',* New Delhi, Penguin (India).
- ________, (2005): 'India's Black Economy: The Macro-economic Implications'. *South Asia: Journal of South Asian Studies,* Vol. 28, No. 2, August 2005. pp. 249-263.
- ________, (2007): 'Macro Overview'. Chapter in the Alternative Economic Survey Group (Ed.). *Alternative Economic Survey, India 2006-07: 'Pampering Corporates, Pauperising Masses',* pp. 37 - 46. New Delhi, Daanish Books.
- ________, (2012): 'Measuring Illegal flows from the Indian Economy: Some Methodological Issues'. *Economic and Political Weekly,* Vol. XLVII, No. 39. September 29, pp. 71-74.
- ________, (2013): *Indian Economy Since Independence: Persisting Colonial Disruption*, New Delhi: Vision Books.
- NIPFP (1985): *Aspects of Black Economy in India*, New Delhi, National Institute of Public Finance and Policy.
- RBI. (1993): *Report on Securities Transactions*. (Final), (Chairman: Janakiraman).
- Sarma A., A. Vasudevan, K. Kanagasabapathy, M. Narayan and M. Roy. (1992): "Gold Mobilisation as an Instrument of External Adjustment: A Discussion Paper". Development Research Group, Department of Economic Analysis and Policy, Reserve Bank of India, Mumbai.
- Rishi, M., and J.K., Boyce (1990): "The Hidden Balance of Payments: Capital Flight and Trade Misinvoicing in India, 1971-1986", *Economic and Political Weekly*, Vol. 25, No. 30, 28 July, pp. 1645-48.

# 3

# *Pampering Business Houses at the Cost of the Nation*

*C.P. Chandrasekhar*

Opinions on the social, political and economic fallout of the policy of neo-liberal reform pursued since 1991 may differ. But there is a broad agreement that whatever economic gains have been made in this period have been disproportionately shared, with the overwhelming share going to businesses. That is not all, there is also a large body of opinion that this redistribution of income and wealth in favour of corporate capital was not merely the result of autonomous tendencies characterising the neoliberal growth path, but was consciously engineered by the State in order to incentivise private capital in the hope of making it an engine of growth. There is evidence that the government sought to catalyse growth with multiple concessions at central and state levels for private investors, important among which were easy access to and low taxes on imports of technology, capital equipment and intermediates, low cost access to land and minerals and other scarce resources and open and hidden subsidies to the corporate sector.

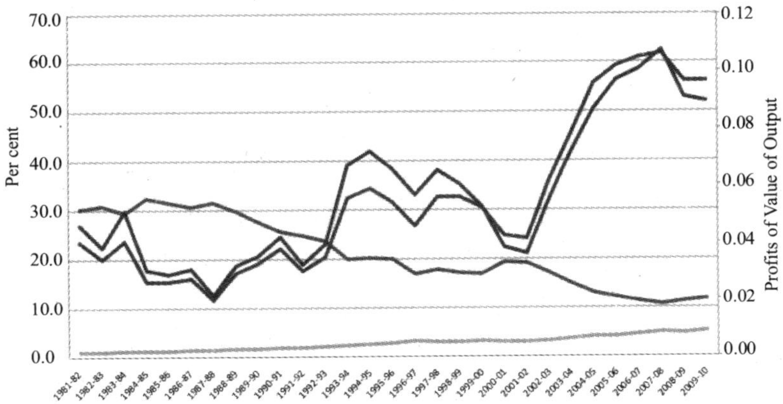


**Chart 1: Profits, Wages and Productivity in Organised Manufacturing.**

The result was an increase in the private sector's ability to garner higher profits. Consider trends emerging from the official Annual Survey of Industries relating to the organised manufacturing sector depicted in Chart 1. To start with, since the early 1990s, when liberalisation opened the doors to investment and permitted much freer import of technology and equipment from abroad, productivity in organised manufacturing has been almost continuously rising. Net value added (or the excess of output values over input costs and depreciation) per employed worker measured in constant 2004-05 prices, rose from a little over Rs. 1 lakh to more than Rs. 5 lakh. That is, productivity as measured by net product per worker adjusted for inflation registered a close to five-fold increase over the 30-year period beginning 1981-82. And more than three-fourths of that increase came after the early 1990s.

Unfortunately for labour, and fortunately for capital, the benefit of that productivity increase did not accrue to workers. The average real wage paid per worker employed in the organised sector, calculated by adjusting for inflation as measured by the Consumer Price Index for Industrial Workers [CPI(IW) with 1982 as base], rose from Rs. 8467 a year in 1981-82 to Rs. 10777 in 1989-90 and then fluctuated around that level till 2009-10 (Chart 2). The net result of this stagnancy in real wages after liberalisation is that the share of the wage bill in net value added or net product (Chart 1), which stood at more than 30 per cent through the 1980s, declined subsequently and fell to 11.6 per cent or close to a third of its 1980s level by 2009-10.

A corollary of the decline in the share of wages in net value added was ofcourse a rise in the share of profits. However, the trend in the share of profits is far less regular than that of the other components in net value added. Between 1981-82 and 1992-93, the ratio of profits to net value added fluctuated between 11.6 per cent and 23.4 per cent. During much of the next decade (1992-93 to 2002-03) it remained at a significantly higher level, fluctuating between 20.4 per cent and 34.3 per cent, but showed clear signs of falling during the recession years 1998-99 to 2001-02.

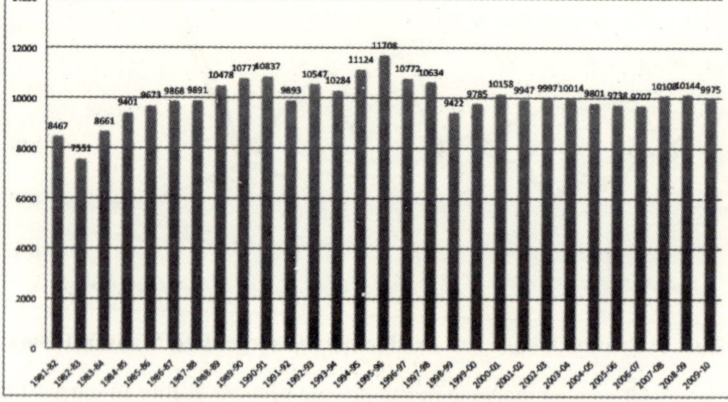


**Chart 2: Average real wage (Rs per year in 1982 prices).**

However, the years after 2001-02 saw the ratio of profit to net value added soar, from just 24.2 per cent to a peak of 61.8 per cent in 2007-08. What needs explaining is the remarkable boom in profits at the expense of all other components of net value added. An interesting feature that emerges from the chart is that the ratio of profits to value of output, or the margin on sales, tracks closely the irregular trend in the share of profits in value added described above. Increases in profit shares have clearly been the result of a rise in the 'mark-up' represented by the profit margin to sales ratio, or the ability of capital to extract more profit from every unit of output.

Interestingly, the periods in which the ratio of profits to the value of output has risen, leading to sharp increases in profit shares, were also the years when the two post-liberalisation booms in manufacturing occurred. The first of those was the mini-boom of the mid-1990s, starting in 1993-94 and going on to 1997-98, which was fuelled by the pent-up demand in the upper income groups for a range of goods that had remained unsatisfied prior to the liberalisation of imports and foreign investment rules. The second was the stronger and more prolonged boom after 2002-03, led by new sources of credit-financed demand. That boom lasted till the global financial crisis in 2008-09. The coincidence of the rise in profit margins and profit shares and the output booms suggests that, in periods of rising demand, the organised manufacturing sector in India has been able to exploit liberalisation in two ways. First, it has been able to expand and modernise using imported technologies, raising labour productivity significantly in the process. Secondly, it has been able to ensure that the benefit of that productivity increase accrues almost solely to profit earners, because of the conditions created by the "reformed" economic environment. As a result, the mark up rose significantly or sharply in these periods and delivered a profit boom.

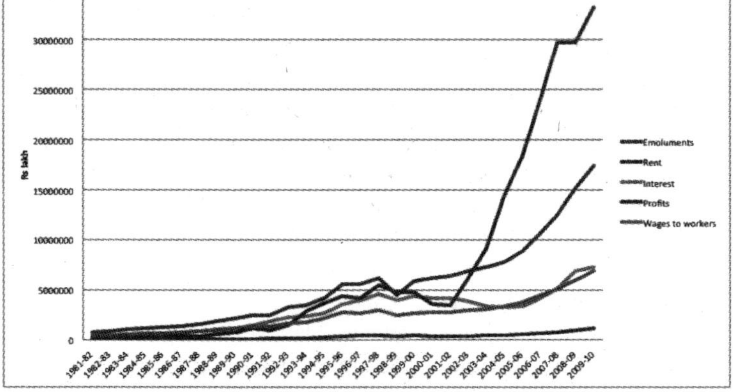


**Chart 3: Components of Net Value Added.**

An interesting feature is the way in which this process feeds on itself. As Chart 3 depicting trends in the different components of net value added shows, while the nominal value of rent, interest and wages rose only marginally over a long period, the increase in emoluments, which include managerial salaries was substantial. Profits of course soared as noted earlier. The increase in non-wage salaries and incomes not only directly drives manufacturing demand, but also provides the basis for the expansion of credit-financed investment and consumption expenditure. Thus the boom creates conditions that also help prolong that boom.

**Engineered Redistribution**

The sharp spike in profit margins and profit shares have not been just the result of the operation of "market forces". A feature of the neoliberal era in India, as elsewhere in the world, is the role played by the state in redistributing assets and incomes in favour of a small elite, including specially chosen business groups. There are many ways in which this redistribution has been engineered. One is through disinvestment. Not only has the government divested equity in some of the most profitable enterprises, but it has done so at prices that have been found (as in cases such as BALCO sold to Vedanta, IPCL sold to Reliance or Centaur Hotel, Mumbai sold to Sahara) to be way below the true value of the assets involved. Moreover, in many cases, under the policy of strategic disinvestment, business groups acquiring a minority stake of 26 per cent or more; were handed over complete control of the company. In the case of VSL, this allowed Tata's to access the large cash reserves that were available with the company to facilitate its own expansion. Thus Centaur Hotel, Mumbai Airport which belonged to the ITDC, was sold to Batra Hospitality for Rs. 83 crores, and within six months, the entire property was resold to Sahara for Rs. 115 crore.

Another route through which surpluses have been transferred to the private sector is the hand over of mineral resources, including oil and gas, to be exploited by the private sector, often at exorbitant prices. A major controversial beneficiary of such hand-outs has been Reliance Industries, with the recent example being in the gas business. As of now there are multiple pricing regimes prevailing in India's gas market. The ones that matter most are the prices charged by the principal producers, consisting of the public sector Oil and Natural Gas Corporation Ltd. (ONGC) and Oil India Limited (OIL) and the private sector Reliance Industries Limited (RIL). They, together, account for more than 85 per cent of the domestically extracted and delivered natural gas.

The prices charged by ONGC and OIL for much of the gas they sell are based on an administered pricing mechanism (APM), wherein prices are ostensibly calculated on a cost-plus basis. The price charged by RIL (of $4.2 per million British thermal units (mmBtu)), on the other hand, is an "arm's length" price linked to the price of oil and arrived at in consultation with the government as per the terms of the New Exploration and Licensing Policy

(NELP). As of now the price of APM gas varies from $2.52 to $4.2, while the price of non-APM gas varies from $4.2 to $ 5.25 per mmBtu.

In December 2012, one more of many official committees headed by C. Rangarajan, Advisor to the Prime Minister, recommended that India should shift over time to a single gas pricing formula for all forms of gas and all the consuming sectors with domestic gas prices being determined on an "arm's length" basis. Based on that recommendation and a version of the pricing formula suggested by the committee, the Petroleum and Natural Gas Ministry had reportedly moved a Cabinet note recently, recommending that the price of domestically produced gas be fixed at $6.7 per mmBtu, which amounts to a 60 per cent increase in the currently most prevalent non-APM price. This would benefit the public sector oil companies immediately, and Reliance Industries from April 2014.

The recommendation has stirred a controversy, because while it would deliver a bonanza to the current producers of natural gas in India, it would have damaging consequences for the user industries, which include the all important power and fertiliser sectors. According to one estimate, every dollar increase in the price of gas can impose a burden of as much as Rs. 3000-4000 crore a year (depending on production volume) on urea producers and as much as Rs. 10,000 crore on gas-based electricity generation units. Many of these units are in the public sector. Hence, much of the benefit that the public sector oil companies derive from a higher gas price will be wiped out by the high costs incurred by other public sector units or by the government burdened with a higher subsidy bill for fertiliser and power. If that is to be avoided, end-product prices would have to be raised substantially.

Reliance would be a major beneficiary. And this at a time when it is being accused of having inflated capital costs to garner a larger share of profits (as compared to the government) and of having failed to ensure gas output levels and therefore shareable revenues promised in the original contract. The loser has been the government. And the winner, till now and in the future, is seen to be RIL.

**Fiscal Policy and Profits**

Another way in which the government has favoured profit earners and contributed to the profit boom is by providing them with a host of tax concessions. Revenues foregone through various concessions and tax preferences have become a significant part of fiscal policy. Although the Kelkar Committee Report on Direct Taxes (2003) had recommended reducing or eliminating such concessions while reducing tax rates, this has not happened. Indeed, while the tax rates have been reduced progressively since then, various concessions were also continued and then even expanded especially in the wake of the global crisis in Budget 2009-10. As a result, such concessions have grown significantly in value. For 2012-13, they have been estimated at a total of Rs. 5,73,627 crore - as much as ten per cent higher than the total fiscal deficit of the central government.

These "tax preferences" include a range of measures — such as special tax rates, exemptions, rebates, deductions, deferrals and credits — that are provided in accordance with certain policy priorities of the government, and obviously affect both the level and distribution of tax revenues.

As the Finance Ministry has noted, these tax preferences may be "viewed as an indirect subsidy to preferred taxpayers". These are essentially equivalent therefore to subsidies or expenditures, and so are often called 'tax expenditures'. They are provided in various ways: as concessions on direct tax payments to companies and individuals, as well as reductions or rebates in customs and excise duties. Here we will consider specifically the impact of corporate tax concessions in the recent past.

The latest Statement on "Revenue Foregone under the Central Tax System" (part of the Budget Papers of 2013-14) provides data on such tax expenditures in 2011-12. The concessions on corporation taxes amounted to Rs. 61,765 crore, which was 61 per cent of the total benefits given to direct tax payers and around 12 per cent of the total amount of estimated tax expenditures. (It should be borne in mind that most of the indirect tax concessions are also effectively preferences given to companies, especially if they do not result in declines in retail prices faced by consumers.)

Since 2006-07, the Ministry of Finance has been providing estimates of revenues foregone through various concessions on tax payments and related fiscal measures. The data relating to corporate taxes are provided from the database of electronic returns filed by companies. In the last few years these have accounted for 90 per cent of the total corporate returns expected in that year. The number of companies has been increasing over the years, suggesting improved coverage of the sample. The effective tax rate also rose, particularly for the year 2009-10 and 2010-11, but declined again for 2011-12, the latest year for which actual data (rather than projections) are available. Even in 2011-12, the effective tax rate of 22.9 per cent was well below the statutory corporation tax rate of 32.4 per cent. Table 1 shows how these rates varied by size of company, in terms of amount of profits. All sizes of companies (by amount of profit) paid much less than the statutory taxes. As expected, the largest companies with annual profits of more than Rs 500 crore accounted for the bulk of the profits and the greater amount of the tax payable. However, the effective burden of tax paid was among the lowest for them — only 21.67 per cent, substantially lower than the 26.26 per cent paid by smaller companies with less than Rs. one crore of profits.

In previous years, the incidence of tax has been least on middle to large sized companies with Rs. 50-100 crore of profits, but in 2011-12 the giant companies with more than Rs. 100 crore of profits clearly paid the lowest rates of effective tax. They also showed the lowest rates of taxable income to profits before tax, indicating that they were the best placed to take advantage of the various fiscal concessions offered.

**Table 1: Profile of sample companies in 2011-12**

| | *Number of companies* | *Share in profits before taxes (per cent)* | *Share in total tax payable (per cent)* | *Total taxable income to profits before tax (per cent)* | *Effective tax rate (per cent)* |
|---|---|---|---|---|---|
| Less than zero | 184653 | 0 | 0.41 | | |
| Zero | 30910 | 0 | 2.3 | | |
| Less than Rs 1 crore | 249567 | 2.96 | 6.11 | 85.79 | 26.26 |
| Rs 1-10 crore | 23339 | 7.1 | 7.82 | 79.2 | 25.16 |
| Rs 10-50 crore | 4330 | 9.31 | 9.46 | 73.11 | 23.21 |
| Rs 50-100 crore | 755 | 5.28 | 5.21 | 71.24 | 22.54 |
| Rs 100-500 crore | 739 | 15.86 | 15 | 68.23 | 21.63 |
| More than Rs 500 crore | 252 | 59.49 | 56.4 | 68.99 | 21.67 |
| All sample companies | 494545 | 100 | 100 | 70.6 | 22.85 |

## Concession to Finance Capital

It needs to be noted that a substantial share of these concession have been given to finance capital, especially international financial capital, which has had a field day in India's equity and debt markets after liberalisation, just as it has had in many other 'emerging markets'. A striking example is the income earned from equity investment. There are two principal ways in which income is garnered through such investment: dividends and capital gains. Both have benefited from recent tax concessions. To start with, on the grounds that corporate taxes are already taxed so that taxing shareholder dividend income would amount to a form of double taxation, it was decided in 1999-2000, that dividends paid-out to share-holders should be made tax free. Being controversial, this decision was reversed in the budget for 2002-03, only to be reinstated again in the Budget for 2003-04. What has been the fall-out of this exemption? An extremely revealing analysis by B.G. Shirsat (2006) of 1,050 major dividend-paying, listed companies had found that dividends paid out during the three years ending 2005-06 amounted to Rs. 29,532 crores. Since the beneficiaries of these dividends were likely to be in the highest marginal tax bracket, if this dividend income had been subject to tax, the revenue earned by the government over those three years would have been an additional Rs 10,000 crore (if we assume that the dividend pay-out rate would have been the same even if the tax was effective). This is by no means a small sum. What is noteworthy is the inequality in the distribution of this tax benefit. It is known that a miniscule proportion of the domestic population invests in equity. But even among them, the distribution of dividends and therefore the benefit of the tax exemption tends to be highly skewed. For example, of the close to Rs. 30,000 crore of dividends paid out by these companies in 2005-06, Rs. 14,000 crore, or around 45 per cent accrued to the promoters of the companies themselves. In fact, small or so-called "retail" shareholders received a relatively small share of this benefit. Over ninety per cent of the shareholders holding up to 500 shares each received just over Rs. 4000 crore of dividend income, while public shareholders with equity holding in excess of 500 shares garnered Rs. 7,575 crore as dividends. A significant amount of the dividend paid to public shareholders went to foreign investors. Foreign institutional investors (FIIs) received Rs. 12,808 crore of dividend income during this period and investors in GDRs and ADRs, NRI investors and other overseas bodies received Rs. 4,567 crore. In sum, a combination of promoters, high net worth domestic investors and foreigners were the main beneficiaries of the dividend tax hand out.

There remains the argument that the exemption of dividends from taxes was not a hand out but the redressal of an unjust scheme of double taxation. Even if this is accepted, there remains the fact that there is a high degree of inequality in the distribution of incomes in the country, which the accrual of record dividend incomes seems to aggravate substantially. If the government really wished to garner a fair share of the surplus for social and capital expenditure, then the removal of the tax on dividends should have been accompanied by an increase in the marginal corporate tax rate or the reduction/ removal of various exemptions. The fact that the government did not choose such measures only strengthens the perception that it has failed to tax a section of the rich adequately and effectively.

The evidence on unwarranted benefits to investors in equity does not end here. It is visible in the case of the other form of returns from equity holding-capital gains-as well. The budget for 2003-04 also decided that, "in order to give a further fillip to the capital markets", all listed equities that were acquired on or after March 1, 2003, and sold after the lapse of a year, or more, were to be exempted from the incidence of capital gains tax. Capital gains made on those assets held by the purchaser for at least 365 days were defined for taxation purposes as long-term gains. Up to that point in time, long-term capital gains tax was levied at the rate of 10 per cent.

An analysis of share price movements of 28 Sensex companies found that if we assume that all shares purchased in 2004 were sold after 365 days in 2005, the total capital gains that could have been garnered in 2005 would have amounted to Rs. 78,569 crore. If these gains had been taxed at the rate of 10 per cent prevalent earlier, the revenue yielded would have amounted to Rs. 7,857 crore. That reflects the revenue foregone by the state and the benefit accruing to the buyers of these shares. It is indeed true that not all shares of these companies bought in 2004 would have been sold a year-and-one-day later. But some shares which were purchased prior to 2004 would have been sold during 2005, presumably with a bigger margin of gain. This estimate relates to just 28 companies, so the actual revenues foregone were presumably much greater. Clearly, a more appropriate tax policy relating to dividends and capital gains could have yielded substantial revenues for the government.

**At the Cost of Hunger**

The concessions to the corporate sector have to be seen in the light of the government's aversion to provide support to the poor. Consider the argument, which has been the focus of the case against an extensive or universal food security programme that the cost involved is too high for a government already burdened by a high fiscal deficit. It may be useful to reiterate once more that a fiscal deficit can also be pruned by mobilising more resources through increased taxation, reduced tax concessions and better implementation. The controversy surrounding the capital gains demand made on Vodafone makes clear that this government is committed more towards incentivising investors, including foreign investors, than to mobilising resources to finance crucial expenditures.

The Rangarajan Committee estimated that the subsidy required to support the National Advisory Council's food security scheme could go up to Rs 92,000 crore and the Parliamentary Standing Committee report on Food Security estimates the subsidy required to support its recommendations at Rs 1.12 crore. The latter would amount to 1.35 per cent of GDP in 2011-12.

Compare this with the numbers giving the ratio of actual food subsidies over the last decade relative to GDP. In most years subsidies have amounted to between 0.6 and 0.8 per cent of GDP, and touched 1 per cent in only a single year. Raising this figure to more than one per cent is a reasonable demand given the fact that the World Food Programme estimates that, despite high growth over two decades and more, a quarter of the world's hungry population resides in India and around 43 per cent of children under the age of five years are malnourished.

More importantly, during the 2000s, when corporate profits were soaring, tax concessions in different forms provided to the corporate sector amounted to well above one per cent of GDP. Thus the sum estimated by the Parliamentary Standing Committee as needed to support its recommendation was, at 1.35 per cent of GDP in 2011-12, less than the 1.36 per cent of GDP transferred to the corporate sector through these concessions in 2007-08. And corporate tax rebates are only one form in which the corporate sector is favoured, as the controversies over spectrum sale, coal blocks and even gas pricing suggest. Anyone with a sense of social priorities should, in the circumstances, recognise that the argument that the money is not available to address them is without much basis.

**The Concealed Subsidy**

This brings us to the most important way in which the corporate sector has been favoured in recent years: concealed subsidies that are not treated as such as they are seen as illegitimate transfers made by corrupt government officials and politicians who receive a quid pro quo or a 'bribe'. The view that the record of graft and corruption during the two-term, nine-year rule of the UPA is the worst in India's post-Independence history is widespread. The reason is obvious. While corruption has always been with us, and is by no means only an Indian disease, the period in question has seen an almost respite-less, spate of allegations of corruption, many of which have stuck. The terrain in question is wide, with allegations of kickbacks for procurement for games events and the army, of procedural errors and malfeasance in the distribution of resources varying from land, non-reproducible raw material reserves of coal and iron ore and of spectrum, of suspect disinvestment and privatisation, and of violations such the 'sale' of government positions to the highest bidder interested either in the regular incomes they afford or the opportunity for graft they provide.

Across this wide terrain, the allegations suggest, the scale of each instance has been on the rise. Petty corruption, such as those of a clerk or constable is now almost forgotten though widespread. A few hundred rupees make no bribe when payments amounting to crores, tens of crores, or even hundreds of crores are routinely quoted in the media. What is at issue today is large-scale corruption. Moreover, the allegations are against those at the top, involving senior bureaucrats, high level public sector executives, ministers, and, even if tangentially, the Prime Minister. The bribe givers too are allegedly big, including some of the top and hitherto unsullied businesses and captains of industry. Does this then mark a new phase in the ubiquity and intensity of an old problem? That seems to be the case even if difficult to prove.

However, the visibility of corruption may be greater because of more transparency and better reporting. It is true that the number of allegations in any given time period is much larger. There are many factors that may be contributing to this rise in the number and significance of the "revelations". One is of course the proliferation of the media and competition within a media space that increasingly depends on sensationalism to attract readers and viewers. With defamation laws still weak, such competition results in a willingness to deliver an exposé even when the evidence is not complete. The language and method is also in many cases in the nature of a media trial without adequate investigation. Moreover, the media too is not free of corruption, with allegations not just of paid news parading as editorial content, but also of the investigative story being used as a weapon to extract advertising revenue. So there is reason to believe that there is far more reporting of alleged corruption today than in the past. This tendency is aggravated by the fact that politics today is a far more contested terrain and the politicisation of the bureaucracy has increased. Selective leaks to the media to discredit opponents helps trigger a scandal and force an investigation. More the leaks; greater are the evidence of corruption.

A more encouraging reason for the spate of revelations of corruption is increased access to information. Not only has civil society activism yielded a Right to information Act that is being exploited to garner information that puts errant officials under scrutiny, but statutory bodies have also played a role. Obvious examples are the office of the Comptroller and Auditor General of

India, which has investigated and questioned dubious practices in areas varying from the sale of Spectrum to the allocation of coal blocks, or of Lokayuktas, such as in Karnataka, that have exposed malpractice in the issue and use of mining licences.

While these reasons for greater reporting and increased revelation of the corruption phenomenon may suggest that the problem need not be worse than it was, the fact of the matter is that even the revealed tip of the corruption iceberg is far too large for comfort. Moreover, there are other reasons to infer that the space and potential for corrupt practices have increased after liberalisation, rather than decreased. The 'urge' to engage in such practices also seems to have been enhanced in the new environment.

Advocates of liberalisation had long held that state control and regulation during the pre-liberalisation years between the 1950s and 1970s allowed for corruption. Given the detailed physical and financial controls in place, bureaucrats and policy makers were seen as capable of using their control over the levers of policy, in areas varying from licensing through tariffs and foreign exchange allocation to provision of credit, to favour those whom they wanted to privilege. While this was done in the name of plan objectives, it was claimed; it also provided the grounds for demanding and receiving a quid pro quo.

There were, of course, many sensational instances of allegations of large scale corruption. The cancer of corruption that pervaded the East India Company had indeed affected even early leaders of Provincial Councils, forcing Gandhi to declare in the late 1930s that: "We seem to have weakened from within. I would go to the length of giving the whole Congress a decent burial, rather than put up with the corruption that is rampant." However, Gandhi's standards were high, and the number of individuals, the instances and the magnitudes involved were small relative to later trends. The problem persisted in the post-Independence period. The Jeep Scandal of 1948, involving the purchase of army jeeps for Rs. 80 lakh, through a process that bypassed established procedure, and the Mundhra Scandal of 1957, involving the sale of fraudulent shares to LIC by businessman Haridas Mundhra, were two among the well-known post-Independence corruption controversies. The first was closed, but the second led to Mundhra's arrest and the resignation of Finance Minister T. T. Krishnamachari.

But there was much in the system that seemed to make these the exception than the rule. Political leaders in early post-Independence India had won their spurs through the national movement, as part of which they had engaged in much sacrifice. They were unlikely to turn to corruption so easily. Moreover, as Feroze Gandhi's role in the Bennett Coleman acquisition, the LIC-Mundhra and the Jeep scandals showcased, parliamentary scrutiny of the (mis)use of authority was considerable. Besides parliamentary scrutiny, the ethos of the time was such that a majority of the bureaucracy saw itself as part of a common national project. Corruption was not the norm, and peer example discouraged it. Moreover, the income levels and life styles of the bureaucracy did not induce a desire for large additional incomes on the side. So even if petty corruption was significant, big corruption was not too widespread. Nor was it always very big. In the old days, allegations of corruption were inevitably associated with the unearthing of wealth beyond that warranted by known sources of income. Given the size of those incomes the magnitude of corruption could not have been large.

Matters seemed to have changed since the 1980s, with the Bofors scandal involving kickbacks from Bofors AB in return for orders of its 155 mm howitzer almost symbolising the transition. This change cannot be attributed to just a change in the value system as the nationalist fervour and commitment to social change associated with the freedom movement wore out. Social behaviour of the kind that leads to an escalation of the scale of corruption must be a result of systemic influences associated with a change in circumstances with time.

Two changes occurring in this period are of relevance here. The first was political: the destruction of the Congress as a mass party under Indira Gandhi, the associated end of one-party dominance and the emergence of competitive politics. Not only did central leaders and vote-getting local satraps become important, but competitive politics saw the increase in the use of money power in the electoral process. The second was socio-economic: a transition in the social vision underlying the trajectory of development, from one in which the focus was on regulating capitalism to ensure that the fruits of development were more equitably shared, to one where the emphasis was on unfettering capitalism in the hope of realising capitalist success.

The first was an obvious encouragement to corruption among the political elite. If money has to be outlaid to win elections, it must be mobilised: either from those who expect favours from politicians benefiting from their donations or garnered by the politicians themselves during past periods when power had been held and exercised. That provides the basis for increased corruption. The second involved state functionaries favouring capital as part of the development project, making it easier for them to push policies in return for which they can expect illegitimate payments. Since this occurs in a period when the social ethos is one that celebrates the wealthy and the economically successful, sudden increases in the wealth position of individuals is not seen as abnormal. For even a suspicion of corruption, it is not enough that an individual's wealth exceeds what can be built based on known sources of income. What matters is direct and adequate evidence of illegitimate acquisitions of income that violate existing laws.

It is in this light that we need to examine the argument that liberalisation should result in a reduction in the extent of corruption. The premise underlying that argument is that it is only under regulated capitalism of the 1950s kind in India that the state, which rationed access to commodities, services or finance, can, by favouring some, lay the ground for a quid pro quo. That is not true. In all societies, there are scarcities of one kind or another: access to the best free hospital facilities; access to land; access to a scarce 'intangible' resource like the air waves; or rights to extract limited and non-reproducible mineral resources, to name just a few. In a regulated regime there are well-defined rules on how this is to be done. Those rules can be violated, but there are well-defined procedures and benchmarks to decide whether unwarranted access has been provided to one or other agent. In a liberalised economic order, on the other hand, while the government still has the right to determine the level of access, its role is seen as one of providing such access as part of a process of encouraging private sector-led growth.

State involvement can lead to corruption from both the 'buy' and the 'sell' side. Bribes can be paid when orders are placed by the state for military equipment, purchase of goods for consumption or investment or for provision of a host of services. Since liberalisation involves an increasing emphasis on getting the state out of production and on outsourcing services of different kinds, corruption from the buy side is bound to increase. But bribes can also be received when public assets are disposed off by the state: through the disinvestment of public equity or privatisation of public enterprises, provision of land for various "development purposes", or sale of Spectrum or coal blocks. Since these can be sold only to some and at a price decided by politicians and bureaucrats, there is much profit to be made. A "small" fee for the agents delivering such profit is not a high price to demand.

This increases the space for the misuse of power. The result is large-payoffs for two groups. The first is for those occupying high positions in the state apparatus. The second for the business interests which derive gains from decisions purchased at a small price. If we go by the Comptroller and Auditor General's estimate, the loss of revenues to the state from the mispricing of 2G Spectrum alone is Rs. 1.76 lakh crore or close to 10 per cent of Gross Fixed Capital Formation in the economy in 2008-09. If much of that is a transfer to those acquiring Spectrum it points to huge illegitimate benefits for the private sector. There is here clearly a link between public and private corruption.

It needs to be noted that transfers of this kind to private capital are not always the result of corrupt practices. There have been many instances where sections of the private sector have made huge gains through means that are "unfair", even if not illegitimate and not associated with credible allegations of corruption. One such, involving Spectrum again, was the implicit bail out of investors who made irrational bids for cellular bandwidth during the first round of auctions. Though these bids were irrational, the government helped the bidders meet their initial commitments by allowing them to retain a few of the multiple circles in which they had, not surprisingly, won licences. However, when these bidders turned operators, they discovered that they could not operate profitably if they were actually required to pay the amounts they had bid to obtain even these licences. The government, therefore, allowed them to migrate to a revenue sharing regime rather than a specific licence fee system, allowing them to make huge profits subsequently.

The point to note is that the irrational bids made by these operators had kept out a number of rational bidders who may have been more efficient suppliers. Yet, by allowing the irrational bidders to substantially reduce their commitments the government rewarded them. This was to say the least unfair, even if not illegitimate because no clear evidence of corruption emerged. This was one more instance where unfair business practices and state patronage at the expense of the exchequer permitted sections of the private sector to garner huge profits. But no allegations of corruption were involved.

However, when discussions of corruption occur, the possibility that it serves as a mechanism for private aggrandisement receives little attention. The tenor of the discourse is that the virus of corruption afflicts only the government officials and politicians who control and misuse state power. But increasingly corruption appears to reflect payments made by the private sector to realise illegitimate gains that are not merely violative of fair practice and/or the law, but damaging from the development, environmental or fiscal points of view. Given the large amounts that can be garnered in this fashion the state seems to have emerged an important site for primitive accumulation for the private sector during the phase of liberalisation and economic reform.

The essential point is that corruption tends to be greater in periods when there is a state engineered redistribution of wealth in favour of a few and at the explicit or implicit expense of the many. Liberalisation is one such period, whether it is of the 'shock therapy' kind in a largely state-controlled Russia or the (relatively speaking) moderately-paced kind adopted in the so-called 'mixed economies' like India. In such periods corruption is not just an aberration involving a few wayward individuals overcome by greed. It is systemic and reflects an aggravation of the tendency towards primitive accumulation of capital characteristic of capitalism throughout its history and more rampant in the distorted capitalism superimposed on the partially destroyed, pre-capitalist formations in the underdeveloped world.

With the transition to a neoliberal order electoral democracy too has its cost. Evidence of the wealth amassed by elected representatives reporting their assets when they stand in consecutive elections is quoted to show what corruption could be delivering to politicians. But what is also noteworthy is that increasingly it is extremely difficult to participate in the electoral process without access to wealth, irrespective of the rules that the Election Commission frames. This intensifies the drive to adopt corrupt practices.

In sum, there are two systemic causes for corruption in today's India: the political and the economic. By ignoring the latter what is being concealed is that neoliberalism is a class project aimed at pampering and transferring wealth to business. In many ways this implies a huge cost to the nation. Resources are diverted away from projects with high social returns to those that enrich a few. Income inequality increases depriving many of the ability to participate in economic activity and wasting the human resources of a demographically young nation. Revenue that can be garnered to finance much-needed infrastructure that would promote development is transferred to the private sector which privileges profit above nation development. And the fiscal room needed to combat hunger, create employment, reduce poverty and advance human development is lost.

# 4

# *Access to Justice: The Case for Judicial Reforms*

*N.R. Madhava Menon*

## The Challenge of Access to Justice

Article 14(1) of the International Covenant on Civil and Political Rights describes the right to fair trial as follows:

> "All persons shall be equal before the courts and tribunals. In the determination of any criminal charge against him, or of his rights and obligations in a suit at law, everyone shall be entitled to a fair and public hearing by a competent, independent and impartial tribunal established by law".

> "Justice, Social, Economic and Political" is the promise of the Indian Constitution. It is the duty of the State to secure a social order in which the legal system promotes justice, on a basis of equal opportunity, and in particular ensures that opportunities for securing justice are not denied to any citizen by reason of economic or other disabilities (Article 39-A).

Through a set of Fundamental Rights, the Constitution guarantees to every citizen basic freedoms (right to equality and non-discrimination, right to freedom, right to life and personal liberty, right to religion, right to constitutional remedies) and provides that the right to move the Supreme Court for the enforcement of these rights is in itself a Fundamental Right. To guard against illegal arrest and detention, the Constitution provides the Fundamental Right of every arrested person being informed of the grounds of such arrest and being allowed the right to consult; and to be defended by, a legal practitioner of his/ or her choice.

In respect of social and economic rights, the Constitution has adopted a different approach under which certain Directive Principles of State Policy are stipulated on condition that — though not justiciable, they shall be "fundamental in the governance of the country" and the State shall apply them in making laws. Under these principles the State is obliged to enact laws and adopt policies to secure a social order in which opportunities for securing socio-economic justice are not denied to any citizen by reasons of social, economic or other disabilities. The State is thus obliged to secure adequate means of livelihood, minimise inequalities in status, facilities and opportunities, equal pay for equal work, free legal aid, living wages, just and humane conditions of work, etc. (Article 39,42,43).

In short, the Constitution of India through restrictions on State power (Fundamental Rights of citizens) and positive obligations on the State (Directive Principles), provides a legal framework for citizens to access justice. Under this arrangement, access to justice is both a means to ventilate grievances and seek remedies on the basis of equality before law as well as a product of State policies directed to the welfare of the poor and marginalised sections of people.

How does the promise of equal justice for all, under the Constitution translate on the ground? In other words, how effectively does the system protect the rights of the disadvantaged groups? Are the disadvantaged groups able to seek and obtain remedy through the formal and informal institutions of justice?

Despite sustained economic growth and the reduction of the number of people living in poverty, the fact remains that the poor and under-privileged are still struggling to access justice even when their rights over their land and natural resources are taken away in the name of development. Many of them are further impoverished in the process and their ability to access justice is reduced. Illiteracy and poverty are rampant among Scheduled Castes and Scheduled Tribes. Sexual and domestic violence against women continue to rise despite progressive legislations providing for stringent punishment. Rural areas fare much worse because of having lower income levels and weaker human development indicators. No doubt poverty and illiteracy result in denial of access to justice because the justice system expects people to be aware of their rights and be able to seek their enforcement when threatened. A Bulk of India's poor are not aware of their legal rights and entitlements. Many of those who are aware do not have the economic capacity or command the technical know-how to process their grievances through the formal judicial system.

There are institutional barriers in the system of administration of justice which tend to work against the interests of the poor and marginalised. These structural factors first need to be resolved in strengthening access to justice.

**Adversarial Legalism and Structural Constraints**

As observed by Robert A. Kagan (Adversarial Legalism, Yale 2003) "adversarial litigation inspires legal defensiveness and contentiousness, which often impede socially constructive co-operation alienating many citizens from the law itself .... Its outcome is shaped more by the delays and opportunity costs of extended adversarial processes.... It is lawyer-dominated, markedly inefficient, unnecessarily complex and unpredictable method of Dispute resolution.... Its procedural tools exacerbates its potential for inconsistency and unequal treatment. It encourages and rewards manipulative lawyering and extortive demands. It is a two-fold source of inequality: sophisticated litigants gain an advantage not only because they are better at withstanding the costs and uncertainties of adversarial litigation but also because they are better able to devise ways of circumventing it".

These observations on the American litigation scene hold true in India with greater force particularly vis-à-vis the marginalised sections. The huge backlog of cases (over 30 million cases) pending in courts, some of them for over 10 years is a standing testimony of the inappropriateness of the system to provide access to justice to all. The problem is compounded by the inadequacy of courts (18,000 for a population of 1.2 billion) and the inability of the system to fill the vacancies of judicial officers as they arise.

Acknowledging the implications of adversarial legalism and the impact of backlogs and delays due to technicalities of procedure, Government of India has launched a National Mission for Justice Delivery and Legal Reforms with a view to strengthen access to justice. The object of the Mission is to strengthen the judicial sector towards reducing pendency and delays and thereby enlarge access to timely delivery of justice. It is a Mission spread over five years 2011-2016 and has five major strategic initiatives. These include: (i) policy and legislative changes; (ii) re-engineering procedures and promoting alternative methods of dispute resolution; (iii) strengthening the system through human resource development; (iv) leveraging Information and Communication Technology (ICT) for better justice delivery; and (v) improving the judicial infrastructure.

It is for the first time in Indian legal history, the judicial sector is receiving such co-ordinated attention from all branches of Government. It all began with the thirteenth Finance Commission (2008) recommending a number of initiatives to improve judicial outcomes saying that the inordinate delay in disposal of cases results not only in immense hardship to litigants, but also hinders economic development. On the basis of Finance Commission's recommendations an initial sum of Rs 5000 crore was allocated for six set of reforms proposed by the Justice Department. These included (i) increase in the number of court hours using the existing infrastructure by holding shift courts, (ii) scaling up Lok Adalats (People's courts where disputes are disposed of through negotiated settlements), (iii) increased funding for free legal aid to indigents to enable wider access to justice, (iv) establishment of ADR mechanisms in every district to promote out of court resolution of disputes, (v) enhancing capacity of prosecutors and judicial personnel through better education and training, (vi) setting up judicial academies in every State to institutionalise training for capacity development, and (vii) appointment of court managers in every judicial district to assist the judiciary in their administrative functions. As part of the package of reforms the Finance Commission also recommended that Central and State Governments should frame state litigation policies aimed at more responsible approach to litigation. In India, the Government is the single largest litigant which significantly adds to the burden of arrears. The State Litigation Policy is supposed to include steps for (i) reviewing the existing cases and wherever necessary, withdrawing cases identified as frivolous and vexatious, (ii) formulating norms for defending cases as well as for filing appeals, and (iii) setting up of Empowered Committees in Government to eliminate unnecessary litigation.

The Department of Justice with the funds allotted not only pushed the reforms with the State Governments and the Judiciary but also integrated them with the National Mission on Justice Delivery now under implementation. The Department could also succeed in persuading the Central Planning Commission to incorporate judicial sector reforms as part of the XIIth Plan (2013-18) so that the funding support will continue to be available even after the Mission ends. The Prime Minister has gone on record saying that for each step the judiciary takes to expedite justice his Government would take two steps to facilitate the process. In short, it appears that India is going to see discernible changes in administration of justice in the next few years despite the institutional challenges and old mindsets.

**Technology Adoption for Delivery of Timely Justice**

Since 2005, the judiciary has embarked upon large scale computerisation of court records and functioning of court systems. The object of the E-Courts project is to provide designated services to the citizens by ICT enablement of all courts in the country by internet connectivity and installation of standard application software at each court complex. The project has provision for supply of laptops to every judicial officer with broadband connectivity and laser printers and imparting ICT training to them. The project is expected to be completed by 2014 and the Department of Justice with an Empowered Committee is monitoring implementation through the National Informatics Centre (NIC).

Meanwhile a National Judicial Data Grid is being developed with up-to-date judicial statistics on cases pending in the 16,000 and odd courts spread throughout the country. As on October, 2012, 11,165 District and Subordinate courts, all High Courts and Supreme Court have been computerised and the rest is expected to be completed by March 2014. The ICT enabled courts would render several services to litigants, lawyers, court staff and judges through Judicial Services Centres in court complexes. The Information Software is reportedly ready and is under experimentation in select districts. Process re-engineering for greater efficiency in trial procedures is said to follow the computerisation in select districts. Delhi High Court reportedly accomplished several procedural reforms to speed up the processes with the ICT enabled services.

It is expected that the E-Court project once completed, judicial efficiency and productivity will be considerably enhanced to the advantage of litigants generally and the poor in particular. Justice delivery will become more transparent, less dilatory and further cost effective. By reducing the need for litigants repeatedly visiting courts and their advocates, it will mitigate possible harassment and inconvenience as well as costs involved.

**National Court Management Systems (NCMS) for Expediting Justice**

Another parallel initiative of the Supreme Court under way is a framework for enhancing court performance addressing issues of equality, timeliness and responsiveness. A user friendly case management system, a court development plan and a human resource development strategy will form the core activities of the NCMS. The Chief Justice of India has constituted an Empowered Committee and an Advisory Council of sitting judges for overseeing the implementation of modernized court management systems.

According to a note prepared by the NCMS Committee, it is estimated that the number of judges/courts will increase six-fold (75,000 Courts/Judges from the present 16,000 Courts/Judges) while the number of cases grow twelve-fold (15 crore cases each year compared to two crore currently), when the population figure reach 1.5 billion. This is an assessment based on increases in literacy and economic growth as well as new legislations adopted which impact on number of new cases filed. The note also calculates that only 74 per cent of cases pending are over five years old and NCMS will address the remaining 26 per cent cases (over five years old) also to become "five plus free" status in judicial administration. In other words, when NCMS is fully operational, no case will remain pending in Indian courts beyond five years! At the same time NCMS will aim to shorten the average life cycle of a case in a given court to not more than one year!

An ambitious plan indeed, that is now directly supervised by the Chief Justice of India and the Advisory Council of sitting judges and the Chief Justices of High Courts.

**Pendency Reduction Campaign**

On a joint action by the Government and various High Courts, a campaign for clearing long pending cases and cases pertaining to senior citizens, minors, disabled and marginalised groups was undertaken in the country between July-December, 2011.

It is reported that the results are encouraging in as much as High Courts could reduce over 78,000 cases pending for over five years during the period and the subordinate courts 7.5 lakh cases pending beyond five years. Nearly 2.6 lakh under-trial prisoners got released or discharged during the campaign period. And above all, 1.36 lakh cases involving senior citizens, minors, disabled and marginalised groups pending in the judicial system got resolved by disposal of their cases by the respective courts.

**Development of Physical Infrastructure of Courts**

Under a Centrally-sponsored scheme in which the Centre and States share the expenses, the Department of Justice is implementing a programme of building physical infrastructure of subordinate courts throughout the country. The scheme includes construction of new court buildings, accommodation for judges and development of Model Court complexes in select districts.

The Model Courts project is intended to increase access by reducing delays and pendency in the system and to enhance accountability through structural changes and by setting performance standards and capacities. Among other things, Model Courts will adhere to minimum standards in terms of building, ICT enablement, staffing, training, and guidelines on how to function efficiently. Initially, the Model Courts project is proposed to be implemented as a pilot in select courts at the trial level. An amount of Rs. 130 crore for a two year period is allocated for the purpose.

**Gram Nyayalayas (Village Courts) for Affordable and Quick Access to Justice in Rural Areas**

A major initiative for access to justice to the rural poor has been the Gram Nyayalaya Act, 2008 under which village courts are established at the level of intermediate Panchayat or for a group of contiguous Panchayats. The judge is supposed to visit villages and hear the parties (mobile court) and dispose of the cases without having to adjourn the matter or to put litigants in difficulties for seeking justice. It has limited civil and criminal jurisdiction and is empowered to follow summary procedure in criminal trial. Conciliation is the preferred procedure in Gram Nyayalayas and the technical rules of evidence under the Evidence Act are not binding on them. Only principles of natural justice have to be followed. The Schedule to the Act gives the offences trialable and includes offences punishable with less than two years of imprisonment, theft (Sec. 379, 380, 381) where the value of the property stolen is less than Rs. 20,000, Section 411 where the value of property received is less than Rs. 20,000 and offences under Sections 454, 456, 504 and 506 of Indian Penal Code. Furthermore, Gram Nyayalayas can try offences and grant reliefs under Section. 20 of the Cattle Trespass Act, Payment of Wages Act, Minimum Wages Act, Protection of Civil Rights Act, Bonded Labour System (Abolition) Act, Equal Remuneration Act, Protection of Women from Domestic Violence Act and Order of Maintenance under Chapter IX of Cr.P.C.

On the civil side, Gram Nyayalayas have jurisdiction in matters of use of common pasture, regulation of taking water from irrigation canal, right to purchase property and disputes on money suits either arising from trade transaction or money lending, disputes arising out of the partnership in cultivation of land and disputes as to the use of forest produce by inhabitants of Gram Panchayats. Plea bargaining under Chapter XXI-A of Cr.P.C. is applicable in Gram Nyayalaya. Judgment of Gram Nyayalaya is deemed to be a decree and it shall be executed by it without being bound by the C.P.C. procedure for the purpose guided only by principles of natural justice.

A scheme of Central assistance to States for setting up Gram Nyayalayas has also been announced. It is reported that over 150 Gram Nyayalayas are now functioning in a dozen States providing access to quick justice to the rural people at their doorsteps.

**Legal Aid and Legal Empowerment**

Legal aid is recognized as a guaranteed fundamental right, part of right to life and personal liberty (Art. 21) in criminal cases and trial conducted without representation by counsel is declared by the Supreme Court as null and void. There is an elaborate system of State sponsored free legal aid to marginalised people under the Legal Services Authorities Act, 1987. The National Legal Services Authority is headed by the Chief Justice of India himself and State Legal Services Authorities by the High Court Chief Justices. Women, Scheduled Castes, Scheduled Tribes and Children are entitled to free legal aid irrespective of income. Legal aid includes not only lawyer's services but also litigation costs like court fee, process fee, etc.

District Legal Aid Committee and Taluka Legal Aid Committees headed by the District Judge and the Civil Judge respectively maintain panels of legal aid lawyers who are assigned to eligible persons who are paid by the Committees. Besides, they organise Lok Adalats, legal awareness camps, pre-litigation mediation, legal counseling and public interest litigation.

Though the Act envisages a dynamic system of legal aid for widening access to justice for the poor, there are gaps and failures in the delivery of services. The emphasis seems to be on litigative aid through assignment of counsel and settlement through Lok Adalats. There is a vast area of unmet legal needs in rural areas where lawyers are hardly available. Because of low remuneration of panel lawyers, the quality of services suffers. The tradition of pro bono work is still not popular among legal practitioners. The involvement of the bar is not substantial and the system breeds delay and incompetence leading to alienation of people from the system. Occasional attempts to improve the system by enlightened Chief Justices keep the system functional at least to the urban and middle class litigants.

At the same time, initiatives by the legal services authority as well as by civil society organisations to campaign for legal empowerment of weaker sections by bringing welfare programmes and developmental activities of the Government within their sphere of activity have helped the rural communities to have greater control over their lives and livelihoods. They are rights-based campaigns generating awareness and consequent increase in demands for benefits and entitlements under Government programmes of poverty alleviation. The legal aid apparatus is compelled to respond by strengthening the supply side and hence access to justice. There are several examples of legal empowerment strategies enabling the poor to access rights to which they are entitled and to avoid exploitation in the process. Social mobilisation for legal action is becoming a mainstream strategy for access to justice. This is facilitated by law school-based legal aid clinics, civil society-based para-legal outfits and media-based social activists.

**Public Interest Litigation and Access to Justice**

The Indian Supreme Court is credited with popularising certain tools for wider access to justice particularly for the poor and marginalised communities. The jurisprudence of Public Interest Litigation (PIL) enabled millions of marginalised people access courts without their being present in court or being parties to the litigation. Public spirited citizens could move the court on their behalf and seek remedies and reliefs. Court relaxed the rule of locus standi, organised verification of facts through court-appointed commissions, negotiated with State agencies involved through conciliation processes, designed remedies and reliefs appropriate to the circumstances and reached justice to the needy without the beneficiaries having to pursue the matter. The Court has held that legal redress for the deprived should not be encumbered by the restrictions of the adversarial system. Together with the expansive reading of Article 21, the court could deliver social justice in several dark areas where the implementation of welfare laws was neglected for long. In fact, employing the doctrine of continuing mandamus, the court saw to it that its orders are implemented and the beneficiaries received their entitlements.

**The Criminal Justice System: An Area of Continuing Concern**

Talking about access to justice for the poor and marginalized, one cannot escape saying that the way police, prosecution and custodial institutions function is a source of continuing concern despite repeated interventions by the Supreme Court and High Courts laying down standards and guidelines. The legal aid services could not do much in this sphere. Policy changes on arrest, bail, search, interrogation and detention did make a difference in the law governing police powers of investigation; but on the ground, business is as usual. Terrorism and insurgency have added another dimension to the problem keeping the poor and disadvantaged sections at the receiving end. Institutional incapacities are being addressed by improved training and service conditions. However, given the power equations and inherited biases that play out in criminal proceedings, the system becomes unfair to rape victims, child abusers, dowry victims, forest dwellers, migrant workers and others who do not have money or political clout to influence the system.

**Key Areas of Reform for Strengthening Access to Justice**

Apart from the number of initiatives already under implementation as part of the National Mission for Justice Delivery and Legal Reforms (2011-16), one would like to draw attention on certain segments of the justice system which continues to be out of the reform loop despite being critical to the reform strategy. These include the following:

1. Police investigation and criminal prosecution;
2. Juvenile Justice and Child Welfare;
3. Victim orientation in criminal proceedings;
4. The Private Bar: Competence and Accountability;
5. Legal Aid Administration and Non-Litigative Legal Aid;

6. Corruption and Justice Delivery;
7. Adversarial Legalism and Equal Justice;
8. Community Rights and Public Interest;
9. Demystification of law and its processes;
10. Enhanced public participation in law making and justice delivery.

**Conclusion**

Justice system essentially stands on three pillars — the LAW (substantive and procedural), the INSTITUTIONS through which rights and duties under the law are processed, and the PERSONNEL who provide the human resources to operate the institutions and implement the laws. The system receives the inputs in the form of laws and claims of litigants, gets them processed through institutions by the personnel who manage them depending on their capacities and produces the output called justice. It is supposed to be justice according to law and it is believed that rule of law is thus maintained. There are many myths and distortions in this story of administration of justice. For example, laws are taken to be just, fair and reasonable though, sometimes they are not as fair as one would expect. Adversarial adjudication is taken to be the best method for finding the truth on disputed questions of fact though; very often they work to the advantage of the rich and the powerful. Legal aid to the poor is supposed to enable them access justice though, very often it does not result that way.

Yet, in the absence of a better system for justice delivery, all that one can expect is to see better laws are enacted with participation of people, institutions of the law are strengthened by greater transparency, accountability and good practices, and the personnel of the law are so trained to perform in such a manner that the inadequacies of the laws are overcome in order to advance the cause of equal justice particularly to the weaker sections of society. So long as human beings are imperfect, the justice they administer will remain imperfect. Nevertheless, it is the obligation of every democratic State to ensure that barriers to justice are removed and access improved to ensure equal justice under law, a reality to every section of the citizenry.

# 5

# *Top-Heavy Administrative Structure: A Case Study*

*C.P. Nair*

The enormous hierarchical state apparatus, described in popular parlance by the term 'bureaucracy' has been part of the social landscape of India from the dawn of history. Even in the days of the Mahabharata there were high-ranking functionaries like Mukhyamatya (Prime Minister), Nyayadheesa (Chief Justice), Kosadhyaksha (Chancellor of the Exchequer) and Mahasenapati (Commander-in-chief), serving the monarch. At the bottom of the bureaucratic ladder there were the equivalents of the present village officer and police constable. Of course it was far from an institution with democratic ethos in the modern sense. On the contrary it was meant more or less to look after basic bureaucratic functions like collection of tax, maintenance of law and order and apprehending and bringing before the seats of justice offenders against the law. This state apparatus was meant to look after the interests of the citizenry at large and regulate social life according to the law codes, custom and usage, though it hardly bothered to identify the hopes and aspirations and needs of the public and to take proactive steps to answer them.

There is an oft-quoted verse in Kalidasa's magnum opus Raghuvamsa, which may be translated as follows:

> "He (emperor Dilipa) collected tax from them (the public) for their own prosperity, even as the sun draws up water to return (it) a thousand-fold" (Canto I, verse 18)

This, however, has to be viewed as a rare, ideal, stand-alone case: the great Dilipa was a glorious exception to the general run of potentates. Till recently their hallmark was extravagance, ostentation, profligacy, and an obsession with wealth, luxuries and sensual pleasures. Not even in their remotest dreams did the welfare of the people figure.

As centuries passed, the concept came to be accepted, however slowly, that bureaucracy should have an undeniable commitment to society at large, that its interests should be reflected in its programmes and performances, that the concerns of the '*aam aadmi*' (a term popularised by the Prime Minister and the UPA Chairperson) have necessarily to be not only factored in its policies and projects, but fully realised in practice. To put it differently, it was by and large accepted that at least in theory; the bureaucratic apparatus should be, as famously spelt out in President Lincoln's classic definition of democracy, of the people, for the people and by the people. The administrative structure that exists in India today, both at the Centre and in the States, is the product of a continuous process of evolution of democratic principles. Our Constitution itself mandates that it is the solemn duty of the State to safeguard the interests of the poor, the underprivileged and the marginalised, the dalit and the tribal, the exploited and the deprived, and work out and implement programmes that would ensure their all-round development and well-being.

**The Governance Deficit**

Nevertheless, even after the progressive growth of a democratic ethos, it is today widely accepted that the Indian bureaucracy is obese and top-heavy, that a lot of flab has accumulated in it in the course of the last one century, that it has become prohibitively costly, and most of all, it has become self-centered and self-seeking, and has all but lost its commitment to the people. This criticism, unsparing and oft-repeated, emanates not only from social activists, academics, media gurus and senior politicians, but even from those who are part and parcel of the huge, faceless, amorphous, amoral thing called bureaucracy — be they politicians or civilians. To downsize drastically the bureaucratic equipment, to vastly step up its level of professional competence and social commitment, and to convert it into an effective and competent instrument that can translate into reality the policies and programmes adumbrated in the tomes that emerge periodically from Yojana Bhavan and the OMs and Circulars from the innumerable bureaucratic salons, comfortably ensconced in the heavily guarded, lavishly appointed chambers in North Block and South Block — such has been the theme of many a lecture, seminar, workshop and Committee Report. The number of 'high-level' 'expert' committees that have enquired into and reported upon administrative reforms (at enormous cost to the public exchequer) since Independence is disconcertingly large. Far from implementing their well-meaning recommendations even on a selective basis, no serious effort seems to have been made even to make an in-depth appraisal of these proposals (The Government of India (GOI) today has 85 Secretaries and 87 Departments — at least a six-fold increase from the Nehru days!).

In fact, in India the bureaucracy has always been an elite service. The bureaucrats are rich, highly privileged and in many ways, more powerful than most politicians. During the recent economic downturn, the bureaucrats with a Sixth Pay Commission – granted bonanza remained highly secure, where those in the private sector including top CEO's even in MNCs went through a harrowing time. As India is chasing a nine per cent growth story, hardly anyone has raised the issue of an ever-increasing number of bureaucrats and even the inflated kitty to sustain them-this, against the backdrop of the global trend of down-sizing bureaucracy and regular objections to their fat salaries.

**The Ongoing Process of Expansion**

An article by A.K. Bhattacharya dated March 21, 2012 (accessed from the Internet) makes the astounding observation that "over 10 years, the actual reduction in the number of employees is just 10,000." Serious thinking on downsizing bureaucracy had begun in the early 1990s. A sub-group set up by the Planning Commission had suggested in 1993 that the Union Government should weed out at least 20,000 senior positions in various Ministries. The 5th Pay Commission had also recommended that the number of employees should be reduced by three per cent annually. Then there was the recommendation of the Geetha Krishnan Committee to wind up several Departments. However, the real gain in terms of reduction of employees' strength is "almost insignificant at less than 10,000 over a 10 year period". Since reducing the number of employees does not seem to be figuring in any specific Ministry's agenda (the last time one heard of this was when Yashwant Sinha spoke of this in his Budget speech in 2001), it seems most desirable that the Prime Minister's Office itself takes over the task of monitoring closely each Department's staff strength and see what kind of reduction can be effected in a specified time-frame. Indian Railways, the Department of Posts and a few other Ministries / Departments have made a beginning in this direction; there is no reason why other Ministries cannot adhere to the target of reducing their staff strength by three per cent annually.

We may now consider at some length the scenario in Kerala State which may be taken as typifying the situation that obtains in most, if not all, of State Governments. Let us start from the apex of the bureaucratic hierarchy. Kerala's cadre of All India Service Officers is as follows:

| | | |
|---|---|---|
| IAS | – | 148 |
| IPS | – | 100 |
| IFS | – | 100 |
| (Indian Forest Service) | | |

(The late E.M.S. Namboodiripad who headed the first Communist Ministry in India (April 1957 - July 1959) protested in vain that little Kerala should not be burdened with too many A I S officers. That was when Kerala's IAS and IPS cadres were less than one-third of what they are today!)

Kerala has 35 IAS officers in the grade of Chief Secretary, Additional Chief Secretary, Principal Secretary or Secretary. The number of Additional Secretaries, Joint Secretaries, Deputy Secretaries and Under Secretaries in the State Secretariat (forget the more fortunate ones in these grades who have been able to land in plum 'deputation' posts outside the Secretariat, often nearer home!) is legion. Finance Department (entrusted with the solemn task of 'strictly' regulating public expenditure) has 15 Additional Secretaries, with 10 Joint Secretaries to boot. The Law Department has seven Additional Secretaries and 10 Joint Secretaries (These examples have been selected at random) The Secretariat, with a very spacious Annexe, is literally bursting at the seams! The sad fact is that the contribution of most of these busybodies is just a lazy, clichéd minute mention in the 'note file'- "A and B may be approved"! Evidently these precious pearls of wisdom leave the Secretary none the wiser- that, of course, doesn't matter; what matters is that every year, there should be a minimum addition to each cadre, reminding one of the amoeba multiplying! This writer, while holding the office of Chief Secretary, issued an order that no file should traverse more than three levels before it reaches the Secretary concerned. It was honoured more in the breach than in observance by the 5,000 - strong army of Additional / Joint / Deputy / Under Secretaries / Section Officers and Assistants!

As indicated above, there is a consensus today that any meaningful attempt to revamp the administrative apparatus should start by trimming this lazy, sluggish, somnolent behemoth. Here it has to be pointed out that while obviously the concept of downsizing has primarily to be applied to the lakhs of employees manning Government offices as such, it has necessarily to be extended pari passu to agencies and institutions fully or partly funded by Government that are chronic, systematic fund guzzlers. No attempt seems to have been made, at least in recent times, to assess objectively the actual necessity or justification to continue them, and to wind up unceremoniously at least those that have proved to be so many 'non-performing assets' in banking vocabulary, no more, in fact, than an enormous, endless drag on the public fisc. The following table is quite revealing in this context:

| | | | |
|---|---|---|---|
| 1. | Commissions | – | 16 |
| 2. | Public Sector Undertakings | – | 86 |
| 3. | Universities, other Autonomous Bodies and Cultural Institutions | – | 93 |
| 4. | Welfare Fund Boards | – | 28 |
| 5. | Co-operative Organisations | – | 28 |

(It is strange but true that Kerala's (population: 3.34 crore) Public Service Commission has 21 Members - reportedly, twice the number in the UPSC! Three Members were recently added to the already jumbo-sized Commission of 18 Members, unabashedly to 'accommodate' certain constituent parties of the United Democratic Front in power in Kerala!)

Apart from generous honoraria, the Chairmen and CEOs (they receive fat salary packets) are granted allowances, conveyances (expensive cars) at Government cost, telephones and some times even official residences. The staff receives the same emoluments and perks as Government employees. No wonder these multifarious agencies eat heavily into the revenues of Government!

One cannot, in this context overlook the enormous body of functionaries in various classes and categories — their number has swollen alarmingly in recent years — who are designated as the 'Personal Staff' of Ministers, the Speaker, the Deputy Speaker and even the Chief Whip. They enjoy the same pay and allowances and perquisites as Government servants, including a pension if only one has put in just two years of service — an act of munificence from their political masters.

The sheer inevitability of reducing the size of this 6 lakh (approximate) strong privileged class that gobbles up the vast bulk of the income of Government without providing corresponding benefits becomes all the more glaring if we consider, even in macro terms, the continuing dismal, crisis-ridden financial landscape of this "debt-stressed state" (an honour it shares with West Bengal and Punjab). Kerala's Public debt in 2011-12 was a whopping Rs 96,562 crore — one of the highest among Indian States. The chronic resources crunch afflicting the State has cascaded on to its social sector - once a 'pride of place' for Kerala, in health care and education in particular. Today the liquidity crisis is undermining the unique achievements of the State in social development, on account of sheer lack of funds. The reasons for this crisis are not hard to find — the runaway growth of 'revenue expenditure' is the biggest among them. Kerala's Public Debt profile is alarming:

| *Year* | *Total Debt (Rs in Crore)* |
|---|---|
| 2005-06 | 45929.05 |
| 2006-07 | 49875.18 |
| 2007-08 | 55410.00 |
| 2008-09 | 63270.00 |
| 2009-10 | 70969.00 |
| 2010-11 | 78673.24 |
| 2011-12 (BE) | 88746.69 |

The per capita debt of Kerala (2009) was Rs 18042 as against Rs. 11256 for AP, Rs 10182 for Karnataka and Rs. 9780 for Tamil Nadu (The all-India average is Rs 11086).

The trend in Revenue expenditure is equally ominous:

*(Rs in Crore)*

| *Year* | *Amount* | *Annual Growth Rate* |
|---|---|---|
| 2005-06 | 18423.58 | 7.30 |
| 2006-07 | 20824.57 | 13.03 |
| 2007-08 | 24891.64 | 19.53 |
| 2008-09 | 28223.85 | 13.39 |
| 2009-10 | 31132.38 | 10.31 |
| 2010-11 | 34664.82 | 11.35 |
| 2011-12 (BE) | 44961.41 | 29.70 |

Fiscal deficit has gone up during this period from Rs. 4181.72 crore in 2005-06 to Rs 10506.99 crore (BE) in 2011-12. It uneasily hovers around 3.43 per cent of GDP.

A 2001 'White Paper' put out by the Government to "help the people of Kerala assess the malaise that has set in to the financial system of the state" makes the following sharp observations: "The reasons for the crisis are not hard to find — the runaway growth of revenue expenditure in particular did foreshadow the crisis.... The inexorable growth of revenue deficit, an inordinate increase in public debt as a proportion of the domestic product, increasing reliance on debt for financing current expenditure (not capital expenditure) an unsustainable salary and pension bill that has been building up over time, the commitments on account of debt servicing — all manifest in the imbroglio that we have got ourselves into".

The 'imbroglio' continues to be as serious today as it was twelve years ago; and this single fact underscores the critical importance of reining in unproductive revenue expenditure by a drastic downsizing of the overgrown bureaucratic equipment, including of course, its adjuncts and appendages like State - funded agencies and institutions listed above. For, as the White Paper somberly warns us : "No easy options are available to Government. It is no longer possible to keep accumulating liabilities and incur debt in the hope that the future will take care of the problem. No extent of further borrowing or book adjustment affords a solution to the financial impasse. Development efforts under the aegis of Government are simply petering out. The development machinery of Government has virtually come to a standstill."

**The Rapid Growth of Bureaucracy and Fiscal Crisis**

It is necessary to examine in a little more detail the strong correlation between the continuing fiscal crisis of Government and the exponential growth of the bureaucracy in terms of sheer numbers. The growth of Public Debt (outlined above) by itself need not have been a cause for alarm or concern, had the funds involved in this staggering figure, or the bulk of it, been spent on development. Unfortunately this has not been the case over the last several decades. The last decade in particular (as already shown above) has witnessed an enormous growth in unproductive Revenue expenditure. During the ten-year period 2001-2011, Gross Revenue Receipts went up from Rs. 7,942 crore to Rs. 31,181 crore — an impressive growth of 293 per cent. However, Revenue Expenditure rose from Rs. 6028 crore to Rs. 19,195 crore — a growth of 318 per cent almost pari passu. During this period, it should be further noted, development expenditure was often less than 50 per cent of Revenue Expenditure. Thus the very substantial growth in Revenue Receipts was almost completely neutralised by the staggering growth in Revenue Expenditure, which, we should remember, is after all, only another name for non-developmental expenditure.

The total commitment of the State on salary, pension and interest payments is today about 76 per cent of Revenue Receipts. That is to say, out of every rupee that goes into the coffers of Government, just 24 paise is available to alleviate the poverty and distress of the downtrodden. The rest goes as fuel to the ever-growing, gigantic machine called the civil service. This extreme inequity becomes more patent and stark when we find out that Government servants constitute less than 2.5 per cent of the population of the State. It is a very rare type of democratic socialism indeed, when 76 per cent of the State's income straightaway goes into the pockets of a fast-growing army of Government employees!

In 2011 there was the inevitable quinquennial pay revision for the State Government employees (it is only decennial for Central Government employees). This regular exercise has brought out some revealing facts. The additional annual commitment on pay revision this time is a whopping Rs. 2,000 crore. Expenditure on pension payment has reached the staggering figure of Rs. 4,900 crore per annum. Interestingly enough, the number of pensioners has out stepped the number of those in service — 5.42 lakh as against 5.33 lakh! The moral is very clear — at least to rectify the gross anomaly of an unsustainable salary and pension bill that has been building up over time, it is a matter of the highest priority to downsize the bureaucracy. This is especially so since the resource base of the state is far too limited to meet the growing expenditure commitments. In fact, this is the first and most compelling raison d'etre for the downsizing proposed.

**Flaws in Personnel Administration**

We now come to the second factor that makes the downsizing of bureaucracy not just desirable but inescapable. The system of promotions that now prevails in Government is inconsistent with reason, equity and even commonsense. The so-called comparative assessment of merit and suitability has long since degenerated into a routine exercise that verges on the farcical. The seniority-cum-merit principle of evaluation evolved with the best of intentions a century ago has now been reduced to an empty ritual. While seniority based on recorded facts cannot be disputed, scrutiny of relative merit suffers from very grave flaws and inadequacies. The position today is that an officer who has not been convicted of a serious criminal offence and has, in his dossier of annual confidential reports, no major adverse observation, is more or less assured of his elevation to the next higher post. The Departmental Promotion Committee is indulgent to a fault: no one wants to court unpopularity with his subordinates, especially when discipline and decorum are at a very low ebb, and physical assaults on superior officers during strikes and other forms of violent protests are nothing unusual, the sheer strength derived from numbers and political clout emboldening the militant cadres of employees. This highly unsatisfactory situation is compounded by the absence of objective and comprehensive criteria of honesty and integrity, efficiency and devotion to duty. The relative assessment of merit, therefore, boils down to a highly subjective exercise, often vitiated by prejudices and pre-dispositions. The system of promotions, even in the case of All India Service officers that is in vogue today is perfunctory and lackadaisical, no conscious and unsparing effort being made to weed out dead wood. Worst of all, no thought whatsoever is bestowed to pause for a moment and ponder whether a particular promotion post is at all necessary. The cumulative result of this all-round deficit of discipline is that while ineptitude and incompetence are perpetuated on the one hand, more and more flab accumulates on the other, on an already obese and lethargic machine.

This leads us to the obvious question of a ban on future recruitment. Often talked about vaguely by the political and administrative executive, it is very rarely that this desperate remedy has been actually resorted to. The same weakness and vulnerability for cheap popularity (and vote bank politics) that hold back policy-makers from resorting to a drastic cut on the ever-swelling numbers at all levels due to the continuous and unregulated induction of more chunks of employees, is seen in the reluctance to prohibit recruitment to particular classes or categories at least for a limited period. This failure has come into sharp focus with the spread of computerisation to substantial sections of public offices. Computerisation is progressing fast (as indeed it should), the ultimate goal being a 'paperless system'. Viewed against this background, there is no credible reason why a policy decision should not be taken to ban recruitment at least selectively. The A.K. Antony Government that came to power in 2001 famously published a White Paper immediately on assuming office (already referred to above) and loftily announced a temporary ban on recruitment, only to hastily beat a retreat and abandon the resolution, in the face of massive direct action by militant cadres of leftist service organisations. Since then, any thought of such a prohibition has remained a forlorn hope (but then, it is incumbent too on the Government to provide enough work to the jumbo 21-member Public Service Commission!).

Not as drastic, unpalatable and unacceptable as an interdict against all recruitment is a slow, step-by-step programme of downsizing the bureaucracy, by progressively abolishing redundant posts. The modalities are simple: a small, compact team of knowledgeable officers may be entrusted with the job of identifying 'surplus' posts along the whole gamut of the service. The next step would be to unambiguously declare them as such, and abolish them one by one as and when superannuation vacancies arise. It goes without saying that all pressures to fill up such retirement vacancies — the shrill cries about 'stagnation' are only too familiar - should be firmly resisted. A single exception, "as a special case" as the sarkari lingo goes, is sufficient to topple the whole effort, as 'precedents' are inviolable in Government service, as the edicts and decrees of the hoary smritis go, and are conveniently quoted to justify every exception, however irregular and unjustified on merits. If scrupulously implemented, the procedure outlined above can produce very satisfactory results during a time-frame of ten or fifteen years.

Because of laxity and inadvertence, the distribution of personnel manning the various rungs of the administrative ladder is often found to be lopsided and anomalous. Again, in the same office, some 'seats' may be very 'heavy' and some very 'light'. This can only mean that the distribution of work is not rational and balanced. On a larger scale, by the same logic, some offices / departments may be over — staffed while some others may be inadequately staffed. A patient and careful exercise has to be undertaken to ensure that anomalies and imbalances in the overall distribution of staff, inter-department and intra-department, are rectified, and surplus personnel, wherever found, are re-deployed. This has to be an integral part of the downsizing exercise.

**Revamping the Administrative Apparatus**

Decentralisation of administrative powers on a generous scale is yet another important measure inevitable in any meaningful endeavour to reduce bureaucratic obesity. Serious efforts have been made to this end, following the Balwantrai Mehta Committee report dating back to the early 1960's. In Kerala the E.K. Nayanar Government launched a major programme of decentralized planning in 1996, taking formulation and implementation of Plan programmes to the lowest rung, viz, the grama sabha. The 'Kerala experiment' came in for warm praise from President K.R. Nayaranan and Vice-Chairman of the Planning Commission Prof. Madhu Dandavate. Naraynan, in fact, enthusiastically commended it for adoption at the national level. Tragically enough the tempo generated during the first two years was not consciously kept up by succeeding Governments, with the result that once again, the politician-contractor-bureaucrat axis came back with a vengeance! Be that as it may, the present situation is that the aam aadmi is driven to cooling his heels at the door of the *taluk* office to get a petition sanctioned, a task that properly has to be done at the level of the Village Officer, and waits on the Collector to get a grievance redressed that falls actually in the domain of the *Tahsildar* and so on, endlessly, until a harassed and tired Minister *sahib* has willy-nilly to answer his hoarse cry for help. This absurd, irrational, senseless waste of time, effort and money can be given the quietus only through a comprehensive, well-orchestrated decentralisation of powers; that should be not only well-formulated but also well-implemented. Such a step will go a long way to relieve the sheer burden on the common man. Ipso facto, it would also pave the way to downsize governmental machinery.

Equally important is the weeding out of antiquated, outdated, irrelevant rules and orders and procedures, which were the inevitable by-product of a system based on distrust, a cardinal feature of both the British administrative set-up and the one that held sway in the 'native' sates (which was no more than an unimaginative copy of the former). It is more or less accepted today that the earlier we jettison this archaic, irrelevant baggage, the better for the speedy and cost-effective functioning of the administrative apparatus. A small committee may be formed to take up the job of examining the huge, accumulated mass of rules and orders department-wise that still find a place on the statute book, and sweep away ruthlessly those that have lost their relevance and utility. Simultaneously another exercise may also be undertaken to examine to what extent the existing delegation of administrative and financial powers in individual departments may be liberalised in order to facilitate speedier and easier transaction of business, consistent with the need for propriety and regularity. This systemic overhaul, if properly carried out, will go a long way to ultimately eliminate the need for 'additional staff' whenever a new scheme is taken up.

One welcome development in recent times that augurs well for the progressive democratisation of bureaucracy and its transformation into an efficient and cost-effective apparatus consistent with the ethos of a welfare state, is the fact that 'Charters of Citizens' Rights and the Right to Services Act have all become part of the common man's equipment to deal with governmental machinery that touches his daily life at several points. It has been universally accepted that it should by definition subserve the needs and interests of the common man who supports it after all, and that he can no longer be left helpless and frustrated at the portals of a public office. It has to respond proactively and adequately to his concerns. The seats of justice have risen to the weltgeist as a bulwark to protect his rights and prerogatives against authoritarianism and arbitrary and mala fide action, whether of the executive or the legislature. During the last three or four years in particular, the Apex Court has asserted its authority against corruption and ineptitude in the highest citadels of power. More than ever in the past, the media are using their enormous influence against lack of probity and propriety among those in authority, both politicians and civil servants, and against arbitrary abridgement or denial of a citizen's rights. The time, it seems, cannot be more propitious for a serious, well-meaning endeavour to comprehensively revamp and re-design the administrative equipment of the Government, so that at far lesser cost and with more efficiency and speed, it will optimally subserve the interests of the people and promote the common weal.

# 6

# *Challenges Before India's Relations with Neighbours*

*V. Suryanarayan*

Speaking in the National Defence College in New Delhi few years ago, then US Ambassador to India, His Excellency William Clark Jr, referred to the "evolving, but radical, change in the way the peoples and nations of the world relate to each other". He quoted the distinguished American historian Thomas Kuhn, who pointed out something startling about the way "we understand the world around us and are willing to accept what we understand". Thomas Kuhn pointed out that the Copernican model of the universe, Newton's Laws of Motion, Albert Einstein's Relativistic Revolution — were all frowned upon by their contemporaries. It took a long time for people to accept these changes as "normal". This process of acceptance has been referred to as "paradigm shift". We are today faced with the same startling phenomenon. Accustomed as we were to Cold War conflict, ideological rhetoric and peculiar mindsets, we fail to understand the meaning and significance of the revolutionary changes taking place around us today.[1]

**How to Measure Success of Foreign Policy?**

An important yardstick for measuring the success of foreign policy is to pose the question: Can the foreign policy makers correctly anticipate the turn of events and adjust the country's policy accordingly? If we apply this yardstick to India's foreign policy before and after independence, the result presents a mixed picture. Given below are illustrations of correct assessment, which paid the country rich dividends as well as incorrect assessments which tarnished the image of the county very badly.

Jawaharlal Nehru's keen interest in international affairs and his conviction that India should make its stand clear on crucial global issues was a logical corollary of the manner in which the Indian foreign policy thinking originated during the long years of freedom struggle. Nehru underlined the need for a reorientation of Indian outlook on international affairs and was mainly instrumental in making the Indian National Congress take positive stance on issues relating to freedom from colonial domination and fight against Fascism and Nazism. As his well-known biographer Sarvepalli Gopal has written, "Jawaharlal Nehru played a decisive role in the history of the twentieth century-as the leader of the Indian people, as a representative of the new mood of Asia and as a spokesman of international conscience".[2] A keen student of international affairs, Nehru foresaw the emergence of new imperialist powers, especially US Imperialism. In his report on the Brussels Conference, he explained how the United States, "with its tremendous resources and immunity from external attack" was taking a "stranglehold of Central and South America".[3]

During the height of the Cold War Nehru was convinced that communism was not a monolith. An intensely nationalist country like China will not remain subservient to Soviet Union for long. Therefore, Nehru made a distinction between Chinese expansionism and communist ideology, which enabled India to get the solid support of Soviet Union in the years following the outbreak of the Sino-Soviet dispute. No other nationalist leader of the twentieth century, except perhaps Ho Chih Minh, was able to understand the cross currents of history and fashion the foreign policy of his country in the backdrop of changing international events.

In retrospect, Nehru's idealism and conviction that India should strive for a world without war made him make friendship with China the sheet anchor of India's foreign policy. Despite growing differences with China he never envisaged a situation when the two countries would drift into an armed conflict. As a result national defence was neglected. The Chinese breach of faith and the diabolic attack on India in October-November 1962 not only shattered Nehru, it also made Indians realize that we were living in an artificial world of our own creation.

Let me now turn to negative aspects of foreign policy. Accustomed to Soviet support on crucial foreign policy issues, it took a long time for our policy makers to evaluate the consequences of the disintegration of Soviet Union. Some were even hoping that orthodox communists would once again regain power in Kremlin. To Illustrate in August 1991, there was an attempted coup against Gorbachev. A rebel group claimed that it had taken over from Gorbachev, who was at that time in Crimea on vacation. They held him confined to his Dacha. Yeltsin took the leadership to reverse the coup and he succeeded in three days. However, Indian Embassy in Moscow reported that the coup was successful. The Indian Prime Minister publicly welcomed the coup just before it was reversed. Naturally, the Indian Prime Minister was hoping that Soviet Union would revert to the old days and once again Indo-Soviet friendship would be back on the cards.[4]

Even when New Delhi's assessment of the international situation was correct and our foreign policy was based on solid basis, South Block did not have the courage of conviction to explain the nuances of Indian foreign policy cogently and boldly. India's policy on the Cambodian issue during the Third Indo-China War was based on its correct evaluation that Pol Pot backed by China was a threat to Vietnam's security. New Delhi was suspicious of the short term and long term consequences of China's policy of fighting Vietnam to the last Cambodian soldier. It was in Peking's interest to continue the leechcraft so that Vietnam remained weak, disunited and internationally ostracised. What is more, there was appreciation both in Indonesia and in Malaysia that Vietnam could be the bulwark against Chinese expansionism in Southeast Asia. Despite these plus points India failed to bridge the differences between Hanoi and ASEAN. What is more, on several occasions, the Indian diplomats were defensive about New Delhi's policy on Cambodia. The decision at the last Moment not to participate as a dialogue partner in the ASEAN Foreign Ministers meeting in Kuala Lumpur in June 1980 did in no way enhance the prestige and standing of India in Southeast Asia. In fact, India would have been ASEAN's first dialogue partner from the Third World.[5]

What is more tragic, on a few occasions, the highest officials in the Ministry of External Affairs did not have a grasp of the complexities of the situation. In his book, Assignment Colombo, Amb. J.N. Dixit, former Indian High Commissioner in Sri Lanka, provides an illustration to drive home this point. As part of its mediatory efforts to find a solution to the vexed ethnic problem, New Delhi had prepared a "non-paper". On the instructions of Romesh Bhandari, then Foreign Secretary, Dixit had conveyed the contents of the non-paper to the Sri Lankan Government. In the course of a dialogue, Bhandari asked Dixit whether he had informed the moderate Tamil leaders of the contents of the non-paper. To quote Dixit: "I told him that I had not, because I had no such instructions. This was where his vague knowledge about Tamil leadership found expression. He said, "Mani, as soon as you reach Colombo, hand over the documents to Chelvanayakam". I pointed out that Chelvanayakam had died nearly two decades ago. So handing over the papers would not be possible. I said perhaps he meant I should hand over the papers to Dr. N. Thiruchelvam. Bhandari was impatient. He said, "Mani, give the papers to Chelvanayakam, Thiruchelvam, whosoever it is. All these South Indian names are very confusing".[6] With such an ignoramus as Foreign Secretary, no wonder, India's Sri Lanka policy drifted into a quagmire.

**Knowledge is Power**

The United States was the first country to realise that knowledge is power. American universities recognized the salience between scholarship and foreign policy. It is well known that the Area Studies pogrammes, initiated during the height of the Cold War, were the creation of the national security state. These programmes were structured and financed, and their research agendas and methodologies set by the state/intelligence/foundation nexus. Their research agendas were blindly followed by many universities in the developing world. I recall that when I was a research scholar in the Indian School of International Studies in mid-1960s the reading lists which were prescribed for us for the study of Theory of International Relations were all books written by American and British scholars. The syllabus did not include the analytical study of the teachings of Kautilya or Sun Tzu. The Indian Universities blindly accepted the American terms of reference, especially those relating to the division of the world into different areas. The artificial division between South Asia and

Southeast Asia, which we follow in India, is a clear illustration of our intellectual dependence on the West.

Though teaching and research in international relation and area studies commenced in India in the mid-1950s, the academic pogrammes in the Indian university system "are not fully able to cope with the demands and opportunities facing a modernising and rising India". India, which had relatively "more developed" programmes in area studies and international relations in the 1950s "has since fallen behind East Asian countries, particularly China".[7] Even after six and a half decades of independence, as far as Southeast Asian Studies is concerned, we do not have a research institution comparable to the Institute of Southeast Asian Studies in Singapore or Monash University in Australia.

The term Southeast Asia came into vogue after the Second World War as a defence connotation. Countries, South of the Tropic of Cancer, were placed under the Southeast Asia Command, with its headquarters in Colombo. Its objective was to liberate the colonial territories of Britain, Holland, France and the United States that came under Japanese Occupation. The term caught on and gained currency in the post war period. The term South Asia was also used in a similar fashion. According to the International Encyclopaedia of Social Sciences, "the term South Asia which covers the countries of India, Pakistan, Ceylon and some smaller autonomous and semi-autonomous states in the Himalayas, came into use after the partition of India in 1947.[8] In the late 1950s and 1960s South Asia programmes were started in an organised way in the United States. Invented by the Pentagon and financed by the defence establishment in the post-sputnik Cold War era, the United States did not want to lag behind in academic scholarship. One of the earliest publications was South Asia: An Introductory Bibliography edited by Maureen L.P. Patterson and Ronald B. Inden. Published by the syllabus section of the University of Chicago, the book had a sub title: Introduction to the Civilisation of India, which brings out the indo-centric nature of the region. The emphasis on India, the colossus of the region, is naturally resented by the smaller countries of South Asia.

India has land and maritime boundaries with Myanmar and maritime boundaries with Indonesia and Thailand. Few people in India realise the fact that distance between Indira Point and Pu Breush in Northwest Sumatra is less than the distance between Chennai and Tirupati. Few people are conscious of the fact that the distance between Indira Point and Phuket in Thailand is less than the distance between Chennai and Madurai. But since the two countries belonged to a different area, they became intellectually distant from us. These countries are not only our immediate neighbours, they were in the past profoundly influenced by Indian political ideas, institutions, religion, language, art and architecture. It is also necessary to remind ourselves that Indian historians like R.C. Majumdar, K.M. Panikkar and Nilakanta Shastri used the term Southeast Asia to include what we today refer to as South Asia and Southeast Asia. By accepting the American concept that Southeast Asia -

countries stretching from Myanmar to the Philippines - is a different entity, we intellectually distanced ourselves from countries with whom we share so many cultural attributes in common.

**Prospects of a Bay of Bengal Community**

The concept of Ocean as a unifying force and focus of regional co-operation has not yet been fully grasped. Throughout history sailing was an import means of communication between India and the distant lands. In fact India was a bridge between East and the West. Hence the Arab name for the Southwestern coast of India- Ma'abar — the Arabic word for bridge or causeway. We in India should redefine the concept of area taking into consideration both historic realities and political imperatives. From early 1990s the author, along with Prof. K. R. Singh, former Professor in Jawaharlal Nehru University, have been advocating the concept of a "Bay of Bengal Community". The underlying idea is not to replace SAARC or ASEAN, but to have an additional organisation, which will bring together India and its southern and eastern neighbours.

Historically, all members of the Bay of Bengal Community — India, Bangladesh, Thailand, Malaysia, Singapore, Indonesia and Sri Lanka - have witnessed dynamic interaction between maritime trade and cultural evolution. What Kenneth McPherson wrote about the Indian Ocean in general applies with greater validity to the Bay of Bengal. To quote "The Indian Ocean region is the home of the world's first urban civilisation, and the center of the first sophisticated commercial and maritime activities. The ocean as great highway and source of food and raw materials was a vital force moulding the many societies on its shores long before people maintained written records".[9]

The Bay of Bengal is the gift of "Mother Nature" and co-operation among the littoral states can lead to a win-win situation for all. Exploitation of marine resources, promotion of tourism, weather forecasting, prevention of maritime terrorism — take any subject, fruitful interaction can benefit all littoral states. What is more, two counties with which we have not so friendly relations — China and Pakistan– are absent in the area. Despite these plus points, it took a long time for New Delhi to support the concept of Bay of Bengal Community. In the course of a conversation with the author, Amb. Ranjit Sinha, former Indian Ambassador to Thailand, said that when he mooted the idea to then Foreign Secretary J.N. Dixit, the response was that it was a "non-starter". Ranjit Sinha did not give up hope; he was able to sell the idea to the Thai Foreign Office. And the suggestion for the formation of BIMSTEC came from Bangkok, India, naturally, had to support the idea.

BIMSTEC (Bangladesh, India, Myanmar, Sri Lanka Technical Co-operation) came into existence in June 1997. It was renamed Bay of Bengal Initiative for Multi-Sectoral Technical and Economic Co-operation and was expanded to include the landlocked states Nepal and Bhutan. It has identified certain priority areas for co-operation, but the overall progress had been very slow.

What is more, no attempts are being made to include the Andaman Sea and the Malacca Straits into the ambit of the organisation. Such an initiative is immediately called for because Andaman Sea and the Malacca Straits are adjuncts of the Bay of Bengal. It will also bring in Malaysia, Singapore and Indonesia into the organisation.

**Regional Co-operation – Which Way?**

It needs hardly any emphasis that in the contemporary world, no country, however powerful, can chart its destiny absolutely alone. It had been the lesson of history that governments can optimise their opportunities and enhance their capacity to shape events if they join with a group of countries with shared political and economic interests. Despite these advantages, the contemporary South Asian scene presents a picture of a region sharply divided. The international relations of South Asia, since the advent of independence, have been characterised by mutual suspicions, unfriendly relations and, at times, even open conflict.

Of equal relevance is the fact that in the beginning of the new century, two contradictory tendencies can be seen in the international system. At one end is the re-assertion of national identities. The Soviet Union, which was bound together by one ideology and one centralised leadership, disintegrated paving the way for new state formations. At the other end, free and independent states are coming together to form a larger association and, in that process, ceding some of their sovereign rights. The classic example is the European Union. These two contradictory tendencies of disintegration and integration have to be kept in mind in any analysis of success or failure of regional co-operation in our part of the world.

The most striking feature of the South Asian scene is the pre-eminent position of India, which bestrides the region almost like a colossus. The largest and the most populous, it has all the potentials of emerging as one of the world's major powers. In terms of area, demographic structure and economic resources India is bigger than all other countries put together. In 1982, according to the World Development Report, India had 78 per cent of the area, 73 per cent of the population and 77 per cent of the gross domestic product of the region.[10] What is equally interesting is the fact that India is at the very centre and other countries are bordering on its periphery. India's neighbours among themselves have very few common attributes and their relations with each other – both economic and political — are very minimal. The crux of their diplomacy is how to gain maximum leverage vis-à-vis India, the central power in the region. In other words India is the axis around which the wheel of South Asia is revolving.

One of the underlying causes of instability in South Asia is the inability of India and Pakistan to settle their differences amicably. Since independence in 1947, the relations between the two countries have taken a *zig-zag* course, leading to hostilities on a few occasions. The two countries still remain trapped in a vicious circle of mistrust and suspicion. In the context of mutual suspicion, the talk of a no war pact, balanced reduction of forces, mutual inspection of nuclear energy facilities, declaring South Asia as a nuclear free zone etc. were intended more to score debating points in international forums than any sincere steps to build mutual confidence. What is more, the hope entertained by many observers that a nuclearised India and Pakistan, keeping the inherent dangers of nuclear proliferation, would usher in an era of stable relations have also been dashed to the ground. Raj Mohan Gandhi describes the culture of suspicion that prevails in South Asia as follows: "We can, in fact, picture South Asia as a large ground containing number of open air theatres where ancient scenes are continually being re-enacted, not sadly to learn from the past, but in order to avenge it. The call is to fight yesterday's battles and reverse yesterday's results — while much of the world prepares for the 21st and 22nd centuries, South Asia wishes to enter and re-arrange the 12th century".[11]

How long can India afford to be trapped in the Pakistani conundrum? Should New Delhi continue to be a prisoner of India-Pakistan differences? Should India allow the slow moving camel to stall the onward march of the caravan? I submit that the best option available for India, under the present circumstances, is to follow a four- fold policy. While befriending the political forces in Pakistan which wants good relations with India, make it clear to Pakistan that New Delhi would not tolerate cross border terrorism. Second, efforts should be made to consolidate and strengthen bilateral relations with other South Asian countries — Nepal, Bhutan, Bangladesh, Sri Lanka and Maldives. It would also be useful to give a push to sub regional organisations, for example, co-operation among Sri Lanka, Maldives and Southern India, and also among Southern China, Northeastern States and Myanmar. Finally, as mentioned in the earlier section vigorous efforts should be made to expand BIMSTEC into Bay of Bengal Community (BOBCOM) and infuse flesh and blood into the organisation.

**Northeast India: Gateway to Southeast Asia**

Northeast India — comprising the States of Arunachal Pradesh, Assam, Manipur, Meghalaya, Mizoram, Nagaland, Sikkim and Tripura – shares land borders with four countries. To the North is China and Bhutan, to the East is Myanmar and to the West is Bangladesh. Northeast India is linked to the Indian mainland through the Siliguri corridor, which is only 21 kilometers wide and is flanked by Bangladesh, Bhutan and Nepal. Northeast India accounts for 7.6 per cent of the area and 3.6 per cent of India's population. However, it makes up for 40 per cent of India's land borders with China, Bhutan, Myanmar and Bangladesh. India's bilateral relations with few neighbours have not been cordial which occasionally led to situations, where militants could find sanctuary and support in foreign soil.[12]

The inter-state boundaries in many Asian countries are artificial creations. Instead of uniting people who speak the same language, follow the same religion and belong to the same ethnic group, they have tended to divide them between two countries. Northeast India is a good illustration. There are Nagas both in India and in Myanmar; certain Naga groups have been clamouring for an independent Nagaland comprising of all those areas where Nagas live, which, if conceded, would imply the redrawing of the maps of India and Myanmar. There are also Mizos in India and in Myanmar. There are Meities both in Manipur and in Myanmar. It was only after independence that the Government of India, guided mainly by security considerations, began to push the administrative borders to geographical limits. The transition, as B.G. Verghese rightly puts it, "was not without trauma — civil wars, insurgency, conflicting nationalisms, foreign intervention, refugee movements, gun running, smuggling, narcotics, AIDS, trafficking in women".[13]

I became conscious of the connectivity between Northeast India and the neighbouring States when I was working in Shillong as a faculty member in the North Eastern Hill University (NEHU) during 1975-77. There is an area in Shillong known as Laban, where the Bengalis are concentrated. Every afternoon, the hilsa fish, brought from Bangladesh will be available in the Laban market, an illustration of traditional trade in full swing. In the summer of 1975 I went to Mizoram to evaluate the academic progress of a college located in Champai, near the India-Burma border. I visited the market and was surprised to find Chinese made goods coming via Myanmar. Clothes and battery operated radios were in great demand. During a recent visit to Shillong I found that the market is full of Chinese and Burmese goods. I am tempted to mention another incident which happened more than a decade ago. I went to the University of Manipur to hold a Ph.D viva voce examination and was surprised to find a Naga student who had come from Myanmar for higher studies. In my naiveté I asked him, "was it difficult for you to get a student visa from the Indian Embassy in Rangoon?" The student laughed. When I asked him why he was laughing, he said, "I just cross the mountains and come to Imphal. During vacation, I cross the mountains again and go home".

Can the underlying connectivity between peoples straddling across borders be exploited meaningfully for regional co-operation? Such co-operation will not lead to the undermining of sovereignty. As B.G. Verghese had put it, it will constitute "building blocks of regional co-operation. Cross-border co-operation could invest hitherto peripheral marches with a new dynamism and centrality, a sense of purpose and belonging that makes for political stability, friendship and peace through regional co-operation".[14]

During recent years New Delhi's interest in Northeast India has further enhanced due to the realisation that this region could be a bridge between India and the mainland Southeast Asian countries, for Northeast India is where India ends and Southeast Asia begins. Pranab Mukherjee, then Minister for External Affairs, highlighted this point in a Seminar in Shillong on 16 June 2007.

To quote Mukherjee, "India is aware of the geo-economic potential of the Northeast region as a gateway to East and Southeast Asia. I am convinced that by gradually integrating this region through cross market access, the Northeastern States can become the bridge between the Indian economy and what is beyond doubt the fastest growing dynamic region in the world".[15]

In a conversation with the author the distinguished former civil servant M.R. Sivaraman provided the background to the formal opening of trade between India and Myanmar through Northeast India in 1994. There were powerful forces within the Government of India and the State Governments, in addition to business community, who were opposed to it. Their argument could be summed up as follows. The bureaucrats in New Delhi were state-centric in their approach; they felt that the opening of trade would give a fillip to drug smuggling from Golden Triangle to India and through India to other counties. The local leaders did not want to lose a lucrative income emanating from illegal trade. The business interests were hand in glove with administrators and did not want to forego the enormous profits. Sivaraman informed me that he personally undertook an extensive tour of the India-Burma border, exchanged views with the people concerned and came to the conclusion that the opening of trade would give a fillip to economic development in both counties. This was the background to the conclusion of the Border Trade Agreement which was signed in 1994. It gave a legal framework to the customary traditional trade carried on head-load basis. The Moreh-Tamu point in the Manipur sector was operationalised in April 1995. A second border point was opened in Champai-Rhi in the Mizoram sector in 2004. A third border trade point at Avakhung/ Pansai/Omrai would be opened soon. The list of items to be traded has been increased from 18 to 40. The border trade was worth US Dollars 12.8 million in 2010-11. But according to informed sources it is an under-estimate and the trade may be worth about US dollars 600 million. The major items of trade include pharmaceuticals, cotton yarn, auto parts and vegetable products like betel nut, dried ginger, etc.

The keen interest in exploiting the northeast connection is apparent from a number of initiatives taken to strengthen relations with Southeast Asian countries. Connectivity will be speeded up if the Trilateral Highway Agreement and the Trans Asian Railway Initiative get implemented. In the ASEAN Summit in Bali in 2003 Prime Minister Vajpayee announced an "open skies" policy which would connect all ASEAN capitals with major cities in India. In Phnom Penh in 2002 Vajpayee brought up the idea of linking New Delhi with Hanoi by a railway line. During Manmohan Singh's visit to Myanmar in May 2012, an agreement was signed to set up a joint committec to explore the possibility of developing rail infra-structure from India, through Myanmar, to Hanoi.

The sad fact, however remains that there is a big hiatus between intention and reality. I have described elsewhere that India's Southeast Asia policy is a story of "missed opportunities".[16] The same holds true of India's Myanmar policy. In a chapter included in the book, Two Decades of India's Look East

Policy: Partnership for Peace, Progress and Prosperity, Amb. Shyam Saran has given two illustrations to prove this point. After the Asian Economic Crisis of 1997, India had a good opportunity to build up relations with Myanmar in the field of gas exploration. To quote Shyam Saran: "This was a great window of opportunity for energy starved India. Despite persistent efforts with our own Ministry of Petroleum and Natural Gas and the public sector giants, ONGC, Indian Oil and GAIL, these opportunities were ignored and we have now joined the ranks of rejected suitors. If India had grasped the opportunities then, the situation today would have looked very different".[17] The second relates to hydro-electric projects in the Chindwin river. General Than Shwe was very keen that India should implement the project. The project will be located very near India-Myanmar border adjoining Nagaland. The entire generated power could be transferred to India. To quote Shyam Saran: "It was an uphill task getting our own government to think strategically and pursue the project expeditiously". Flimsy reasons were put forward that Northeast does not require any power, since it was "surplus in power". Shyam Saran concludes, "It appears that after much dilly-dallying the Thamanthi project is finally poised to take off. I certainly hope so".[18]

As an academic I am tempted to mention the enormous potentials for educational co-operation between India and Myanmar. Northeast India has made tremendous strides in the field of higher education and there are a number of good universities located in various states. On the Myanmarese side, there are no good universities. If the power for issuing student visas is delegated to various universities they could attract large number of Naga, Mizo and Meitei youngsters living in Myanmar. This would go a long way in strengthening bilateral relations.

If Northeast India is to become an economic hub and break out of its landlocked isolation and fruitfully engage in benign interaction with its eastern neighbours, it is essential that it should become an area of peace and tranquility. This pre-supposes reconciliation among various ethnic groups and between ethnic groups and the government. This requires an imaginative approach and the ushering in of a political system where multiple identities can co-exist harmoniously. The same holds true of Myanmar. If Myanmar continues to be at war with itself, India's efforts to forge links with mainland Southeast Asia through Myanmar will be a non-starter. The pre-requisite for cordial bilateral relations is for Myanmar to become a vibrant democracy, having a government committed to find an amicable solution to the problems of ethnicity and nation building. During her visit to India last year, the iconic pro-democracy leader Daw Aung San Suu Kyi declared, "I was saddened to feel that we had drawn away from India, or rather India had drawn away from us, during our very difficult days, but always I had faith in the lasting friendship between our two countries, faith in the lasting friendship between our two peoples". She laid emphasis on "friendship between peoples", not "friendship between governments", because, she added, "governments come and go, and that is what democracy is all about".[19]

**Palk Bay: Not Contested Territory, but Common Heritage**

If India is to keep pace with other developing regions of the world, we must take initiative and give momentum to bilateral and regional co-operation. It is unfortunate but true, that at the present moment regional co-operation occupies a very low priority in our interaction with our regional environment. India should immediately follow up on Prime Minister Man Mohan Singh's pronouncement about "asymmetric reciprocity" in relation to our smaller neighbours. In this connection, I want to take up one of the ticklish issues which vitiate relations between India and Sri Lanka, namely the travails of the Indian fishermen in the Palk Bay region and suggest a possible solution to the problem.

The state centric approach to the problems of fishermen ignores the symbiotic relationship between the fishermen and the sea. To the fishermen maritime boundaries are government made creations. Throughout history, they have been fishing in those waters, where there is plenty of fish. It is a universal phenomenon. The Sri Lankan fishermen fish in Indian and Maldivian waters. Indian fishermen enter into Pakistani waters and Bangladeshis into Myanmar and Thai, Taiwanese and Japanese trawlers roam around the whole of Asian waters. The restrictions imposed by the governments on cross border movements of the fisher folk have led to strains in bilateral relations, loss of human lives and destruction of fishing crafts.

The intimate ties between the fishermen and the sea have affected the history, economy and culture of the coastal communities of both Tamil Nadu and the northern and eastern coasts of Sri Lanka. The shallow waters of the Palk Bay and the geographical proximity between the two countries facilitated the movement of ideas, goods and men. The rich cultural heritage of the island was the cumulative outcome of benign cultural interaction spread over several centuries. In the 19th and 20th centuries, thousands of Indian Tamil labourers were ferried across the Strait to provide the much needed labour for the development of tea plantations. In a strange twist of history, after the communal holocaust of 1983, there was a reverse flow. Sri Lankan Tamils came to Tamil Nadu in large numbers through Kallathonis or what was popularly known as Eelam Shipping Service. After 1983, Tamil Nadu became the sanctuary and support base for the armed conflict and through the Palk Strait arms and ammunition and guerrillas moved freely intensifying the ethnic conflict. Since fishing was banned by the Government on the Sri Lankan side, that area began to be frequented by Indian fishermen. When the ceasefire agreement was signed in 2002 and the Sri Lankan fishermen resumed their vocation again, they found poaching by Indian fishermen to be a major hindrance to their livelihood. After the decimation of the Tigers and the return of normalcy to the Tamil areas, the problem was further accentuated. Fanned by chauvinist elements, the fishermen started viewing each other with suspicion and hatred. This was in sharp contrast to the earlier period when there was closeness and camaraderie between the two communities.

The Indian and Sri Lankan Tamil fishermen, like most artisanate fishermen around the world, are a migratory species. Crossing the sea borders is their way of life. The conflict of interests arose when the maritime boundaries were demarcated. As far as India-Sri Lanka maritime boundary was concerned, the situation was rendered complex by the desire of the Government of India to befriend the Sri Lankan Government. As a result, despite strong historical claims, the island of Kachchatheevu was ceded to Sri Lanka. In order to facilitate the transfer, the median line was adjusted so that the island could fall on the Sri Lankan side. Articles five and six of the Agreement, however, safeguarded the rights of the Indian fishermen to fish in and around Kachchatheevu, but these rights were also sacrificed by the Maritime Boundary Agreement of 1976. However, as far as fishermen were concerned, the Agreements were only scraps of paper. They continued to fish in each other's waters as they had done for several centuries. But the situation changed with the security dimension coming to the fore after 1983.

The present policies pursued by the Governments in New Delhi and Colombo could be compared to a fire fighting exercise. As soon as Indian fishermen get detained in Sri Lankan waters, the Tamil Nadu Chief Minister shoots off a letter to the Prime Minister. The Ministry of External Affairs and the Indian High Commission in Colombo get into action and Colombo releases the fishermen in the International Maritime Boundary line. In other words, when there is a fire, take steps to extinguish the fire. But what is required is to extinguish the causes of fire once and for all. Keeping this cardinal principle in mind, in the early 1990s I had suggested two solutions to find an amicable solution to the travails of the Indian fishermen. Given the strong feelings in Tamil Nadu that the ceding of the island of Kachchatheevu was a betrayal of India's historical claims, I had suggested that New Delhi should get the island back on "lease in perpetuity", Tin Bigha in reverse. It could guarantee that the Indian fishermen could fish in and around Kachchatheevu as they had done for several centuries. The second was to come to an agreement with Sri Lanka by which licensed Indian fishermen could fish in Sri Lankan waters up to five nautical miles. As a quid pro quo licensed Sri Lankan fishermen could be permitted to fish for Tuna in the Indian Exclusive Economic Zone. I am happy that both the DMK and AIADMK Governments had accepted these suggestions and, on several occasions, requested the Government of India to persuade the Sri Lankan Government to concede these demands.[20]

During recent years I have modified these ideas still further and have pleaded that an amicable solution could be found only if fishermen in the two countries are made the major stake holders. Their livelihood should form the major focus of negotiations. I maintain that India should project a vision that

Palk Bay constitutes the common heritage of the fishermen of both countries. The foremost requirement for arriving at an amicable solution is to recognise that apart from the Government of India and the Government of Sri Lanka, there are other important stakeholders. There are the State Governments in India and the Provincial Governments in Sri Lanka as well as littoral fishing communities on both sides of the Palk Bay. I have suggested the constitution of a Palk Bay Authority to co-ordinate and implement the policies of the two governments. The Palk Bay Authority could consist of the representatives of the two countries, including those who have specialised in fisheries and marine environment. With the assistance of specialists, the Palk Bay Authority can determine what will be the ideal sustainable catch, what type of fishing equipment could be used, allot equitable fishing dates, three days each to be earmarked for India and Sri Lanka with one day as a holiday etc. Specific areas could be declared as non-fishing zones, so that the area can enrich itself. Special provision should be made for safeguarding the interests of traditional fishermen. The programmes initiated by the Government of Tamil Nadu and organisations like the M.S. Swaminathan Research Foundation like sea ranching commercial shrimp species; installation of artificial sea reefs and promotion of alternate livelihood should cover the whole Palk Bay region. Prof. Swaminathan has embarked on an ambitious programme of "blue revolution" which means "fish for all and fish forever". Instead of restricting these pogrammes to Tamil Nadu alone, the canvas should be widened to cover both sides of the Gulf of Mannar and the Palk Bay. According to specialists, there is considerable scope for joint ventures and bilateral co-operation in the field of introduction of multi-day boats for deep sea fishing in the Indian Ocean region. The focus of co-operative development and sharing of know how should be the enrichment of marine resources and brining about qualitative improvement in the livelihood of fishermen.[21]

**Federal Units and the Making of Indian Foreign Policy**

India borders on Pakistan, China, Nepal, Bhutan, Bangladesh, Myanmar, Thailand, Indonesia, Sri Lanka and Maldives. India's relations with each neighbouring country will have its immediate fallout on contiguous Indian States. Thus India- Pakistan relations will have its fallout on Gujarat, Rajasthan, Punjab and Jammu and Kashmir; India-China relations will affect Kashmir, Uttarakhand, Himachal Pradesh, Sikkim and Arunachal Pradesh; India-Nepal relations will spill over to Bihar, Uttarakhand, Uttar Pradesh, Sikkim and West Bengal; India-Bhutan relations will impinge upon West Bengal, Sikkim, Arunachal Pradesh and Assam; India-Myanmar relations will have its fallout on Arunachal Pradesh, Nagaland, Manipur and Mizoram; India-Sri Lanka relations is closely intertwined with the politics of Tamil Nadu and India-Maldives relations will have an impact on Minicoy islands. I have not mentioned Thailand and Indonesia, because relations with these countries have yet to take off in a big way.

During the era of one-party dominance, New Delhi pursued a neighbourhood policy which it considered to be in India's national interest. On several occasions, the interests and sensitivities of the contiguous Indian states were not taken into consideration. Two illustrations are given below to substantiate the point.

(1) In the years immediately after independence, a point of discord between India and Sri Lanka was the legal status of the people of Indian origin in the island. During his stewardship as Prime Minister Jawaharlal Nehru emphatically maintained that all, except those who voluntarily opted for Indian citizenship, were the responsibility of Ceylon. Taking into consideration their long period of residence and contribution to the economy, Nehru advised Colombo to confer citizenship on them. From the mid-1960's this time tested policy was sidetracked and eventually derailed. With Lal Bahadur Shastri as the Prime Minister and C.S. Jha as the Commonwealth Secretary, New Delhi reversed its earlier principled stand and began to adopt a new approach on the question of stateless people in Sri Lanka. New Delhi was eager to come out of the diplomatic isolation in South Asia following the defeat in the Sino-Indian border war. The astute politician that Sirimavo Bandaranaike was, she made the best use of the situation and clinched the deal. According to India-Sri Lanka Agreements of 1964 and 1974, India decided to confer Indian citizenship on 6,00,000 persons, plus their natural increase and Colombo agreed to confer citizenship on 3,75,000 persons plus their natural increase. The two pacts reduced the people of Indian origin to the status of "merchandise" to be divided between the two countries in the name of good neighbourly relations. It was not only a betrayal of Gandhi-Nehru legacy; it also constituted a bad precedent for India's policy towards Indians Overseas. It is the tragedy of India-Sri Lanka relations that these two agreements which had a bearing on the lives of thousands of estate Tamils of Indian origin were finalised by the two Governments without taking into consideration the feelings and views of the affected people. All trade unions in the plantation areas, though rivals amongst themselves, were unanimous in their opposition to the Sirimavo-Shastri Pact. Of equal relevance is the fact that all political leaders of Tamil Nadu – C. Rajagopalachari, Kamaraj Nadar, C.N. Annadurai, V.K. Krishna Menon and P. Ramamurthy — vehemently criticized the inhuman agreement.[22]

(2) The ceding of the island of Kachchatheevu in 1974, like the earlier Sirimavo-Shastri Pact, is another illustration of New Delhi bending backwards to placate its southern neighbour. Despite strong historical claims, New Delhi adopted the stance that it was a disputed territory. What is more, though the principle of equi-distance was followed in demarcating the maritime boundary line, a deviation was made so that the Island would fall on the Sri Lankan side. Though the island was ceded, articles four and five of the agreement provided for the continuation of the traditional fishing rights enjoyed by the Indian fishermen to fish in and around Kachchatheevu, but these rights were also

bartered away in the subsequent agreement of 1976. Both Jayalalitha and Karunanidhi have filed cases in the Supreme Court challenging the ceding of Kachchatheevu, the Supreme Court has yet to commence hearing on the cases.[23]

May I give an example of how constructive suggestion made by the State Government was ignored by the Mandarins in the South Block. The suggestion was made by Tamil Nadu Chief Minister C.N. Annadurai, who was very concerned with the developments in Burma, especially the forcible repatriation of Tamils and related issue of compensation due to them. In a conversation with the Author, Thomas Abraham, then Minister Counsellor in the Indian Embassy in Rangoon, recalled his meeting with Annadurai in the Chief Minster's residence in Mambalam. The meeting was arranged through the good offices of common friends. After discussing the pros and cons of the matter, Annadurai wrote a letter to Prime Minister Indira Gandhi suggesting that India should enter into a long term agreement with Burma for the import of rice and the compensation due to the Burmese repatriates could be adjusted in the proposed deal. It may be recalled that during 1967 India was facing an acute shortage of food grains. On his return to Rangoon, Thomas Abraham also made a similar proposal to the Ministry of External Affairs. It is unfortunate, but true, that these concrete proposals did not elicit any favourable response from New Delhi.[24]

With the formation of coalition governments in New Delhi and the regional parties becoming alliance partners a qualitative change took place in the centre-state equation with particular reference to India's neighbourhood policy. The alliance partners began to make their inputs into the making of Indian foreign policy. For example, the inclusion of the Sethusamudram project in the policies and programmes of the Man Mohan Singh Government was due to the tireless efforts of the DMK. Of equal relevance, the Central Government exerted its benign influence and softened the hard line stance of its regional allies. Thus during the 4th Eelam War, the DMK was a willing partner of New Delhi. At the same time, New Delhi, for tactical reasons, permitted Karunanidhi to indulge in theatrics so that he could continue to pose himself as the champion of overseas Tamils. But the fact remains that Karunanidhi did not rock the central government while the Fourth Eelam War was being fought to the finish and gross human rights violations were taking place in Sri Lanka. Karunanidhi did a reappraisal of the Sri Lankan situation; he realized that the DMK has lost the good will among the Tamil diaspora. Therefore, in order the regain their support he revived the Tamil Eelam Soldarity Organisation (TESO) and also instructed his colleagues to resign from the central cabinet.

How to bring about harmony in the thinking of the central and state governments with reference to neighbourhood policy will be a litmus test for the policy makers in New Delhi in the years to come. As far as India's Sri Lanka policy is concerned, differences have come into sharp focus during recent months. On the travails of the Indian fishermen in the Palk Bay, on human rights violations in Sri Lanka and on training of Sri Lankan military personnel in defence establishments located in Tamil Nadu, Chief Minister Jayalalitha had been very critical of the policies of the central government. Jayalalitha's postures can be understood only if we keep in mind the competitive nature of Tamil Nadu politics where the two Dravidian parties are vying with one another in championing the cause of the overseas Tamils. This slinging match will gather momentum in the days to come, as the political parties will be chalking out their strategies for the parliamentary elections due to be held this year.

I.K. Gujral, during his stewardship In the Ministry of External Affairs, was very keen to associate the state governments in the formulation and implementation of neighbourhood policy. Rehman Sobhan, the Bangladeshi economist turned diplomat, in a tribute to I.K. Gujral, has provided glimpses into Gujral's eagerness to take along the West Bengal Government on the question of sharing of the Ganges waters with Bangladesh. Rehman Shoban mentions that at the end of a dialogue in New Delhi, Gujral asked him to stay back for a private conversation. He said that since West Bengal has vital stakes on the Ganges waters, it is necessary to take Jyoti Basu on board. Gujral made the "quite extra-ordinary suggestion" to Rehman Shoban that the Awami League Government should open its own "channel of communications" with the West Bengal Government, "drawing on our shared geography and cultural heritage". Instead of proceeding to Dhaka, Rehman Shoban went to Kolkata, met his old friend and class mate Asim Das Gupta, the Finance Minister. To quote Rehman Shoban, "Asim responded very positively to my suggestions and indicated that his leader was not unaware of the mutually beneficial opportunities on offer". Jyoti Basu and Sheikh Hasina displayed exceptional statesmanship. The rest, as they say, is history. The Government of West Bengal was formally invited to be a party in the negotiations with Bangladesh. In fact, Asim Das Gupta led the Indian delegation. The statesmanship of Gujral and Jyoti Basu stands in sharp contrast to the intransigent attitude of Chief Minister Mamata Bannerjee on the question of the sharing of Teesta waters.[25]

**Rise of China—Implications for India**

The independence of India in August 1947 and the emergence of China as a united country in October 1949, in both cases after years of subjugation and relentless struggle, are momentous events in world history. In his book, Asia and Western Dominance, ambassador historian K.M. Panikkar mentions that these two events brought to an end the "Vasco da Gama epoch of history".[26] And, as the two countries develop, pursuing their own unique paths of development, they are destined to play significant roles in international affairs. The future of countries in South and Southeast Asia would depend on the impact that China and India would exert on them in the years to come.

The remarkable transformation taking place in these two countries has to be highlighted in the beginning itself. As India's leading strategic specialist

Late K. Subrahmaniam has pointed out, "Who would have predicted within three decades after the death of Mao Zedong, China would be a citadel of capitalism with inequalities greater than those prevailing in India, or that China should be able to hold the United Sates as an economic hostage? Similarly who would have predicted that within 18 years of initiation of economic reforms the Indian economy would be a trillion dollar economy and India and China would be considered as emerging rivals, moving up in the global hierarchy of economies?".[27] The Peoples Republic of China, according to a publication of the Institute of Policy Studies, Singapore, is the second largest economy in terms of Purchasing Power Parity (PPP), the world's sixth largest merchandise trading nation, the twelfth largest global exporter of commercial services and the largest recipient of foreign direct investment (FDI) among developing countries. India is catching up, at a slower pace; it is ranked fourth largest in terms of GDP at purchasing power parity (PPP) and has been, according to World Bank estimates, one of the fast growing economies of the world. The two countries together number 2.4 billion, 40 per cent of the world's population and given proper leadership and vision; can transform themselves from demographic giants to economic and political super powers. It was this common commitment which made Deng Xiao Ping to tell Prime Minister Rajiv Gandhi that when India and China attain their full potential, the world will witness the "Asia-Pacific century".[28]

The development models of China and India hold important lessons for developing countries. But one important point should be highlighted. The economic performance of China since 1949 was accompanied by political and economic upheavals at regular intervals. The Great Leap Forward, the upheavals during the years of the Cultural Revolution and the massacre at Tiananmen Square shocked even sympathetic observers of China.

Broadly speaking China watchers in India could be divided into three camps. First is the optimistic view of the Government of India that Chindia (Jayaram Ramesh's picturesque phrase) can be a beacon of hope and cheer for mankind. Prime Minister Man Mohan Singh echoed these feelings when he addressed the Chinese Academy of Social Sciences in January 2008. To quote: "We must ensure that India and China co-operate in creating a world of positive externalities and mutual prosperity rather than one based on balance of power calculations and animosity. This involves India and China working together clearly to ensure a global order in which our simultaneous development will have positive influence not only on our own economies, but also on the rest of the world".[29] At the other extreme, there are Cassandras who portray China as a country besieged by traditional "Middle Kingdom mentality" waiting for an opportunity to impose its hegemony on the rest of the world. In this connection, the statements of Prof. Brahma Chellaney are worth repetition. Chellaney pointed out that the PRC began its international debut through wars even when it was weak and poor in the 40's and 50's. Dr. Chellaney asked,

"What did they do when they were poor and weak? They annexed Xinjiang in 1949, occupied Tibet in 1950-51, joined Korean War and invaded South Korea in 1950; attacked India in 1962 and took on the Soviet Union in border conflicts in 1969 and Vietnam in 1979". Dr Chellaney exhorted, "One should, especially the policy makers should look at the track record".[30] The third group of scholars, to which the author belongs, maintains that the relations between the two countries will be simultaneously characterised by co-operation, competition and conflict. It must be pointed out that the success of Indian diplomacy vis-à-vis China would depend upon how we maximise the areas of co-operation and minimise the areas of conflict.

How can an observer describe the present stage in India-China relations? Beset by a "siege mentality", there are powerful forces in both countries, which are eager to adopt confrontationist postures. We, in India, are yet to recover from the catharsis of October-November 1962. Instead of adopting a "consensual" approach towards China and trying to expand and consolidate the gains in bilateral relations since Prime Minister Rajiv Gandhi's visit to Beijing in 1988, the two major political formations led by the Congress and the BJP are indulging in "one upmanship". An atmosphere of dangerous hysteria is being whipped up by visual and print media. There are reasons to be concerned about China's recent moves — incursion into Lhasa; the stepping up of the territorial claims in the whole of Arunachal Pradesh which the Chinese refer to as "Southern Tibet"; China's continuing support to Pakistan's ongoing military programmes; Beijing under writing the tyrannical military regime in Myanmar; China's growing influence in Nepal, Bangladesh, Sri Lanka and Maldives; the misuse of work permits issued to the Chinese workers; Beijing's criticism of growing strategic co-operation between India and Vietnam and the issuance of stapled visas to visitors from Jammu and Kashmir. An analysis of China's foreign policy postures clearly reveal that in order to promote its national interests, it is prepared to go to any extreme and adopt a cynical approach to democratic struggles, whereas despite certain glaring aberrations, the Indian Foreign Office has to take into consideration fundamental values like upholding human rights and supporting democratic aspirations. In this connection, the differing cultural traits of the Chinese and the Indians need to be highlighted. As the Singapore statesman Lee Kuan Yew has pointed out, "In China 90 per cent are Han Chinese and speak Mandarin. And they have simplified the Chinese characters and educated everyone to master Chinese. So CC TV is understood throughout the country. Compare the Indian and the Chinese cultures. The Chinese are doers. The Indians are contemplative and argumentative. Nobel Laureate Amartya Sen entitled one of his books The Argumentative Indian. When the Chinese decided to make Chongquing a prosperous centre in the Western region, they gave the necessary resources. Then you find Chongquing quickly blossoms".[31]

During recent years, PRC has made tremendous strides in winning friends and influencing people in different parts of the world. China's economic assistance to the developing countries is more than that of the World Bank. Lying between India and China, Southeast Asia is one region where India and China is competing for influence. Therefore, in this section, I shall concentrate on this region. The main contributory factor in China being viewed as a benign power had been the result of astute diplomacy. When the process of economic liberalisation began, the Chinese leaders were keen to have a peaceful environment. Therefore, Beijing lent its support to the process of détente and was keen to avoid tensions which may undermine economic development. However, the brutal suppression of pro-democracy movement in June 1989 is an illustration that China's ruling elite will be prepared to go to any extent in order to cling on to power. While there was understandable concern and criticism in the United States, the Southeast Asian countries were less inclined than the West to allow the Tian An Men Square incident to disrupt relations with China. China's dilemma is apparent. In a world of shrinking geographical boundaries and widening intellectual horizon, how can China insulate itself from the winds of democracy sweeping across the world?

When Southeast Asian countries were engulfed in a serious economic crisis in the late 1980s and the international financial institutions and developed countries like the United States, Japan and Singapore were not forthcoming in extending assistance, China played its cards cleverly. There was general fear that China may devalue its currency to boost up its exports. Not only China resisted the temptation, it entered into long term trade agreements with Southeast Asian countries to stabilise their economies. A friend in need is a friend indeed. The Southeast Asian ruling elite realised this truth. This was also an excellent opportunity for India to enter into long term trade agreements with both Malaysia and Indonesia for the import of palm oil. But New Delhi missed this golden chance to consolidate relations with Southeast Asia. The author cannot resist the temptation to highlight another missed opportunity to gain the good will of South Asian countries. When the Iraqi invasion of Kuwait took place in August 1990 a large number of workers of Indian origin were stranded in West Asia. New Delhi mobilised its resources and quickly evacuated the Indians stranded there. It was a feather in the cap of Indian foreign office. But, at the same time, there were workers from Nepal, Sri Lanka and Bangladesh, who were also in the same predicament. If New Delhi had evacuated them also India would have earned the eternal good will of these countries. But the mandarins in the South Block were keener not to lose the profits earned by Air India, which had to divert flights from commercially profitable routes for the sake of evacuation. Another illustration of a missed opportunity.

Southeast Asian countries hope that the United States would retain its credible military presence in the region and there will be no major frictions between Washington and Beijing, which will upset the strategic equilibrium. But will this trend continue for a long time? China is convinced that the United States is a disengaging power and in that situation it will be able to fill the vacuum. At the same time, Beijing is conscious of the fact that the United States is building up a broad united front of countries against China, consisting of Australia, Japan, ASEAN and India in a broad security framework. In order to counteract this move, China is endeavouring to build bridges with India's neighbours -Pakistan, Myanmar, Nepal, Bhutan, Bangladesh, Sri Lanka and Maldives.

With China emerging as a major power, Beijing has started to emphasise certain core issues, where it will not be willing to compromise its stance. From the Southeast Asian perspective, the stepping up of the territorial claims in the South China Sea has emerged as an important source of discord. China's relations with Vietnam and the Philippines are being subjected to severe stresses and strains. In its approach towards China, ASEAN is no longer homogenous. China has successfully divided them. India's growing friendship with Vietnam is also a matter of concern for China. China has severely criticised India for assisting Vietnam in oil exploration in the South China Sea. China does not want India to enter a region which it considers as a "disputed territory". This comment is an obvious illustration of China's double standards. As is well known, Azad Kashmir (Pakistani occupied Kashmir) is a disputed territory between India and Pakistan, but China has entered into several agreements with the Government of Pakistan and is involved in the implementation of several projects.

From an Indian perspective, the question naturally arises how will Southeast Asian countries respond in case of a hypothetical rift between India and China or between China and the United States? It may be recalled that during the Sino-Indian conflict, 1962 Federation of Malaya, Thailand, South Vietnam and the Philippines extended their support to India. Burma, Cambodia and Indonesia were neutral in the dispute. The only country which supported China was North Vietnam, the reason for which was Hanoi's dependence on Beijing for military and economic support.

Two illustrations are given below which will give a clue to the changing perception of Southeast Asian countries towards China and India. In his Memoirs, S.R. Nathan, the former President of Singapore, describes an incident during Lee Kuan Yew's first official visit to China in 1976. The highlight of the visit was Lee Kuan Yew's meeting with the Chinese Prime Minister Hua Guofeng. During the discussion, Hua presented Lee Kuan Yew with a book, saying, "This is the correct account of the war between India and China. Hope you will find it useful". Lee Kuan Yew looked at the book, looked at the front cover, looked at the back page, and said, "Mr. Prime Minister, this is your version of the war. There is another version, the Indian version. And, in any case, I am from Southeast Asia. It has nothing to do with us". He handed the book back. "For me this was a very important moment, a clear confirmation that Lee Kuan Yew, though ethnically Chinese, was his own man, in no way subordinate to China or to the Chinese communists. We, in Singapore, had a separate, multi-racial identity. What we made clear is that we should not be taken for granted. The Chinese Foreign Minister Qiao Guanhua was rather agitated, but kept his cool; his wife did not, and walked out of the room in a huff"[32]. Another incident took place when George Yeo, then Singapore Foreign Minister, visited China two years ago. The Chinese authorities arranged a meeting between their nominee of Panchan Lama and George Yeo. It may be recalled that George Yeo had visited Tibet during his earlier visit and was in full praise for China's efforts to bring about massive economic transformation. What does this event signal? Does it mean that in the post-Dalai Lama phase Singapore would extend support to China's nominee as the leader of the Tibetan people? B. Raman, one of India's leading strategic specialists, posed the question as follows: "The action of the Singapore Foreign Minister in providing legitimacy to the actions of the Chinese Communist Party in interfering in the religious affairs of the Tibetan Buddhists and tampering with their traditions cannot be missed".[33]

How does Malaysia which extended spontaneous support to India in the Sino-Indian conflict and started a "save democracy fund" perceive China today? In his Memoirs, A Doctor in the House: The Memoirs of Tun Mahathir Mohammad, Dr. Mahathir, former Prime Minister, expressed his views in a forthright manner. To quote: "I stuck up good relations with the Chinese leaders, in particular, with Ziang Zemin. Malaysia's goodwill and support are well known to most informed Chinese citizens. China has now become the world's factory, churning out all kinds of manufactured goods which are very quickly achieving world standards. Their per capita income is well below that of Malaysia but their population makes China a huge market. Malaysia is China's largest trading partner in Southeast Asia and our China friendly foreign policy will continue. We must not fall into the American trap of regarding China as a potential enemy. When you regard a country as a potential enemy, you can be sure that the country will regard you as its current enemy".[34] It is also interesting to note that though Malaysia has territorial claims in the South China Sea, unlike Vietnam and the Philippines, Kuala Lumpur has not adopted an antagonistic posture towards Beijing.

Until very recently when Indian academics used to point out that China is one country which has used force to buttress its territorial claims — against India in 1962, against Soviet Union in 1968, against Vietnam in 1974 and in 1979- the argument used to be received with understanding and sympathy. I do not know whether Singapore, Malaysia, Cambodia and Myanmar will respond in the same way today. ASEAN is sharply divided on the question of China's intentions and capabilities. While Vietnam, Indonesia and the Philippines share Indian perception, Cambodia is pro-China and other countries are ambivalent. India must step up its diplomacy in Southeast Asia and enter into dialogue with governments and leading think tanks. We must follow a calibrated policy towards China and continue the dialogue to broaden the areas of convergence and minimize the areas of dissonance. At the same time, we must be vigilant, for eternal vigilance is not only the safeguard of democracy; it is the only guarantee for our survival.

**Notes**

1. V. Suryanarayan (ed.), (1992) : 'Preface', *South and Southeast Asia in the 1990's: Indian and American Perspectives*, New Delhi, pp. vii-viii.
2. Sarvepalli Gopal, (1976) : *Jawaharlal Nehru: A Biography,* (Part I), New Delhi, p. 5.
3. 'Report on the Brussels Conference', *Selected Works of Jawaharlal Nehru*, Vol. 2, pp. 270-2.
4. K.P. Fabian, (2012) : *Diplomacy: Indian Style*, New Delhi, p. 245.
5. V. Suryanarayan, 'The Kampuchean Crisis', P. N. Haksar, (ed.), (1987): *Nehru's Vision of Peace and Security in Nuclear Age*, New Delhi, pp. 181-99.
6. J.N. Dixit, (1998) : *Assignment Colombo*, New Delhi, p. 37.
7. Muthiah Alagappa, 'Guest Editor's Note', *International Studies*, Vol. 46, January and April 2009, pp. 3-6.
8. *International Encyclopaedia of Social Sciences* (1968): New York, p. 412.
9. For further details, refer V. Suryanarayan, 'Prospects of Bay of Bengal Community', *Seminar*, March 2000, pp. 58-61.
10. For details refer V. Suryanarayan, 'Neighbourhood Diplomacy in South Asia - Partners in Progress or Uneasy Co-existence', *Asian Studies*, Vol. 3, Nos. 3 and 4, 1985, pp. 1-6.
11. For details refer V. Suryanarayan, 'Plea for a New Regional Organisation', *South Asian Survey*, Vol. 9, No. 2, 2002, pp. 263-73.
12. For details refer B.G. Verghese, *Re-orienting India: The New Geo-Politics of Asia*, New Delhi, 2001.
13. *Ibid.,* p. x.
14. *Ibid.*
15. Speech by the Hon'ble Minister for External Affairs, Shri Pranab Mukherjee at *Seminar on 'Look East Policy'*, Shillong, 16 June, 2007 (Website of the Ministry of External Affairs, Government of India).
16. V. Suryanarayan, 'Looking Ahead: India and Southeast Asia in the 1990's: New Perspectives, New Challenges', Baladas Ghoshal (ed.), (1996) : *India and Southeast Asia: Challenges and Opportunities*, New Delhi, pp. 10-27.
17. Shyam Saran, 'Re-Engaging the Neighbourhood: A Personal Perspective on India's Look East Policy', Amar Nath Ram (ed.), (2012): *Two Decades of India's Look East Policy: Partnership for Peace, Progress and Prosperity,* New Delhi, pp. 131-40.
18. *Ibid.*
19. Text of Aung Saan Suu Kyi's *Jawaharlal Nehru Memorial Lecture*.

20. For details, see V. Suryanarayan, *Kachchatheevu and Problems of Indian Fishermen in the Palk Bay Region,* Madras, 1994.
21. V. Suryanarayan and R. Swaminathan, Contested Territory or Common Heritage? Thinking out of the Box (Occasional Paper Number 1, *Center for Asia Studies*, Chennai, 2009).
22. V. Suryanarayan, 'Tamil Nadu and Ethnic Conflict in Sri Lanka', in M.L. Sondhi, (ed.), (2000): *Terrorism and Political Violence: A Source Book*, New Delhi, pp. 118-45.
23. For details refer V. Suryanarayan, (2005): *Conflict over Fisheries in the Palk Bay Region*, New Delhi.
24. V. Suryanarayan, 'Forgotten Children of Mother India', Commodore R.S. Vasan and Jacob Ashik Bonofer, (eds.) (2010): *Developments in Myanmar: Implications for India*, Chennai, pp. 99-110.
25. Rehman Sobhan, 'I.K. Gujral: A Tribute from Bangladesh', *Mainstream* Annual 2012, December 22, 2012, pp. 11-14.
26. K.M. Panikkar (1953): *Asia and Western Dominance: A Survey of the Vasco Da Gama Epoch of History*, 1498-1949, London.
27. For details refer V. Suryanarayan, 'China and Southeast Asia: An Indian Perspective', D.S. Rajan, R.S. Vasan and J.A. Bonofer, (eds.), (2012): *Rise of China: Implications for Asian Neighbours*, New Delhi, pp. 29-48.
28. *Ibid.*
29. Quoted in *Ibid.*
30. Brahma Chellaney, 'China and South Asia: An Overview', M. Rasgotra, (ed.) (2012) : *China and South Asia: Developments and Trends*, New Delhi, pp. 23-30.
31. Quoted in No. 27.
32. S.R. Nathan (2011): *An Unfinished Journey: Path to Presidency*, Singapore, p. 424.
33. No. 27.
34. *A Doctor in the House: The Memoirs of Tun Dr. Mahathir Mohamad* (2011): Petaling Java, p. 432.

# 7

# *Environmental Issues and Peoples' Concerns*

*R.V.G. Menon*

**Whose Concern is Environment?**

With increasing economic development, a class is emerging in Kerala, which consists of people who think that they can build a high wall around them and protect themselves not only from the society to which they belong, but also from the vicissitudes of environmental destruction and even climate change. Gated communities with sentries and security systems, children transported in air conditioned buses from home to expensive and exclusive private schools, self-contained shopping malls which obviate the necessity of rubbing shoulders with the *aam admi* in the market place, private entertainment (including vacationing in exotic locales), and a habit of resorting to private solutions for all the problems of the deteriorating public services which plague the society, by patronising private schools, private hospitals, private transport- and even private policing, are all signs of this emerging culture. They are the least concerned with environmental destruction, and consider environmentalists to be the enemies of development. At the same time, they will profess much concern for the environment, because it is fashionable to do so, and wouldn't mind engaging in some 'politically correct' ceremonial activities like tree planting, paying lip service to environment, etc. But they would consider those who campaign against any 'developmental' project, which might result in the large scale cutting down of trees or destruction of paddy fields, to be 'environmental extremists' who carry things too far.

This is the contradiction of our times.

As a matter of fact, much of what goes on the name of development these days, are destructive of environment. Laws which are meant to safeguard the environment, like the Forest Conservation Act, Environmental Protection Act, Coastal Zone Regulation Act, Paddy Land Protection Act, Land Utilisation Act, Mining and Geology Act, etc., are being flagrantly flouted, for the sake of construction of resorts, restaurants, hotels, highways, shopping malls or airports. Almost all this, one may point out, are meant for the benefit of the richer sections, and with may be a handful of poorer people getting some employment. On the other hand, the destruction of the environment results in an impoverishment of the basic ecosystems, on which the poorer sections of the population depend directly for livelihood. For example, the extent of paddy fields in Kerala came down from about ten lakh hectares to just below 2.5 lakh hectares over the last twenty five years. Since one hectare of paddy land provides about 150 person-days of employment, one can imagine the tremendous loss to the farm workers in terms of workdays. Even allowing for the fact that there has been a shortage of farm workers in the area of paddy cultivation, there cannot be any dispute that for those who have opted to remain in the agricultural labour sector, the diminishing paddy fields have posed a serious threat to livelihood. This is felt acutely in the paddy belt of Palakkad, for example, where alternative employment opportunities have not grown fast enough to offset this impact. The destruction of the bamboo wealth of our forests as a result of over exploitation for the sake of our paper and rayon industries, has culminated in a scarcity of this resource, and consequential hardship for traditional bamboo craftspeople, who depended on it for their livelihood. In all these cases, it can be argued that this kind of sector-wise unemployment is unavoidable in an economy which is in transition from an agrarian one to an industrial one.

However, it is one of the fallacies of Economics to argue that those who find themselves displaced from one sector can be easily accommodated in another sector, which is fast growing. This does not happen in practice, because of various human factors. On the one hand, the displaced workers may be lacking in the new skills which are in demand in the emerging sector, which is cited as its replacement. It is also usual for agricultural people to prefer to remain where they are, and to scavenge for the available labour opportunities, scarce though they are, rather than to migrate to alien cities where the new jobs are likely to be. It is thus that we find the seeming paradox of rampant unemployment in some areas, while some other sectors suffer from shortage of skilled labour.

Pollution of the water bodies, as well as over-exploitation of the sea wealth with the aid of inappropriate mechanisation, again has resulted in loss of productivity of the marine resources over the past few decades. While Boat owners and merchants have prospered, the traditional fisher folk have suffered. This is yet another instance of 'development' turning some people into 'development refugees'.

It may be noted that while the more intensive exploitation might have resulted in greater revenues from exports, the plight of the traditional fisher folk would definitely have deteriorated.

All this shows how the so-called development results in exacerbating inequalities. No wonder that Kerala, which was for long known for its equitable and just model of development, is now exhibiting a larger inequality than the National average, as evidenced by its Gini coefficient. The effect of inequality on development is an area which has received considerable attention in academic circles, lately, the most notable work being the book "The Spirit Level: Why More Equal Societies Almost Always Do Better" by Richard

Wilkinson. Prof. Wilkinson shows graphically, and on the basis of irrefutable studies, how less prosperous but more equitable societies like Japan and the Scandinavian countries perform much better on Human Quality indices than the more prosperous but inequitable USA or UK, where more people are in jail per million population, and the incidence of more mental health problems, more suicides, more drop outs in schools, and more crime. It is ironical that even the better off segments of the population are not able to insulate themselves from the general deterioration in the social fabric. In other words, high walls wouldn't help! Thus it transpires that environment concerns not only the poor who depend directly on its bounty, but also the rich who believe they have a right to a separate future! As Gro Harlem Brundtland's Report for UNCED aptly put it, it is "Our Common Future." We either swim together, or sink together!

## Some Universal Environmental Concerns

### *Global Warming and Climate Change*

After the publication of the IGPCC report, it is now almost universally accepted that global warming is a fact. Opinions may differ as to its rate or impact, but there is no doubt that the planet is warming up.

- Average temperatures have climbed 0.8°C around the world since 1880, much of this in recent decades, according to NASA's Goddard Institute for Space Studies.
- The rate of warming is increasing. The 20th century's last two decades were the hottest in 400 years and possibly the warmest for several millennia, according to a number of climate studies. 11 of the past 12 years are among the dozen warmest since 1850.
- The Arctic is feeling the effects the most. Average temperatures in Alaska, western Canada, and eastern Russia have risen at twice the global average.
- Arctic icecap is rapidly disappearing.
- Glaciers and mountain snows are rapidly melting-The Himalayan Glaciers are receding at a frightening rate.
- Coral reefs, which are highly sensitive to small changes in water temperature, suffering severe bleaching, and are dying off.
- An upsurge in the amount of extreme weather events, such as wild fires, heat waves and tropical storms is also attributed in part to climate change by some experts.

A rise in sea levels is also predicted, which might inundate much of the low lying coasts all over the world.

Climate change might also cause variation in rain patterns and distribution, resulting in significant impact on agricultural yields.

## Some National Issues

All these issues are very much relevant in the Indian context also. We have "developed" enough to become the No. 3 emitter of Carbon dioxide in the world, overtaking Japan (China is No. 1 and USA, No. 2). But we are trying to hide behind the statistics that our per capita emission is still way behind that of the US (2 Tons per person per year, as opposed to 5 Tons for US). But what we conveniently forget is the fact that almost all our petrol consumption and electricity usage (for which we burn most of our coal) take place for the sake of our burgeoning urban population, especially those who live in the metros. The life-style of our urban elite is approximating that of the western affluent class. In fact that is what we call development. The emphasis on privatized transport rather than mass transit systems, the transition from a culture based on long use, reuse and recycle to one based on 'use and discard', the consumerist frenzy, which identifies possessions with satisfaction, are all signs of this transformation.

While this frantic rush for consumerism vitiates the urban middle class, the rural poor is being pushed into the depths of despair and destitution. What passes for wealth creation is an unscientific and unsustainable exploitation of natural resources. These are the same resources based on which the poor were eking out a living. The millions who have been dispossessed to make way for our developmental projects have never been rehabilitated in a satisfactory way (It has been estimated that more than 60 million people have been driven away from their habitats since independence, on account of development projects!). Farmers' suicides have ceased to make headlines in the mainstream media, due to their sheer regularity (According to government statistics, 2,90,740 farmers committed suicide between 1995 and 2011). The over-exploitation of ground water for meeting the ever increasing demands of the cities; has lowered GW levels to dangerous proportions, again adversely affecting the poor and marginal farmers the most severely, thus exacerbating their poverty. It was Indira Gandhi who said that poverty is the worst pollution, and we are having that in plenty! The gap between the rich and poor is steadily widening, and the worsening condition of the small and marginal farmer and the dispossession of the rural poor, seem to be the essential features of our development paradigm, rather than accidents or oversight.

**Some Kerala Specific Issues**

Privatisation of public spaces, over exploitation of limited natural resources, pollution and degradation of the environment, unscientific land use and resulting disruption of life support systems, are all evident in Kerala also. Land reclaimed from the Vembanad lake, under the pretext of Port Development, is being handed over to a private agency for building a Convention Centre. The Kovalam Palace, taken over form the Travancore Royal family, has been handed over to a private agency for operating a Hotel. Large tracts of land, acquired ostensibly for industrial development, is handed over to Inkel, a PPP agency in which "26 per cent of the shares of INKEL Limited are owned by Government Agencies and PSUs and investors and NRI industrialists and businessmen. The remaining 74 per cent is owned by Non Resident Keralites, individuals and banks...." See how fragile the government control is, in this crucial agency!

A crass case of over exploitation of a natural resource is the unscientific mining of river sand, which has converted most of our rivers into mere storm water drains. The rivers are dying, the embankments are collapsing, ground water level in the neighbourhoods is dropping, and salinity incursion during summer has spread to far interiors, upsetting the local ecology. But the mafia dominated sector remains 'untouchable', having support from corrupt politicians, officials and also criminal elements. Honest officials and people's representatives who venture to challenge them are intimidated, assaulted or even liquidated!

Sand mining is only one of the threats which our rivers are facing. Pollution has reached fatal proportions in many rivers, resulting in frequent reports of massive fish kill. Municipal wastes, household wastes, chemical effluents from factories, all contribute to this.

Kerala has stringent laws to prevent the conversion of paddy lands for non-agricultural purposes, but these are violated with impunity by the rich and the powerful. The case of the Aranmula Airport Project is illustrative of this aspect. The District Collector has passed an order that the initial land purchase by the party was illegal. A case is pending in the Court against the diversion of paddy field. The Hon. Minister for Revenue has stated in the floor of the Legislature that action is being taken against the perpetrators of this crime. In the meantime, we find the State Government taking shares in the Project, making it another PPP! Moreover, the President of India includes this as a prestigious project in his inaugural address to the Parliament. Such is the power of money and contacts in this country! Paddy fields are important, not only from the point of view of food security, but also for their role in replenishing ground water, and preserving biodiversity. Wanton filling up of paddy fields for real estate development, and the associated leveling of nearby hillocks, have already created severe drinking water problems and altered local micro climate in those regions.

Encroachment of backwater shores and canal banks as well as marshes is another major threat to our environment. Unlike other poramboke lands, kayal lands are scarcely accessible to outsiders and most encroachments go unnoticed until they have become fait accompli. Quite often these involve violation of Coastal Zone regulations also, but the authorities often look the other way. It has been reported that the extent of our water bodies have been reduced by one third, during the past half century due to encroachments and diversions.

Illegal quarrying and rock crushing are responsible for a lot of hardship to local residents. Indiscriminate quarrying also threatens our fragile ecosystem and needs to be carefully monitored. These rocky outcrops and their overburden are often rich repositories of ground water and their destruction often leads to local water shortage. When local residents and environmentalists raise protests, one finds local functionaries of all political parties as well as officials, protecting the perpetrators for obvious reasons.

**Conclusion**

Thus it follows that environment is everybody's concern, and those who believe that they can insulate themselves from the consequences of its deterioration by virtue of their money power, are living in a fool's paradise.

# 8

# *India's Investment in Science and Technology-Challenges Ahead*

*V.N. Rajasekharan Pillai*

The relative investment in scientific research and development as a fraction of the Gross Domestic Product has remained stagnant in India for the last five successive five year plans. It is in the 0.6 to 0.9 per cent range of the GDP during this quarter century. A striking contrast is that of China which has increased the investment in science from 0.5 per cent to almost 1.5 per cent during this period. In the European Union Countries it has been almost consistently in the range 1.5-1.8 per cent, in Japan, 2.5-2.8 per cent; OECD Countries, 2.3 per cent and in the United States 3-3.5 per cent. In absolute terms, today India's budget for Science Departments is about 21,000 crore, about 5 times than that of 25 years back. As a country, we could have invested much more in Science and Technology in the last 15 years of rapid economic growth. More than three fourths of the national research and development expenditure in India comes from the Central Government and a quarter from the industry. In the federal system, the States' contribution to the research and development is relatively small. Even though Indian industry is spending more on research and development in absolute terms, it is much less relative to the gross national product. In 1985 it was 0.38 per cent of GNP, whereas currently it is only 0.20 per cent. Indian industry does not make major investments in Indian Science, except in drugs and pharma sectors. The industry in India is also not making much demand on Indian Science.

The economic reforms initiated in 1991 have only begun to influence the Indian Science and Technology system. It was only during the 11th plan period that a new set of Indian Institutes of Technologies (IITs) have started almost 50 years after the establishment of the first five IITs. During the last five years we have seen the establishment of a new kind of high quality science teaching and research institutions, the Indian Institute of Science Education and Research (IISER) across the country. There are five of them as of now, Pune, Kolkata, Mohali, Bhopal and Thiruvananthapuram. They come under the higher education sector of the Ministry of Human Resource and Development. There is a similar institution under the Department of Atomic Energy, the National Institute of Science Education and Research (NISER) at Bhuvaneswar. Another such specialised institute under the Department of

Space is the Indian Institute of Space Science and Technology (IIST), Thiruvananthapuram. The creation of the Indian Institute of Information Technologies (IITs) in the government sector, as well as in the public-private participation mode, are also parts of the new wave of science and technology development in the country. While it can be argued that the public investments which have gone into these and other new institutions during this period is huge, considering the population of the country and a drastic increase in the number of potential science and technology higher education seekers, the numbers of the new high quality institutions are very low. A systematic and gradual enhancement of the central and state budgetary provisions during the last 25 years could have addressed this issue positively. We should take stock of this situation and ensure that a quantum leap is happening at least now in the number of high quality state-of-the-art higher education institutions in science and technology.

**The Current Budget**

In January 2013, Prime Minister Dr. Manmohan Singh said that country should aim to double its scientific research expenditure by 2017, to reach two per cent in India's Gross Domestic Product. Under the new Policy on Science, Technology and Innovation, India is planning to increase the number of scientists by 66 per cent by 2017 and enhance private sector participation in research and development. These spending targets were also proposed in the five-year plan released in December 2012. The Government's proposal in 2013-14 budget indicates that it is actually trying to cut research spending. Nine research departments, viz., the Departments of Atomic Energy, Health Research, Agricultural Research, Earth Sciences, Space, Defence Research and the Ministry of Science and Technology's Departments of Biotechnology, Scientific and Industrial Research and the Department of Science and Technology share a little over Rs. 20,000 crore, a mere four per cent more than budgeted for 2012-13, and below the rate of inflation.

**Resource Needs for a Strong R&D System**

Substantial public and private investments are necessary for creating a strong research and development base in India. As indicated earlier, the R&D expenditure in the country today is only 0.9 per cent. Almost 80 per cent of this is from the public sector and 20 per cent only from the private sector. The plan to enhance the total expenditure in research and development to two per cent of Gross Domestic Product by the end of the 12th plan should be realised. Half of this should come from the corporate sector including the Public Sector undertakings. Present resource allocations for research and development in our large public sector organisations are very small. The recent Act on Corporates promotes incentivisation to make much larger provisions for scientific research and development. Such enhanced provisions in Corporates should not just be for in-house research and development. They should support and invest in research institutions and universities, both public and private.

A major intervention possible through the enhancement of private sector R&D expenditure is the interaction and cooperation of public science and technology institutions with industry. Securing private financial flows supporting and a demand-driven research and development path by leveraging the public funds and other financing channels can play a catalytic roll in the industrial support of public research and development institutions. The public and private industries need to be incentivised to invest at least two per cent of their sales turnover in research and development. Research and Developmental activities of Multi National Corporates (MNCs) in India have created certain hubs of world class technological development. This has facilitated the creation of a pool of a highly skilled scientists and technologists. The 12th Plan document from the Planning Commission of India delineates steps to encourage large Indian companies to establish research and development centres across the country. Many of these Indian companies are now global establishments with large interests with a world-wide presence in sectors like minerals, metals, engineering, energy, drugs and pharmaceuticals. These Indian companies have the organisational and financial capacity to recruit high-quality science and technology research personnel from across the world. The central and state governments need to take proactive steps for facilitating such centres to come up in various locations in the country. These places should have an academic ambience and high-quality human resource development institutions like engineering colleges and universities.

**Sectoral Allocation in Various Departments**

Over 60 per cent of scientific research and development expenditure by major scientific agencies goes to just three government departments, the Indian Space Research Organisation (ISRO), the Defence Research and Development Organisation (DRDO) and the Department of Atomic Energy (DAE). The distribution among these agencies is 34 per cent, 17 per cent and 11 per cent respectively. The share of other departments are: Indian Council for Agricultural Research (ICAR), 11 per cent; Council of Scientific and Industrial Research (CSIR), 9 per cent; Department of Science and Technology (DST), 8 per cent; Department of Biotechnology (DBT), two per cent; Indian Council of Medical Research (ICMR ), two per cent; Indian Council of Forestry Research and Education (ICFRE), two per cent; Department of Earth Sciences, two per cent; and Department of Information Technology, two per cent. These figures relate only to the scientific research component of these various institutions.

The three strategic departments of atomic energy, defence research and development organisation and the department of space are developing technologies primarily for their own respective needs. In order for them to trigger mechanisms to encourage innovation and to impact on social, industrial and other development sectors focussed funding and enhanced investments are necessary. This potentially high-yielding side of spin-off technologies are not given the right kind of priority in budgeting. While it is true that these technology-transfer can create an impact only by participation by big Corporates or private industries, resource allocation or mobilisation supported by governments is highly necessary for at least venturing into these areas. We have clear indications of successful spin-offs like automative weather stations, fleet monitoring equipment, tele-education and tele-medicine systems developed by the Indian Space Research Organisation. Similarly, there are the instrumented pipeline inspection gauges and food processing irradiation technologies developed by the department of atomic energy. The biomedical instruments, life science technologies, medical diagnostic kits and bio toilets for water-scarce areas developed by the DRDO are also successful spin-offs. Such technology transfers in the areas of water purification, seawater desalination, waste disposal and alternate energy systems also hold great promise. This area needs much larger focussed investments from the public sector. Public-Private-Participation in the area of Technology-Transfer needs to be regarded as a priority area of funding by the Central and State Governments.

**New Funding Avenues for Public and Private Agencies - Expectations**

The Science and Technology R & D system in the country is currently input-driven. This pattern should undergo a paradigm shift to an output-driven developmental strategy. The felt-needs of the Indian society and the industry need to be addressed by our scientific and technological establishments. Such a transition is imperative for reorienting the direction and priorities of the science and technology sector. This can only lead to opening up new funding avenues for public and private establishments, expecting and securing benefits from their association with science and technology sectors. Over the years, several areas of science and technology have been adopting suitable institutional frameworks to enhance the research and development capabilities. The 12th Plan Report of the Planning Commission has recommended a critical review of the continuing relevance of these institutional research and development frameworks. Such a step is crucial for the much-needed human and financial resources for the identified priority areas. In this context, the report has also recommended moving some of the research programmes to the university system from the national laboratories. This is very important for the right kind of human resource development in the science and technology sector in the country.

We need to create an ecosystem that encourages research and innovation in a self-sustaining manner. There is an urgent need for bringing back the lost research culture of Indian Universities helping them to create new knowledge. Collaborative research, setting up industry incubation parks in Universities, enhancing research fellowships and providing more of them, promoting innovation through interdisciplinary and trans-disciplinary research in new emerging fields and strengthening inter-university centres are being continuously emphasised in our plan budgets for higher education. However these are not getting really materialised due to the severe shortage of faculty in the system. Hence many such budgetary provisions are not getting converted into real activities.

**Framework for Holistic R & D Funding**

In the science and technology sector, it is necessary to create and follow a framework that takes into account the entire life cycle of ideas starting from discovery or creation to commercialisation, extension and value addition. The funding patterns should take care of these requirements. A holistic approach to public funding of research and development for socially relevant projects needs to be engrained in the current institutional structures and mechanisms. Here the entire knowledge domain of research and development needs to be interconnected. A much larger base of full-time researchers and greater flexibility in engaging them can only ensure the quality utilisation of the much-scarce financial resources. Greater autonomy with fixed accountability and assured outcomes can only bring about effective use of public funds for research. There needs to be much more facilitation for young scientists to pursue their research ideas. Maximum mobility and interaction among industry, academia and the research and development institutions has to be ensured. Promotions of big science and technology missions through the combined efforts of different sectors have to be supported. We need to strengthen gender parity initiatives in the research and development sector by way of facilitating mobility and by providing for suitable parameters for women re-entry programmes in science and technology. The scope of inter-institutional and international collaborative research programmes has to be enhanced. Participation of the different States and socio-economic ministries in technology deployment processes has to be ensured. A well-articulated strategy for technology acquisition in high-tech areas needs to be worked out and implemented. Radical changes are needed in human resources, financing and procurement policies. A transparent performance appraisal and incentivisation system needs to be in place.

**Funding of New Research and Innovation Universities - Planned, yet to be Realised**

Substantial funding for new research universities and innovation universities has been envisaged in the 12th Plan. This funding mostly for scientific research and innovation in the university system is in addition to the funding through the various science and technology related ministries. The Ministry of Human Resource Development (MHRD) in the Central Government is the nodal ministry for this funding which is through the University Grants Commission and also through the newly created Rashtriya Uchchathar Shiksha Abhiyan – RUSA – (National Higher Education Commission). So far no significant activity in this regard has happened mainly due to delay in getting the Innovation University Bill passed in the Parliament.

Research Universities are crucial to the 21st Century global knowledge economy and serve as flagships for higher education. Advanced research in frontier areas of various branches of sciences and technology is the major thrust of the research universities. These institutions are proposed to provide the key link between global science and scholarship and the country's knowledge system. The number of undergraduate (below Ph.D. Level) students in the research universities will be limited. The brightest students selected from all over the country will only get the opportunity for undergraduate education in such universities. The research universities are expected mainly to offer highest quality doctoral programmes and to produce the bulk of the research output. The United States have the largest number of research universities. They have over 150 globally relevant research universities out of about 5,000 higher education institutions. India has only less than five universities which can be considered as some sort of research universities; there are about 40,000 tertiary higher education institutions in India. In contrast, China has more than 100 research universities, from among its over 50,000 post-secondary higher education institutions. The organisational structure, reward patterns and the proposed academic profile of these universities are oriented towards research. The budgets of these universities are several hundred times larger than that of other universities. The financial support for these institutions is largely from public sources in most of the countries.

Research Universities play a critical role in training and developing professionals, high-order specialists and researchers in the core areas of science and technology. These institutions promote research needed for the economic growth. The 2002 World Bank Report gives a critical overview of the relevance of the Research Universities in the perspectives of various countries. The salient features of these research universities are abundant resources to offer a rich learning environment, state-of-the-art facilities for conducting advanced research and favourable governance features to encourage leadership, strategic vision, innovation and flexibility. At the core of the research university is its teaching and research faculty. Even though their research appears to be for creating knowledge for its own sake only, we see the concrete applications of their research achievements at a later stage. The research universities are designed to be 'elite and meritocratic' in the areas of hiring faculty, admission policies and promotion requirements. Academic freedom is at the core of the idea of a research university. The key element here is the concept of open inquiry as central to the objectives of the research universities. The governance structures are also totally different from the existing universities.

**RUSA Funding for Research Universities in Various States**

In the recently approved pattern of higher education funding to the States through the Rashtriya Uchchathar Shiksha Abhiyan (RUSA), funds for setting up of new research universities by the States have been provided. This is in addition to the existing central funding through the University Grants Commission. This is based in the felt-requirement of creating a research ecosystem complimenting the high volume of tertiary education, mainly teaching, happening in the universities and colleges in the different States. The present research scenario in the state universities and colleges is not very promising primarily because of the totally inadequate funding. The RUSA proposals, which are slated to be implemented from 2013-14 fiscal year onwards, envisage seeding and nurturing of one research university in each of the States in the country. There are a set of preconditions, formulated on the basis of the characteristics of global research universities, for availing these funds. In view of the limited timelines for fulfilling these preconditions, RUSA suggests that it is pertinent to upgrade the existing institutions to research universities, rather than creating institutions afresh. Existing state universities which have achieved a critical standing in terms of establishment, enrolment, rating and research are the potential institutions for upgradation to research universities, according to these guidelines. The academic dimension of the existing institutions can be gauged from the quality and number of the post-graduate teaching and research departments. Along with other stipulations, the RUSA also insists that the existing institutions should come up with agreed benchmarks on governance and possess a high degree of compliance with the quality framework in order to be eligible for up gradation to Research University. For the vast majority of the state universities in the country, fulfilling these conditions as such is a formidable challenge. However systematic attempts to fulfil these criteria by the state universities would be great steps forward for enhancing the quality and relevance of the higher education system in the country.

**Conclusion**

Strengthening scientific and technological interventions in the country requires substantial additional funding from the public and corporate sectors. In addition to the major science and technology departments, several other sectors like agriculture, health, industry, information technology, environment and skill development needs funds for sector-specific areas of scientific interventions. While focusing on the set objectives of these developmental sectors, a coordination of the core science activities of these institutions at the national level is desirable. Even when we advocate for much higher levels of funding for Science and Technology, we see the limited absorption of funding and low-quality utilisation of even the available funds. Systemic corrections are needed to address these issues. The most important factor in this context is the development of right kind of higher level human resources in science and technology in the country. The fact that we require 66 per cent more full time equivalent of scientists and technologists in the next five years illustrates the gravity of the challenge. This is in addition to about 55 per cent existing vacancies of teaching and research faculty in our existing universities and various other institutes of science and technology. Consolidation and strengthening of the conventional universities by way of providing them state-of-the-art scientific and technological infrastructure and recruiting quality faculty are essential for revamping the science education in the country. De-bureaucratisation of higher education and science is a noble idea which we have been hearing all these years. This should happen. The academic freedom and the ambience which is there in some of the premier scientific and research establishments in the country should be a model for the existing universities, particularly state universities. The financial investment in the undergraduate and postgraduate science and technology education in the several thousands of colleges and hundreds of University Departments in the country are deplorably poor. This is the reason why they cannot attract best faculty or motivated students in science and technology. Higher education in science and technology and scientific research in the University system require extensive additional funding. If we can realise 10 per cent of the per-student funding in the national institutions like IITs, IIMs, IISERs or Central Universities, for the students in our affiliated colleges and universities, there would be a revolutionary change in the performance and outcome of science education and research in the country. While reinforcing the advocacy for enhancing from the 0.9 per cent to two per cent of the GDP for science and technology in the country, we need to look at the ground realities objectively and ensure quality and out-come based allocation, distribution and utilisation of funds.

# 9

# *Police Reform: All Eyes on the Apex Court*

*P.J. Alexander*

**Chasing an Elusive Agenda**

Reforming the Police, insulating the Central Bureau of Investigation from political interference, strengthening the different components of the Criminal Justice System and thus ensuring the Rule of Law, are issues that have again forcefully surfaced in public discourse in this Country. The context which pushed the issues to the fore however does no credit to us. In fact it is a matter of national shame. But even the darkest of clouds has a silver lining. What else can we say about the sad and unfortunate incidents which have brought the above issues to the very epicenter of the public square? The rape and murder of a young girl in New Delhi, rape and murder of very young female children, wanton neglect of law and order while ensuring the highest category of security to a very rich industrialist, the 'Coal-Gate' and the 'Rail-Gate', the soaring crime graph, and the mounting disorder, have stirred, yet again, the public conscience and there is pressing demand for reforming the police and strengthening the Criminal Justice System. There has been public outcry on police ineptitude on many occasions in the past. But there has not been any satisfactory response from the State. What gives room for optimism is that this time the Apex Court is deeply involved in the issues. It may be recalled that it was the Apex Court again, through the directions issued in Prakash Singh's case that resurrected the Report of the National Police Commission. With Police and Law and Order in the State List, the Centre could look the other way and the States have their own reasons to keep the police under their control. The last time the Centre responded to the demand for police reform was in the aftermath of the Internal Emergency of June 1975. The Shah Commission and the National Police Commission were two responses of the Janatha Government to the massive misuse of police and the criminal law. The National Police Commission submitted its First Report in February, 1979, and the Eighth and concluding Report in May 1981. But hardly anything was done to implement any of its recommendations either by the Centre which appointed the Commission, but was practicing what could be called 'political apartheid' or the States to whose share the Constitution had given public order and police but were never active players in the game of police reform. As years rolled by, almost every one had given up hope that the recommendations of the Commission would ever be even selectively implemented. The very cold response to the attempt by the Union Home Minister Indrajit Gupta to revive interest in the recommendations had convinced even the most incorrigible optimist that the chapter was closed tight. It was into this 'Slough of Despond' that the Supreme Court breathed hope and life. The closed doors are now open and a whiff of fresh air is blowing the cob webs away. Thus is the justifiable optimism in the title of this Paper. All eyes are not on the Committee of Ministers attempting to design a system to insulate the premier Investigating Agency from being interfered with, but on the Apex Court which said while dealing with the Coal scam that "We should liberate CBI from interference".

**Police Commissions – 1860, 1902-03, 1978**

Under the British there were two Police Commissions – that of 1860 and 1902-03. The First Commission set up immediately after the National Revolt of 1857 gifted to us the ever living Police Act of 1861. Like Banquo's ghost it refuses to go away and is the most potent tool in the hands of the political executive to keep the police under tight control. The Frazer Commission of 1902-03 did not deal with issues germane to the present discussion. When the reins of power came to Indian hands on August 15, 1947 reforming the police was not a pressing or serious enough issue to the new leadership. They seem to have not noticed the total break down of the District Administration in most of North India, where people who were till yesterday, neighbours and friends, suddenly became citizens of another country and bitter enemies. People, in hordes, large masses, started moving from one country to the other and there was murder and mayhem and total breakdown of civil administration. It is an ugly blot on the 'Steel Frame' that it failed to anticipate the consequences of the Radcliff Award and the emergence of new boundaries between the two countries. The lives lost, the families scattered, the property lost and destroyed, the total breakdown of the governing apparatus, particularly the law and order machinery, did not prompt the new political masters to search for better alternatives, to what has been bequeathed to them by the British. They opted for continuity than change and it suited them well. The police continued to be under their control dancing to their tune. That a new society needs a new police was a vision they did not find compelling or attractive. They opted to preserve the status quo. The ICS and the IP were christened IAS and IPS. While distributing powers, between the Union and the States, Public Order and Police went to List II, State List. The Union in List I, had Other Armed Forces of the Union, and the Central Bureau for Intelligence and Crime. This arrangement did not prevent proliferation of para military units or other organisations/agencies under the Centre. The States were to look up to the Centre for help when large scale law and order situations erupted. E. M. S. Namboothiripad as Chief Minister of Kerala, faced with the mass upsurge called 'Vimochana Samaram' drew the Centre's attention to Article 355 - 'Duty of the Union to protect States against external aggression and internal disturbance'. There were also academic discussions like the present author's Dissertation while at the Central Police Training College, Mt. Abu, (1966) and in the Police Science Congress (1968) on placing police and public order in the Concurrent List. The distribution of powers in the Constitution literally absolved the Union from any direct responsibility for reforming the police. The States also did not take Police Reform as important. Thus there was not even a whisper for police reform in the country during the first two decades - a sad neglect indeed.

**The Kerala Initiative, 1959**

It is a matter of satisfaction that among the States it was Kerala which took the first step to reform the police. The Kerala State with E.M.S. Namboothiripad as Chief Minister and V.R. Krishna Iyer as Home minister, appointed a Police Re-organisation Committee on 15 January, 1959. The Terms of Reference were very progressive and anticipated issues and problems Police face today. Many States took the cue and constituted Police Commissions, but not with such a wide or progressive Terms of Reference. These Commissions were flooded with former police officers and brother bureaucrats and did not have the presence of an Ashok Sen, Mohan Kumaramangalam, Gurumoorthy or P.N. Krishna Pillai. The need to change the police and to give them a re-orientation to be in tune with the aspirations of the people too did not emerge prominently among the concerns behind the appointment of these Commissions. Further, no Commission or State dared to suggest steps to free the police from political interference and be accountable to the Law of the land. Most of the Commission Reports were all about the shine of the shoes and the starch of the uniform. They threw no doubt some sops to the harried man inside, but forgot to attempt to transform him to be a friend of the people and a servant of the Law of the land.

The Kerala Police Re-organisation Committee which was forced to wind up its work abruptly, (on the government being dismissed and President's Rule imposed as a sequel to the Vimochana Samaram) had this to observe in conclusion — "The role of the police as guardians of law and order has undergone an important change after the attainment of independence. The Police Force in the Country was organised nearly a century ago by a foreign Government and during the struggle for freedom by the people, the police as the coercive arm of the Government had to subserve the interests of the Government then in power. They came to be looked upon with distrust and antipathy by the people who considered them the instrument of aggression used by an alien government. After the attainment of independence and the adoption of the Constitution, greater awareness of civil liberties, and rights of the people guaranteed by the Constitution changed the attitude of the people towards the police. They expect a different approach by the police towards the maintenance of law and order and want them to play a new role in a progressive and enlightened democracy. It therefore became a matter of increasing importance that the method of functioning of police which was codified in the previous regime should be examined for re orientation to enable them to function as friends and guardians of the people animated by a spirit of service towards the common people which is essential in a Welfare State".

The Report did not find favour with the Government which succeeded the E.M.S. led government. It was also an exercise in 'political apartheid'. But what was unbelievably strange was that even the three Left Democratic Governments which came to power subsequently did not bother to implement any of the recommendations in the slim volume. It would not have cost the Exchequer much to implement the recommendations. The same fate, curiously, awaited the Second Police Reforms Commission constituted by a Congress Home minister and Chief Minister-led Government also (1984 - 88). The present author was the Member-Secretary to this Commission. Earlier, even the Report of the Gore Committee on Police Training, an initiative of the Union Government, did not receive here the enthusiastic welcome it received in other States. What emerges out of these instances is that while many pay lip service to police reforms there is an abject lack of political will to really change and reform the police. This would appear to be the case with the recommendations submitted by Commissions appointed by other States also.

The following extract from the Report of the Royal Commission on the Police (1962) in the United Kingdom is of immense interest in this context as the Government in the U K, the mother of Parliamentary democracies, did not find it difficult to accept the recommendations making the police accountable to the Law and to no one else.

> 57–The police in this country are the instrument for enforcing the rule of law; they are the means by which civilized society maintains order that people may live safely in their homes and go freely about their lawful business. Basically their task is the maintenance of the Queens' Peace that is the preservation of law and order. Without this there would be anarchy. Policemen, like everybody else, are accountable to the law. They are also the laws' agents: and the uniformed policeman has for many years been recognised and accepted as the embodiment of the laws' authority. In a general sense it can be said that the purpose of the police is unchanging....
>
> 59–The policeman works in a changing society and there is nothing constant about the range and variety of police duties, just as there is nothing constant about the pattern of crime, the behaviour of criminals, the State of public order or at deeper levels, the hidden trends in society that dispose men to crime, to civil and industrial unrest or to political demonstration.

This picture is true of this country also. The society underwent rapid change and new trends and pressures emerged. The State also moved forward, expanding its activities and spheres of involvement. The police organisation remained static, although there were sporadic attempts at tinkering with it. Police service and functioning deteriorated and with increasing political interference, the police in India were not generally accepted as the agents of Law and were being branded as the agents of the government in power. There was a widening gap between police precepts and practice. Even the few unwilling steps to check police excesses, misuse of power, brutality or misuse of authority were soon circumvented. Police ingenuity was versatile enough to devise, every time, short cuts and alternatives. The Indian situation thus was a classic case of adequately effective provisions in the statutes, but wanton disregard to all such provisions in practice. The divide between precepts and practice became too wide and invited frequent strictures from the Judiciary and also from the media and the public.

**Terms of Reference of the National Police Commission-Vision for Reform**

The 'Emergency' of June, 1975 to March 1977 saw the police at their deteriorated worst. It has to be observed that the Emergency could be imposed only with the collusion of the police. In States where non Congress Governments were in power, misuse of power by the police was minimal. Obviously the political executive was working through the police. On the lifting of Emergency there was a hue and cry against the police and demands for dismantling the Central Police Organisations and other Units which had blotted their copy book with excesses. As mentioned above, the two specifically targeted initiatives against misuse of the police machinery by the Government during Emergency were the Shaw Commission of Enquiry and the National Police Commission – (Dharma Vir Commission) 1978. The Terms of Reference of the Police Commission is reproduced below in full to give a clear picture of the changes the Government desired to bring about in the police.

1. Re-define the role, duties, powers and responsibilities of the police with special reference to prevention and control of crime and maintenance of public order.
2. Examine the development of the principles underlying the present policing system, including the method of magisterial supervision, evaluate the performance of the system, identify the basic weaknesses of inadequacies, and suggest appropriate changes in the system and the basic laws governing the system.
3. Examine, if any changes are necessary in the existing method of administration, disciplinary control and accountability.
4. Inquire into the system of investigation and prosecution, the reasons for delay and failure; the use of improper methods and the extent of their prevalence; and suggest how the system may be modified or changed and made efficient, scientific and consistent with human dignity; and how the related laws may be suitably amended.
5. Examine methods of maintaining crime records and statistics and suggest methods for making them uniform and systematic.
6. Review policing in rural areas, evaluate any new arrangements that have been made and recommend changes that are necessary.

7. Examine the system of policing required in non-rural and urbanized areas including metropolitan areas, and suggest the pattern that would be the most suitable.
8. Examine the steps taken for modernising law enforcement, evaluate the work of police communications, the computer network, scientific laboratories and agencies for research and development, and examine whether modernisation can be speeded up; examine to what extent, as a result of the modernisation of Police forces, streamlining of its functions and its re-structuring, it would be possible to economise in the manpower in the various areas of its activities.
9. Examine the nature and extent of the special responsibilities of the Police towards the weaker sections of the community and suggest steps to ensure prompt action on their complaints for the safeguard of their rights and interests.
10. Recommend measures and institutional arrangements:
    (i) to prevent misuse of powers by the police and to examine whether police behaviour, out-look, responsiveness and impartiality are maintained at the correct level, and if not the steps such as recruitment and training which should be taken to improve them;
    (ii) to prevent misuse of the Police by administrative or executive instructions, political or other pressure, or oral orders of any type, which are contrary to law;
    (iii) for the quick and impartial inquiry of public complaints made against the police about any misuse of police powers;
    (iv) for the quick redressal of grievances of police personnel and to look after their morale and welfare; and
    (v) For a periodic objective evaluation of police performance in a metropolitan area/District/State in a manner which will carry credibility before the public.
11. Examine the manner and extent to which police can enlist ready and willing co-operation of the public in the discharge of their social defence and law enforcement duties and suggest measures regarding the institutional arrangements to secure such co-operation and measures for the growth of healthy and friendly public-police relationship.
12. Examine the methods of police training, development, and career-planning of officers and recommend any changes that are required at any time in their service, to modernize the outlook, and to make the leadership of the force effective and morally strong.
13. Examine the nature of the problems that the police will have to face in the future, and suggest the measures necessary for dealing with them, and for keeping them under continuous study and appraisal.
14. Consider and make recommendations and suggestions regarding any other matter which the Government may refer to the Commission; and

15. Any other matter of relevance or importance having an impact on the subject.

**National Police Commission Report–To the Cold Storage**

The Commission submitted their Report in eight volumes between 1979 and 1981 and it carried enough recommendations to re-organise the police and give them a new face, a new style of functioning, functional independence, strict accountability and professionalism. In their Second Report submitted in August, 1979, the Commission in Chapter XV dealt with: Interference with and misuse of Police by Illegal or Improper orders or Pressure from Political Executive or other extraneous sources — 'Remedial Measures'. In their Eighth and Concluding Report they appended a draft Police Bill to replace the Police Act of 1861. They said "We have in our Reports recommended certain basic reforms for the effective functioning of the police to enable it to promote the dynamic rule of law and to render impartial service to the people. This presupposes a professionally competent and attitudinally impartial police force. For the incorporation of our new recommendations, it is necessary to replace the existing, outmoded Police Act of 1861. We have, therefore, drafted a new Police Act incorporating our recommendations".

With the fall of the Janata Government and the return of the Congress under Indira Gandhi to power the Reports of the National Police Commission and the draft Police Bill were sent to the morgue of police reform initiatives. Nothing was done to implement the recommendations by the States, and the Centre felt that it had really no role to play under the Constitutional plan of distribution of powers. A valiant attempt was made to resurrect the Police Commission Report by the then Home Minister in August 1997 who wrote to the States on the pressing need to reform the police. The Home Minister while echoing the overall popular perception that there has been a general fall in the performance of the police as also deterioration in the policing system as a whole in the country, expressed that the time had come to rise above limited perceptions to bring about some drastic changes in the shape of reforms and restructuring of the police before the country is overtaken by unhealthy developments. It was expressed that the popular perception all over the country appears to be that many of the deficiencies in the functioning of the police had arisen largely due to an over dose of unhealthy and petty political interference at various levels starting from transfer and posting of police men of different ranks, misuse of police for partisan purposes and political patronage quite often extended to corrupt police personnel. The Union Home Minister expressed the view that rising above narrow and partisan considerations, it is of great national importance to insulate the police from the growing tendency of partisan or political interference in the discharge of its lawful functions of prevention and control of crime, including investigations of cases and maintenance of public order. It is of great interest to note that this Home Minister was none other than Indrajit Gupta of the Communist Party of

India, the first Communist to occupy the post of Union Home Minister. But his cry of anguish also fell on deaf ears.

**Prakash Singh's Case and After**

It was when nothing appeared to work that Prakash Singh, a member of the IPS and a former DGP, approached the Supreme Court. His petition remained before the Supreme Court for long. Why Prakash Singh and others approached the Supreme Court is best answered in the orders of the Supreme Court itself. "When the recommendations of National Police Commission were not implemented, for whatever reasons or compulsions, and they met the same fate as the recommendations of many other commissions, this petition under Article 32 of the Constitution of India was filed about 10 years back, inter alia, praying for issue of directions to Government of India to frame a new Police Act on the lines of the model Act drafted by the Commission in order to ensure that the 'police is made accountable essentially and primarily to the law of the land and the people'. The Supreme Court acted and issued certain directions.

**Enter the Apex Court**

The Supreme Court did not suggest anything new; their directives were all based on the Report of the National Police Commission. They directed that (1) a State Security Commission, a Police Establishment Board and a Police Complaints Authority be constituted, (2) a new selection process for selecting the Director General of Police be introduced, (3) the Director General and some other functionaries given a minimum tenure of two years, (4) and investigation and law and order to be functionally separated – all steps towards implementing the Report of the National Police Commission. Their reasons for issuing these directives are however very important.

"Having regard to (i) the gravity of the problem; (ii) the urgent need for preservation and strengthening of Rule of Law; (iii) pendency of even this petition for the last over ten years; (iv) the fact that various Commissions and Committees have made recommendations on similar lines for introducing reforms in the police set-up in the country; and (v) total uncertainty as to when police reforms would be introduced, we think that there cannot be any further wait, and the stage has come for issue of appropriate directions for immediate compliance so as to be operative till such time a new model Police Act is prepared by the Central Government and / or the State Governments pass the requisite legislations. It may further be noted that the quality of Criminal Justice System in the country, to a large extent, depends upon the working of the police force. Thus, having regard to the larger public interest, it is absolutely necessary to issue the requisite directions".

It is a matter of great satisfaction that in Prakash Singh's case, a three member Bench headed by the Chief Justice of India, Y.K. Sabharwal, painstakingly went through the annals of police reforms in this country, the Reports of the Law Commission, Report of the Human Rights Commission and a host of material relevant to Police and Criminal Justice reforms. The Court noted that 'police' is a State subject, and quite candidly asked themselves: "The question however is whether this court should further wait for Government to take suitable steps for Police Reforms" and concluded, most logically, that they should not wait any further.

Even these directions did not bestir the political executive to act for police reforms. The States went to bargain for time. The Supreme Court while giving some more time to implement some of the directions, stated without mincing words that — "review of judgment cannot be ordered in the garb of modification of the order" and set 10 April, 2007 for filing affidavits of compliance. The Court added "that the elections have been ordered in any State would not be ground not to comply with the directions in the time frame in this order". This was in Record of Proceedings in Writ Petition (C) 310 of 1996 dated 11 January, 2007.

For any government with commitment to the Rule of Law and to a strong Criminal Justice System, a desire to maintain law and order, to arrest the burgeoning crime trend and to preserve order for the sake of the fruits of development, reaching the intended, especially, the marginalized, the message was loud and clear. But what followed were again steps aimed at, delay, and dilution of the directives of the Highest Court of the Country. In almost all States, except in a few small States, the most cunning and ingenious exercise to circumvent the directions of the Apex Court was employed using a clause from the directives of the Supreme Court "till such time a new model Police Act is prepared by the Central Government and / or the State Governments pass the requisite legislations" as the excuse. This in sum was to cobble up legislation as the prerogative of the Executive, incorporating whatever they wanted to make the directions of the Apex Court ineffective, leaving ample room for interference and manipulation. A classic instance is the Police Act 2011 legislated in Kerala. (Act 8 of 2011).

**The Great Kerala Betrayal**

Close on the directions of the Supreme Court, the State Government promulgated Ordinances to set up the State Security Commission, the Police Complaints Authority, the Police Establishment Board, etc. and constituted a Committee of serving senior Police Officers to draft a Police Bill. The Government had earlier appointed the Law Reforms Commission-Kerala with the eminent Jurist Justice V.R. Krishna Iyer as Chairman. The Commission had appointed a Sub Committee with former Judges of the High Court, outstanding lawyers of the High Court and the present author to draft a Police Bill. There was no move to combine the two and as a result two Bills were prepared, one by the Committee of Police Officers and the other by the Law Reforms Commission. The Chairman of the Commission Justice Krishna Iyer forwarded the draft Police Bill prepared by the Commission in his letter No. 188/LRC/08, dated July 16, 2008 to the then Chief Minister of Kerala, V. S. Achuthanandan. He pleaded that the draft Kerala Police Bill prepared by the Commission may be considered instead of going ahead with the Bill prepared by a group of serving Police

Officers who were obviously under very severe constraints. It is necessary to reproduce this letter to expose the attitude of the Government in regard to police reforms.

> I am forwarding herewith the draft Kerala Police Bill prepared, at my instance, by a sub-committee of the Commission and substantially aided by Dr. Alexander, an able former DGP. The Commission has 'generally approved' the bill at its meeting held on 12 July, 2008. The bill itself is based upon all possible materials, including one the Central Law Minister sent to me, the Policy Paper by the Central Committee headed by Shri Soli Sorabjee prepared with the directions given by the Supreme Court in a recent ruling. A number of others have been consulted, including the Commonwealth Human Rights Committee. The Commonwealth Human Rights Chief in Delhi and Shri Justice K.T. Thomas have been furnished its copies. It is comprehensive and excels the draft prepared by the Police Department of the State Government. It is, therefore, important that instead of rushing to the House with an imperfect Bill, at least consider a far more accomplished version which has absorbed ideas from Police Bills from other Countries. Kindly acknowledge the receipt of this letter and enclosures. Let the people of Kerala benefit by the Commission's work on Police jurisprudence....

However the Political Executive did not pay any heed to the request of Justice Krishna Iyer and took steps to legislate the draft Bill prepared by the Committee of serving Police Officers, a draft which satisfied the political executive.

The present author realising that the Government was bent upon enacting its own draft, along with his colleagues in the Centre for Criminal Justice Research (CCJR) prepared and published a Draft Kerala Police Bill and forwarded the same to the Government. He had earlier joined hands with the Law Reforms Commission, Kerala, under the Chairmanship of Justice V.R. Krishna Iyer to draft a Kerala Police Bill satisfying the directives of the Apex Court. The following, reproduced from the introduction to the Draft Kerala Police Bill 2009, would be of interest in this context.

> The Draft Kerala Police Act 2008 now proposed to be tabled before the Legislature has every directive of the Supreme Court. It is a clever exercise to pull wool over the eyes of the Supreme Court and to ensure that the political executive continues to control the police and its functioning, to subserve narrow political interests. This has to be resisted. When for the first time after 1861 a new Police Act is being legislated, it should be ensured that we have a Police which has none of its past traits, habits and deficiencies. A new Police for a new Society, a Police which our Society deserves and not one that hogs all space in media headlines, all for the wrong reasons. Hence this Draft Bill. Except for minor and cosmetic changes, it is

substantially the same which the Law Reforms Commission, Kerala under the Chairmanship of Justice V.R. Krishna Iyer, submitted to the Government of Kerala.

The Centre for Criminal Justice Research went ahead and circulated the Draft Bill among various stakeholders. As Director, the present author extensively campaigned among lawyers, law students and civil society activists and partnered with NGO's and other similar organisations to plead with the Government to incorporate the directives of the Supreme Court in their Draft Police Bill. He also gave evidence before the Select Committee and later forwarded to the Chairman of the Select Committee and the Secretary, Legislature Secretariat a recent decision of the Madras High Court emphatically reiterating the position that the directives of the Apex Court have to be complied with. All this fell as usual on deaf ears.

This in short, is an account of what happened to police reforms in this State under governments led by the UDF as well as the LDF from 1959. It is very disappointing to note that even the LDF led Governments, which probably would have suffered more under a partisan police, did not opt to liberate the police and make it independent and accountable to the Law. The story of police reform for the Country as a whole too is none too different. Despite the National Police Commission Report and the directives on it by the Apex Court in Prakash Singh's case and subsequent orders of the Supreme Court dated 11 January, 2007, there was hardly any genuine attempt to reform the police.

**A Martyr for Police Reforms**

The heinous crime perpetrated on 'Nirbhaya' in New Delhi stirred the national conscience as never before and public anger erupted into the streets of the country. The common denominator was police inability to give security to the life and property of the people, particularly to the very poor and defenseless and the call for police reform again came to centre stage. Subsequent events like mindless assaults on female children, the attempt to cover up the Coal Gate Report and to tamper with the Investigating Agency made the case for Police Reforms stronger.

Justice Verma Committee constituted to suggest amendments to the Criminal Law in the wake of the 'Nirbhaya' rape and murder case has strongly argued for Police Reforms as can be seen from the following extracts from their Report: "(5) Police Reforms that are recommended and directed for the autonomy and better quality of the police force must be urgently implemented for the preservation of the rule of law, which is a basic feature of our Constitution. (6) The Law enforcement agencies must be insulated from any political or other extraneous influence, which impedes their performance. Law enforcement agencies must not become tools at the hands of political masters". The Committee which did an excellent job, within the time limit, without waiting for Government support facilities have concluded their Report with a quote from the immortal words of Panditji in his 'Tryst with destiny' speech.

Alerted by the mood of the Country and particularly that of the Apex Court, the Union Home Minister convened a conference of State Home Ministers to review the progress of police reform and the new Police Act to be legislated in the wake of Prakash Singh's case and the issues that came before the Apex Court subsequently in different litigations. It was sparsely attended. Even Chief Ministers and Home Ministers of States with Congress Ministries did not care to attend, in an eloquent display of supreme indifference to the call for change in the police structure and functional dynamics. A hurried Balance Sheet prepared by the Press gave the most disappointing picture of willful disdain to the directions and the spirit behind the directions of the Supreme Court in Prakash Singh's case. It has come out that many States have enacted Police Acts completely diluting the directions of the Apex Court in Prakash Singh's case and there was really no commitment to carry out the directions of the Apex Court in letter and spirit. A living instance is the Police Act of the State of Kerala.

**A Word of Caution**

My experience as a campaigner for police reform and good governance compels me to draw the attention of the readers to an article by C.P. Joshi in the Hindu of 3 May, 2013, captioned 'From Hawala Scam to Coalgate, Full Circle for Supreme Court' and another by Harish Khare in the Hindu of seven May 2013 captioned 'The False Allure of Liberating CBI'. While my very exclusive exposure as an insider, a member of the IPS, and as a serious student of Politics and Public Administration caution me against being over optimistic, my faith in the Indian people and the Judicial System tells me that the Apex Court would not fail us.

**Directions of Police Reform**

What should be the directions of Police Reforms in this Country is a legitimate question. The National Police Commission Reports are over 30 years old. These recommendations would not therefore be adequate to reform the police to be in tune with the State and society today. It is not assumed that with a new Police Act, faithfully incorporating the directives of the Supreme Court, the police would be reformed. It requires great many efforts. The entire process of application of criminal law has to be reviewed to reduce the grey areas and the vast discretion and consequent scope for misuse, at the disposal of the police. The Reports of the Law Commission of India provide strong indicators to the directions of these changes. It would not be easy to bring about required transformation with a stroke of the pen. It requires careful planning and introduction of structural changes and infusion of ethical and legal concerns that govern our Society. The objective should be to transform the police in to a service, from being a force and made accountable to the law and not to the political executive. Police reforms are an unfinished national agenda and have to be treated as a national priority. The Criminal Justice System hinges heavily on an honest and efficient police system which respects the rule of law and human rights. The Criminal Justice System, in generic terms, connotes interlinked agencies — the police, prosecution, the courts penitentiaries and reformation institutions — that perform complementary social defense functions. The individual and his aberrant behaviour are matters of serious concern for society. Society's concern expresses itself in its enactments, enforced by the investigating agencies and adjudicated by the judiciary. Penal institutions take care of those who are found remiss; others are thrown back, hopefully, for reformation and reintegration. The different agencies are therefore not separate entities, but part of a whole, designed to fulfill complementary objectives. The strength of one strengthens others and the weakness of one disables everyone. This is the focus from which Police Reform and Criminal Justice Reform have to be viewed.

Well known writers on Police Science subjects like Critchley, Coatman and Ben Whitaker in England and Bayley in the U.S. and P.D. Sharma, Iqbal Narain and others in India and the massive literature produced by the National Police Academy have all pointed out that the police is much larger than the space they occupy in the Governmental structure. Critchely has rightly observed "Total freedom is anarchy, total order tyranny. The police, who represent the collective interests of the community are the agency which holds a balance somewhere between. Their standing is a rough index of society's own attitude towards the regulation of civilised living: regard for the police, which should not of course be uncritical, is regard for the law and order". In Coatman's view "the police have come to mean today the operative agency for ensuring the essentials of civilised life and the touch-stone for testing the spirit and quality of civil administration". Bayley with focus on the Indian situation has said "the number of contacts most rural people have with Government is still comparatively slight, although there is no question that they have increased enormously since the beginnings of the five year plans. Still, the police are there all the time; development experts and advisors come and go, their presence is occasional and unpredictable. The police are there for the Government, day in and day out... one would certainly be unjustified in discounting the possibility that police, by virtue of their ubiquity and the relative lack of other sorts of official contacts, may be playing a much more important socialising role in political development in India...." Therefore reforming the police cannot be treated as reforming a department within the Government. It is rather an effort to reform the regulatory administration itself and consequently the social defense agenda of the State.

**All Eyes on the Apex Court**

The outline I have etched above hardly gives reason to be optimistic about the prospects of police reforms. But Prakash Singh, who brought the issue of Police Reforms back to centre stage by taking it to the Apex Court, has this to say about Police Reforms "The process of the police reforms has started and is unstoppable. It will take two decades but it will certainly happen. Several NGO's have also taken up the cause".

I may add that the matter is now seized by the Apex Court and therefore Police Reforms are inevitable. The question before us is how to make this happen within a short span of time and how to make the Civil Society more deeply involved?

# 10

# *Internal Security in India: The Present and the Future*

*Jacob Punnoose*

At the outset, we may specify what we mean by Internal Security. For the current discussion, it may be taken as the situational condition in which the Sovereignty and Integrity of the State is protected against threats from disruptive and anti-national forces acting within the State.

Threats to Internal Security can arise[1] from:

(a) Insurgency which includes waging of armed struggle by a group or a section of the population against the State with the political objective of autonomy;
(b) Militancy which includes any violent widespread activity of a group using explosives, fire arms, lethal weapons or hazardous substances in order to achieve its political objectives;
(c) Terrorism which includes any sensationally violent activity of a person or a group against any target, usually chosen for publicity value, with the aim to strike terror in the society or any section thereof, and with an intent to demonstrate the striking power of such person or group against the Government established by law or against the society at large;
(d) Organised Crime, which includes any type of crime committed by a group or a network of persons in pursuance of a common primary intention of unlawful economic gain by using violent means or threat of violence, the unchecked growth of which destroys the efficiency and credibility of the State apparatus and the criminal justice system.
(e) External Forces, outside the country but which are in a position to patronise and encourage all the above different types of activity with a view to attack or weaken National Sovereignty.

The paradox of India has been its unitary multiplicity[2]; it has been the source of our strength – and resilient survival in the face of adversity. It has also, unfortunately, been the cause of our sorrows. 'Unity in Diversity' has been an abiding theme — a Dream and a Reality simultaneously. But Diversity, of which we are so justly proud, can often be manipulated to cause divergence first, then discord, then conflicts and eventually militancy, insurgency and terrorism.

When Sub-national and Sub-cultural identities become more potent than the National Identity itself, such Identities could pose a challenge to Internal Security. Conversely when the dynamic social processes which continuously shape and reshape National Identity do not allow sufficient elasticity, mutuality and respect towards Sub-national and Sub-cultural Identities, they would marginalize and alienate different sections, inviting and fuelling rebellion.

The threats to Internal Security in India have, at various times, arisen due to Religious Bigotry, Regional Chauvinism fuelled by backwardness, Ethnic Loyalty, Linguistic Affinity, Casteist Rivalry and the Deficiencies in the Criminal Justice System. Truly, some of these problems have proved endemic and nearly intractable. But we can be legitimately proud of the fact that we are still a vibrant democracy and a reasonably successful economy. No major alteration in our political geography had been occasioned by internal strife.

This was despite the prophets of doom who, right from the bloodbath during partition, had predicted failure — of Democracy itself, as a form of government; of Nationhood itself, due to complexity of Identity; of India itself, as a Union of States. They were not exaggerating. Glancing around in the subcontinent, — at Sri Lanka, Pakistan, Afghanistan, Nepal, Burma, Bangladesh, Maldives, etc., — we see a host of struggling Nations[3], facing the challenge of domestic discord to such a degree that either Democracy or Nationhood itself is in danger. In such a neighbourhood, India holds the torch for Democracy, with its Nationhood intact, with the State very much in command[4].

Several factors have helped us succeed against tremendous odds. Usually these are not openly acknowledged — and even opposite strategies are recommended by those who thirst for sudden solutions. Recognising them as such is important for resolving outstanding and future problems.

**1. Democratic Space**

The Indian style of Governance, though often condemned for vacillation and absence of ruthlessness, had always left space for Democratic Dissent and Democratic Dialogue. The parliamentary and the judicial systems, acting both independently and together, have actually helped nurture democratic institutions. This ensured that disadvantaged and disgruntled sections, as a whole, never felt totally excluded and isolated from the System. Among disturbed populations, even during the worst of times, there was considerable hope that the problems can be resolved through democratic reconciliation. This factor helped the coalescence of diverse interests and emergence of common interest and helped solve many problems in different parts of India.

**2. Police Operations and Sacrifices**

Consistent and determined low-intensity police operations, always taking care, though not always successfully-to distinguish between civilians and militants/insurgents, succeeded in the continuous consolidation of State authority in affected areas. Often the persistence of operations had simply tired the other side out. The police forces, including Central Paramilitary forces, suffered heavy casualties. More than 60,000 among them have died while actively defending internal security. Such disciplined and systematic policing operations have few parallels elsewhere in the world. Conquest by a marching army had seldom solved any civil strife. The trouble spots in contemporary South and Central Asia, Africa and Europe are examples of such failures. Herein lies the merit of the low intensity policing strategy that India had adopted.

### 3. Professionalism of Bureaucratic and Military Leadership

All India Services and the Leadership of the Armed Forces have contributed immensely to the preservation of Internal Security. In essence, both are legacies from the British. But significantly, the Indian Constitution allowed the continuation of the British Indian Civil and Police Services and the British Indian Army as All India Services for the Administration and Policing (IAS and IPS) and as the Indian Armed Forces.

The tradition and standards of the Indian Army in maintaining political neutrality and high discipline, the strategies by which the Army reflected the integrated diversity of our population, and the professionalism of the Officer Cadre of the Armed forces drawn from different parts of India and assimilated into different Regiments contributed to the evolution of a professional military establishment, rising above caste, religion, region and politics. The armies in our neighbouring countries — or elsewhere in the world other than those in long established democracies— have seldom shown such high standards. Due credit must go to them in any discussion on India's Internal Security. Simultaneously it is always good to remind ourselves from the experience of our neighbours that military rule is no guarantee for Internal Security.

The new born Indian Federation sought a Pan-Indian identity and structures consonant with the same while allowing regional autonomy. The broad unification of the administration and police forces of the different states and the Union is vital to that effort. For this task, reliance was placed on the two All India Services. Their members were selected and assigned by the Centre, by a well recognised, widely respected and impartial process. Their presence in every corner of India in positions of authority prevented centrifugal tendencies from creeping into the local administration and police forces of different States. Very often senior officers occupying critical positions in State administration and Police Service do not even belong to the States concerned. So the national goals and concerns were never forgotten. At the same time legitimate regional aspirations found space in the administration at the Centre because, officers nurtured and having personal stake in different states occupied key positions in the Centre also. Therefore administrative unification with regional autonomy, a key factor in ensuring Internal Security in a multi-faceted Federation was achieved relatively painlessly.

Any strategy to resolve the contemporary issues must take note of the strategies which gave us success in the past and must take into account the special features of the existing insurgencies and the global security scenario.

**Internal Security — General Concerns**

We must note that the dividing line between external and internal security threats is getting obliterated. Non-State actors have become the bane of the global security order. News reports about Al Qaeda projecting India as a key player in the 'US- Zionist conspiracy' and the activities of the affiliates of Al Qaeda in the region, e.g., LeT and JeM in Pakistan and HUJI in Bangladesh are of great concern.

The role played by foreign intelligence agencies in sponsorship of insurgent and terrorist activities remains a challenge and has been discussed for long. Infiltration into India has for long been attempted by hostile groups. In addition, training camps are organised across the border and some of our misguided young men are believed to be taken for covert arms training abroad and sent back.

The specter of Urban and Transport Terror looms large. The Internet transcends territorial boundaries and undermines traditional concepts of national sovereignty. Growth in Technology and the spread of the Internet have empowered even the isolated disgruntled evil mind to commit acts of terror and cause widespread public panic. If such individuals are motivated by some cause, then it can cause serious problems for Internal Security.

Left Wing Extremism is the most serious internal threat facing us. It combines a dangerous intellectual appeal with strong pockets of mass support. It is based on an effective propaganda machinery in favour of the 'poorest of the poor', specially the tribal and the dispossessed. It capitalises on the failures of local administration to provide good governance. There has been consolidation of like minded forces also in this regard. Various Naxalite splinter factions have merged to form the CPI (Maoist). They also have a well-developed military organisation and are executing military type operations against security forces, leading to large casualties.

Internal Security can also be seriously compromised by covert techniques of economic, psychological warfare using drug-generated funds and fake currency. These go hand in hand with the techniques of organised crime. It is to be understood that Hawala transactions, as per current trends, are ideally the most reliable means of terrorist financing leaving virtually no paper trail for investigators. 'Fake Currency Notes' is also another widely prevalent mode of terror financing. They are also double edged in that they are good for destabilising the country, economically as well as by undermining the faith of the common man in its 'legal tender'. The quality of Indian Fake Currency printed abroad is very high but several recent seizures have made us conscious of the threat.

The networks for Counterfeit notes and Hawala are highly evolved and can lend themselves as infrastructure for gunrunning, transportation of explosives, hideouts and communication channels for terrorists. Narcotics and its linkages to organised crime and terrorist networks represent another issue of crucial importance. Opium, grown in south-western Afghanistan, is said to have a street value in excess of $10 billion. Diverting even a fraction of that to funding of terrorist operations would have disastrous consequences to national security. It is also known that foreign intelligence agencies actually use drug money to finance anti-national organisations.

Coastal Security is essential to Internal Security. But traditionally, security of the coastline was neglected, perhaps because of the feeling that 'there is no one out there in the sea'. But it is to be noted that the conquest of India by Europeans took place from the Coastline. They first developed trading posts and then centres of authority all along the Coastline. When they did so in the 16th and 17th Century, India was a powerful empire. India then was far mightier than what the United States appears today with respect to the rest of the world. Despite our great stature, the Europeans were able to politically and militarily subdue India making use of the coastal footholds. The vulnerability of the Indian coastline is both a historical fact and a contemporary reality.

Admittedly, the State must dominate its territory by the political process and the effective administration of justice. The State must necessarily claim the monopoly of physical force within its territory. This is to be primarily ensured by an efficient and effective criminal Justice System. The primary reasons for the backwardness of the system are lack of strength, lack of proper training and lack of modern facilities. There is not enough infrastructural investment taking place within the Criminal Justice System and the per capita investment on Criminal Justice Enforcement in India is far below the percentage figures prevalent in any modern democracy. Structural and procedural reform has also been slow. Several Commissions, and the Hon'ble Supreme Court itself, have taken note of this.

When the justice system fails due to the failure of the police or the prosecution or the courts, the people in general lose faith in the System. This is likely to be exploited by anti-national forces. Safety is fundamental to existence. The need for it prompts men to seek security. Social organisation evolved and flourished because membership in a group gave greater security to the individual. Security is, therefore, the ultimate rationale of State authority. No State can survive unless it retains the confidence of its citizenry in its ability to provide safety and security. Breakdown of the criminal justice system implies the breakdown of the very social compact which is the foundation of State authority. Breakdown of Law and Order will prompt people to take the law into their hands — and public lynching, of the type witnessed in Bhagalpur, and not orderly judicial process, will be the order of the day. We will go back to the jungle, as many collapsed African societies have already done. No progress is possible unless security is preserved. Where there is no peace, there can be no progress.

**Internal Security Strategy**

One striking common feature of the major problem areas — whether in Naxalite infested areas or the Northeast or Kashmir — is that they are all basically inaccessible areas, cut off geographically or otherwise from the national mainstream and backward in development. The strategy must therefore be to end the isolation of these areas and quicken the development process. Inaccessibility and remoteness are by themselves reasons for insurgency when it combines with relative sense of deprivation and underdevelopment[5].

Persons from areas affected by insurgency should be encouraged to live in other parts of India and study in institutions of higher learning in different parts of India. This is to ensure that the intellectual elite gets a broad feeling of India and realize the opportunities that can come to the group by aligning with India. Employment in different parts of India must be deliberately promoted. For several states in the North East this is already happening. We must also remember that one of the factors that helped prevent the success of the Sikh separatism was the fact that the Sikh economic interests in India outside the Punjab were huge and were almost comparable to their assets in would-be Khalistan. This is the kind of situation that every community must be encouraged to find itself in, so that inter-dependence — and not exclusivity and relative deprivation — become the potent prescription for pursuit of progress and community interest.

Physical isolation also must be sought to be reduced, wherever possible. Improvement of transport facilities must get priority. The lack of such infrastructure can fan insurgency and inhibit intermixture with other segments of population besides contributing to economic isolation. If we take the quadrilateral bounded by Chennai, Trivandrum, Ahmedabad and Hyderabad on the one hand and compare with the other quadrilateral bounded by Vijaywada, Bhopal, Siliguri and Calcutta on the other, we can see for ourselves (by counting airports, railway stations, and municipal bus stands therein) why extremism could spread so rapidly in one area and not in the other. If insurgency is to be contained, the areas must literally be opened up in greater density, with greater extent of general services, so that the reach of the rest of India even to remote areas in the region is easier.

But the strategy for the development of such areas is fraught with an inherent danger. The primary reason for backwardness, despite 60 years of developmental effort, is the corruption among the local political elite and the local bureaucracy. Corruption encourages insurgency in two ways. On the one side it exacerbates the frustration of the disadvantaged and motivates them more towards rebellion. The funds siphoned off from development allocations are taken off by the corrupt and invested elsewhere. This money makes the corrupt even more powerful and in a better position to get more allocations and steal more, progressively making the relative poverty of the area more demonstrable. On the other side, the insurgent realising the mechanism of corruption, himself becomes a blackmailer of the official or the beneficiary and takes a cut from the official himself. So a portion of the developmental funds can possibly reach the insurgents themselves to finance the insurgency efforts.

Thus, in two ways, in an insurgency affected area, corruption helps insurgency. So far corruption had never been given much importance in discussions on Internal Security. But as it sets at naught our efforts to contain the threat, the issue of corruption in administration must be seriously addressed by the State and effective course of action implemented by strengthening both the law and the machinery for Anti-corruption.

There must also be great stress on improving the technological and human quality of security infrastructure. If internal security is to be protected then the security infrastructure must be commensurate with the challenges to be faced. Proper investment must be made in this sector to bring the Criminal Justice System on a par with that obtaining in modern democracies. We cannot have a nineteenth century structure to face the problems of the 21st century. Therefore systemic and procedural reforms are also needed.

The funding for the Criminal Justice System comes basically from the State Budgets; the States, saddled with heavy developmental and service-related responsibilities in health and education, cannot always find any sizeable allocation for improving security services. The best that they can do is to provide for the status quo and engage limited strength of manpower. The expenditure itself is also very low as a percentage of the per capita income. Nearly 90 to 95 per cent of the relatively low expenditure on security by the State Government goes on salary, with the per capita salary of the policeman being at the lower end of the salary spectrum as a whole. Security infrastructure improvement must become a Plan item, with adequate provisioning from Plan Funds for the sound reason that security is the pre requisite for any progress at all.

**Security with Freedom — the Democratic Ideal**

Colonialism had fragmented our domestic Statehood itself. Our first challenge, in continuation of the struggle for Independence, was to build up Statehood, brick by brick, in such a way that all the fragmented units felt the confidence, ability and security to appropriate the new Nationhood as their own. And the police had to uphold the Peace - the Peace, not of Empire, but of Democracy. Securing Peace in a society that polices itself under democratic governance — policing by consent — was a new experience and a challenge.

More pertinently, there is a difference in the kind of security we seek today from that of the past. Security with the personal freedoms that we enjoy today is different qualitatively from security without such fundamental rights. Now, we seek the security given by the State, not merely for the prolongation of vegetative existence or for silent acquiescence in structural straitjackets inducing individual indignities, but for the proactive exercise of all our freedoms including free speech, travel, education, civil rights, social rights, protests and what not[6].

The purpose of security now is to ensure that every human being is enabled to realize his full human potential in dignity and equality. And the manner of ensuring security is also extremely important. The maturity of any culture is now judged by the degree of permeation of human rights principles in its criminal justice system. What is sought is security in the midst of dynamic activity, with the citizen exercising every right and developing every talent.

When we face the difficult challenges in maintaining Internal Security, the severity of the difficulties should not deter us from viewing Security in the democratic context. Proper levels response also needed to be calibrated to tackle each situation. The guiding principles of governance must recognize the pluralistic democratic society in India, while managing discontent. In discharge of duties, the police forces must not be seen to be damaging the fabric of secular democracy. At all times the principle of social justice be upheld. The cure must not be worse than the disease.

**Notes**

1. India is facing all these types of threats.
2. Europe as a single nation might resemble India without the Caste System. The Constitution recognises 23 official languages while the EU has 20. Mother tongues that are spoken in India number more than 1600. Our social, cultural, religious and ethnic spectrum is more varied than that of EU.
3. Afghanistan and Pakistan remained a concern for India. Pakistan faces opposition to the Army's authority, resulting in turbulence, particularly, in Baluchistan, Waziristan and FATA. The prevailing situations in Nepal, Bangladesh and Maldives are also very delicate and are of great concern to India.
4. We have triumphed over most of the serious conflicts and insurgency threats during the past 60 years. The partition riots were quelled. Communal riots, though still a worry, do not threaten to dismember the nation. The Punjab problem, despite its support from foreign soil, has been solved. The language riots and agitations have been resolved satisfactorily. The Tamil problem has become a thing of the past, never having deteriorated into militancy or insurgency of the type witnessed in Sri Lanka. Naxalite problems in Kerala and West Bengal were solved. Naga Insurgency has been largely contained. And even in the continuing problem areas like Kashmir, or North East or the so called Naxal Corridor in the East Central India, we are still in control despite great difficulties and severe challenges.

5. Remoteness results from inaccessibility due to geography or extreme climate or absence of transportation infrastructure. Government servants dislike being posted in such areas; often the least influential or the disgruntled tend to get posted there, leading to bad image of the State in the locality. Inaccessibility also inhibits economic development, which generally is facilitated by high connectivity. Economic developments would have encouraged variety, non-traditional patterns of interdependence and new life-styles, greatly reducing the hold of caste, religion, linguistic group or tribe. Meantime progress takes place elsewhere. But the inhabitants of inaccessible areas do not find any progress around them. This induces the sense of relative deprivation which increases proclivity to violence. Inaccessibility also causes the relative marginalisation of local politicians in national politics and the local population would therefore feel further excluded and neglected. The State becomes unpopular. The Insurgents move in with advantage.
6. A few decades back, the citizen had neither fundamental rights nor freedoms. So the security then given was security within the system of limited freedoms.

# 11

# *India: The Changing Alchemy of Politics and Erosion of Institutions*

*J. Prabhash*

**Introduction**

The alchemical promise of democratic politics is its ability to moderate and contain conflicts to transform them from something base to something richer [Khilnani, 2004: 26]. The implication here is that democratic politics not merely resolves conflicts of interests inherent in human societies amicably, but makes use of their dialectics to enrich the democratic order itself. This happens when such conflicts are converted into opportunities to distill consensus on national priorities and establish norms based governance. Having said this, a rejoinder is in order here. 'Consensus on national priorities' does not, in any way, mean that democracies have to do away with conflicts in the realm of public policies nor that they (public policies) have to be placed in a de-politicised context. In fact, it has to be the other way round-politics is inherent to policies and hence they are prone to contending claims and counter claims. Therefore, what is alluded to here is the need for a shared vision about the future of the country - 'a vision aspirational enough, uplifting enough for the [country] to march ahead' [Bagchi, 2013: 34 - 35]. Needless to say political parties play a crucial role in all these issues.

Democratic order essentially puts a high premium on political parties though, in many instances, democratic constitutions hardly make any direct reference to them. Basically, they have to act as conveyor belts between the state and society so much so that social issues get political attention they deserve and eventually even get settled in a democratic manner. Interestingly, it is through activities like these that political parties could provide organic leadership to the citizens and 'safeguard the rights and interests of all sections' [Joseph, 2007: 3217]. Here the democratic project enters its substantive phase which is a combined function of the enforceability of constitutionally guaranteed equal rights within a universal legal system, the social condition which makes their effective exercise possible [Jayal, 2000:99] and the high degree of synergy between the state and society.

However, this is easier said than done as political parties often become prey to power struggles, class conflicts (in certain cases caste and religious conflicts also), and factional wrangles with the result that they degenerate into a bunch of power seekers and power brokers. With this, they get alienated from the people (cease to be the conveyor belt connecting state and society), develop feet of clay and gradually lose touch with social reality. As such, political parties rather than becoming agents for transforming conflicts from something base to something richer, themselves generate conflicts and become something base. Here the alchemical promise of democratic politics is made to stand on its head. Consequently, not only political society loses its moral timber and becomes corrupt, but the institutional and political architecture of the democratic order lose their robustness and get denuded. Net result, politics becomes parasitical and manipulative, brokers unfair decisions for a price and legitimises every illegitimate deed including indiscriminate criminality and corruption. Contemporary Indian politics has to be located in this theoretical context.

**Congress and the Metamorphosis of Indian Politics**

Nobody would dispute the proposition that Indian politics today is in the throes of a deep crisis which fundamentally — though not exclusively — stems from the rot of political parties. With exceptions apart, parties have become opportunistic and asylums for corrupt and mafia groups, power seekers and power brokers with the fatal consequence that they suffer from a chronic deficit of popular trust. Any analysis on this, however, has to begin with the metamorphosis in the nature of the Indian National Congress from a loose coalition of social groups (both in a class and caste/ religious sense) with a peculiar texture of openness, conflict and consensus to one which has lost its federal - coalitional character, mass appeal and openness and became dynastic and leader centric.

It may be recalled that Indian politics during the formative period since independence was characterized by two apparently contradictory trends — conflict and consensus. Initially both these trends were enacted within the Indian National Congress as it was the central pillar of the country's politics then and a couple of decades thereafter. The conflicts though became personal on certain occasions — for instance between Vallabhai Patel and Jawaharlal Nehru — went beyond their narrow confines and frequently took the form of ideological differences, caste/class rivalry and divergent perceptions on development and social change.[1] This was natural as Congress was a grand coalition of groups and interests [Khilnani, 1997: 79; Guha, 2009: 42 - 43] held together partly by the absence of a viable political alternative and on the other part by Nehru's charisma, and the leadership provided by the party bosses at the regional level. Nehru's socialist commitments further broadened Congress' social base by promising progress to India's downtrodden [Kohli, 2010: 501]. Additionally he also ensured internal democracy within the party, though it was one in which he reigned the supreme — a sort of 'guided democracy'. With this internal structure, the party could easily mediate between state and society [Hassan, 2000: 18] and also represent every shade of public opinion from that of business and land owning groups to the poor peasantry and the urban middle class. The conflict of interests which is inherent in such an amorphous social base was moderated by Nehru who successfully converted them into consensus through his carefully crafted left and centrist policies and his control over both the party and government machinery. Sudipta Kaviraj puts this role of the Congress during this period thus:

> Congress, it was sometimes argued, ruled India well precisely because it was internally diverse like India. A better way of putting it would be to recognize that there was a duality in the nature of the Congress System: it was, at one level, rule by a single political party; but, in fact, inside, it was a coalition. Plural interests could seek and receive attention within it precisely because of its ideologically heterogeneous character; yet the fact that these negotiations took place inside the institutional boundaries of a single party meant that the conflict of interests rarely exploded into overt political violence, or that the bitterness and disappointments they generated went out of control [Kaviraj, 2010: 235-36].

This arrangement, however, did not last long. An important reason for this was the failure of Jawaharlal Nehru in institutionalising inner party democracy within the Congress with the result that the party could be manipulated and swiftly moved into a centralized/authoritarian organisational mode depending on the personal predilection of the leadership. This was what exactly happened during the term of Mrs. Indira Gandhi and thereafter. Her discord with 'old guards' (commonly described as 'Syndicate') encouraged her to destroy every trace of internal democracy within the organisation and centralize, in her person, both governmental power and reins of party leadership. Within a decade (1970s) this resulted in the weakening of the regional roots of the party [Khilnani, 1997: 182] and it (Congress) morphed from a vibrant grass root organisation into a fawning, imperial court, appointed by and adoring of its leader [Zakaria, 2003: 107].

Interestingly, while this was happening within the Congress party, a different kind of churning was taking place in the national politics. Two-and-a-half decades of democracy and developmentalism had mobilised a large chunk of the marginalised social groups (It is another thing that a majority of these people were left out of the development process) to the national mainstream through the electoral process. There was also a noticeable increase in the density of representation of these groups in the structures of state power, both at the regional and national levels. These newly mobilized sections who were the products of what Christophe Jaffrelot described as 'silent revolution' and who were earlier accommodated by the federal — coalitional structure of the Congress now found it difficult to get along with it in the changed context of the party's internal dynamics. They, therefore, either migrated to other parties including regional outfits or, in some cases, formed their own parties, often based on caste and ethnicity. As a result, Congress ceased to be the 'axis of connection between the Indian state and society' and at the same time no other party emerged to perform that role. Thus the old degenerated without giving birth to the new, and, if at all, a new alternative (for instance BJP) emerged, it was (is) worse than the old 'Congress System'.

National parties like BJP, Janata Dal, Nationalist Congress Party and the organised left waxed and waned or, in certain instances, got fragmented or remained with growth stunted. At the other end, regional and state- based parties that emerged and grew in relative strength and entered into coalitional arrangement with the aforementioned national parties including the Congress, kept (keep) them in tender-hooks, extracting even the last pound of flesh in terms of patronage and power. With the exception of the Left — that too to a certain extent only — no parties have any ideological shibboleth to take care of or any real social justice agenda to bother about or any trace of internal democracy to showcase. They spoke about all these things, but practically remained perfectly at ease with power politics and neatly enmeshed in personal aggrandisement. The degeneration of Indian politics today is the cumulative by-product of all these. The neo-liberal policies, implemented overtly since the 1990s, have aggravated the situation.

**Politics as Family Enterprise**

The degeneration of politics has reached such a stage that it has ceased to be public, accountable and one that conjoins state and society. Most of the parties today are run like family enterprises rather than institutions in which the general public has a stake. As Perry Anderson points out, they have become something other than the oligarchic organisations into which Ostrogorsky and Robert Michels thought all political parties must sooner or later turn, and instead have become family firms competing for market shares of the electorate and so access to public office [Anderson, 2012: 159-60]. This 'family touch' is not merely confined to positions in the party organisation, but even in representative bodies of the state as well. The present Lok Sabha is a clear case in point as proved by the following table.

**Table: 1. MPs with Family Ties: Fourteenth Lok Sabha (Party wise Break-up)**

| *Name of Party* | *No. of MPs* | *Total No. of MPs in the House* | *Percentage of distribution* |
|---|---|---|---|
| Indian National Congress | 86 | 208 | 41.35 |
| B.J.P. | 28 | 115 | 24.34 |
| SP | 9 | 22 | 40.91 |
| JD(U) | 3 | 20 | 15.00 |
| DMK | 7 | 19 | 36.84 |
| Trinamool Congress | 4 | 18 | 22.22 |
| CPM | 4 | 17 | 23.53 |

| | | | |
|---|---|---|---|
| Biju Janata Dal | 6 | 14 | 42.86 |
| Shiv Sena | 1 | 11 | 9.09 |
| NCP | 8 | 9 | 88.89 |
| AIADMK | 1 | 9 | 11.11 |
| TDP | Nil | 6 | NA |
| RLD | 5 | 5 | 100.00 |
| Akali Dal | 3 | 4 | 75.00 |
| RJD | 2 | 4 | 50.00 |
| CPI | Nil | 4 | NA |
| National Conference | 2 | 3 | 66.67 |
| JD (secular) | 2 | 3 | 66.67 |
| Others | 6 | 32 | 18.75 |
| **Total** | **185** | **545** | **33.94** |

(*Source:* Chandra and Umaira, 2011: 19).

According to the above table, 33.94 per cent of MPs in the current Lok Sabha have family connection. They are the people whose family members - fathers, mothers, siblings, husbands, wives, grandparents, uncles, aunts, cousins or in-laws-preceded them in politics [Chandra and Umaira, 2011:14]. Most interesting point to note here is that the regional political outfits have outwitted the national parties in this regard. For instance, this is cent per cent for Rashtriya Lok Dal (RLD), 75 per cent for Akali Dal, 66.67 per cent each for National Conference and Janata Dal (S), and 50 per cent for Rashtriya Janata Dal (RJD). Among the major national parties, Indian National Congress tops the list with 41.35 per cent followed by BJP - 24.34 per cent. Significantly, even CPM has 23.53 per cent of its MPs with family tag attached to them. All these show that family connection as a mode of political recruitment has become pervasive in Indian politics, though its magnitude changes with parties.

As a natural corollary to the above, parties have been reduced to hotbeds of power brokers and artificially foisted leaders — those who are anointed to various organisational / ministerial positions by the dynasty in charge of the respective parties. Needless to say, these are the very same people who have little popular clout. Congress party is a typical example in this regard with backroom specialists becoming party functionaries and ministers[2] [Subrahmaniam, 2008]. Party activists with genuine track record of public service end up as the real loosers in the process. The extent to which this has affected the organisation is clear from the words of Sheila Dixit, former Chief Minister of Delhi:

> ... with the exception of a few, the party leadership is far removed from the grassroots and has more in common with the elite and middle classes than with the poor who vote the party to power... consequently it lacks a critical mass of leaders who enjoy political support of their own... Very often, party workers who join the party

do so for economic reasons. For them, party work is a business proposition and they enter the party to earn money [Hassan, 2012: 114].

With the exception of the Left, this is the case with regard to a very large number of political parties. These parties have ceased to be political vehicles for mobilising people around their quotidian concerns. In a situation in which personal contact with and loyalty to top leadership rather than public contact with mass of the people decide political fortunes of party men, it is only natural that they have little incentive for social mobilisation. There is, thus, paralleling the unorganised sector in the economy, what may be described as an unorganised sector in the Indian polity - ordinary people [Jayal, 2000: 119]. This has produced two disastrous consequences for the country's democratic order: politics has come to be devoid of its social context, and has started hobnobbing with moneyed interests and corrupt and criminal forces.

It goes without saying that politics in order to be democratic has to be rich in social content, i.e., it has to reflect the social discontents that plague the society. It is through strategies like this that parties mint fresh impetus and ideas for governance, and become protean and reinvent themselves. However, it is in this very respect that India's political parties have failed. There is a noticeable disconnect between them and the grass root social realities so much so that they have become grass without roots. This has even robed them of meaningful electoral issues which primarily explains the reason for the emergence of caste, communal and ethnicity based politics in the country since 1980s. For winning elections parties also came to depend on some 'waves' or, in an increasing number of cases, on money and muscle power [Kothari, 1992: 16].

When 'money, muscle and waves' decide the fate of elections, they become issueless. They become less a choice between alternative political programmes and more a referendum on personalities and slogans with professional fund — raisers and public relation consultants playing a greater role [Joseph, 2007: 317]. Today, the cost of contesting elections has gone up enormously. The idea is 'campaign to millions of voters for millions of rupees' [Sainath, 2010]. It is stated that, on an average, a candidate has to spend anything between three to fifteen core rupees in a single Lok Sabha constituency[3] [Ray, 2009: 36]. This is true of State Assembly elections as well. As a result, representative bodies have become exclusive clubs of multi-millionaires[4]. Where does the money come from is the basic question here and its answer is to be found in the unholy nexus between politics, business and corruption.

**Politics, Business and Corruption**

Linkage between politics and business and corruption in politics are not new phenomena. But what is of great concern is the influence of big business over the political class and the magnitude of corruption. Further, there is also a tendency for the political class and the businessmen to poach on each other's turf. Recall the statement of former Prime Minister, V.P. Singh that, 'the crown of the highest political office lies in the treasure chest of a large industrial house in Mumbai and not in Delhi' [Godbole, 1997: 2051]. Now, after two decades and more of neo-liberal economic policies, state (by implication politicians) has become an agent directly and openly promoting private enrichment, through the sale of state property 'for a song', through handing over to private hands of the control over national resources and offering guaranteed rates of return on private investment in certain sectors [Patnaik, 2000: 149]. As Jacques Ranciere said, "it is now an obvious fact... the absolute identification of politics with the management of capital is no longer the shameful secret hidden behind the forms of democracy; it is the openly declared truth by which our governments acquire legitimacy" [Ranciere, 1999: 113]. It is important here to note that this is often done by the politicians in a lawful manner through the large plethora of discretionary powers they enjoy. Big corruption in India is a by-product of this—a quid pro quo - and has grown in geometrical proportion.

**Table: 2. Major Corruption Scandals (1992-2009)**

| *Year* | *Amount (rupees in crore)* | *Increase / decrease from Previous Year* | *Percentage of Increase/ Decrease* |
|---|---|---|---|
| 1992 | 5,000 | Not applicable | Not applicable |
| 1994 | 650 | –4,350 | –87.00 |
| 1995 | 5,700 | +5,050 | +776.92 |
| 1996 | 2,383 | –3,317 | –58.19 |
| 1997 | 3,474 | +1,091 | +31.40 |
| 1998 | 8,000 | +4,526 | +130.28 |
| 2001 | 6,645 | –1,355 | -16.94 |
| 2002 | 600 | –6,045 | –90.97 |
| 2003 | 172 | –428 | –71.33 |
| 2005 | 19,141 | +18,969 | +110.28 |
| 2006 | 1,675 | –17,466 | –91.25 |
| 2008 | 1,25,095 | +1,23,420 | +7368.36 |
| 2009 | 13,630 | –1,11,465 | –89.10 |
| Total | 1,92,165 | Not appiicable | Not applicable |

(*Source:* Dasgupta, 2009: 41).

This is particularly so in the neo-liberal era. The money swindled by the political class during the 17 year period from 1992 to 2009 is pegged at a mind boggling Rs. 1,92,165 lakh crore compared to which the greatest pre-liberalisation scam - Bofors (Rs. 64 crore) - pales into insignificance [Dasgupta, 2009: 41]. Except on three occasions (1994, 2002 and 2003), the amount involved touched four digits and upwards (Table 2).

A much more grave issue is the one which pertains to politicians developing business interests and businessmen enlisting themselves as politicians and getting elected to representative bodies. In fact many politicians are turning politics into business, i.e. — they are making use of state power to establish business empires. Many big names in politics could be pointed out as examples to this including politicians like Sharad Pawar, Jayant Patel (Maharashtra Finance Minister), Pratik Patel (Former Union Minister of State for Coal), Manohar Joshi (Former Lok Sabha Speaker), Raj Thackeray (Shiv Sena leader), Dayanidhi Maran (DMK leader), former Karnataka Infrastructure and Tourism Minister, Jenardhana Reddy and former Union Minister for Railways, Pavan Kumar Bansal, [Manish, 2012:17; Bhanutaj, 2009: 32-34; Khare, 2005].

**Table: 3. Business Representation in Parliament (1991-2013)**

| *House* | *Business representation* | *Non-business representation* | *Data not available* | *Total* |
|---|---|---|---|---|
| | | **Lok Sabha** | | |
| 10th House | 82<br>(15.97) | 440<br>(80.88) | 22<br>(4.04) | 544<br>(100) |
| 11th House | 109<br>(20.19) | 421<br>(77.96) | 10<br>(1.86) | 540<br>(100) |
| 12th House | 78<br>(14.80) | 441<br>(83.68) | 8<br>(1.52) | 527<br>(100) |
| 13th House | 99<br>(17.43) | 449<br>(79.05) | 20<br>(3.52) | 548<br>(100) |
| 14th House | 119<br>(22.33) | 393<br>(73.73) | 21<br>(3.94) | 543<br>(100) |
| | | **Rajya Sabha** | | |
| 1994 | 8<br>(9.88) | 69<br>(85.19) | 4<br>(4.94) | 81<br>(100) |
| 1998 | 31<br>(12.60) | 211<br>(85.77) | 3<br>(1.22) | 246<br>(100) |
| Current House | 38<br>(15.90) | 192<br>(80.33) | 9<br>(3.77) | 239<br>(100) |

[Note: Figures given in brackets indicate percentage distribution].

(*Source:* Sinha, 2010: 472).

**Table: 4. Revenue Forgone under various heads by the Central Government (2005-2013)**

| *Financial year* | *Corporate Income Tax* | *Excise Duty* | *Customs Duty* | *Total* |
|---|---|---|---|---|
| 2005-06 | 34,618 | 66,760 | 1,27,730 | 2,29,108 |
| 2006-07 | 50,075 | 75,475 | 1,37,105 | 2,62,655 |
| 2007-08 | 62,199 | 87,468 | 1,53,593 | 3,03,260 |
| 2008-09 | 66,901 | 1,28,293 | 2,25,752 | 4,20,946 |
| 2009-10 | 72,881 | 1,69,121 | 2,07,943 | 4,49,945 |
| 2010-11 | 57,912 | 1,92,227 | 1,72,740 | 4,22,879 |
| 2011-12 | 61,765 | 1,95,590 | 2,36,852 | 4,94,207 |
| 2012-13 | 68,008 | 2,06,188 | 2,53,967 | 5,28,163 |
| Total | 4,74,359 | 11,21,122 | 15,15,688 | 31,11,169 |
| % increase in 2012-13 over 2005-06 | 96.45 | 208.85 | 98.33 | 130.53 |

[Note: Rupees in crore].

(*Source:* Sainath, 2013: 50).

At the other end, is the case of businessmen turned politicians. Their number is rapidly increasing, particularly in the Parliament (Table 3). While there is a 7.26 per cent increase in their representation between the 10th and 14th Lok Sabha, the same is 6.02 per cent between 1992 and 2010 in the Rajya Sabha [Sinha, 2010: 472]. Importantly the representation shows an increasing trend with each succeeding House. If one looks at Lok Sabha, for instance, this was only 15.07 per cent in the Tenth House, moved a few notches higher in the Eleventh House to reach 20.19 per cent, and went to 22.33 per cent, in the Fourteenth House. The same pattern is seen repeated in the case of Rajya Sabha as well - from 9.88 per cent in 1994 it progressed to 12.60 per cent in 1998 and 15.90 per cent currently. The writing on the wall is thus clear.

This connection between the two has proved to be an explosive mix from the vantage point of democracy as it has turned politics into a lucrative business instead of committed public service. Needless to say, the ultimate beneficiaries of this are the business houses. A few indicators are enough to prove this. One clear instance in this regard is the revenue foregone under corporate income tax, excise and customs. The total revenue loss to the exchequer in this regard, between the term 2005-06 to 2012-13 is actually very huge - 3,11,1169 rupees (Table 4). Percentage increase in 2012-13 over 2005-06 is 130.53. The split up of this loss also makes interesting reading. Revenue loss in corporate income tax is Rs. 4,74,359 and in the case of excise duty the same is Rs. 1,12,1122. However, the highest loss pertains to customs duty — Rs. 1,51,5688. The percentage increase in 2012-13 over 2005-06 is the highest for excise duty — 208.85 – followed by customs duty, 98.83. All these show that businessmen's preferences have become government's policies and government's policies have become their (businessmen's) business. Much worse, this has resulted in a systematic neglect of the public realm and a tendency has also developed to treat power as a means of personal aggrandisement and state as an instrument of patronage and profit [Kothari, 1975].

With the state degenerating into an important site for primitive accumulation for the private sector [Chandrasekhar, 2013: 13] and with the political class losing its organic linkage with the people, a new class of fixers[5] who act as middlemen between the state/political parties and the people / vested interests have emerged in Indian politics. They function like leeches and feed on corruption this unholy alliance generates. These fixers have not only institutionalised corruption but act as gatekeepers of the ruling classes influencing their decisions and, in certain cases, even taking decisions on their behalf. Such extra-constitutional centers of power, thus, bargain with the state on behalf of special interests and strike illegal deals for a price. As a result of this, problem of graft which was earlier confined to individual politicians has now become rampant affecting the whole government, party leadership and its cadres. [Anand, 2013: 18]

Interestingly, as in the case of businessmen and politicians, here also one could point out innumerable instances in which a change of role taking place between fixers and politicians – politicians acting as fixers, and fixers masquerade as politicians, blurring the boundaries between the two. Neera Radia case offers the best example not merely of the extent of penetration of such elements into the system, but also of how the change of role between the fixers and politicians takes place. That the Indian state itself promotes such a transformation– particularly politicians becoming fixers – is the moot point here. The provision of MP/MLA fund by the state is a case in point.

It may be recalled that each MP is provided with 2 crore rupees annually (Rs 10 crore for a full Lok Sabha tenure) by the Government of India which he/ she could use for 'developmental' purposes in his/ her constituency at his/ her discretion. When this is computed for 540 MPs, it comes to Rs 5400 crore which is a hefty amount by any standard. Needless to say, this is a sure recipe for corruption which starts at the level of individual politicians. Like the politician — business nexus, this paves the way for another kind of linkage: Politician – contractor nexus. Actually through these kinds of wheel-deals and business connections, an average politician amasses huge fortunes without any questions being asked by the sate.[6] It is not that the state doesn't have with it or feels shy of asking such questions, but it reserves them to be used at a future date when the need for exercising such an option arises. Recall here the story repeatedly told about the Central Bureau of Investigation that the agency activates or put on back burner cases against politicians depending on the needs of the ruling dispensation [Ramakrishnan, 2013: 8, Tripathi, 2013: 6].

The Indian state here plays a double ball game — provides ample scope for perpetuating corruption and then makes use of it to tame opposition against it. This — corruption and rule — is the new edition of the old colonial policy of 'divide and rule'. The state, thus, depends on this parasitical politics for its sustenance.

**Conclusion**

Under duress of these developments, politics has become parasitical and predatory in nature with the sole objective of maximising the take from the economy by those who are involved in the political processes. Parties, rather than solving the problems of the people, became their problem. In other words, parties themselves are creating more problems to the marginalized social groups than solving any. At no other point in time in the country's history the political parties remain so thoroughly disconnected with the ground reality as they are today.

This is not a mere decline of the party system, but a total degeneration of the democratic process itself. This is quite natural as degeneration of politics everywhere has a serious spillover effect for the system as a whole with the consequence that the credibility of the institutions of the state including Legislature, Executive, Judiciary and Bureaucracy get eroded. They are closed to democratic negotiation by vulnerable categories of citizens but at the same time are permissively open to bargain by special interests [Jayal, 2000: 121]. Therefore, what is at stake is the legitimacy of the entire system.

However, the implication here is not that because of the aforesaid reasons the institutions of governance should be de-politicized. What is actually required is to strengthen democratic inputs into the political process while restoring a sense of collective good and shared future [Joseph, 2007: 3217]; and a forceful political leadership that can listen to and respond to the voices from the grassroots and civil society and assimilate them democratically into the parties' organisational system and governance structures [Hassan, 2013: 63]. All these, in turn, point towards the greater need for reforming the party system and, in a larger sense, the electoral system itself. Parties have to be made democratically accountable and the most important step to achieve this is to restore inner party democracy in them. On the other side, the electoral system should be cleansed of money and muscle power. Once these two are put in place other issues become much more easier to address.

**Notes**

1. The best example in this regard was the conflict between Patel and Nehru which bordered on both the personal and ideological. On the one side, Patel wanted the state simply to express and tend the existing pattern of India's society with all its hierarchy, particularity and religious tastes. On the other side, stood Nehru who hoped to use the state actively to reconstitute India's society, to reform it and to bring it

in line with what it took to be movement of universal history [Khilnani, 1997: 33, 41; Muralidharan, 2007: 40 - 41]

2. Even the Working Committee of the party — highest decision making body - is packed with men and women who have little contact with the mass of the people. For instance, of the 19 members of the Committee in 2006, only one was from Lok Sabha. Of the rest, 13 were Rajya Sabha members, two were those who had lost the 2004 Lok Sabha elections, one lost the 2003 Madhya Pradesh Assembly elections, and two others were former Chief Ministers. [Subrahmaniam, 2008].

   The same is true of other party functionaries. Of the seven party General Secretaries, for example, three were Rajya Sabha members, two lost the 2004 Lok Sabha elections and the rest were former Chief Ministers. Of the five who held independent charge, two were from the Upper House while the other three lost the 2004 general elections. A rising number of powerful cabinet ministers also belong to this genre whereas during the Nehru era most important cabinet posts went to Lok Sabha members. It is pertinent to remember that, Rajya Sabha is not the ideal abode of 'real political activists', as this reflects 'a growing disinclination to engage with the risks of mass politics (Chatterjee, 2006; Hassan, 2012: 115].
3. According to a very conservative estimate, in the 2009 general elections to the Lok Sabha, Congress party has officially spent Rs. 1500 crore, BJP Rs. 1000 crore, BSP and NCP Rs. 700 crore each, DMK Rs 400 crore and AIADMK Rs 300 crore [Ray, 2009: 36]
4. It is estimated that one-fifth of the MPs in the current Lok Sabha is a dollar millionaire and the total assets of its 543 members is reckoned at $ 2 billion, in a society where over half the population lives on less than $ 2 a day [Anderson, 2012: 159]
5. Fixers are middlemen who serve as crucial political intermediaries between the localites and powerful figures at higher levels... These people are political operators who do not hold any formal political or administrative positions, but who practice 'the art of approaching officials for favours and making the wheels of administration move in support of such favours'.

   Upto 1970, the fixers had little role in Indian politics. For, in those years, the organisational strength of major parties, especially the Congress Party, left little room for them. But the decay of party organs over the years since 1970 has created openings and a need for such fixers. Decay undermined the capacity of parties to penetrate into local areas, and to respond to mounting demands from the grass roots [Reddy and Haragopal 1985: 1148 - 62; Manor, 2004: 67].
6. Shiv Sena leader and former Speaker of Lok Sabha, Manohar Joshi, and the one time Member of Parliament, Phoolan Devi, offer two classical examples in this regard. Joshi, a school teacher turned

politician, who, while contesting the 2004 Lok Sabha polls, declared the total value of his assets to be Rs. 2.5 crore, secured, one year after the declaration (2005), a bid for a NTC Mill property in Mumbai worth Rs. 421 crore in partnership with another Shiv Sena leader, Raj Thackeray [Khare, 2005].

Phoolan Devi's case is also equally illustrative. Born in poverty, she had accumulated assets estimated at Rs. 2.5 crore (official valuation) to Rs. 10 crore (market valuation) in a short political career [Wilkinson, 2001: 24].

## References

Anand (2013): 'Which Democratic Value Reigns Today', *Bhashaposhini* (M), Vol. 37, No. 6, June.

Anderson, Perry (2012): The Indian Ideology, New Delhi: Three Essays Collective.

Bagchi, Subroto (2013) : 'Match Action with Vision', *India Today*, Vol. XXXVIII, No. 5, February 4.

Bhanutaj, N (2009): 'Rape of Bellary', *The Week*, Vol. 27, No. 43, September 14-20.

Chandra, Kanchan and Wamiq Umaira (2011): 'India's Democratic Dynasties', *Seminar*, No. 622, June.

Chandrasekhar, C.P. (2013): 'Age of Graft', *Frontline*, Vol. 30, No. 10, May 31.

Chatterjee, Manini (2006): 'Upper House, Upper Hand', *The Indian Express*, April 1.

Dasgupta, Debarshi (2009): 'After the Burial, At the Wake', *Outlook*, Vol. XLIX, No. 46, November 23.

Guha, Ramachandra (2009): 'The Past and Future of Indian Elections', *Outlook*, Vol. XLIX, No. 15, April 20.

Godbole, Madhav (1997): 'Democracy at What Cost?', *Economic and Political Weekly,* Vol. XXXIV, No. 30, July 24.

Hassan, Zoya (2000): 'Introduction: The Political career of the State in India', in Zoya Hassan, Reading in *Indian Government and Politics: Politics and the State in India*, New Delhi: Sage.

_______, (2012): Congress After Indira, *Policy, Power, Political Change* (1984 - 2009), New Delhi: Oxford University Press.

_______, (2013): 'Congress and its Future', *Seminar*, 641, January.

Jayal, Niraja Gopal (2000) : 'The State and Democracy in India or What Happened to Welfare, Secularism and Development' in Vinita Damodaran and Maya Unnithan - Kumar (eds.), *Post Colonial India: History, Politics and Culture,* New Delhi: Manohar.

Joseph, Sarah (2007): 'Neoliberal Reforms and Democracy in India', *Economic and Political weekly,* Vol. XLII, No. 31, August 4.

Kaviraj, Sudipta (2010): *The Imaginary Institutions of India: Politics and Ideas,* Ranikhet: Permanent Black.

Khare, Harish (2005): 'Audit the Political Class As Well', *The Hindu,* July 27.

Khilnani, Sunil (1997): *The Idea of India, London*: Hamish Hamilton.

_______, (2004): 'Branding India', *Seminar,* No. 533.

Kohli, Atul (2010): 'Politics and Redistribution' in Niraja Gopal Jayal and Pratap Bhanu Mehta (eds.), *The Oxford Companion to Politics in India,* New Delhi: Oxford University Press.

Kothari, Rajni (1975): 'The Failure of a System: Politics as Private Enterprise', *The Times of India,* April 10.

_______ , (1992): 'Area of Darkness', *Seminar,* No. 399.

Manish, Sai (2012): "This Sugarcane Season, Crush the Farmer', *Tehelka,* Vol. 9, No. 48, December 1.

Manor, James (2004): 'Towel Over Armpit: Small Time Political Fixers in India's States', in Ashutosh Varshney (ed.); *India and the Politics of Developing Countries: Essays in Memory of Myron Weiner,* New Delhi: Sage.

Muralidharan, Sukumar (2007): 'The Tyranny of Identity, Party Politics in India and its Changing Forms of Authoritarianism' in Arvind Sivaramakrishnan, *Short on Democracy: Issues Facing Indian Political Parties,* Gurgaon: Imprint One.

Patnaik, Prabhat (2000): 'The State in India's Economic Development', in Zoya Hassan (ed.) : *Readings in Indian Government and Politics: Politics and the State in India,* New Delhi: Sage.

Ramakrishnan, Venkitesh (2013): 'Drowning in Scams', *Frontline,* Vol. 30, No. 10, May 31.

Ranciere, Jacques (1999): *Disagreement: Politics and Philosophy,* Minnesota: University of Minnesota Press.

Ray, Shantam Guha (2009): 'Offer Valid Till Votes Last', *Tehelka,* Vol. 6, No. 17, May 2.

Reddy, G. Ram and G. Haragopal (1985): 'The Pyraveekar: The Fixer in Rural India', *Asian Survey* Vol. XXI, November.

Sainath, P (2010): 'The Empire Strikes Back - and Low!' *The Hindu,* August 5.

_______, (2013): 'The Feeding Frenzy of Kleptocracy', in Chandra Dutt and V. K. Sharafudheen (eds.), *Indian Economy, Politics and Society,* Thrissur: Nirmala Hiprint.

Sinha, Aseema (2010): 'Business and Politics' in Niraja Gopal Jayal and Pratap Bhanu Mehta (eds.), *The Oxford Companion to Politics in India,* New Delhi: OUP.

Subrahmaniam (2008) : 'Mass Leadership and Backroom Politics', *The Hindu,* April 8.

Tripathi, Purnima. S. (2013): 'Small Players, Big Games', *Frontline,* Vol. 30, No. 10, May 31.

Wilkinson, Sven. I (2001): 'Cleansing Political Institutions', *Seminar,* No. 506, October.

Zakaria, Farid (2003): *The Future of Freedom: Illiberal Democracy at Home and Abroad,* London: Viking.

# 12

# *Democratic Revival — Agenda for Electoral Reform*

*Jayaprakash Narayan*

**Introduction**

Among the nations liberated after the Second World War, India has a unique record of successive elections and stable and peaceful democracy. Many countries, which emerged as nascent democracies with high hopes over the past fifty years, have fast succumbed to authoritarian impulses and army coups. The experiences of our own neighbours - Pakistan and Bangladesh - illustrate the difficulties in running a democracy. Indian democracy has shown refreshing capacity to adapt to conditions and uphold democratic institutions and practices. People have been voting in large numbers, and democracy has broadened its appeal, though it may not have struck deep enough roots. There is wider representation of various castes and social groups in legislatures. By all accounts, the bold experiment of universal adult franchise since the inception of our republic has paid off.

However, it will be useful to pause and examine the record of post-colonial India in the light of the democratic institutions and practices as commonly understood in contemporary liberal democratic world. Myron Weiner has listed four such institutions and practices as follows:

(i) Government leaders are chosen in competitive elections in which there are opposition political parties.
(ii) Political parties - including opponents of government - have the right to openly seek public support. They have access to press, freedom of assembly, freedom of speech and freedom from arbitrary arrest.
(iii) Governments defeated in elections step down; winners do not punish losers; defeated leaders are not punished unless in the act of governance they have broken the law; their punishment is based on due process.
(iv) Elected governments are not figureheads; they exercise power and make policies and are accountable to the electors - not to the military, the monarchy, the bureaucracy, or an oligarchy.

Judged by these yardsticks, many countries, while having elections, fail to qualify at varying periods of time as true liberal democracies. Zambia and

Argentina had for some time, competitive elections for public office, but gave unlimited power to elected leaders. In Argentina for some time there was also limited electoral competition with major political forces banned. In apartheid South Africa and white-dominated Rhodesia, while there were regular elections, large sections of people were forcibly prevented from participating in them. In fact, even in the Southern states of the United States, the blacks, while legally permitted to vote, were in practice denied the franchise until the Civil Rights Movement of the 1960s. In countries like Mexico for decades, and in Pakistan and Bangladesh often, there was theoretical electoral competition, but massive state sponsored rigging was practiced. In Turkey, Pakistan, Bangladesh, and Philippines periods of electoral competition are interspersed with authoritarianism. In Algeria and Burma there was electoral competition but the winning parties were prevented from assuming office, and are in fact persecuted. Erstwhile Soviet Union, and most of the Eastern European countries until their adoption of democracy about a decade ago, had authoritarian communist regimes in which only one party could control government. China continues to be under an authoritarian, one-party rule. Several South East Asian countries too have witnessed limited electoral competition or outright authoritarianism for decades.

Judged by these standards, as Myron Weiner points out, "India is one of a handful of post-colonial countries that could be regarded as having a stable democratic regime. The list is very small and one could quarrel with the inclusion of several of the countries in it: Malaysia, Sri Lanka, Jamaica, Trinidad/Tobago, Papua New Guinea, and a variety of mini-states: Bahama Islands, Barbados, Botswana, Gambia, Mauritius and Surinam. In the main, post-colonial regimes have been one-party states, military bureaucracies and dictatorships, communist, or personalized autocracies. The new regimes typically restrict opposition parties, limit freedom of assembly and freedom of the press, do not permit competitive elections, restrain the judiciary from performing an independent role, and limit freedoms of their citizens in a variety of ways - to speak out, to travel abroad, to criticize the regime and to change the government peacefully. In most post-colonial regimes, political participation is restricted and leaders are not held accountable; and, in the worst cases, governments are tyrannical. India, along with a handful of smaller countries, is a notable exception."

**Electoral Reforms in India**

Undoubtedly, Indian experience with democracy has been a remarkable success story. Never before did a poor, largely illiterate, extremely diverse society dare to accept universal adult franchise, liberty and rule of law as the guiding principles of its nation-state. Not only did democracy and liberty endure in India, but the nation also achieved several notable successes. The largely peaceful integration of over five hundred princely states of every conceivable form of diversity into the Indian Union is an unmatched accomplishment in human history. In a world in which most nation-states are struggling with multi-lingual societies, India built a stable framework for coexistence of eighteen languages, and linguistic reorganisation of states proved to be a great triumph of common sense and pragmatism. While India was only quasi-federal in the early years of the republic, a true federal republic has been built over the past two decades, with states coming into their own. All these have been accomplished while preserving liberty, peace and harmony. At the same time, modest economic growth was witnessed, though we continue to perform below our potential. All these are significant successes in the working of our democracy.

**Distortions of Democracy and Growing Crisis**

Nevertheless, there are many distortions increasingly evident in our democracy which are undermining our accomplishments and impeding the twin national goals of poverty eradication and rapid economic growth. The most glaring distortion relates to the deployment of vast sums of money in elections illegitimately. While the legal ceiling on election expenditure incurred by a candidate is Rs. 16 lakhs for State Legislative Assembly in most large states, and Rs. 40 lakhs for Lok Sabha, the actual expenditure often reaches twenty to thirty times the limit. In many states an expenditure of Rs. 5 crore (50 million) is quite commonly incurred by candidates of each major party for State Assembly. Most of this expenditure is to buy the vote with money, liquor or other inducements. Increasingly money is lavishly distributed to a large proportion of voters. Voters take money from all the major candidates, and vote for whomever they want. What it means is large expenditure for vote-buying does not guarantee victory. But if a candidate does not spend money lavishly to buy the vote, there is very little chance of his being elected. Large expenditure may not ensure victory; but non-expenditure guarantees defeat. Huge investment in elections has thus become an entry fee to have a realistic chance of success. Rich man's money is thus chasing poor man's vote, and whoever gets elected then controls the levers of state and earns multiple returns. Land, mining, other natural resources, contracts, police cases, transfer of officials, government approvals and clearances - all these become sources of making money once elected. A vicious cycle of vast expenditure to control levers of power, and abuse of power and corruption to earn multiple returns is established. As people see more corruption and abuse of office, they become even more cynical and demand more money at the time of election. Honesty has become increasingly incompatible with survival in office. A dangerous equilibrium of money power, electoral success, monopoly over state resources and corruption has been established and perpetuated. While the unscrupulous practitioners of power politics benefit hugely, the poor are lulled into complacency through short term freebies that mitigate the pain of poverty without actually enhancing incomes and ending poverty. Short-term palliatives like employment guarantee, subsidized food etc. have become a substitute to quality education, healthcare, skills, jobs and incomes. Not surprisingly, in a 2009 survey of educational outcomes of fifteen-year olds among 74 countries (PISA - Programme for International Student Assessment), India stood 73rd, just one rank above the lowest ranked Kyrgyzstan Republic. This plunder can be perpetuated only by undermining rule of law, and by short-term freebies at the cost of real empowerment, incomes and economic growth. The state's primary role of 'improving' rule of law, infrastructure, basic amenities and human development have been largely neglected in the quest for votes, short term populism and plunder of state resources.

**INEXHAUSTIBLE DEMAND FOR ILLEGITIMATE FUNDS**

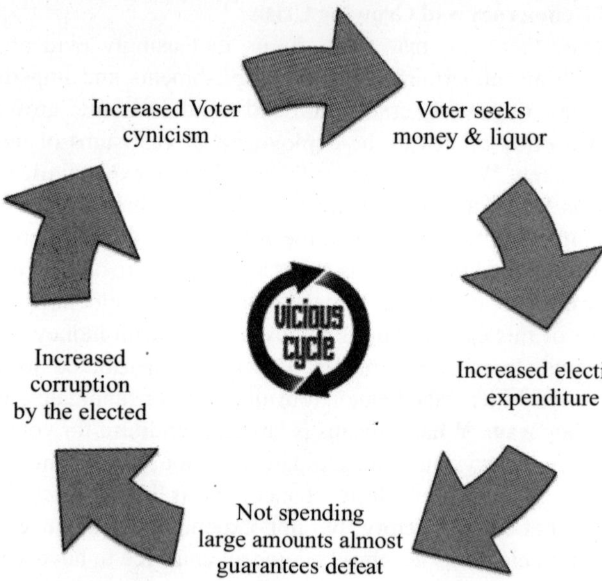


**Politics Becomes a Big Business**

In this climate, a class of political entrepreneurs has emerged. Politics has become big business for the bulk of these individuals. The truly public spirited citizens who want to make a difference find politics increasingly inhospitable, and are relegated to the background in most cases. In place of them, political fiefdoms have emerged in most constituencies. Unscrupulous individuals commandeering vast, often ill-gotten resources has established strong local networks of patronage and caste, and made themselves very powerful and increasingly indispensable to the political parties. These status-quoist, wealthy individuals seek access to state power and resources at any cost. Parties and ideologies are inconsequential to them. Not too long ago, they depended on a party for their political future. Increasingly the parties depend on them for vote mobilisation, and they make or unmake a party's political fortunes as they switch their loyalties with consummate ease. This shift of power from parties to locally powerful individuals is the key feature of politics in recent years. This behaviour of powerful individuals is further complicated by the rise of primordial loyalties for political gain. In the early decades of our republic, parties and leaders have consciously built the idea of India and promoted harmony. But now, promoting loyalties and animosities based on caste, region, religion or language has become increasingly acceptable in the quest for votes and political power. Instead of mobilising people for fulfilling legitimate aspirations, 'the other' is sought to be portrayed as the enemy, and a feeling of separate identity is deliberately promoted for gaining votes. Politics of zero-sum game, in which the gain of one group is always seen at the cost of another group, has gained ascendancy, fragmenting our society and polity increasingly. This made our political system increasingly fragile and fragmented, and harmonious reconciliation and interest aggregation have become more and more difficult. Political fiefdoms and primordial loyalties have together accentuated political volatility.

As a result, the national parties are declining continuously for over two decades. As a few powerful individuals leave a national party in a state, or a caste or religious group switches loyalties on account of a single, emotive issue, the major national parties suddenly fall below a threshold of vote required in the state to be politically viable. Once a party's vote share falls below the threshold, it gets far fewer seats than vote share. Once people realise that the vote for a party does not translate itself into seats, the vote share plummets, and the party is marginalised in the state.

**DECLINE OF CONGRESS IN MAJOR STATES**

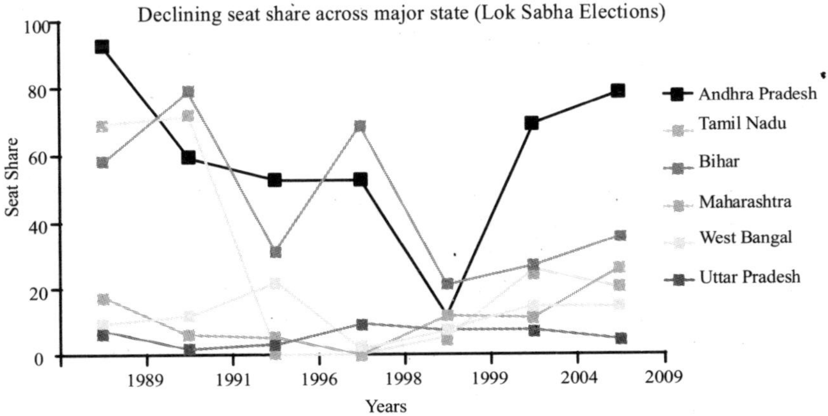


Note: *Only UP & Bihar do seats and votes reflect Congress' own strength; in other states alliances have given Congress better results.*
*Also, Congress could not win a single seat in AP in any of the by-elections since 2009*

**DECLINE OF BJP IN MAJOR STATES**

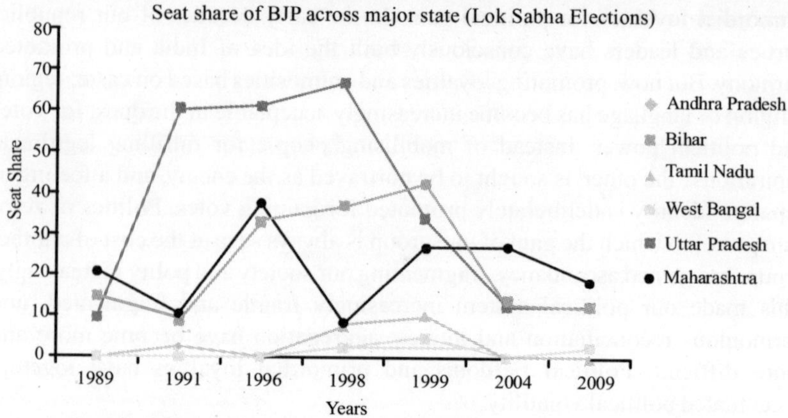


Note: *In Bihar and Maharashtra BJP is in alliances with regional parties.*

This process has been at work for the large national parties in many large States. Both Congress and BJP are increasingly marginalized in Uttar Pradesh, Bihar, West Bengal and Tamil Nadu. In Andhra Pradesh BJP has a marginal presence, and as per current indications, with the rise of YSR Congress, Congress is marginalized at least for the time being. In Maharashtra both Congress and BJP rely on their allies — NCP and Shiv Sena — for political viability. These six largest States account for 55 per cent of our population, and 292 of the 543 Lok Sabha seats in India. In Karnataka, Yedyurappa's departure has seen the decline of BJP in the only major state in which a national party gained significantly in the last decade. Increasingly the familiar pattern of decline of national parties, and rise of regional or sub-regional political outfits based on individual ambitions or primordial loyalties are visible in most parts of India. In the world's most diverse and complex society, the political idea of India seems to be in retreat.

All these factors are leading to increasing de-legitimisation of the Indian state, and alienation of the youth, middle classes, farmers, dalits, *adivasis* and other sections of the population. Defiance of authority, street marches and protests, ready recourse to abuse of politics and politicians, assertion of narrow groups at the cost of the whole society, intense unsustainable populism- all these have been recurring features of the Indian street. The street is pitted against the state, and governance has become more and more difficult.

As imperatives of political survival gain precedence over good governance, corruption has become ubiquitous, rational public policy has become a casualty, and poverty eradication and long-term economic growth have been neglected at the altar of short term political expediency. As education, skills, infrastructure and sound policies for job creation have been neglected, and economic growth itself is in jeopardy, leading to more volatility in the midst of rising expectations and satellite television.

**Recent Democratic Reforms**

In the face of this mounting crisis, there have been concerted attempts over the years to improve things. While these reforms are inadequate to address the growing challenges, they do indicate that the political parties, legislature and constitutional authorities are alive to the need for reforms. Not all changes are positive or flawless, but cumulatively they certainly help improve the situation. A brief outline of some of these developments will be of value in understanding the present situation.

The Seventy Third and Seventy Fourth Amendments enacted in 1993 are ambitious in scope, and were aimed at creating the third tier of federalism. While the intention was sound, unfortunately these amendments ended up creating over-structured, under-powered local governments. The net result is, we have elected local governments without real or substantive devolution of powers and resources. In a few States like Kerala there is more genuine devolution, but in most States the legislators and bureaucracy forged a formidable alliance to resist decentralisation. Increasingly, the state legislator became the disguised executive taking control of all local issues. This exercise of power without authority undermined local governments, made bureaucracy unaccountable, and rendered service delivery ineffective. As a result, public dissatisfaction, and in large parts of India, public disaffection, continue to mount.

Years of civil society activism and judicial pronouncements finally made it mandatory in 2003 for candidates for elective office to disclose their antecedents, including education, financial information and criminal record, if any. Experience of disclosures for about a decade shows that constant public pressure on political parties can improve candidate choice in the long term. Established politicians with criminal record have struck deep roots in politics, and have successfully erased their criminal record using a pliable system. But major parties do refrain from nominating new candidates with criminal record, provided citizens' movements are strong enough to make candidate choice a key issue.

The year 2003 saw a significant improvement in political funding. The law now provides for full tax exemption to individuals and corporates on political contributions to parties. Thus an incentive is now provided for legitimate funding of political activity. All contributions over Rs. 20,000 should now be disclosed along with a party's annual accounts. The law also provide for equitable sharing of time by recognized political parties on the cable television network and other electronic media (public or private). This last element has not yet been implemented as rules have not been framed. Once this law is implemented in full, in the long term, a robust and viable mechanism would be in place to meet the legitimate campaign needs of political parties. However, as most contributions are in cash and unaccounted, and as most expenditure is for illegitimate purposes like vote-buying, mere campaign finance reform is not sufficient to change the nature of politics.

Through the 91st amendment to the Constitution, the size of the Council of Ministers in the Union and States is now restricted to 15 per cent of the strength of the lower house. The days of jumbo-jet cabinets are now gone. With smaller cabinets, parties are now constrained in doling out ministerial positions in return for political support.

The anti-defection provisions of the Xth Schedule have been strengthened considerably, and 'splits' and group defections are no longer possible. A defecting member is now compelled to resign from the legislature and seek re-election. This has certainly brought greater stability and reduced defections. However, as party whip is not limited to a vote affecting survival of the government – money bills and no-confidence motions – and therefore healthy debate and legitimate dissent are stifled. Also past evidence shows that partisan presiding officers loyal to the government cannot always be trusted with the power to decide on disqualification.

In 2003, the Parliament amended the Representation of the People Act removing domicile requirements for election to the Rajya Sabha from a State, and mandating an open ballot in Rajya Sabha election. While critics argued that removal of domicile requirement violates federal character, many observers felt that the parties have tacitly acknowledged the need to get competent persons elected to Rajya Sabha, as Lok Sabha elections have been beyond the reach of all but a few very wealthy candidates. Removal of domicile requirement enables parties to get desirable candidates elected from states where they have strength, and open balloting eliminates horse-trading. While these changes in Rajya Sabha election do not address the real crisis affecting our legislatures, they are nevertheless real, short-term responses to growing problems of governance.

In 2005, the Parliament enacted the landmark Right to Information Act, strengthening accountability and empowering citizens. Similarly, the Election Commission has improved voter registration over the years, making the system cleaner and more accessible. However, there still is no permanent, citizen-friendly, transparent, verifiable mechanism for voter registration. If post office becomes a permanent nodal agency for voter registration, things will improve considerably. The 2009 law on Gram Nyayalayas now makes justice delivery in simple cases accessible, inexpensive and citizen-friendly. However, many states are slow to creating local courts despite central assistance. The 97th amendment to the Constitution, enacted in 2012 has now protected the citizens' right to form and run cooperatives as a fundamental right without undue interference from governments.

In recent months, the Lokpal Bill and Service Guarantee Bill providing for time limits for service delivery and compensation for delays are two robust responses improving accountability. Similarly, a National Judicial Commission and an Indian Judicial Service are in the pipeline to improve the quality of higher judiciary.

All these reform initiatives indicate that our political and governance system is alive to the challenges and capable of addressing them. But these responses are insufficient to address the underlying structural problems deepening the political crisis.

**Structural Challenges to the Political System**

There are many in India who are deeply distressed about the nature of our politics. There is growing revulsion of politicians, parties and the political process. Much of our public discourse is dominated by the popular distaste for politics. But this deeply anti-political attitude assumes that our political crisis is an issue of morality and values. Most of the middle classes and youth have developed contempt for the politicians, and blame all those who are part of the political process for our current ills. Revulsion of politics, a daily dose of protest, a perpetual anti-establishment approach, the ubiquitous notion that defiance of law and authority is somehow heroic and noble, a mindset that those who are elected can do nothing right, and a belief that the citizen is always right when he shows contempt for law and due process — these features of our contemporary society are making India increasingly ungovernable. Rise of anarchy and failure of rule of law are making the poor, the weak and the underprivileged ever more vulnerable.

But even a cursory examination will reveal that this contempt for politics is a flawed approach. During freedom struggle and in the first few decades after independence, our political process threw up some exceptional men and women into positions of leadership. Public life and politics were marked by nobility and passion for public good and nation-building during those decades. Even today there have been, and continue to be, great leaders who made a phenomenal contribution to public good at various levels in many sectors. It would be absurd to assume that everyone in public life is a scoundrel, and all those who eschewed politics are angels. Clearly there are deep-rooted structural issues which have led to the political and governance crisis in India in recent decades. In fact, many mature democracies did go through a difficult period of transition. It took a civil war and massive bloodshed to accept that slavery was immoral, despite the fact that the American founding fathers passionately believed that all men are created equal. The machine politics of Chicago, New York and Philadelphia took decades of reformist zeal and relentless struggle to clean up. Britain took many reform efforts, notably by the great liberal Gladstone and his successors, to clean up the 'rotten boroughs' and make politics a respectable and noble endeavour in the public eye.

In many ways, the travails of Indian democracy are by means unusual, except that India's republican era coincided with a period of breath-taking technological and economic revolution. The industrial revolution in Britain witnessed an average annual growth rate of about 1 per cent and in an era of centuries of stagnation, that steady growth was seen as a miracle. But now five-six per cent growth rate in India is seen as failure. Clearly, Indian democracy does not have the luxury of many mature democracies which had decades and centuries of time to improve institutions and meet emerging challenges successfully. Therefore, the notion that our democracy has failed is erroneous. We only need to rapidly internalise the lessons of the past seven decades, and correct the distortions.

In order to understand the nature of our crisis and resolve it, we need to focus on our unique initial conditions when democracy and universal adult franchise were institutionalised in India. No other nation before us dared to embrace the revolutionary idea of total equality of all citizens across caste, region, religion, language, gender, class, education, status and wealth from its very inception. That we succeeded as well as we did under the circumstances is nothing short of a miracle. But certain institutional and cultural flaws which are inimical to democracy have not been adequately corrected during our republican journey, and the resultant distortions have undermined our democratic process.

There are three crucial initial conditions which, uncorrected had grievous consequences. The first is the asymmetry of power between the colonial subject and an all-powerful bureaucracy. Our public servants were never taught humility, and they never saw themselves as individuals who delivered services to the people, the tax payers. Even the lowliest public servant was more influential, economically more secure, and more powerful than the vast majority of the people, who were the notional masters in a democracy. In this climate, getting even a simple service like a birth certificate, a land record or a water or electricity connection was then an excruciatingly painful and difficult process. Without red-tape and bribes, harassment and delays, and without influence-peddling and *sifarish* of some big wig, almost nothing got done. With some improvement of literacy and economic status of sections of people, and with the advent of technology, there is some improvement in delivery of services; but even now for most basic services and amenities most people continue to rely on bribes and *sifarish*. This sense of abject helplessness and dependence is accentuated by an intrusive state in a socialist era. Citizens had to approach the state functionaries for practically everything — a ration card, sugar, kerosene, cement, telephone, electrical connection, etc. The state monopoly combined with inefficiency and corruption made the public servants even more powerful and unaccountable in independent India than during the colonial era.

The second complicating factor was the absence of the notion of citizenship. After centuries of oppression most people saw themselves as subjects, not citizens. While universal franchise and liberty were real enough in democratic India, they were merely superimposed on the existing notions of authority and power. While earlier hereditary maharajahs and colonial masters were the unchallenged rulers, in the new era the elected leaders and high officials became the new 'monarchs'. Just as a monarch's word was law, and complete surrender and appeal to his mercy was the safest option in the earlier era, the elected monarchs would 'somehow' fulfill all their needs and expectations.

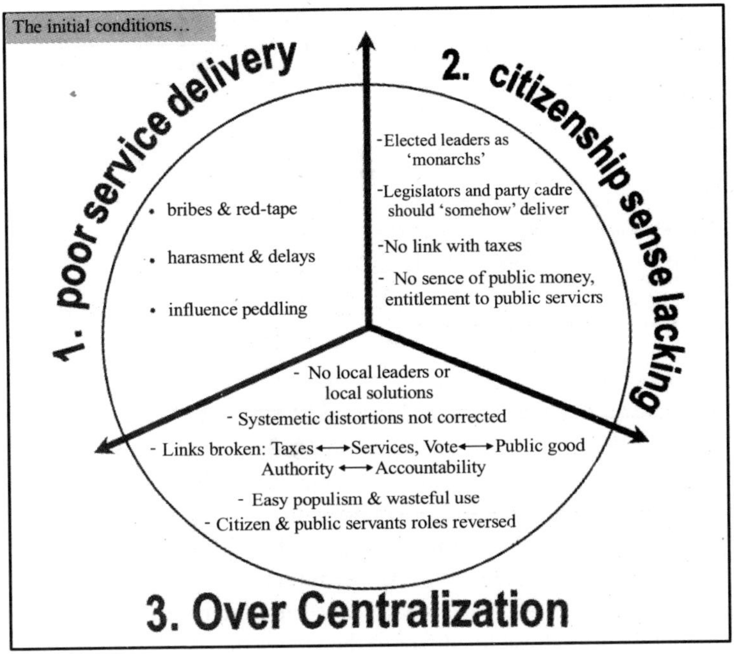


We were never enabled to realise that there is a link between taxes we pay and services we get, and that public money is meant for public goods and services. By some magical process called the 'election', and the 'ballot box', the new maharajahs are chosen with our vote; and now these legislators and their party cadres would 'somehow' deliver everything we need. In this climate there was no space for the notion of rule of law and due process to take roots. Everything is linked to an individual's access to those in power, particularly the legislator who sought your vote, and therefore is beholden to you, and is more accessible than the aloof, arrogant bureaucrat.

This over-reliance on the elected legislator and party cadre to deliver in a dysfunctional and recalcitrant system imposed an enormous burden on them. A vast parallel party bureaucracy had to be built to address people's needs and grievances. During the freedom struggle many, many people sacrificed their time, energy and resources willingly in the service of the nation. The romance of freedom struggle, an idolatrous sense of patriotism, and the relatively low opportunity cost in a stagnant, agrarian economy made such sacrifice relatively less painful. But to expect a similar sacrifice in the mundane task of day to day service delivery in a free republic would be unrealistic.

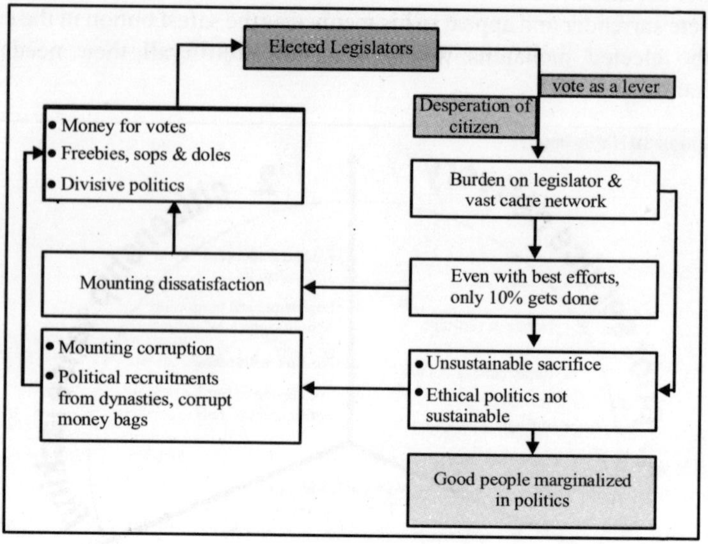


This is especially true when many are feathering their nests in the newly emerging license-raj. As the agrarian stagnation is giving way to modest economic growth and therefore the opportunity cost of giving up a career is very high, such sacrifice is highly unsustainable. The new-found power over levers of state and arbitrate the license-permit raj gave many opportunities for the elected legislators and party cadres to secure their own economic future. The legislators who chose to adhere to the values of sacrifice and morality of the freedom struggle were either marginalised in time, or chose to leave politics. Abuse of office, corruption, politics and service delivery, based on a patron-client system have been institutionalised for years. Even as license-permit raj is dismantled to some extent, the rise of populist culture of transferring individual benefits to the poor and not so-poor ensured that political patronage networks are intact.

But there are two problems with this form of service delivery. First, there was no effort to make bureaucracy more effective and accountable. Therefore despite the most strenuous efforts of legislators and party cadres, the service delivery was inadequate and very unsatisfactory. This led to mounting dissatisfaction, and the voters are increasingly sullen and resentful at the time of election. Second, the system is sustained by massive corruption and abuse of office. Transfers and postings, licenses and permits, contracts and tenders, land grants and mining, police cases and file movements - everything is greased by corruption. This again eroded the legitimacy of both the politician and bureaucrat, and made people ever more mistrusting of the politicians and the system.

The third distortion was centralisation of power. While half-hearted efforts were made to involve the local communities in some decision making for sometime, in general the post-independence Indian state is highly centralised with little local initiative and empowerment. There was no link between taxes and services. Everything is based on the patronage and good will of the players in the centralised state. There is no link between vote and public good. In a wooden, inflexible, centralised system, no matter who is elected, nothing really changes. Therefore vote ceased to have a positive value. Authority is totally divorced from responsibility. Therefore, a system of realistic and plausible alibis has come into being, in which most things fail, but nobody is held accountable. Once the possibility of emergence of local leadership and implementation of local solutions is denied, the centralised government had to resort to both easy populism and wasteful use of resources to retain the loyalty and vote of people, or coercion and control to keep them in line. Either way, the roles of citizens and public servants are reversed, and people became mendicants.

These three initial conditions - poor service delivery, absence of citizenship, and over centralisation — led to many familiar distortions of democracy. Increasingly vote had a price, and people are enticed to vote for money and liquor. In many states, it costs about Rs. two to six crore for every major party candidate to be able to seriously compete for a Legislative Assembly seat. Increasingly, more and more voters are seeking money and other inducements from all candidates. Large expenditure is a necessary condition for serious competition, but does not guarantee victory. More expenditure complicated by paid news and other pernicious practices, results in more corruption, more cynicism and even more vote-buying. The best and brightest individuals increasingly shun politics, and they are seen as unelectable. As all mainstream parties are indulging in vote-buying, more is needed to get votes: a culture of reckless, competitive populism and endless freebies at the cost of the essential functions of government has now become endemic. Rule of law, justice, infrastructure, basic amenities, education, and health care have been largely neglected in favour of direct, individual, short-term benefits. Most of these benefits are transient, and they neither enhance the capacities of the poor, nor empower them. Therefore poverty is perpetuated, and with failed public services, the poor who depend on government infrastructure and services disproportionately suffer the most.

As most parties resort to populism for votes, even that has become an equalizer. Therefore, wherever possible, parties skillfully fomented divisions in a disparate society, and fashioned vote banks based on primordial loyalties of caste, region, religion and language. Money for vote, freebies and divisions became the three most common currencies for vote, fragmenting our polity, undermining growth and harmony, and debasing our democracy.

All these tendencies have been accentuated by the dependence on the marginal vote in our first-past, the post (FPTP) system. In FPTP system, the winner-takes-all, and one more vote means victory, and one less vote means defeat. In such a system, the marginal vote a candidate or party gets is all important. Decades of democratic reform, robust internal democracy, decentralisation, strong systems of accountability and a spirit of public service pervading society and politics ensured that FPTP served the needs of society well in countries like Britain. No system is in itself good or bad; it is the initial conditions and accompanying institutions and practices which will determine the outcome. In Britain, competent and honest citizens are put up as candidates by parties; parties offer clear alternative agendas; elections are clean without vote buying, inducements, freebies or divisions; voters generally respond to politics of individuation rather than primordial loyalties; and elected governments set out to implement their declared agenda. The key functions of framing policies and choosing leaders are well-served in FPTP system under British conditions.

But given the different initial conditions and the trajectory of politics and society, FPTP and dependence on marginal vote have had radically different consequences in India. Dependence on marginal vote in our conditions led to vote buying, phenomenal corruption and abuse of office, and marginalisation of the best and brightest elements in the political process. Again imperatives of marginal vote forced almost all parties to overemphasise freebies and reckless populism at the cost of rule of law, infrastructure, education and health care, resulting in deepening fiscal crisis and erosion of nation-building and economic growth. Fear of losing marginal votes, and loss of power also made most parties embrace sectarianism and policies to pander to narrow primordial loyalties. This led to fragmentation of the polity, erosion of national ethos, and decline of national parties. Loss of support of a few individuals or caste groups could easily upset the balance of power, and both parties and governments have become increasingly fragile and volatile. Society is more and more polarised as vocal minorities vociferously promote sectarian agenda in their efforts to browbeat the political parties and governments into submission.

Electoral systems have profound consequences in the evolution of politics in a society. The exact consequences may vary depending on the nature of a society, level of democratic maturity of institutions of governance, the political culture, and the practices internalised in a society and polity. Members of the Constituent Assembly were aware of the importance of electoral systems, and several of them felt that a proportional representation system was better suited for India. Two members, Mahboob Ali Baig Sahib Bahadur and Mohamed Ismael Saheb (3 January, 1949), quoted Lord Howard of Penrith and Sir Samuel Hoare in support of proportional representation by means of the single transferable vote in India. Mohamed Ismael Sahib argued "It is said that this (proportional) system of election will lead to fissures and divisions amongst the people. But, in reality, it would not be leading to that result or effect at all, because people know that under this system of election every group of people has got an effective say in the election. Therefore every group will be drawn towards the other group. It will make each group seek the franchise of other people. Therefore it would really work for unity rather than for disunity". On 4th January 1949, Kazi Syed Karimuddin (CP & Berar) moved an amendment incorporating proportional representation (PR) with multi-member constituencies by means of cumulative vote.

**CONSEQUENCES OF MARGINAL VOTE**

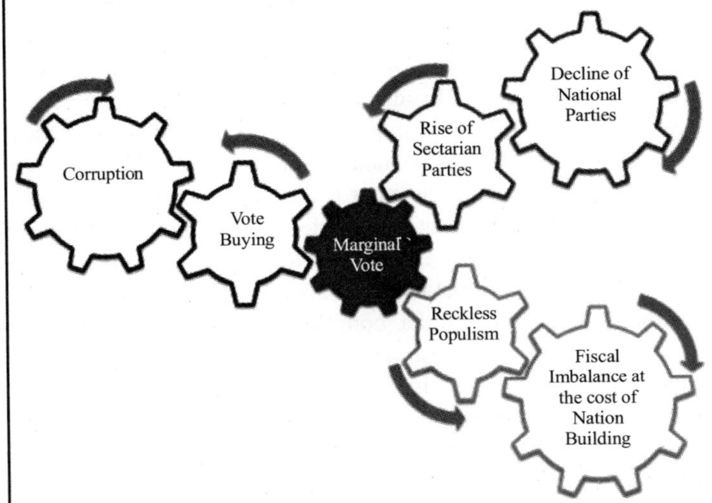


But much of the debate on electoral systems was largely centered round the issue of reservation of elective offices. Dr. Ambedkar opposed proportional representation: "I think, it might be said that one of the disadvantages of proportional representation is the fragmentation of the legislature into a number of small groups". Then Ambedkar cited the British Parliament's rejection of a Royal Commission recommendation in 1910: "The reason which was given for not accepting it was, in my judgment, a very sound reason, that Proportional Representation would not permit a stable government to remain in office, because Parliament would be so divided into so many small groups that every time anything happened which displeased certain groups in Parliament, they would, on that occasion, withdraw their support from the Government, with the result that the Government losing the support certain groups and units, would fall to pieces.... I am therefore, very hesitant in accepting any system of election which would damage the stability of government". Dr Ambedkar also argued against Proportional Representation on the ground that it may not accommodate reservation of seats for Scheduled Castes and Scheduled Tribes. He argued: "I submit that this proportional representation is really taking away by the back-door what has already been granted to the minorities by this agreement, because proportional representation will not give to the minorities, namely, a definite quota. It might give them a voice in the election of their representatives. Whether the minorities will be prepared to give up their quota system and prefer to have a mere voice in the election of their representatives, I submit in fairness ought to be left to them". The amendment on Proportional Representation was thus negatived.

As E. Sridharan pointed out, "both the traditional justifications for the FPTP system, in general and in India, including in the Constituent Assembly debates ..., which are namely that it produces stable single-party majority governments, and that its aggregative imperative leads to national integration as against splitting the party system along 'ethnic' (broadly defined, including religio-communal, cast, regional-ethnic, cultural etc.) lines, have been belied in practice for a decade now". Sridharan summed up: "The single-member constituency, FPTP system was adopted in the Constituent Assembly and early Parliamentary debates, not so much from a focused debate on the merits of alternative electoral systems as regards their effects on the representation of parties and social groups, but from a default assumption that the FPTP system was somehow natural, carried forward largely unconsciously from British and British colonial practice since 1935".

It is ironic that in today's India, both the justifications for FPTP – stable majority governments, and aggregative imperative leading to national integration transcending ethnic differences — proved to be unfounded. The political fragmentation and inherent instability of governments over the past two decades, and the proliferation of parties with a narrow social base, appealing to primordial loyalties based on caste, region and religion were clearly not anticipated by the Constituent Assembly while adopting FPTP system.

Even then, interestingly, Article 81 (2) (b) of the Constitution permits Proportional Representation through cumulative vote in multi-member constituencies. The Article says in respect of Lok Sabha: "Each State shall be divided into Territorial constituencies in such a manner that the ratio between the population of each constituency and the number of seats allotted to it is, so far as practicable, the same throughout the State..." A similar provision exists for elections to Legislative Assemblies under Art 170(2). In fact in 1951 and 1957 Parliamentary elections, there were several multi-member constituencies for Lok Sabha to accommodate reserved seats. In the first Lok Sabha, out of the 401 constituencies, 314 were single-seat constituencies (304 general, and 10 ST seats), and 86 were double-seat constituencies, with the second seat reserved for SCs (71 constituencies) and STs (15 constituencies). There was also one triple-seat constituency in West Bengal, with a seat each for General, SC and ST categories. Thus, while there were 401 constituencies, there were 489 seats filled in the election. Similarly in 1957, (Second Lok Sabha), there were 312 single-seat constituencies (296 general and 16 ST seats) and 91 double-seat constituencies (in 76 of them second seat reserved for SCs, and in 15 of them for STs). Thus 494 seats were filled from 403 constituencies. Multi-member constituencies with proportional representation are permissible in the

Constitution, and only the laws and rules need to be amended to facilitate proportional representation, provided there is political consensus.

Given the fact that the FPTP system did not result in the two advantages of governmental stability and national integration promoted by the aggregative imperative, we are saddled with FPTP for no sound reason except tradition and habit. While the benefits of FPTP did not flow to us as a nation, the disadvantages of seeking marginal vote in a poor and largely illiterate country of India's complexity have now remained with us. Rise of abnormal and illegitimate money power in elections and the phenomenal corruption, the un-electability of enlightened, competent and public-spirited citizens, the decline of national parties in large parts of India, the fragmentation of polity, the reckless populism and freebies culture at the cost of core functions of state, the rise of primordial loyalties and divisive politics for short-term political gains, and increasing erosion of state's authority - all these can be directly traced to FPTP system under Indian conditions.

It is in this context that we should examine closely alternative electoral systems capable of addressing our challenges. In the Indian situation, given the vastness, diversity and complexity of our society, a parliamentary system of election with executive drawn from, and accountable to, the legislature seems to be the best available option. There is a broad agreement that a directly elected executive for the whole nation, and embodying all executive authority, may not be acceptable in India, given the deep fissures on account of religion, language (Hindi vs Non-Hindi) and region (North vs South). But within the parliamentary framework, we need to design a system best suited to our conditions, and capable of overcoming the many distortions and dysfunctional features that have crept in over the decades.

Both proportional system and FPTP are parliamentary systems with the executive drawn from the legislature. However, FPTP system is essentially candidate-based and constituency based. FPTP demands a high threshold of voting requirement in a constituency. Even parties and candidates with very narrow social or political base can succeed in constituencies, as long as they can get a high vote share locally. Equally, for broad-based parties, the threshold requirement in a state is very high, and a party will not achieve significant success unless it can command a high vote share and is one of the top two parties. As a result, marginal vote becomes all important in electoral success. But Proportional Representation, however, does not reward a large, but narrow base in a constituency. It rewards a moderate base in a whole state. The threshold requirement in a whole state is moderate, and local candidate strength and marginal vote become unimportant.

As threshold requirement varies and marginal vote becomes unimportant, the electoral outcomes and incentives change considerably in the PR system. As marginal vote is not critical, there is far less incentive to buy the vote. Competent, honest and public-spirited politicians with good image become electoral assets. Rational, long-term, policies can be pursued by parties in PR system without yielding to the temptation to resort to short-term populism for fear of losing marginal vote. National parties and parties with a broad, non-sectarian political agenda become viable in PR system even with moderate base and voting support across a whole state. Once voters realise that their vote will translate into seats for a party of their choice, there is much less tactical voting. In FPTP, tactical voting is common as a preferred party or candidate may not have a high percentage of votes, and therefore vote for such candidates or parties is 'wasted'. Therefore most voters vote for one of the two top parties, often with an intention to deny victory to the party they dread most. But in PR, there is no need to vote 'against' a party; instead, the voter can much more freely exercise her choice with the secure knowledge that her vote will be translated into seats, and her voice is represented and vote is not wasted. As a result of broader choice, in PR systems the voter participation is generally significantly higher. In FPTP, national parties are often compelled to forge alliances at the cost of party's long term viability, in order to maximise the short term gains. As a result, national parties, once they fall below a high threshold of vote in a state, get increasingly marginalised. PR prevents this fragmentation and marginalisation of national parties, because with a moderate share of vote, a party is viable in pursuit of its goals.

Clearly, in a suitably designed PR system, most of the distortions of FPTP system can be overcome. The challenge lies in retaining the best features of both FPTP and PR systems, and avoiding the pitfalls of both. In PR system, there are certain concerns which need to be addressed. The foremost concern in a very complex, heterogeneous society is the danger of further political fragmentation as each caste/ethnic group forms its own political party, and seeks vote on the basis of a primordial divisive agenda. This tendency is already pronounced in FPTP system in India, and the design of PR should address this problem. The solution to such a problem lies in imposing a reasonable threshold requirement of voting, say 5 to 10 per cent of the vote in a large state, as the minimum required vote to give the party seats in Legislature from the state. Such a threshold has to be at state level, since a national threshold of even two to five per cent will exclude most established regional and other recognised parties from the contest. But a state level threshold of 5 to 10 per cent of the vote is reasonable, will protect the interests of all recognised parties, and is at the same time difficult to achieve unless a party has a wide base, and can appeal to various interest groups. The imperative of vote aggregation is preserved, and the temptation to play to primordial loyalties will be resisted.

The second major concern in a list-based PR System is that the link between the voter and the elected legislator will be broken. In a constituency-based FPTP election, the voters depend on the local legislator for intervention on their behalf. The ideal solution to this problem is effective empowerment of local governments, so that voters approach local governments for most things that matter to them. However, with feeble local governments, most voters depend on the local legislator to act as disguised executive and to ensure delivery of simple services and to address grievances. This felt need should be addressed in PR system. A simple solution to the problem would be formal allocation of a territorial seat to each elected legislator in the PR system, so that, that member would be accessible to local voters and address their problems. This allocation of a territory to the elected members in a multi-member constituency can be made on the basis of the vote share of a party, and the preference of the members elected on behalf of that party.

A third concern relating to PR is the stability of governments. It is true that FPTP did not ensure stability, especially at the national level. It can be argued that in PR system there is greater stability in coalitions, as parties are much more secure in their support base, and volatility of a small segment of voters would not grievously affect the electoral prospects of a party. However, when electoral system is sought to be improved, we need to make it more stable to the extent possible. There are two institutional measures which will enhance stability of governments in PR System. First, a provision can be incorporated to the effect that a government cannot be voted out of office on the floor of the House unless an alternative government with majority support is in place. Article 67 of the German Basic Law provides for such Constructive No Confidence: "The Bundestag can express its lack of confidence in the Federal Chancellor only by electing a successor with the (support of the) majority of its members". Spain and Hungary too have similar provisions. In addition, a second measure which facilitates filling of vacancies in legislature without having to resort to by-elections will greatly enhance stability of governments and continuity of policies. Article 48 of the German Federal Electoral Law states that if a vacancy arises in Bundestag, "The vacant seat shall be filled by an appointment from the Land (State) list of that Party for which the departed member stood for election". These two provisions of Constructive No-Confidence, and filling vacancies in legislature from the Party list without resorting to by-elections will greatly enhance stability of governments.

A simple PR model with these safeguards should eliminate the need for marginal vote and propensity to buy the vote or resort to reckless populism or divisive politics. Such a model would have the following features:

- State as a unit for PR threshold for State Assembly and Lok Sabha
- About five-10 per cent minimum vote for the Party in the State to be eligible to have its members in the legislature from that State.
- Multi-member constituencies, each having 6 to 10 seats.
- Each voter will have a single vote for a party of her choice.
- Each party will offer a list of candidates for each multi-member constituency in order of preference.
- Parties get seats in proportion to their votes in a State, provided they cross the minimum required vote, of say 5 or 10 per cent of the total vote.

- Required number of SC/ST candidates and women candidates will be elected as per reservation by suitable adjustments in the lists.
- Each elected member is allotted to an Assembly /Lok Sabha segment by preferential choice based on party vote share in the multi-member constituency.

No electoral system in itself is a panacea in any society. Ultimately the suitability of a system depends largely on the nature of society, and the context in which it operates. In a perfect world of moral giants and men and women of virtue without vice, any system will work well. But in reality there are no guarantees ever in any society that only moral giants and men and women of unimpeachable integrity with an eternal sense of public purpose will always occupy public offices. Therefore wisdom demands that a set of rules and institutions is designed to ensure that persons with right qualities will operate the Constitution and once they ascend to public office they will function within certain parameters without over-stepping the limits of their authority. If a Constitution is merely a declaration of good intentions and has no role in shaping the nature of the state, then such a Constitution is a worthless scripture. Thomas Jefferson is closer to reality when he argued that Constitutions are living documents. "Some men look at Constitutions with sanctimonious reverence and deem them like the Ark of Covenant, too sacred to be touched. They ascribe to the men of the preceding age wisdom more than human and suppose what they did to be beyond amendment.... laws and institutions must go hand in hand with the progress of human mind.... As new discoveries are made, new truths discovered and manners and opinions change with the change of circumstances, institutions must advance also and keep pace with the times". Each generation has the benefit of experience of the past and should have the capacity and the right to build upon the foundations of this experience.

A dispassionate and objective examination of the evidence of the past six decades leads us to the conclusion that our democratic institutions have performed creditably, but they are increasingly finding it difficult to cope with growing challenges. We need to learn from past experience and strengthen our institutions, and where necessary, reform our system to ensure the best outcomes possible. Proportional representation system with suitable safeguards and sensible design to suit our requirements offers us a great opportunity for democratic revival. The opportunity is immense, and the risks are minimal. But we must realise that while a change in the electoral system will improve the outcome that alone is not sufficient to address our political and governance crisis. Proportional system of representation should be accompanied by two far-reaching, long-overdue reforms. First, the local governments should be substantially empowered in a manner that the third tier of federalism becomes a reality. Such empowerment with accountability at the local level will unleash the energies of our people, and generate new leadership which can innovate, inspire and transform our society. Second, accountability must be institutionalised by a series of measures including strengthening rule of law through police and judicial reforms, an effective service guarantee law backed by delivery mechanism and penalties for delays to enable citizens to reclaim the republic they have lost, and several institutional measures to curb corruption and prevent abuse of office at every level.

Indian republic had embarked on democracy project in unusual circumstances, and we achieved a fair measure of success. Now is the time to improve our institutions and practices to suit our changing requirements. With the right kind of incentives and well-designed system, our people are capable of overcoming all the great challenges we face, and build a great future for the next generation. As Gladstone said, "the purpose of a government is to make it easy for people to do good and difficult to do evil". The eternal challenge of human history has been to find the balance between liberty and order, and freedom and discipline. A few sensible changes with adequate safeguards and checks and balances will radically alter our future and India can find her destiny. Status quo is not an option. History beckons us.

**Note**

1. E. Sridharan, 'The Origins of Electoral System' in Zoya Hasan, E., Sridharan, R., Sudarshan (eds.), *India's Living Constitution: Ideas, Practices, Controversies,* Delhi, Permanent Black, 2011, p. 348.

# 13

## *Decline of Elected Democratic Bodies*

*N.A. Karim*

How did our founding fathers happen to overlook the need for democracy at the village level in a country of continental size and vast number of its people living in the traditional villages far removed from centers of power, often both state and central, the life of whom was based on agriculture and rural economy, is still a mystery. During the period of struggle for independence particularly on arrival of Gandhi on the political scene of the country there was a perceptible shift in the social focus of the freedom movement to villages and their problems.

Gandhi always glorified the simple life and social fabric of our traditional villages which he wanted to preserve intact. This romanticisation of Indian villages was seen by Dr. B.R. Ambedkar as Gandhi's subtle plan to perpetuate the Indian primitive social order with its cruel stratification of society based on a rigid caste system in which the dalits were the worst victims who were outside the pale of the social life, condemned to lead a sub-human existence. This vice-like grip of the system he wanted to do away with as a necessary first step for the emancipation of his people from this unique form of slavery which had the sanction of religion.

Dr. B.R. Ambedkar who was the Chairman of the Drafting Committee of the Constituent Assembly in his obsession to ensure social justice might have thought the resuscitation of any traditional institution and its integration into the new constitution might defeat the ideal of social justice-social, economic and political–the banner of which has been hoisted at the top of the Preamble of the newly drafted Constitution. The other three ideals Liberty, Equality and Fraternity- were the war cries of the French Revolution of 1789-99

This omission of democracy at the grassroot level was felt and rectified much later by Prime Minister Rajiv Gandhi through two significant amendments of the Constitution. With the three-tier panchayat and nagarapalika systems of democratic governance at the Central, State, District, Block and Village levels are complete. In urban areas municipal councils and city corporations became equal instruments of democratic governance, planning and development.

For a vast country with so many diversities of race, religion, language and caste, the simple system of election based on the first past the post has been found wanting in reflecting the will of the people and in giving fairly due representation to the various groups of people many of which were long-neglected due to the unrelenting caste system and the iniquitous way of development under the British rule. What we inherited from the colonial rulers was a populous country administratively unified but otherwise an unintegrated society and polity with a number of divisive forces most of which were lying dormant. The partition of the country brought in emotions and attitudes which later became decisive forces in determining the nature of the polity and society of this country later. To add to this was the low per cent of literacy. At the time of Independence it was only 16 per cent and consequent social and cultural backwardness.

In the first flush of joy and enthusiasm of attaining freedom from the British rule the spirit of elation reflected in Pandit Jawaharlal Nehru's famous 'Tryst with Destiny' speech at the midnight dawn of political freedom everything seemed to go off well. Under the magic spell of our national and state level leaders with the halo of long service and sacrifice in the cause of freedom, the first general election, though there were several inadequacies was successful beyond the expectation in the then several adverse and a number of unfavourable conditions for a free and fair election.

Since then this process of election has been continuing with decreasing degree of democratic returns in the sense that the quality of candidates, and, therefore the work of Parliament and the provincial legislatures steadily deteriorating. Still the process went on without a complete break down as in most of the countries that became politically free after World War II. In India's case this in itself was something of a miracle in the eyes of the deep-dyed democrats who viewed our performance from a distance. For example the British Prime Minister Anthony Eden in his autobiography spoke of Indian experiment in highly appreciative terms of adopting parliamentary democracy "in one of the most diverse population, poorest and least literate countries of the world". Similar words of praise at the surprise success of India's liberal democratic experiment came from several other quarters in the early days when the country was under the political leadership and democratic guidance of Pandit Jawaharlal Nehru and other eminent stalwarts of the freedom struggle.

**Challenges of Adaptation**

Of the three arms of government, Legislature, its composition, quality and the way of functioning is the most visible one with which people measured the democratic content of the system. There were indeed several deficits as the experiment in this Westminster model was relatively new for the country. While in the cradle of this system, England, it had a long history and tradition of eight centuries if we reckon its history from the Magna Carta which King John was forced to sign as a result of a kind of gherao by the discontented nobles of the realm at Runnymede. The system depended more on healthy conventions and precedents than on laws and rules framed for its functioning.

Charismatic Nehru as Prime Minister showed great respect to the Parliament and unrelenting attention to its productive, meaningful functioning. The brute majority of the ruling Congress in both the houses of parliament was not allowed to smother the small still voice of the opposition, a small group then without even the adequate number to be considered as an official one. This group under the leadership of A.K. Gopalan, veteran leader of many a political and popular struggle and the silver tonged Hiren Mukherji, an Oxford educated ideologue of the Communist Party of India (CPI) was given more than its due right and respect by the Leader of the house always. Thus Parliament functioned both as a free forum to vent grievances of the people that were innumerable and as a responsible law-making body as the first Parliament contained trained lawyers with great skill in legislative work with a clear vision for the future of India.

But Nehru's successors showed little respect to the Parliament and treated it with disdain as an unavoidable institutional check on the work of the executive. On the other hand, though no official opposition of ten per cent of the members of Lok Sabha did emerge until the split of Congress Party in 1969, Nehru believed in the primacy of parliament as the supreme representative institution of the nation and made full use of it as the most important forum to educate people on national issues. To help him in this mission there were eminent members in both the Lower and Upper houses of Parliament, veteran freedom fighters with great political wisdom and debating abilities. In the House there was much less noise than today and more poise and grace in the speeches and conduct of members. Members like A.K. Gopalan, S.A. Dange, Indrajit Gupta, Ashok Mehta, Minoo Masani, H.V. Kamath, Acharya J.B. Kripalini, Nath Pai, Madhu Limaye, Bal Raj Madhok made the quality of debates memorable and the questions posted were pointed and significant and submissions timely and relevant.

After Nehru's death in 1964 the Opposition was gaining political ground till the end of that decade when the Congress Party weakened due to a sense of insecurity of Indira Gandhi which was more pathological than political. In the subsequent several social challenges and political vicissitudes under thirteen Prime Ministers and total fifteen tenures the colour and flavour of Indian democracy underwent a sea change.

**The Post-Nehruvian Period**

Indira Gandhi who was Prime Minister twice, first from 1966 to 1977 and later from 1980-84 till she was assassinated by her own bodyguard unlike her father devalued the role of Parliament and reduced it to a rubber stamp. As she was looked upon by Congressmen in the country as strong ruler with a will of her own Congress satraps in most states treated legislatures with equal disdain or even greater contempt.

In 1971 Indira Gandhi's landslide victory several of her severe critics both in the Congress Party and outside were defeated. This further reduced the importance of Parliament and made it also a hand-maid of her strong-willed executive power. The Emergency she declared in 1975 that continued till 1977 saw the arrest and imprisonment of several of the members of Parliament. There followed a systematic downgrading of all democratic institutions particularly the legislature both at the centre and in the states with varying degrees of deterioration in the status and their work.

In 1984 Rajiv Gandhi won the biggest majority in Parliament and this brute majority of the Congress in the House only contributed to take it for granted all executive decisions. The Prime Minister was absent from the house even on occasions when important matters were being debated. After Pandit Nehru the only other Prime Minister who treated Parliament with great respect and allowed freedom to the members to discuss issues freely was V.P. Singh. But his tenure was short. P.V. Narasimha Rao's period also was no better than that of Indira Gandhi in this matter. On the whole, the history of Indian democracy in the pre-neo-liberal period was one of steady deterioration in the composition of members and quality of work of Parliament at the Centre, and, for more or less for the same political reasons, at the states level also. Had there been democratic system at the panchayat levels too right from the beginning of the Constitution, perhaps there would have grown a democratic culture among people that would have helped democratic institutions and functioning at the state and national levels meaningful. Now, instead of influence going up, it is flowing down to village levels as there is a tendency in the local bodies also to imitate their seniors in state and central legislatures

The canker of corruption had eaten into the vitals of administrative system and the functioning of assemblies and parliament by the time panchayati raj came into existence as a constitutional arrangement of total democracy from top to bottom. All the undesirable trends that had grown in the functioning of state assemblies and parliament had crept into the life and functioning and local bodies also. Virulent political rivalries and narrow partisan attitudes spoiled efforts at meaningful development activities at panchayat levels. This has only aggravated the problem of exclusion of the village poor from the growth that has taken place since Independence.

The mid-1991 balance of payment crisis which forced the government to airlift our gold reserve to London to pledge it in the Bank of England to tide over the immediate crisis necessitated other measures for the long-term survival and the restoration of the solvency of the nation. The then Prime Minister P.V. Narasimha Rao accepted all the conditions of the World Bank, one of which, as Ashok Mitra in one of his autobiographical books has revealed, was the appointment of Dr. Manmohan Singh as the Finance Minister, to facilitate the liberalisation of Indian economy through privatisation and globalisation. Indian economy right from the beginning under Pandit Nehru was a command one of Soviet model which was criticized then by Rajagopalachari and other right-wing leaders as 'quota-license-permit raj'. The rate of economic growth under this regime was slow and painful which was derisively known as the Hindu rate of growth.

There was a spurt in GDP growth with the liberalisation, privatisation and globalisation policies followed by the first UPA government under the Prime Ministership of Dr. Manmohan Singh. But the policies followed by his government brought the executive into direct conflict with the parliament as there was no popular mandate for these radical economic reforms. For one thing, Dr. Manamohan Singh himself was not a popularly elected member of Lower House, Lok Sabha. After becoming, first, the Finance Minister, he got himself elected to the Upper house, Rajya Sabha, which was originally conceived as the Council of States to give special representation to the states the problems of which were different as they were at various levels of socio-economic development lying in far-flung areas of the sub-continent. But eventually it was slowly transformed into another chamber to accommodate those who were not willing or reluctant to go through the process popular election and even those who were once defeated in it.

Dr. Manmohan Singh who was born and brought up in the North West of the country, Punjab, represents the North East, Assam in the Rajya Sabha on the strength of an evidently false declaration in the nomination papers that he lives ordinarily in Assam. This is perhaps one of the less deleterious devices with which the government makes the democratic institutions and constitutional bodies subserve their narrow political interests to meet the exigencies of the political situation. This has contributed considerably to the loss of faith and dignity of those institutions. Instead of setting up good healthy precedents most of the practices that we have adopted have contributed only to add to the deficit of the democratic content of the system.

**The Roots of the Decline**

The character and composition of our elected bodies at all levels have fast deteriorated, and this is the main reason for their malfunctioning in several respects. The process of election and the possibilities of manipulating their outcome in several devious ways is perhaps at the root of the problem. In a country where the vast majority are illiterate, poor and feudal condition of existence it is easy to influence the results of the election with money, muscle power and other forms of intimidations. The question Betrand Russell once raised is very relevant in Indian conditions. "If one man offers you democracy and another offers a bag of grain at what stage of starvation will you prefer grain to the vote?"

Even in the early decades of Indian democracy candidates with no credentials for membership of Parliament or state assemblies managed to get into them, sometimes with impressive majority with the help of criminals and money bags. Later these elements who helped the politicians in the election donned political outfits, managed to get tickets and fought and often won the contests. This change of roles considerably transformed the composition of law-making bodies with a considerable number of members not only with criminal background but also with pending criminal cases including rape and murder charges got themselves elected. It is indeed futile to expect any meaningful contribution from these members in legislative work let alone maintaining parliamentary dignity and decorum.

Till T.N. Seshan's appointment as Election Commissioner the single member institution was in the shadow, mostly a passive spectator of all the goings on in the name of rightful poll campaign to which governments also were indifferent if all unlawful activities were to their advantage. Single handedly, through his high profile aggressive functioning, Seshan put fear in the minds of candidates and the government during elections. He exercised his powers fully and made the existing provisions of the Peoples Representation Act strongly against erring parties and candidates. These new experiments during the tenure of Seshan, forced the government to be on the safer side, to change the Election Commission into a three member body with the chief election commissioner and two members. But the spirit of change that T.N. Seshan brought about remained almost intact even after it became a three member body. However the governments continued to influence the Commission indirectly. Soon after this change was brought about one chief election commissioner was made a member of Rajya Sabha and later inducted into the central ministry who left it in utter discredit. Such undemocratic and unhealthy practices have created doubts about the independence and impartiality of the Election Commission. The first step in making electoral reform and making the electoral process devoid of any corruption and malpractices is to ensure the independence of the Commission. This will go a long way in making the elected bodies true representatives of the people. Now a large section of the people are reluctant to enter democratic life of the country due to the devious means with which the political bullies succeed in manipulating the process.

Another factor that makes our political life unclean is the absence of democracy in the organisation and working of the political parties. The sources of revenue and expenditure of parties are not honestly accounted and properly audited to make the functioning transparent. Black money accumulated through several kinds of dishonest means is a major factor that pollutes the political life and the functioning of our democratic bodies. This unaccounted wealth of the corporate houses earned unlawfully with the help of corrupt bureaucracy of which a sizable portion flow into the election process and vitiate it in such a manner that people have lost faith in the fairness of the whole system. To add to this, of late, the media which has grown considerably in their resources and influence has also begun to play a more devastating role in the form of paid news and other unethical interference in the electoral campaigns of parties and individuals.

Unless the Election Commission and the Press Council of India with the whole hearted support of the government check this menace with sensitively drafted legislation to prevent this new powerful factor from exerting their evil influence creeping further into the electoral system the consequences will be indeed tragic. But the government seems to be in no mood to think of any feasible means to tackle this problem though a few cases of large misuse of this power have been registered against a number of candidates and publications involved in this nefarious collusion. Then there is the case of the visual media more powerful than the print one.

If we want to make our elected legislative bodies to function responsibly with dignity and decorum the politico-electoral system has to be cleansed of the accumulated corrupt, unethical practices that have been taken for granted now. This is indeed a tough job, everybody knows. Ours is the largest democracy in the world. To make it one of the most vibrant one India has to travel a long way clearing the possibly dangerous factors at every step. Democracy is a highly sensitive plant which grows only if conducive atmosphere for its healthy growth is provided unfailingly.

The elected bodies of the representatives of the people at all levels behave in an indisciplined and irresponsible way mainly because the electoral system has become clogged with so many corrupt practices that virtually help only corrupt and powerful to get themselves elected. Some piecemeal reforms introduced from time since Seshan's time by Election Commissioners like Lyngdoh who succeeded had improved the system. Then came new forces like the venal press that could undo the gains made so far. It is not easy to prevent the subtle play of media and their clandestine mode of operations in influencing in favour or against candidates of their choice. A few cases of paid news could be easily brought to light mainly because of the clumsy manner in which they were done leaving a number of trails uncovered.

The way in which the government treats the legislatures is the main reason for their irresponsible behaviour leading to constant disruptions and frequent adjournments of the houses. Dr. Manmohan Singh who has no strong political or popular base, it seems, is fearful of debates and discussions by all and sundry for whom he has as an instructive dislike as an aristocratic technocrat. For example, he wanted to sign the Indo-US Civil Nuclear Agreement, the provisions of which were based on two U S laws: the Hyde Act and the 123 Agreement in conformity with the U S Atomic Law. Fully aware of the foreign policy implications of the Agreement, the Left parties who were the main political prop of the first UPA government wanted the Agreement to be discussed in Parliament which was opposed by the Prime Minister with obstinacy uncharacteristic of the man. Perhaps he knew that the Agreement would be ripped open to shreds by the informed members with remarkable debating skills like Gurudas Das Gupta whose number is steadily shrinking election after election. As Secretary General of South Commission Dr. Manmohan Singh had once spoken of 'Global Perestroika as the spokesman of the Third World'. The same may be after becoming an ardent supporter of the US ever since his association with the Brettonwood twins had become a critic of the Third World view.

The contempt of the parliament was manifested in the bribing of members for enlisting the support of a few opposition members and the ugly scenes of displaying wads of currency notes that changed hands in this utterly immoral deal in the history of Parliament. Nothing of the kind would have happened if the Government had shown a little concern for the democratic patriotic sentiments of the Left party members. True no agreement the Government enters into on any issue with a foreign government need not be endorsed by the Parliament. There are people who believe that it is a constitutional infirmity that is to be removed after total review of the working of the Constitution. This is indeed a dangerous proposition in another way.

The new generation political establishment, both ruling class and the official opposition included, would like to do away with or amend a few of its provisions as they are opposed to its ideals and the implementation of the political agenda. In fact the Vajpayee government appointed a Commission under the chairmanship of retired Chief Justice Venkata Chellaiah to review the working of the constitution. Nothing significant resulted from that exercise as there is a landmark judgment of the Supreme Court that the basic structure of the Constitution is not to be tampered with. The reason for our present day political ills and the impasse of legislative work are due to the electoral process into which all kinds of traditional and new forms of malpractices and corruption have crept in and the whole system has been rendered ineffective. Therefore, a radical reform of the electoral system is needed. Several suggestions for reforms had been put forward from time to time most of which remain unheeded. No amount of sermonising would change the attitude of the elected members who have come to the houses through the present process of elections, vitiated right from the beginning with influence of money, consideration of narrow views of religion, caste and party interests.

The obdurasy of the Treasury benches are met by the opposition with their brand of obstinacy and method of disruption of the proceedings of the House. This was not the situation in the pre-liberalisation period. In 1987, at a formal lunch given by then Prime Minister Indira Gandhi for the visiting French President Francois Mitterand, Indira Gandhi introduced Atal Behari Vajpayee to the visiting dignitary as the man "who makes my life miserable in Parliament" and gracefully added that he was "one of our outstanding parliamentarians". On the other hand the present Prime Minister repeatedly criticized the leaders of the opposition as causing disruption of the House forgetting the fact that it is the arrogance of power of the government that creates such unseemly responses by the opposition. When responsible members feel that their rights to know and discuss the deeds of the government is thwarted, this confrontationist attitude grows. Ever since the tidal waves of corruption came to the public notice, and in their anxiety the governments try to cover up the traces of all misdeeds of the ministers from public eye including the elected representatives of the people clash of the present kind is inevitable.

**Conclusion**

Dr. B.R. Ambedkar who is generally considered the architect of our Constitution in his speech in the Constituent Assembly almost at the end of the work of the Assembly observed in almost a prophetic tone on 24 November, 1947. "However good a constitution may be it is sure to turn out bad because those who are called upon to work it happen to be a bad lot. However bad a constitution may be, it may turn out to be good if those who are called upon to work it happen to be a good lot. The working of a constitution does not depend wholly upon the nature of the constitution". We are now realising the full truth of the words of Dr. Ambedkar when we see the large dominating section of our elected bodies who decide the ethos of these bodies now. That is singularly unconducive to the working of the provisions of the Constitution in its letter and spirit.

All these undesirable trends set in with the neo-liberal market centered economy and development mode. Indeed the very rich and our GDP has grown to the advantage of wider section of middle class but making the lives of the poor all the more miserable. The fiber of morality of the nation is all gone with a new generation of rich and middle class who know the price of everything and value of nothing. In the last analysis it is this change that is reflected in the working of our democratic institutions including elected bodies from parliament to Gram sabhas.

Dr. S. Radhakrishnan in the ccurse of his tribute to the memory of Pandit Nehru remarked that the Indian democratic system is the fittest memorial to the first Prime Minister of independent India. True, but a few of its pillars have since been rendered weak.

# 14

# *Deepening Democracy Through Local Governance*

*M.A. Oommen*

## Introduction

*The people of Thebes! Since when do I take my orders from the people of Thebes?*
*Creon, King of Thebes, in Sophocles', Antigone*

The idea of democracy since its origin in Athens has caught the imagination of the public all the world over. As an ideology it is a triumphant one. It commands the greatest legitimacy among all forms of governments because the ultimate source of authority is derived from the people. Although not always explicit and quite often eclipsed, one can discern a democratic tendency in the social life of human beings in all parts of the world from historical times. The institutional forms that obtain today in Western world evolved in relatively recent centuries. The concept and content of democracy has undergone great transformation and still in a state of flux. Deepening democracy which means making it more meaningful and relevant for the lives that people live therefore assumes significance and requires continuing scrutiny and study. The debates relating to regime types therefore do not matter much in this enquiry. As Amartya Sen points out, the rationale for deepening and promoting democracy depends on three distinct virtues: (1) its intrinsic importance (2) its instrumental contributions and (3) its constructive role in the creation of values and norms. No evaluation of the democratic form of governance can be complete without considering each. [Sen (1999):157-158]. Indeed democracy has to become a way of life in every aspect of human social life so that we make relevant social choices. The recent pioneering initiatives of India's decentralised democracy, Brazil's participatory budgeting and South Africa's developmental local government hold great lessons in building a responsive and participatory local governance system in the future.

## What is Wrong with Representative Democracy?

This is a natural question to be asked in this discourse because in the democratic countries of the world the dominant paradigm is representative democracy. Representative democracy is widely accepted as the most civilised form of governance. Balloting and periodic multi-party elections are quite often equated with democracy by a large number of people all the world over. Among political theorists there are strong advocates of this position. For example, Samuel Huntington says: "Elections, open, free and fair, are the essence of democracy, the inescapable sine-qua non" [Huntington (1991):9].

This certainly is not a comprehensive view of democracy. Not only charismatic leaders, even tyrants have won elections with massive votes. It is generally acknowledged that money, muscle power, media and many other factors influence free and fair elections even in the so-called developed countries. No wonder scholars like Max Weber, John Rawls, Jurgen Habermas, Joshua Cohen, Leonardo Avritzer and Amartya Sen have viewed representative democracy with great misgivings. In the rest of this section (1.0) some arguments to show our strong concerns about representative democracy are given. Representative democracy needs radical reform. The quest for alternative ways of strengthening the practice of democracy has to be a continuing project.

Several institutions of representative democracy including the party systems are not fully answerable and accountable to the people. Too much faith in competitive elections as an accountable mechanism is unfounded. The elected representatives and the executives (cabinet) owe allegiance to their party apparatus and high command rather than to the people who quite often remain remote spectators. There is a growing gap between citizens and state institutions leading to a 'diminished democracy' [Skocpol (2003):11]. Crenson and Ginsberg (2004) who discusses the elite monopoly of American life meaningfully title their work Downsizing Democracy: How America Sidelined its People and Privatised the Public. The sovereignty of people turns out to be a mirage or only an option to be exercised at election times.

In concluding his edited volume that reviews the journey of democracy from 508 BC to 1993 AD, John Dunn ed., (1992:258-66) points out that the present day representative democracy at best can provide three services: physical security, personal security of subjects and the protection of a capitalist economy. Even at the height of its present triumph, he points out that representative democracy does not have any unique claims to political authority. For example, from the perspective of social justice and inclusive development (social, economic and political inclusiveness), representative democracy has no supportive evidence or even arguments as a unique form of organising political life for the common good. John Dunn and colleagues have raised innumerable pertinent questions which representative democracy in retrospect has failed to answer. One challenging question out of them is singled out below to show the deep frustration about representative democracy. "How far is it sane to hope that representative democracy can ever realise for all its vastly expanded citizen body the ferociously demanding value which Greek democrats claimed for their own far narrower demos: the goal of living in freedom together?" [Dunn (1992):262].

"The real development issue in contemporary world is to have an inclusive society with 'the goal of living in freedom together'. The concept of freedom is related to development which consists in removing all unfreedoms, widening choices and expanding capabilities to choose" [See Sen (1999)]. Unfreedoms broadly speaking is the lack of opportunities to exercise one's reasoned agency. The deficits of representative democracy need to be addressed by scholars as well as by the public. Both democracy and development will have to assume newer meaning and added significance.

Although the understanding of democracy in contemporary political philosophy has vastly widened, balloting and competitive elections with four or five years gap remains the overarching salience of democracy. A government of the people, by the people, for the people can never be meaningful with public balloting and competitive elections alone. Yes it is a great right and privilege to choose your government. But it has to be closely related to the analysis and delivery of social justice. In the words of John Rawls: "Justice is the first virtue of social institutions, as truth is of systems of thought. A theory however elegant and economical must be rejected or revised if it is untrue; likewise laws and institutions no matter how efficient and well-arranged must be reformed or abolished if they are unjust" [Rawls (1972):3].

However, a democratic social order informed of justice and fostering fair, responsible, responsive and accountable (to the people) institutions remains a distant dream. In contemporary democracies the voice and power of choice of the poor continue to remain feeble and ineffective. Unprecedented wealth expansion and intolerable poverty coexist. Are we really producing the right or genuine collective good under the various institutional mechanisms we presently live in is a nagging question that needs to be addressed. Endemic unfreedoms like ignorance, illiteracy, treatable illnesses, lack of opportunities for better life and living besides strong human rights violations, lack of civil and political liberties continue to exist.

**Deepening Democracy: Towards a Conceptual Framework**

Deepening democracy is a vague concept and its operational significance obviously depends on the meaning and policy content we give to it. 'Deepening democracy in a fragmented world' was the theme of UNDP's Human Development Report (HDR), 2002. The Report examines how democratic governance can be improved to shape human progress and development in a world where several countries by current reckoning may not achieve many of the targets of millennium development goals by 2015. The Report after evaluating human development in the various countries makes the pessimistic prognostication that "If global progress continues at such a snail's pace, it will take more than 130 years to rid the world of hunger" [UNDP (2002):2]. Poverty which is a multiple deprivation of capabilities is growing in several countries (e.g. Sub-Saharan African countries, Central and Eastern Europe etc.). This is happening in a world where the richest 5 per cent of the world's people have incomes 114 times those of the poorest five per cent as documented in the Report. It is important also to note that although 140 countries have multi-party elections, only 82 countries with 57 per cent of the world's people are really democratic even by conventional reckoning. Obviously there is a strong and compelling need for widening and deepening democracy. While making several recommendations, HDR (2002) argues for strengthening and reforming the working of representative democracy. Local democracy as a policy variable does not seem to have received the attention it deserves in the Report.

In this section, we may spell out two important postulates which should engage any quest for deepening democracy. They are (a) working towards an inclusive society and (b) building a strong public sphere. These are not mutually exclusive.

**Working Towards an Inclusive Society**

Participation in shaping the quality of your common living is an intrinsic democratic value. This can meaningfully happen only as an integral part of the democratic process. The required institutional mechanisms will have to be suitably modified and structured. As Amartya Sen puts it: "Exclusion from the process of governance and political participation is indeed an impoverishment of human lives, no matter what our per capita income may be". [Sen (2000):38].

In other words social inclusion is an integral ingredient of democracy and human progress. That no one should be left out or kept out no matter who you are and where you live is a logical dictum and value. Even so, social inclusion is not a binary model in which some are in and others are out. The terms of inclusion are more important than the fact of inclusion. While one can argue that the caste system was not strictly exclusionary, it is unacceptable obviously because the terms of inclusion are iniquitous. A society where inequality in income keeps widening despite pronounced poverty reduction can never be truly inclusive. An inclusive democracy is expected to ensure dignity, equality and security to all.

In a market mediated society, unless you have the exchange entitlements to participate in the market, you are left out and kept out. Exchange entitlements to ensure minimum needs therefore have to be ensured. The need for public provisioning of health, education, food security including adequate nourishment, adequate credit and so on becomes important. Adam smith's famous observation regarding the basic removal of poverty viz. to appear in public without shame could be considered as the basic norm of freedom from humiliation, participation and social inclusion. The validity of inclusion depends on the development process which should ensure equality of opportunity to all a work a day reality. Therefore the democratic task of fighting unfreedoms becomes the goal and means of development as we have explained already. This is realised best through decentralised local democracy which widens the avenues of direct and indirect participation and improve the well-being of local people.

**Construction of a Democratic Public Sphere**

From the second half of the 20th century, the idea of the public sphere has occupied a prominent place in democratic discourses. As part of this the idea of democracy as the public use of reason has been gaining significance. This means working towards deliberative processes that democratise political practice and economic policy formulation. When you reduce democratisation to the restoration of political competition alone, you miss the dimension of public discussion and deliberation which can influence administrative decision-making. This is precisely where conventional representative democracy has failed. Several scholars have laid stress on the building of a public sphere based on deliberative politics and public reasoning as important for growing democratisation. This is the legitimate way to ensure justice in social living. However we confront the historical and still continuing legacy of gods, kings, customs, tradition, brute force and the like determining 'justice'. Only when public arrives at norms of social justice through deliberative reasoning and practice then only justice becomes legitimate. In recent times John Rawls, Jurgen Habermas, Joshua Cohen, Leonardo Avritzer, Amartya Sen and several others have contributed to the idea of public reason. They argue for a public sphere based on that.

Rawls' Theory of Justice (1972) provides the moral basis for a democratic society where justice is treated as fairness. It is based on 'deliberative rationality'. As John Rawls observes: "[A] society is well-ordered when it is not only designed to advance the good of its members but when it is also effectively regulated by a public conception of justice". [John Rawls (1972): 4-5].

Rawls addresses the problems of social and economic inequality as problems of justice. For him inequalities in the distribution of social and economic goods are justified only if they work to the benefit of the most disadvantaged. Although some scholars like Carol Gould (1988) criticise Rawls on many grounds notably his exclusive concern with distributive justice and his lack of any theory of entitlement, Rawls' idea has gained considerable acceptance.

Habermas has gone beyond Rawls in elaborating the theory of a democratic society. He widens the scope of the concept of democracy and treats democratisation as construction of public sphere. For him, the public sphere emerges historically as the result of a process in which individual citizens are made equal in their capability to demand from the ruling class public accountability as well as moral justification for state actions. Through his various writings Habermas advanced a radical proceduralist model of deliberative democracy in which all major political decision-making is linked to discursive processes of a political public sphere. Here administrative decisions reflect the consensus that emerges at the level of the public opinion. His theory of human rights and popular sovereignty stipulates the creation of political institutions in which a discursive process of opinion-building plays an important role. This is needed to ensure fairness. However in most democracies in contemporary world, the collapse of public sphere is very perceptible. As Habermas puts it: "Tendencies pointing to the collapse of the public sphere are unmistakable, for while its scope is expanding impressively, its function has become progressively insignificant. Still publicity continues to be an organisational principle of our political order" [Habermas (1991):4].

The question of making public sphere meaningful and dynamic in social life is important than ever before and we maintain that as key to democratising democracy. The role of local governments it follows is in building a relevant local public sphere.

In the public sphere new issues, new actors (workers, women, marginalized people etc.) come forward and argue out their case by appealing to the best of reason . This is the only way to break the elitistic democratic traditions. To quote Habermas: "If we assume that the human species maintains itself through the socially coordinated activities of its members and that this coordination has to be established through communication — and in certain central spheres through communication aimed at reaching agreement — then the reproduction of the species also requires satisfying the conditions of rationality that is inherent in communicative action" [Habermas (1984) Vol. 1:397]. In a later work Habermas (1996) points out: "The communication structures of the public sphere must be kept alive by an active civil society. The core of civil society comprises a network of associations that institutionalizes problems-solving discussion on questions of general interest inside the framework of organised public spheres [Habermas (1996):367]. He thus assigns a key role to civil society. He is for a civil society that draws its sustenance from the everyday life of the people.

The quality of public sphere depends on how best it is influenced by public reason without being manipulated by populist leaders, and vested interests which include the media. In the modern world both electronic and print media occupy a major role. Habermas highlights normative standards the media should follow to have meaningful deliberative politics and public sphere. He assumes that the public processes of communication can place with less distortion the more they are left to the internal dynamics of a civil society that emerges from the life-world. The media and political parties also will have to participate in the opinion and will-formation from the public's own perspective rather than patronising them and extracting mass loyalty from the public sphere for staying in power [Habermas (1996): 379]. Sometimes intellectuals and concerned citizens raise issues which find a natural entry into mass media and from that into public agenda. Critical judgment of citizens may have to be mobilized even with civil disobedience. In brief, building and maintaining a key public sphere based on public reason is crucial to a good democratic society. Habermas is criticized for not providing the link between pubic reason and public policy changes. In the words of Avritzer (2002): "Public debate and political deliberation should not be separated because both aim at not only creating societal consensus but also establishing more accountability for the exercise of power. Thus, a stranger mechanism than influence is required to connect the public sphere to the political system". [Avritzer (2002):50]. Not only that Habermas's exclusive emphasis on consensus as the aim of communication and his inadequate appreciation of differences and dissent as something necessarily to be overcome does not seem to be practicable. This is a major weakness of the approach of Habermas.

Joshua Cohen like Habermas is a radical democrat who owes a great deal to the ideas of "discursive democracy" of the latter. The ideal of "self-organising community of free and equal citizens" coordinating their collective ideas through their common reason [Habermas (1996):7) is clearly ambitious. In so far as deliberate public reason influences the performance of legislature, agencies, administration, courts and so on, it is a great step towards deepening democracy. Surely, what we are looking is not aggregation of individual interests, but reasoned public outcome. But this is a formidable task because of the realities of organised social and administrative power. Joshua Cohen suggests directly-deliberative polyarchy as a practical improvement on Habermas. "In directly – deliberative polyarchy, collective decisions are made through public deliberation in arenas open to citizens who use public services or who are otherwise regulated by public decisions" [Cohen (1999):411]. This approach recognises the limits of legislature and administration in problem-solving but seeks to empower and facilitate it through directly-deliberative arenas operating in closer proximity than the legislature to the problem [Cohen (1999):413]. The legislature can even declare certain areas of policy such as education, community safety, environmental health etc. to directly – deliberative polyarchic action. In brief, as a practical proposition there are virtually several areas and ways in which democratic values and problem-solving can be linked.

Leonardo Avritzer (2002) views democratisation as the construction of a democratic public sphere and introduces the concept of participatory public which involves (1) the formation at the public level of face to face deliberation, free expression and association (2) social movements and voluntary associations address contentious issues by introducing at the public level alternative practices (3) they reserve a space for administrative complexity and challenges the exclusive access of technocrats to decision making. Participatory publics reserve the right to monitor the administrative implementation of their decisions (4) they bind their deliberations with the attempt to search for institutional formats [Avritzer (2002):52].

Among the several other scholars who work for improving the quality of democracy, we may mention also Amartya Sen who argues for enhancing the quality of democracy which quintessentially is a 'government by discussion', the latter idea he elaborates in his Idea of Justice. Sen critically supports Rawls, Cohen, and Habermas. He points out how important openness of communication and argument is for formation of value [Sen (2009):336). For him democratic institutions are important for the instrumental role in the pursuit of justice and freedom. Democracy is evaluated and subjected to public scrutiny via public reasoning. That is a profound way of participation by people.

In sum, in this section we have tried to focus on a few democratic values essential for continuing the democratisation process through the writings of some outstanding scholars. Deliberation, building a public sphere and direct participation of citizens and working towards an inclusive society are all fundamental democratic values which are missing under the conventional institution of representative democracy. Deepening democracy cannot be conceptualized without reference to these foundational values.

**Democratising Local Governance**

In the latter part of the 1980s particularly after the fall of the Berlin Wall which discredited the centralised paradigm of development there has been a distinct swing of the pendulum towards decentralised governance. Decentralisation does not mean delegation or deconcentration but larger devolution of powers, responsibilities and authority to the lower tiers of government. It is the empowerment of the people through the empowerment of local governments [Oommen (2005): 223]. Admittedly it has tremendous potential to reduce transaction costs in the delivery of basic services like street lighting, sanitation, drinking water and the like. It is the best way to make social choices that reflect the will and preferences of the local people. There is no better feedback mechanism. Decentralisation also facilitates participation which is a good way for improving the accountability of state besides help to strengthen the ties between citizens and government officials. Participation helps to better civic ties through improved public discussion and resolution of conflicts.

Local governance has a critical role to play in deepening democracy and making it universally relevant and functionally vibrant. Local governance is a broader concept than local governments which are sub-national entities, created either constitutionally as in Brazil, India and South Africa, or by national or state legislations (e.g., United Kingdom, Canada, Pakistan) or even by executive order as in China. Boadway and Shah give a reasonably comprehensive definition of local governance thus: "Good local governance is not just about providing a range of local services but also about preserving the life and liberty of residents, creating space for democratic participation and civic dialogue, supporting market-led and environmentally sustainable local development, and facilitating outcomes that enrich the quality of life of residents" [Boadway and Shah (2009): 242]. Local governance is thus inclusive, participatory, and widens the public sphere and centers around the theme of improving the quality of citizen well-being in an environmentally sustainable manner.

Before we outline in the last part of this section (3.1) some normative or desirable features of a local governance structure that will help to deepen the democratisation in the countries of the world, it is important to note that as of now there is great diversity in the theory and practice of local governance in both the industrialised and developing countries. There is no uniform model. Actually there is no need for one. According to the First Global Report on Decentralisation and Local Democracy in the World (2008) more than half the countries in the Asia-pacific region have own source revenues (OSR) above 30 per cent of the total. The same holds in North America and Europe (around 40 per cent) [World Bank (2008):297]. A high OSR does not mean much if your expenditure responsibilities are deliberately kept low.

**Table 1: The Comparative Role of Local Government**

| *Countries* | *Local expenditure as percentage of total expenditures* |
|---|---|
| Africa | 7.9 |
| Asia | |
| South Asia | 16.0 |
| East Asia | 40.0 |
| South -East Asia | 15.5 |
| Eurasia | 26.5 |
| Europe (2008) | 23.9 |
| Latin America | 11.1 |
| Middle East and Western Asia | 4.6 |
| North America | 26.8 |

(*Source:* Second Global Report on Decentralisation and Local Democracy. 2010, p. 337).

How important are local governments in the governance of the countries of the world? The relative importance of local governments may be measured in terms of (a) the percentage of local expenditure to the consolidated public sector expenditure and (b) local expenditure as a percentage of GDP. Table 1 gives local expenditures as percentage of total expenditure for the major groups of countries and continents. The table shows that percentage ranges from a very low 4.6 per cent in Middle East and West Asia to 40 per cent in East Asia. A more disaggregated country-wise picture may be obtained from Fig.1.

It is evident that the Nordic countries are generally way ahead. Reckoned in terms of most parameters of local governance, one can firmly assert that the Nordic model comprising Denmark, Sweden and Norway constitute the best practice of good democratic governance. Enjoying considerable autonomy even under monarchic rule, as far back as 15th century local governments in Nordic countries "served their residents from cradle to grave", a really inclusive system. The Nordic model emphasizes small local governments (average jurisdiction of fewer than 10,000 inhabitants) that are primarily self-financing [Boadway and Shah (2009):267]. If we take 25 per cent as a global target of spending we set countries like Netherlands, Italy and UK as typical and if 20 per cent is taken as a norm, Latin American countries come out as a model as far as spending goes.

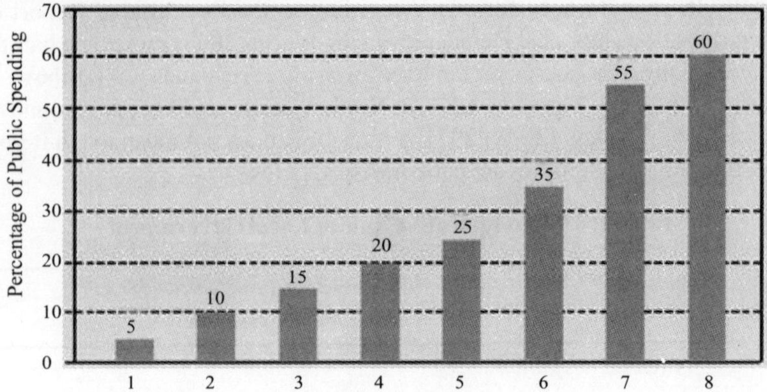


**Figure 1: Local Government Expenditures, Sample Countries**

[Legend: 1. Costa Rica, Nicaragua, Panama; 2. Botswana; Belarus; 3. Israel, France, Belgium; 4. Albania, Bulgaria, Poland; Latin American average; S. Africa; 5. Netherlands, Italy, UK; Uzbekistan; 6. Norway, Sweden, Finland; 7. Denmark; 8. N. Antilles].

(*Source:* First Global Report on Decentralisation and Local Democracy in the world. 2008 p. 296)

Needless to say, expenditure responsibilities must be matched by adequate revenue raising powers and transfer arrangements to those local governments short of funds through revenue-sharing and grants. A well designed transfer system, besides meeting a normatively assessed "vertical gap", can also help to reduce horizontal or inter-jurisdictional imbalances such as fiscal disadvantages or other disabilities due to physical and economic conditions. The State Finance Commission created under Article 243 (I) and 243 (Y) of the Indian Constitution, following the 73rd and 74th Amendments, is an institution designed to rectify the fiscal imbalances at the state sub-state level .

**Table 2: Relative Size of Local Government Expenditure with Reference to GDP in the Asian Pacific Region**

| *Countries* | *Local Public Expenditure (local and meso level only) percentage of GDP* |
|---|---|
| Australia | 2 per cent |
| China | 22 per cent |
| India | 2.42 per cent |
| Indonesia | 6 per cent |
| Japan | 12.3 per cent |
| Malayasia | 4 per cent |

| | |
|---|---|
| New Zealand | 3.9 per cent |
| Pakistan | 2.6 per cent |
| Korea , Rep. of | 16 per cent |
| Thailand | 2 per cent |
| Vietnam | 11 per cent |

[*Source:* First Global Report on Decentralisation and Local Democracy in the world. 2008 p. 68. For India Oommen (2010)].

Table 2 gives the percentage of local public expenditure to GDP of the countries of the Asia pacific region. We do not have corresponding figures for all countries of the world. Even this limited data shows the wide range in the magnitude. The percentage of local expenditure to GDP ranges from two per cent in Australia and Thailand and 2.42 per cent in India to 22 per cent in China. The average in OECD is around 12.75 per cent of GDP (Boadway and Shah (2009):283]. The higher expenditure responsibilities for local governments in China do not necessarily mean that they are essentially democratic. Delegation or deconcentration of responsibilities is different from giving autonomy and participation in decision-making by the people or their duly elected representatives.

**Towards a Responsive, Accountable and Participatory Local Governance**

Given the great diversity in the relative significance as well as in the practice of local governments in the world we may outline below certain basic postulates that must be borne in mind in any effort towards deepening local democracy.

First, there should be clarity about the functional responsibilities of local governments. Second functions should be matched by finance, either through own source revenue or through transfers. Other things being equal, a higher proportion of own source revenue shows greater autonomy and facilitates greater responsiveness to local demands and needs. Autonomy means not only greater freedom in determining spending priorities but also taxing powers and regulatory powers along with adequate authority to hire and fire employees. Without adequate autonomy it is difficult to have performance-based accountability and make innovative improvements in service delivery. It may be pointed out that the tendency of certain central governments to impose larger spending responsibilities unmatched by resources is clearly unhelpful to the growth of proper local governance. Such unfunded mandates are a burning issue in high income countries and some southern countries [World Bank (2008):297]. Third, the autonomy of the local governments should ensure adequate institutional support to harness the energies of the local community (e.g. gram sabha, the assembly of citizens at the village panchayats level in India) for facilitating people's participation and better social outcomes. Fourth, accountability to the local residents is the key to successful local democracy. The outstanding success of local democracy in Nordic countries and several other industrial countries is because local governments are accountable to the residents. The participatory budgeting initiative started in 1989 in Porto Alegre the capital city of Rio-Grande-Do-Sul in Brazil (which has spread to several other cities of Brazil and several Latin American States) has attracted worldwide attention for the participatory accountability outcomes. In the preparation and implementation of municipal Budget, the citizens have a critical role to play. The possibility of elite capture is virtually ruled out in this. Fifth, democratic local governance should never be bureaucratic and technocratic. Being participatory it works to strengthen citizen voice and exit options through direct democracy provisions, citizens' charters, performance budgeting, outcome monitoring, social audit and other participatory mechanisms. Participation is not only intrinsically valuable, it has tremendous instrumental importance in improving the quality of services and ensuring transparency in administration. Participation is facilitated through decentralisation. Therefore decentralised governance and participation should go together in local governance. Sixth, the primary goal of local governance should be social inclusion. Seventh, promoting civic dialogue and expanding the local public sphere should be the dominant approach. Leonard Avritzer's participatory public occurs when societal participatory practices are taken up by and embedded within the state. Eighth, neighbourhood groups (e.g. association of poor neighbouring households called Kudumbashree in Kerala, ward committees in South Africa) can play a key role in bridging the gap between local government and communities. All attempts towards co-option will have to be guarded against. What Buccus and Hicks observe after reviewing the role of ward committees in South Africa offer some useful insights to those concerned with democratisation with inclusion.

> It is clear that ward committees have great potential to bridge the growing divide between communities and municipalities, and facilitate greater community involvement in municipality planning..... this will require more than the allocation of significant resources to fund interventions such as training, consultative process and information disseminations but also the development of appropriate internal systems and guidelines, and appropriate attitudes and responses from municipality councillors and officials [Buccus and Hicks (2008): 536 in Mirjam Van Donketal (2008)].

**Local Governance and Deepening Democracy: The Tasks Ahead**

With the progress of decentralisation well underway in most countries of the world, local governments are increasingly assuming a larger role in public service delivery and even in local planning, budgeting and development [e.g. India (Kerala's People's Plan in particular), Brazil (e.g. participatory budgeting in Porto Alegre, Belo Horizonte, etc.) and South Africa]. Even so, with the exception of countries like Norway, Denmark, Sweden, Brazil and China, local governments continue to play a very small role in people's lives. Although in

China local governments enjoy a great role, from the participatory and democratic perspective, we may not highlight it as an exemplar. The real task ahead is to hasten and deepen the process of democratic decentralisation and participatory democracy.

Political will is critical. India's 73rd and 74th Constitutional Amendments have created the necessary conditions for the devolution of power and authority along with the mandate to 'plan for economic development and social justice'. But the progress since the amendments in 1993 is quite uneven and leaves many things to be desired. There is an evident lack of political will and bureaucratic dominance in many states in India.

A major problem for the local government such as municipalities and village panchayats in India is the lack of adequate fiscal empowerment as we have already pointed out. Unfunded functional responsibilities create serious problems at the cutting edge level. In an important sense taxation is a way of citizen participation in governance. This is generally ignored. What Boadway and Shah note is worth citing: "Political and bureaucratic leaders at the local level show little interest in lobbying for more taxing powers and instead, devote all their energies to seeing higher levels of fiscal transfers. As a result, tax decentralisation has not kept pace with political and expenditure decentralisation" [Boadway and Shah (2009):290]. A local governance system that depends on transfers from higner governments will find it difficult to ensure accountability, because local leaders do not have to justify local spending decisions to their electorates.

Another related question is autonomy a problem which was already discussed. That local governments are incapable and weak is a myth that needs to be exploded. Without that no innovative initiative is possible. Innovation is the essence of the new dispensation of local governance expected to work for social inclusion and public sphere. The three F's widely mentioned in the literature on decentralized governance in India viz., 'functional' autonomy meaning decision-making power in regard to the assigned functions, 'financial' autonomy, authority to spend without waiting for sanction from higher governments and 'functionary' autonomy or administrative autonomy, the power to appoint and make decisions regarding the terms of working of the employees under local governments.

Maintaining and sustaining citizen interest is a challenging task. Without that you cannot hopefully build a public sphere. The discussions made in Section 2.2. relating to the task of building an autonomous local public sphere are significant. It is clear public reason that should influence administrative decisions as well as policy formulation. Here the question of building civil society assumes importance because good citizens are moulded only in civil society. Citizenship is not a bundle of rights but essentially a matter of relationships the quality of which is important for local governance.

Deepening democracy involves wider acceptance at the macro level of the goal of reducing inequality notably income and wealth inequality as a crucial policy choice (See Section 2.1). Two doctors demonstrate with powerful arguments and empirical evidence that poor health and violence are more common in more unequal societies. In their words: "The evidence shows that reducing inequality is the best way of improving the quality of the social environment, and so the real quality of life for all of us" [Wilkinson and Pickett(2009):29]. The idea, arguments and evidence in this book are powerful enough to change political thinking. Will the political class and policy makers listen?

To conclude, deepening democracy through local governance has intrinsic, instrumental and evaluative significance. We have endeavoured to define the concept of deepening democracy and postulate a conceptual framework. It is high time we underscore the serious deficits in the ruling paradigm of representative democracy. World has witnessed a strong shift towards democratic decentralisation. Despite the pronounced shift in several countries towards democratic decentralisation, except in certain prominent countries like Norway, Sweden, Denmark, Switzerland and so on the role of local governments in people's lives is small. The great challenge is to expand and widen the democratisation process so that local democracy succeeds. India, Brazil, South Africa (IBSA), hold out a great promise and a powerful vision because these countries have the best statutory support system for local democracy among the countries of the world. Some powerful participatory initiatives of these countries offer persuasive lessons for all. The following quotation which is the oath of office of council members in the Athenian city is still an inspiring hope because it underlines the quality of citizenship, accountability and commitment needed to make the life of citizens beautiful and great.

> *We will strive increasingly to quicken the public sense of civic duty, that thus... we will transmit this city not only not less, but greater, better and more beautiful than it was transmitted to us.*
>
> *— Oath of office required of Council Members in the ancient city of Athens.*

**Notes**

- See Michael Ross (2006), Haggard and Kaufman (2008), Gupta and Pushkar (2011), among others.
- For Habermas all actors are equally capable of mastering language and introducing arguments at the public level. This indeed is a heroic assumption.
- The Fourth State Finance Commission of Kerala (India) has made an attempt to rectify these imbalances and provides for the inclusion of the excluded as part of state to local government transfers. [See Government of Kerala (2011)].
- Municipalities in South Africa have to be proactively engaged in the initial ground work of establishing, performance indicators and monitoring systems for efficient service delivery.

- Social audit is a method of public scrutiny of local governments. This idea was embedded in the structure of decentralised governance and people's planning of Kerala, in India. A well conducted social audit can be used to subject bureaucrats to scrutiny by the citizenry.
- For e.g., the principle of community participation and accountability is placed "at the very heart of the South African system of local government after 1994". [Fuluthelo G. Netswera (2008):511] in Mirjam Van Dock et. al. (2008).
- Michelle Esau (2007) who supports South Africa's programme of deepening democracy through local participation raises several issues such as elitism, equal participation rendered difficult due to poverty, unemployment, poor awareness and lack of resources for the community.

## References

Avritzer, Leonardo (2002): *Democracy and the Public Space in Latin America,* Princeton University Press, New Jersey.

Boadway, Robin and Anwar Shah (2009): *Fiscal Federalism: Principles and Practice of Multi-order Governance,* Cambridge University Press.

Buccus, Imraan and Janine Hicks (2008): 'Democratisation with inclusion: Revisiting the role of ward committees', in Van Donk Mirjam, ed. (2008); *Consolidating Local Development: Lessons from the South African Experience,* UTC Press. Cape Town

Cohen, Joshua (1999): 'Reflections on Habermas on Democracy', *Ratio Juris,* Vol. 12 No. 4.

Crenson, A. Mathew and Benjamin Ginsberg (2004): *Downsizing Democracy: How America Sidelined its Citizens and Privatised its Public,* JHU Press.

Dunn, John (1992), (ed.): *Democracy The Unfinished Journey 508 BC to AD 1993,* Oxford University Press, New York.

Esau, Michelle (2007): 'Deepening democracy through local participation', paper downloaded from the website http://www.accede.co.za/downloads/DBBS%20Paper%206%20Esau.pdf

Gould, C. Colin (1988): *Rethinking Democracy,* Cambridge University Press.

Government of Kerala (2011): *Report of the 4th State Finance Commission, Vol. I and II Thiruvananthapuram.*

Gupta, Madhvi and Pushkar (2011): 'Democracy and Health: Evidence from Indian States', *Economic and Political Weekly,* Vol. XLVI No. 40, October 1, 2011.

Habermas, Jurgen (1984): *The Theory of Communicative Action,* (Translated by: Thomas Burger with the assistance of Frederick Lawrence) MIT Press, Cambridge, Massachusetts.

_____________ (1991): *The Structural Transformation of the Public Sphere,* (translated by Thomas Burger with the assistance of Frederick Lawrence) MIT Press, Cambridge, Massachusetts.

_____________ (1996): *Between Facts and Norms,* (translated by William Rehg), MIT Press, Cambridge, Massachusetts.

Haggard, Stephan and Robert R. Kaufman (2008): *Development, Democracy, and Welfare States: Latin America, East Asia, and Eastern Europe,* Princeton University Press.

Huntington, Samuel P. (1991): 'How Countries Democratise', *Political Science Quarterly,* Vol. 106, No. 4 (Winter 1991-92) pp. 579-616.

Netswera, G., Fuluthelo (2008): 'A Case Study of Community Participation in Governance and Service Delivery in the City of Johannesburg' in Van Donk Mirjam, ed. (2008).

Oommen, M.A. (2005): 'Rural Fiscal Decentralisation in India: A Brief Review of Literature' in L.C. Jain ed., *Decentralisation and Local Governance,* Orient Longman.

____________ (2010): 'The 13th Finance Commission and the third Tier', *Economic and Political Weekly,* Nov. 27, 2010, Vol. XLV, No. 48.

Rawls, John (1972): *A Theory of Justice,* Clarendon Press, Oxford.

Ross, Michael (2006): 'Is Democracy Good for the Poor?', *American Journal of Political Science,* Vol. 50, No. 4, October 2006, pp. 860-874

Sen, Amartya (1999): *Development as Freedom,* Oxford University Press

__________ (2000): 'Social Exclusion: Concept, Application, and Scrutiny', *ADB Social Development Paper No. 1,* Asian Development Bank, Manila, Philippines.

__________ (2009): *The Idea of Justice,* Allen Lane, Penguin Books.

Skocpol, Theda (2003): *Diminished Democracy: From Membership to Management in American Civic Life.* Norman, OK: University of Oklahoma Press.

UNDP (2002): *Human Development Report*, Oxford University Press, New York.

Wilkinson, Richard and Kate Pickett (2009): *The Spirit Level - Why Equality is Better for Everyone,* Penguin books.

World Bank (2008): *Decentralisation and Local Democracy in the World,* A Co-publication of the World Bank and United Cities and Local Governments.

World Bank (2010): 'Local Government Finance: The Challenges of the 21st Century', *Second Global Report on Decentralisation and Local Democracy,* United Cities and Local Governments.

# 15

# *The Rajya Sabha: To Abolish or To Re-orient?*

*R.L.M. Patil*

Rajya Sabha, the Upper Chamber of the Indian Parliament made its first appearance as the Council of State in 1919 under the Government of India Act, as recommended by the Montague-Chelmsford Report. Hardly has any significant change occurred in its near-hundred years journey. Even when the leading lights of the nation sat together for months to devise a new constitution for independent India in 1946-1949 there was a conspicuous neglect of what should be the role, power and function of the Rajya Sabha or as it was then called the Council of States in the text of Constitution.

It was generally believed inside as well as outside that the role of an Upper House in the bicameral legislature was to hold dispassionate, non-partisan, learned and dignified discussions on several public issues which would not have been possible in case of a single House dominated by elected members who would mostly be hasty, politically-charged, inexperienced, youthful and ambitious. If the single House popularly elected was a tea-cup containing hot tea, the Upper House was to be a saucer which would have tea poured to spread and cool. The respective powers of the two Houses would not and should not be equal but complementary. This is how the utility of the Upper House/ the Council of States/Rajya Sabha was perceived to be by the members of the Constituent Assembly. In a debate lasting for a few minutes, the upper House was at most termed as "acceptable" at the Central level but not at all at the provincial level at which H.V. Kamath described as "pernicious". As if in a state of near-absentmindedness the Constituent Assembly adopted the proposal to continue the Council of State. It is significant that the mover of the resolution as well as supporters of it visualised its nature as an element of democracy rather than a federal apparatus. Compared with any other federal legislature in the world our Rajya Sabha is the least representative of the state units. In the United States, Switzerland and Germany, for example, the federal Upper houses are truly representatives/ guardians of the states' interests. The members are elected or controlled by the people or the Government of their respective states. The German Bundesrat is composed of states ministers or their alternates. The federal Government there cannot constitutionally ignore or override the states' rights or concerns in legislative and executive matters. In fact, the federal lower house elected popularly can be taken for granted by the Prime Minister/ Chancellor since his Government is supported by the majority of the house, but he literally has to beg concurrence from the Upper House in most of the matters federal, executive, legislative or administrative. In India, however, the Rajya Sabha is not intended either by design or by practice to act as the guardian of the rights or concerns of the states; it acts simply as an upper chamber in a unitary Government in a democratic set-up.

It happens often that State legislature which sends its 'representatives' to the Rajya Sabha for a period of six long years, undergoes a change of political complexion within a short period after electing the representatives. An 'opposition' party may come to power in the State either for reason of fresh elections to the State Assembly or defections or coalitional politics. Yet the old selections of the M.Ps of Rajya Sabha continue to hold. This betrays the concept of Rajya Sabha members being the guardians or representatives of their respective states. The ruling parties of the states and the ruling party at the centre often are found to be rivals and settling political scores. Party-politics thus weakens the character and strength of the Rajya Sabha as an upper chamber symbolising States' rights.

It is also noticed that the Rajya Sabha has not always held dignified, learned, dispassionate, nonpartisan discussions as expected of it. Many times there are witnessed undignified, partisan and unproductive debates. Professor of Political Science from Bombay University and a member of the Minority Commission, Prof. Aloo J. Dastur, told the conference of Indian Political Science Association (December 28, 1978):

> The way the Indian Parliament especially the Rajya Sabha has been conducting itself for several weeks reminds one of a similar situation in England in the first decade of the (20th) century. The House of Lords kept on obstructing the work of the popularly elected House of commons and here is the Rajya Sabha obstructing and holding up the entire business of the Indian Parliament. Perhaps the time has come when we as political scientists, teachers and students of parliamentary government, have to give serious thought to the conduct of the elders. Is it necessary, or is it even useful to have a second chamber?... The old English cry 'either mend the House of Lords or end it' raised in the election of 1910 could very well be the rallying cry (here now).

The observation of the learned Professor was not related to an isolated incident. As early as 1954 the Rajya Sabha was angered by the remark of a venerated member of the Lok Sabha N.C. Chatterjee that the Upper House which was "supposed to be a body of the elders seems to be behaving irresponsibly like a pack of urchins". In the eighties the Members of Rajya Sabha who belonged to the ruling Congress party, behaved in such an ugly and unruly fashion that the Presiding Officer, the Vice-President of India, a very much Congressman, Dr Shankar Dayal Sharma, wept, sobbed and wiped off tears from his eyes and begged the elderly members to behave! In recent years another scandalous development is taking place, affecting adversely the stature of the Rajya Sabha. Many business houses, tax-evaders, scamsters and those whose interests are very far from Parliamentary pursuits, are vying to contest elections to the Rajya Sabha from state Assemblies - a proposition which works out to be rather cheap compared to the cost of fighting elections to the Lok Sabha. Often, candidates come from different states: Ram Jethamalani from Karnataka, M.A. Chidambaram from Karnataka, S.R. Bommai from Orissa, Man Mohan Singh from Assam, L.K. Advani from Gujarat and so on. This phenomenon is unique to Indian federation. As observed by Prof. Bhavani Singh: "The Rajya Sabha has become an exotic transplanted on our soil - it represents neither the people nor the Government, nor the State legislatures".

Another Professor of Political Science points out that though N. Gopalaswamy Ayyangar, a leading light in the Constituent Assembly's Drafting Committee, had assured that the proposed Upper House would give an opportunity to seasoned people to participate in the debate with an amount of learning and to hold dignified debates, the House has on several occasions become a refuge for the old, defeated, prestige-hungry, and party-loyalists. As though this was not bad enough, a tendency allegedly to purchase the seats in the Rajya Sabha has been noticed. Maladroit political practices have been observed almost all over the world in all systems: democratic, dictatorial, communist, liberal or any other. Mahatma Gandhi having noticed how his Congressmen were falling a prey to the attractions of the offices of power after 1937 elections, had called for disbandment of the national party famous so far for its sacrifices and ideals. But as power drew nearer, the ideals themselves were being sacrificed. He repeated this call for dissolution of the Congress a few hours before his death. His wishes went unheeded. Corrupt electoral practices in the elections to the popular house, the Lok Sabha, however undesirable is understandable. But in the elections to the Rajya Sabha — a house meant for the elderly, wise, unselfish, learned, dignified, non-partisan and honorable counsels — money power is playing a role which is quite disturbing. Not for all seats in all the states but for a few seats in a few states, from 1952 onwards, various political parties have placed a price for giving support to the aspirants of membership of the Rajya Sabha. This price is not always, but many times, in terms of monetary funds to the political parties or their leaders or their relations. Sometimes, it is a political trade off - say, lending a helping hand in saving a tottering government at the state or at the Centre, communal appeasement, taking away the intelligence agencies' attention on some of the misdemeanor of politicians, etc. It is a sad commentary on the Indian political system that this suave cunningness is practiced by almost all the political parties. Examples of the members who have come or tried to come, to the portals of the Rajya Sabha through these dubious corridors are a plenty.

Some of them have been those who are facing huge income-tax penalty, NRIs who want a firm foothold here, politicians who are rejected by the people in general elections, old never-say-die politicians (one among whom was paralysed and unable to speak or recognize people!), relations of the party heavy-weights, former bureaucrats and judges who had obliged the ruling party in their careers, businessmen and sports administrators who have been generous to their political friends, and so on. Even the nominated members of the Rajya Sabha that is, twelve members who are nominated by the President of India on the advice of the Cabinet/Prime Minister for reasons of their having made distinct and outstanding contributions, and made the nation proud, are not above a murmur of doubt. It includes famous movie stars and singers who never opened their mouths during the debates in the House, internationally famous musicians who did not find time to sit in the House but asked for a chunk of government land to establish music academy, or those who worked for the most influential leaders from behind the scene. They were not corrupt, but were not interested in the activities in the House. On the whole, the Rajya Sabha has come to acquire lot of flab, lost shape and lost sight of the original purpose for which it was created, actually or supposedly. The Constitution-makers obviously did not spend much time or thought on the place of the Rajya Sabha in our Constitutional set-up. The centrality of a federal Chamber of the constituent state units was not in their minds. The shape and character of the Council of State envisaged in 1919 under the Government of India Act, sponsored by the British rulers, continues to be with us even today without any significant changes. B.N. Rau and B.R. Ambedkar in the critical months of preparing the Draft Constitution and even as late as October 1949, toyed with the idea of introducing two key provisions into the Constitution, which would have the effect of (a) Strengthening the states vis-à-vis the centre (b) Strengthening the President vis-a-vis the Prime Minister and (c) Promoting federalisation rather than centralisation. The twin provisions provided for setting out Instrument of Instructions for the President (and Governors of states) and an Advisory Board on Appointments. If accepted, these provisions would have gone a long way in liberating the President of India (and likewise the state Governors) from the vice-like grip which the Prime Minister (Chief Ministers of states) hold on the head of state. For, the Instrument would have given the President a free hand in the choice of Ministers and exercise his own discretion in several important ways. The Board comprising fifteen members of the Parliament (both Houses), elected through proportional representation, would tender advice to the President on the appointment of the Chief Justice, Judges of the Supreme Court and High Courts, Ambassadors, Auditor-General of India, Chairman and Members of the UPSC and Election Commission. These proposals would have eroded definitely the powers and influence of the Prime Minister and Union Government as well as the clout of the ruling political party at the centre. States would also have got a say in influencing the decision of the President to the detriment of the ruling coterie in New Delhi. Perhaps, that is why the suggestions were spiked without full and proper debate in the Constituent Assembly. Dr. B.R. Ambedkar first proposed an amendment to Draft Constitution to incorporate these two provisions when Prime Minister Pt. Jawaharlal Nehru was away touring the United States on his first visit to that country. When the Prime Minister returned, Dr. Ambedkar requested the Constituent Assembly to cancel the amendment which had been advocated by himself earlier. Incidentally, these provisions existed in the Government of India Act, 1935, which was on the whole incorporated into the Constitution of India to an estimated extent of 80 per cent! The details of discussions which were held among the leaders on the subject remain a state secret.

Now that we can assess the working of the Constitution, especially with respect to federalism, it is hoped that the Rajya Sabha's role and functions could be subjected to an in-depth review. A near-hundred old legislative appendix which hardly fulfils a federal requirement could be cut out altogether, without affecting the efficacy of the Union Parliament. Or else, it would be prudent to consider re-orienting the institution towards the achievement of a true-blooded federation as well as full-flowering of democratic system. In this latter option, it would be worthwhile to redefine the composition and functions of the present Rajya Sabha on the following lines, subject to modifications after a full debate.

Firstly, the members of the Rajya Sabha should be named by the constituent states and Union Territories. Big or small all states should send equal number of members (Two, for instance for states and one for UTs). They should be replaceable by a new set of people whenever there is a change in the governments of states. Further, their functioning should be in accordance with the wishes of the states.

Secondly, the President of India should be required to obtain the approval of the Rajya Sabha before or after the dismissal of a State Government and imposition of the President's Rule in that state. The appointment of Governors should also be done by the President in consultation with the Rajya Sabha. The federal Officer/ posts of importance like the Chief Justice and Judges of the Supreme Court and High Courts, Auditor-General, Chairman and Members of the Election Commission, Finance Commission, Planning Commission, U.P.S.C, U.G.C., etc., should be made by the President of India only after the Rajya Sabha endorses his recommendations. This is a time-honored Constitutional practice in the U.S.

The Rajya Sabha need not be burdened with the duplication of work being done by the Lok Sabha. In the matters of legislation, executive, administration or finance if there is a significant impact upon the states, the centre should be obliged to seek the approval mandatorily from the Rajya Sabha, as in Germany for example.

Many myths have come up in connection with making of the Constitution of India. One of them is that it is a totally new Constitution drawn up after a prolonged discussion among the popularly elected members of the Constituent

Assembly. In fact, the 1949 Constitution appears to be a continuation of the Government of India Act 1935, even as Dr. B.R. Ambedkar liked it. A few additions like the Fundamental rights and Directive Principles were added to it, which were not there in the 1935 Act. Many provisions crept into the final text of the Constitution without ever being discussed or raised in the constituent Assembly like the Treaty-making power of the centre or the Inter-state council. The Rajya Sabha or the Council of States as a successor to the Council of State under the Government of India Acts 1919 and 1935, was another instance of institutional survival on account mostly of absentmindedness of the rulers of the state. It is better to re-orient it and make it serve the immanent interest of federalism and democracy before it becomes an object of ridicule.

# 16

# *Water Issues in India: External and Internal Dynamics*

*Uttam Kumar Sinha*

**Value of Water**

There is an adage that says that you don't know the true worth of water till the wells run dry. For that matter even the 'Blue Planet', as the earth is referred to, has an instructive irony to its description. It tells us the value of water which we often tend to ignore. While water covers 73 per cent of the planet only three per cent is fresh water, of which two per cent is held in ice caps and glaciers. The remaining one per cent in the form of rivers, streams, lakes, ponds, swamps and marshes, is non-frozen, salt-free and accessible for human consumption. This amount also includes the ground water available.

The dependence of society on groundwater resources is also growing rapidly. Globally, groundwater accounts for about 50 per cent of pumping for drinking water, and 20 per cent for irrigation. In India, 80 per cent of agricultural production depends on groundwater and in the arid and semi-arid zones, 60 per cent of the water used for irrigation comes from groundwater. Knowledge on groundwater resources is also not exact. For example, are aquifers determined by political boundaries? What exactly are their renewal flows and their stocks? What impact does groundwater have on surface water (river flows, precipitations infiltration, groundwater pollution, etc.)? Importantly, how fast do they replenish?

We live in a world with limited availability of water, which is unevenly distributed. There is approximately the same amount of water on earth today as when it was formed. Since we cannot create more water than what nature provides us or discover it like oil, the 'Blue Planet' teach us not to be wasteful and manage water optimally. As global economic activity and development continues, increase in water demand will be compounded by the decreasing availability of water resources in most major hydraulic basins, either because of deterioration in quality or quantity. This drop in availability affects surface water in a visible and immediate way, and leads to further enhancing the value of groundwater. Competition for groundwater becomes an additional factor of social and political instability, both internally and regionally.

The following facts make water a challenging issue. First, water is indispensable and the ultimate renewable resource. Second, water is being severely impacted by global population increase and economic growth. Together they are extracting and polluting it faster than it can be replenished. Third, the ever-expanding gap between demand and supply will potentially make water a contested issue particularly in densely populated countries. Fourth, since disputes over water are inevitable because of the changes, as described above, understanding the processes of resolution and framing new mechanisms and approaches becomes a necessity.

Water is also an unruly resource and a source of instability because sovereignty over water is not determined by formal international law. Water, unlike oil, is a trans-boundary resource. A large volume of water-over 90 per cent, crosses international borders. It is difficult to determine whether water is a 'public good' (defined as non-rival and non-excludable) or 'private good' (defined as rival and excludable). Such amorphous definitional demarcation subjects trans-boundary rivers to various interpretations. That said, there is, a general view to perceive it as 'collective good' or 'common pool resource.' In spite of the 1997 United Nations Convention on the Law of the Non-Navigational Uses of International Watercourses, which has yet to be ratified, there exists no legally binding watercourse treaty. In the light of this, the Himalayan region's hydro-politics needs to be oriented in a manner that the optimum development of rivers is possible through mutual cooperation and hydrological observation.

**Internal Dynamics**

The World Bank in its 1999 report indicates that the overall water demand for India will increase from 552 BCM (Billion Cubic Metres) to 1050 BCM by 2025, which will require the use of all available water resources in the country. The per capita water availability according to the report has dropped from over 5,000 cubic metres per year in 1947 to less than 2,000 cubic metres per year in 1997 and by 2025, this figure will further drop to 1,500 cubic metres per year, which is well below the level at which water stress is considered to occur. The report also lists six of India's 20 major river basins below the water scarcity threshold of 1,000 cubic metres per year. The Mckinsey Report (2009) suggests that by 2030, water demand in India will grow to almost 1.5 trillion M3, principally driven by population growth and the domestic need for rice, wheat and sugar. According to the Report, the current water supply is approximately 740 billion M3. Clearly, the drivers of future water challenge are essentially tied to development and economic growth with the agriculture sector as the largest water withdrawer. The interplay of food, energy and water (FEW) within the complex context of population increase, rising standards of living and resource constraints poses interlocking challenges to sustainable environmental policies.

In India water security has been high on the national agenda. Prime Minister Manmohan Singh's 2004 Independence Day speech highlighted the importance of water. He identified water as one of the saat sutras requiring special attention. The challenge outlined by him was one of managing water resources as well as ensuring people's participation in water management and conservation. The Prime Minister said: '*Water is a national resource, and we have to take an integrated view of our country's water resources, our needs and our policies and water utilisation practices. We need to ensure the equitable use of scarce water resources...I urge you and all our political leaders to take a national and holistic view of the challenge of managing our water resources.*' Earlier, in his address to the nation on June 24, 2004, Manmohan Singh had observed: '*Water has emerged as a critical and contentious issue across the country...the government will reverse the neglect of public investment in irrigation, addressing the specific problems of each river basin, in an environment and people friendly manner.*'

India has a range of data reports on water. At the national level, a comprehensive document titled "Integrated Water Resource Development: A Plan for Action", published in 1999, by the Ministry of Water Resources, provided a comprehensive summary of data, problems and policies. This was followed by the National Water Policy 2002. One of the latest documents on water is from the Prime Minister's Council on Climate Change, of June 2008, entitled, "National Action Plan of Climate Change (NAPCC)". It envisages eight national missions of which the National Water Mission is central to the action Plan. It states: '*A National Water Mission will be mounted to ensure integrated water resources management helping to conserve water, minimise wastage and ensure more equitable distribution both across and within states. The Mission will take into account the provisions of National Water Policy and develop a framework to optimize water uses and by increasing water use efficiency by 20 per cent through regulatory mechanisms and differential entitlements and pricing.*'

The National Water Mission will encounter varied challenges in the light of rising population, changing expectations due to economic growth and climate change related impacts. The more recent national water document based on new understanding and knowledge and a unified national perspective is the "Draft National Water Policy (2012)" as recommended by the National Water Board of the Ministry of Water Resources.[1] It re-looks, reconsiders and candidly observes some of the earlier water approaches and management practices. For example, it says: '*With a growing population and rising needs of a fast developing nation as well as the given indications of the impact of climate change, availability of utilisable water will be under further strain in future with the possibility of deepening water conflicts among different user groups*'.[2] It further says: '*Low consciousness about the scarcity of water and its life sustaining and economic value results in its mismanagement, wastage, and inefficient use, as also pollution and reduction of flows below minimum ecological needs. In addition, there are inequities in distribution and lack of a unified perspective in planning, management and use of water resources.*'[3] Significantly, it states that internal water management cannot be delinked from the external water approaches: '*Inter-regional, inter-State, intra-State, as also inter-sectoral disputes in sharing of water, strain relationships and hamper the optimal utilisation of water through scientific planning on basin/sub-basin basis.*'[4]

A growing need to synchronise internal water management measures with external riparian policies is thus critical. Although India has low per capita water consumption; it lags in the efficient use of water across sectors. Continued population growth and the impact of global warming along with inadequate conservation and huge wastage are putting enormous pressure on water resources.

Water security for India implies effective responses to changing water conditions in terms of quality, quantity and uneven distribution. Unheeded it can impact relationships at the inter-state level and equally contribute to tensions at the intra-provincial level. Indian policymakers need to be sensitised to the challenges of dealing with such complexities.

It must be remembered that the biggest challenge will be the imbalance between population and available water supplies and this will be a common concern in India where crop production depends heavily on irrigation. This is similar in China and Pakistan as well. Other internal water challenges will be groundwater depletion and resultantly increase of unwanted salts in the soil. Groundwater depletion alone places 10 to 20 per cent of grain production in India at risk.

As farmers lose access to irrigation water and see their livelihoods deteriorate, they may not only resort to violent protest but migrate across borders and to restive and already overcrowded cities. Internal water stresses will add to the burden of humanitarian crises. It is projected that an additional billion people will be added water-stressed countries over the next 15 years with demand for food rapidly increasing particularly in India, China and Pakistan. While these countries are currently grain self-sufficient, it may not remain so for reasons of water and land scarcity. In recent times a new level of water-related tension has emerged over the ownership of water especially from public authorities to private multinational corporations.

**Constitutional and Legal Perspective**

The legal framework of water in India is diverse and has been developed over a long period of time. It draws elements from ancient local customs and traditions and during the Colonial times laws on irrigation was framed. International conventions such as the Helsinki Rules and the 1997 UN Convention also strengthen the water laws. Principles and norms of 'equitable share' and 'no significant harm' help in dealing with inter-provincial disputes. Discourses such as 'water as a human right' and maintaining the 'environmental flow' has equally influenced water laws in India.

Constitutionally water is a state subject (Entry 17 in the State List). Central intervention comes in when there is an inter-provincial water dispute. The provisions (Entry 56 in the Union List) are clearly laid out in the Rivers Board

Act (1956) and the Inter-State River Water Disputes Act (1956). The latter empowers the Centre to set up tribunals to adjudicate disputes over water sharing. The Centre can also intervene in the interest of protecting the environment or for developing a water basin "expedient in the public interest" by enacting a law to give the Union the legislative power over the river. No law till date has been passed to bring any river under the Union. Water has thus been divided in the Constitutional scheme with the Centre and the State having the power to legislate over various aspects and demonstrating in the process the separation of power. Placing water as a State subject was part of the federal exercise to deepen and wider democracy. Since water and people are closely related and connected religiously and culturally it was only appropriate for water to be decentralised.

There has emerged recently the debate whether water should be put in the Concurrent List and whether by doing so would mean centralisation. In fact it opens up the old debate of whether the constitutional provisions over water need to be relooked. Some earlier commissions, particularly the Sarkaria Commission, constituted to look at the Centre-State relations have not favoured any changes. In times of coalition politics, greater claim for decentralisation and enhancing federalism, shifting water to the Concurrent List would clearly be a retrograde step. Water experts like Ramaswamy Iyer strongly feel that the enabling provisions of Entry 56 should be fully utilised and the Rivers Board Act be activated.[5]

There also has been considerable development on the aspect of human right to water and water rights. However, both are legally and conceptually different. First, though not incorporated explicitly in the Constitution, there is a fundamental right to water for every person in India that has been judicially evolved over the years. For example, 'Right to life' under Article 21 has been interpreted as an entitlement for 'pollution free' and 'safe drinking' water for every person. The closest that the law makers have come to incorporating right to water as a fundamental right was when the National Commission in 2002 recommended that a new Article 30D be inserted in the Constitution. It has yet to be enacted.[6] The fundamental right to water may not be forever elusive. After all the right to education of a child from 6-14 years of age was also judicially evolved and eventually became a fundamental right under Article 21A.

Second, the Constitutional space relevant for water rights and management is expressed through parts IX and IXA of the 73rd and 74th Amendments that came into effect in 1993. The two amendments brought in local self-governance as an enforceable ideal and obliges states to create local bodies to "function as institutions of self-government" in rural and urban areas. The panchayats as institutions of self-governance were given power and authority and subjects like drinking water, water management and even minor irrigation and watershed development came under jurisdiction of the panchayats. In the urban areas, municipalities were given similar powers of self-governance looking after matters like water supply for domestic, industrial and commercial purposes. The 73rd and 74th amendments led to what is described as "inspired changes" in the panchayats, Municipal Corporation and Municipal Council laws leading to responsibility and accountability in the services provided particularly water.

**External Dynamics**

Trans-boundary rivers are a significant part of the freshwater biome and contribute to 60 per cent of world's freshwater excluding the Antarctica.[7] There are about 260 river basins of which 200 are shared by two or more countries with roughly 145 sharing treaties in existence.[8] These rivers physically link upstream and downstream users. Since most of the rivers are trans-boundary in nature originating from, flowing through and draining into territorially defined boundaries, riparian relations will be critical. Given that states as actors operate within the constraints of an international system that essentially remains anarchic and that states are not only 'guardians of their own security and independence'[9] but also 'rational egoists',[10] water can assume hegemonic attribution. As major parts of the globe experience high levels of water-stress, the water sector is likely to get contentious. The possession or capture and control of water resources can easily lead to aggressiveness and can equally translate into power and dominance.

While undoubtedly the basins offer ample opportunity for harnessing development benefits serving as a cornerstone for co-operation, it equally, given the competitiveness of the users (riparian states) and the uses of rivers (primarily in terms of consumptive utilisation), can potentially trigger tension and strife. With population increase and corresponding consumption patterns, it is projected that by 2030 the demand for water will be 40 per cent more than at current level and 50 per cent higher in the most rapidly developing countries that include India and China.[11] It is further projected that two out of every three people on the planet will live in water-stressed conditions by the year 2030.[12] According to UN estimates the bulk of population increase (roughly 7.5 to nine billion by 2050) will be in countries that are experiencing water shortages.

**Water in South Asia**

Water is now being increasingly viewed as an issue of urgency in South Asia. The Subcontinent with its rising population, increasing urbanisation and unchecked poverty has added enormous pressure to the existing water sources and with no proportional increase in availability, water challenges seem imminent. The trans-boundary nature of water as seen through the rivers that crisscross the South Asian states makes it intensely political and contentious while simultaneously creates opportunities for hydro-co-operation. Hydro-politics will increasingly factor in state dynamics both between (inter) and within (intra). While there exists no internationally binding watercourse treaty, the allocation of river water at the bilateral and regional level assumes great significance. The shared nature of these challenges requires both macro and micro-level collaborations such as integrated water management efforts between governments.

South Asian states will have to juggle competing and conflicting food-energy-water (FEW) concerns, yielding a set of difficult consequences. A 'perfect storm' of food-energy-water shortages by 2030 has already been predicted.[13] These sets of critical drivers will present difficult-to-manage outcomes and will reinforce each other as never before. First, as population grows, competition for food, energy and water will correspondingly increase. Increasing demand for food grains will claim larger areas of cropland and greater volumes of irrigation water. Second, with the risks that climate change attaches, FEW will be subject to various stresses and strains. Clearly, for South Asian countries food security cannot be achieved without water security. India for example feeds 17 per cent of the world's population but has only 4 per cent of water.

South Asia is home to about 34 per cent of Asia's population (1/6th of world's population) and has about four per cent of world's annual renewable water resources that flows through several river basins.[14] Almost 95 per cent of water in the region is consumed by the agriculture sector as compared to the world's average of 70 per cent. Except for Nepal and Bhutan, the per capita water availability is falling below the world average. It is projected that the per capita water availability in India is rapidly declining. For the year 2025 at a projected population of 1.3 billion, the water availability will be 1341 cubic meter per person per year.[15]

Of significant importance is the fact that planning any water resource utilisation policy will have to take into account the assessment of the impact of climate change in terms of seasonal flow and extreme events. In both direct and indirect ways climate change is related to water as is evidenced through floods, drought and glacial melt.

**Climate Change and Water Resources**

Another factor that needs to be incorporated into water policy is the climate change-connect. It is now being increasingly understood that the effects of global warming will be felt through changes in the hydrological cycle. An effective adaptation policy cannot be delinked from the way water resources are managed and utilized. The impact of global warming on water resources is particularly important for the Himalayan states that are highly dependent on glacial sources of rivers in the Hindu Kush. Initial findings of the ongoing research indicate increased precipitation in some areas and increased variability of precipitation in others. Changes in precipitation and evapor-transpiration will greatly influence groundwater recharge. The expected decline in glaciers and snowfields will affect the flow of rivers, and increase the likelihood of floods due to overall increase in intensity of rainy days. A policy that awaits clear evidence may not be prudent. A precautionary approach and alertness to possible changes is a wiser option.

The role of enforcement and monitoring agencies like the EIA (Environment Impact Assessment) needs to be effectively enforced in respective countries. The purposeful participation of the civil-society will be equally crucial for greater awareness and balance of development and water resources.

In the Himalayan region the GLOF problem, as explained earlier, is compounded by the fact that there is a lack of long-term data. Research on climate change impact on glacial needs to be intensified at a regional level and co-operation should entail sharing of data. The present state of knowledge is inadequate in identifying and assessing the magnitude of potential outbreaks of glacial lakes. GLOF risks has to be soberly assessed and not heightened therefore leading to misperception. Countries in the region with trust deficit can easily misinterpret overstated risks particularly downstream countries. Regional cooperation will need to factor in enhanced and updated forms of an automated early warning system. Also upgraded remote sensing projects are important for flood warning systems because they can detect small changes in lake levels and send immediate signals to alarm systems near villages. Research and risk evaluation will also require ground-level surveys.

Another important feature which each individual state has to consider is to integrate and harmonize external water policies with internal water resource management. Such an approach would require treating river systems, particularly the Ganges-Brahmaputra-Meghna (GBM) and the Indus in a holistic way and reorienting hydro-diplomacy on a multilateral basis than just a bilateral format. This would entail a shift from 'sharing waters' to 'sharing benefits'. Ecological considerations should be the overarching perspective. This would easily allow a far greater understanding on the nature and impact of climate change on water resources. In the past the dominant perspective was engineering and economics now the emphasis should be on ecology and climate change. Keeping the principle of just and wise-use of water, sensible riparian policies can be framed both internally and externally.

The combination of rising population, increased urbanisation, and rapid economic growth compounds the challenges of securing water in the future. Asia, the most populous continent has also the lowest water per capita in the world. Figures indicate that one in five people in the region do not have access to clean water. With an additional 500 million people expected in the next 10 years in the Himalayan watershed states, the stress on food, energy and water resources will only increase. It is thus important to understand the Himalayan region in terms of 'exponential function'-increasing population leading to greater food demand that increases dependence on water for irrigation and energy. The interconnection of food-energy-water (FEW) is crucial, and if not framed sensibly into state polices the cascading effect on food production, livelihood, and migration, will impact political stability in the region. What becomes worrisome is the likelihood of competition over water resources. Though the possibility of water being a direct cause of conflict is unlikely, however, given that the Himalayan watershed is fraught with tensions, water can act as a dangerous trigger and destabilise the region.

**Himalayan Hydrology**

It is being fast established that the Himalayan hydrology will be one of the critical frontlines in the global battle against climate change and water scarcity. The Himalayan mountain system is of crucial importance to the river system of South Asia not only in terms of influencing the monsoon but also in terms of the glaciers which are the source of many of the great rivers in Asia. Geologists often regard all the rivers, including those originating from Tibet, collectively as the "circum-Himalayan rivers".[16] The Himalayan glaciers, regarded as the 'Third Pole', contain one of the largest reservoirs of snow and ice outside the Polar region. Ten major Asian river systems - the Amu Darya, Indus, Ganga, Brahmaputra, Irrawady, Salween, Mekong, Yangtse, Yellow and Tarim have their sources in the Himalayan glaciers contributing to almost 70 per cent of water resources. Almost 2.0 billion people stretching from Afghanistan to the Ganga-Meghna-Brahmaputra basin in South Asia to the Mekong Delta in South-East Asia are dependent on the flows of the rivers from the glaciers of the Himalaya that includes Tibet. The impact of global warming and climate change, as studies indicate, will gradually shrink glaciers resulting in the decrease of water runoff in the long-term. In the short-term earlier water runoff from glaciers when combined with seasonal rains can result in flood conditions.

Of all the evidence showing the impact of global warming, perhaps none is more visible than or as acutely dangerous as outburst flooding in the Himalayas. According to the latest assessment of the Centre for Integrated Mountain Development (ICIMOD) in Kathmandu there are about 200 glacial lakes in the Hindu Kush Himalaya region that are "potentially dangerous": (25 in Bhutan, 77 in China, 30 in India, 20 in Nepal, and 52 in Pakistan). The ICIMOD keeps an inventory of 8,700 glacial lakes in the region. Glacial lakes are recognised as a threat to mountain areas worldwide. The lakes form as glacial melt-water collects behind ridges of loose rock debris called moraines that were deposited by the glaciers themselves.

Over the next 20 years, perceptions of a rapidly changing ecosystem in all likelihood will prompt nations to take unilateral actions to secure resources and territorial sovereignty. Any willingness to engage in greater river basin co-operation will depend on a number of factors, such as the behaviour of other competing countries, the economic viability, and other interests that states are reluctant to either compromise or concede.

In the last two decades, the impact of climate change on water resources cannot be discounted. In fact as a precautionary approach, the awareness to the dangers of climate change on water resources should frame future water policies in the region. Some of the studies/findings indicate increased precipitation in some areas, increased drought in some others and increased variability of precipitation. Long-term trends for Himalayan glaciers under conditions of continued warming clearly point to melting though some reports have tended to exaggerate the situation. The melting in the short term will help liberate melt-water which can be used for agriculture and industry. However, de-glaciation will also lead to rapid destabilisation of mountain slopes causing landslides, rock-falls and mudslides. This would directly impact the livelihood of the people who live on the floodplains of the major rivers spread across Nepal, India, Bhutan and Bangladesh.

The risks and uncertainties over the impact of climate change on water resources are potentially high in many South Asian countries. For example, Bangladesh given its location and geography is extremely vulnerable to any variations in water flow. Being the lowest of the riparian states it shares 54 rivers with India. Bangladesh, geographically speaking, is in a double trap. While on the one hand rivers flow in making it increasingly water dependent on the other it is witnessing sea-level rise. According to a modeling study, the mean global temperatures for Bangladesh may rise by 1.5 to 1.8 degree centigrade by 2050 and correspondingly sea levels may rise by about 30 cm accompanied by an increase in annual rainfall.[17] For India, the middle riparian, decreased snow cover will affect the flows in the Indus, the Sutlej, the Ganges and the Brahamaputra all originating from Tibet. 70 per cent of the summer flow of the Ganges comes from the melt-water and thus can potentially impact the agriculture sector. India's National Communications (NATCOM) in 2004 has projected a decline in wheat production by 4-5 million tones with even a one degree centigrade rise in temperature. Pakistan, like Bangladesh a lower riparian, is vulnerable to access of clean water. The western Himalayan glaciers act as reservoirs that release water into the rivers that feed the plains in Pakistan. The glacial retreat is increasing the flow and the recent devastating flood in Pakistan in July-August 2010 is a stark reminder of the perils of climate change. In the next decade erratic rainfall combined with glacial melt will exacerbate the already serious problems of flooding and draining. After the glacial has receded it is projected that there will be a 30-40 per cent reduction of flow in the Indus basin critically impacting food production.[18]

**Importance of China's Hydrological Position**

From a hydrological perspective China cannot be ignored from the South Asian regional configuration. While China is not member of the SAARC (South Asian Association for Regional Cooperation) it gained observer status along with Japan, South Korea and the US in 2009. Increasingly, and as India's neighbouring countries like Bangladesh, Pakistan and Nepal would like, China is making its presence felt in South Asia and in the process competing directly with India which considers the region to be its sphere of influence. From a hydrological position, India is a lower riparian vis-à-vis China and an upper riparian vis-à-vis Pakistan and Bangladesh. An emphasis that has not been correctly articulated is the fact that India is middle riparian and has concerns over water uses with China and responsibility of sharing waters with its lower riparian neighbours. China's hydrological position, on the other hand, is one of complete upper riparian supremacy. India's middle riparian position increases its dependency on the head waters of the rivers sources such as Indus, Sutlej and Brahmaputra which originate in the Tibetan plateau. Of the nine major tributaries of the Ganges that flow in from Nepal, the three principal tributaries Karnali, Gandaki and Kosi rise from Tibet.

China is equally water insecure but its insecurity relates to the disproportionate availability or uneven distribution of waters within its territory, the majority of which is in the south (Tibet Autonomous Region) with the north and west excessively water stressed. China suffers from an annual shortage of 40 billion cubic meters of water and is expected to face 25 per cent supply gap for projected water demand by 2030.[19] More than anything else, the water shortage becomes an impediment to China's goal of meeting food production and challenges the leadership claims to self-sufficiency in food grains. Electricity is equally crucial in China's economic development. With a GDP growing at the rate of 8-10 per cent a year, China's energy requirement is projected to increase by 150 per cent by 2020. While resource rich in coal and a net importer of oil, both which are climate unfriendly, China is compelled to develop its hydroelectricity as a clean and renewable source of energy. China has already half of the world's large dams including the Three Gorges. China's dams and water diversions are an important component of its rise. Its 'hydro-egoism' or 'hydro-aggression' is intended to secure its massive water requirements in its northern and western regions. But importantly the control over such a valuable natural resource gives Beijing enormous strategic latitude with its neighbours.[20]

**Question of Tibet**

Tibet's water resources raise contesting questions. Should China alone be the stakeholder to the fate of the waters in Tibet? China has rampantly exploited all the rivers from the Tibetan Plateau. With historical disagreement over the territory, Tibet's unresolved political status will be of direct consequence to ways to sustainably manage the water resources. Lower riparian pressure and international attention to defining vital resource as 'commons' would be significant to preserving and sharing the waters of Tibet. While such redefinition is politically sensitive, as it clashes with national jurisdiction, it nonetheless, merits attention keeping in mind future water requirement of the 2 billion people in South and Southeast Asia. International laws on allocating water within river-basin are difficult to implement and often contradictory. The UN Convention on the Non-Navigational Uses of International Watercourses, approved in 1997 by a vote of 104-3 (but not yet ratified), requires watercourse nations (Article 5) to participate in the use, development, and protection of an international watercourse in an equitable and reasonable manner.

It will be fundamentally important to counter China's 'hydro-aggression' with down riparian 'hydro-solidarity'. The rapidly changing Himalayan hydrology will require genuine willingness of states to engage in greater river basin cooperation. However, China the dominant upper riparian has taken unilateral actions to secure resources and territorial sovereignty. The lower-riparian states extending from Afghanistan to South Asian and Southeast Asian countries should form a lower-riparian coalition and show hydro-solidarity to overcome China's hydro-egoism and unwanted resource exploitation in Tibet. It is of existential importance to draw China into a water dialogue and evolve new mechanisms and approaches to solve water problems. The stability of the region will greatly depend upon the stable flow of waters.

**Conclusion: Comprehensive Understanding of Water**

Water requirement has undoubtedly emerged as an issue of great concern and urgency. With multiplying demand on water, the availability of which remains constant, a water crisis is impending. This holds particularly for developing countries, where the requirement of water will rise by 50 per cent by 2030. A comprehensive water policy for these states would need to take into account the rapidly changing water conditions, in terms of quality, quantity, and the uneven distribution of water.

Much of the policy understanding on water has been narrowly framed on the principle of 'water management' that entails manipulation of water for specific uses through water-based projects. Clearly, a more comprehensive policy for protection, development, and utilisation of water resources-including both surface and underground water-needs to be developed. This would mean a shift to a more rational and integrated 'water resource management' that treats water bodies as one hydrological unit and, in the process, embraces the 'conjunctive use' of both surface and underground water resources and their sustainable development. While the developmental focus will remain essentially on the socio-economic uses, it must be noted that water is equally necessary for sustaining the ecosystem. The challenge lies in maintaining the balance.

Regional cooperation will need to factor in an enhanced and updated automated early warning system. The cooperative framework would also require upgrading remote-sensing projects, which are critical for improving flood warning systems. Such enhancement will help in detecting small changes in lake levels, and thereby send immediate signals to alarm systems near villages. While building such capacity is important, what is of greater relevance is repeated risk-evaluation at the ground level, leading to thorough risk assessment. Local knowledge and indigenous understanding are immensely important to the overall assessment. Thus a lot of fresh thinking based on evolving hydrological knowledge and understanding is required-thinking that is sincere, evidential, and scientific; and not alarmist, rhetorical, and misrepresented.

Climate variation and its impact on water resources bind the Himalayan region together. Some of the impacts of climate change are already being observed with glacial melt, seismic activity, and unpredictable weather patterns. States would need to reorient their riparian polices on a multilateral basis. While, on the one hand, a shift from merely 'sharing waters' to 'sharing benefits' is necessary, on the other, it is imperative not to lose sight of the ecological consideration.

**Notes**

1. *'Water, a Shared Responsibility: The United Nations World Water Development Report* 2', Paris, UNESCO Publishing, 2006, p. 128.
2. *Draft National Water Policy* (2012) as Recommended by National Water Board in its 14th Meeting Held on 7th June, 2012 See http://mowr.gov.in/writereaddata/linkimages/Draft NWP2012_English 9353289094.pdf
3. *Ibid.*
4. *Ibid.*
5. Iyer, Ramawamy R, 'Should Water be Moved to Concurrent List?', *The Hindu* (New Delhi), June 18, 2011.
6. Upadhaya, Videh "Water Rights and the 'New' Water Laws in India". *India Infrastructure Report*, 2011, pp. 57-58.
7. Sadoff, Claudia Thomas Grieber, Mark Smith and Ger Bergkamp, Share: 'Managing Water Across Boundaries', *IUCN Report,* Gland, 2008, p. 6.
8. *Ibid.*, p. 6. Also see, *'Transboundary Freshwater Dispute Database',* Oregon University. http://www.transboundarywaters.orst.edu/database/interfreshtreatdata.html
9. Spanier. J, (1978) : *Games Nations Play: Analysing International Politics,* (3rd edition), New York, Praeger Publishers, p. 11.
10. According to Joseph Grieco, "...Neo-liberals see states as 'rational egoists' interested in their own utility, while realist view states as what I describe as 'defensive positionalists' interested in achieving and maintaining relative capabilities sufficient to remain secure and independent in the self help context of international anarchy". See Grieco, 'Understanding the problems of International Cooperation: The Limits of Neo-liberal Institutionalism and the Future of Realist Theory', in Baldwin David, (1993) *Neorealism and Neoliberalism,* New York, Columbia University Press, p. 303.
11. Mckinsey Report, 'Charting our Water Future', November 2009. http://www.mckinsey.com/App_Media/Reports/Water/Charting_Our_Water_Future_Exec%20Summary_001.pdf
12. *Ibid.*
13. As noted by John Beddington, UK Chief Scientist on March 18, 2009. See http://www.guardian.co.uk/science/2009/mar/18/perfect-storm-john-beddington-energy-food-climate.

14. 'Freshwater Under Threat: South Asia', *UNEP Report*, 2008.
15. 'Population Growth and Per Capita Water Availability in India. 1951, 1955, 1991, 2001, 2025 and 2050'. Details available at: http://www.indiastat.com/table/percapitaavailability/24/watersupply/18198/365176/data.aspx.

    Also see *'Water: The India Story', Report by Grail Research and World Bank Report, India's Water Economy: Bracing for a Turbulent Future,* 2005.
16. 'Geochemistry of the Suspended Sediments of Circum-Himalayan Rivers and Weathering Budgets Over the Last 50 years'. See abstract http://adsabs.harvard.edu/abs/2003EAEJA....13617G.
17. Ericksen N J, Q.K., Ahmad and A.R., Chowdhury, (1997) *Socio-Economic Implications of Climate Change for Bangladesh*, Dhaka: Bangladesh Unnayan Parishad.
18. Briscoe J., and U., Qamar, 'Pakistan's Water Economy Running Dry', *The World Bank Report,* Oxford, Oxford University Press, 2008, p. 27, http://www.hec.gov.pk/InsideHEC/ Divisions/FPD/cwf/ Documents/Pakistan's%20Water%20Economy%20Running%20Dry%20Oxford%20University%20Press%202006.pdf
19. Mckinsey Report, 'Charting our Water Future', November 2009.
20. Sinha Uttam Kumar, 'Tibet's Watershed Challenges', *The Washington Post,* June 12, 2010.

## References

Verghese B.G., (1990) : *Waters of Hope: Himalaya-Ganga Cooperation for a Billion People,* Oxford-IBH, Delhi, Reprinted 1998 and in 2007 with an update published by the India Research Press, Delhi.

IDSA Report on Water Security for India (2010) : The External Dynamics, http://www.idsa.in/sites/default/files/book_WaterSecurity.pdf.

Bandyopadhyay Jayanta and Nilanjan Ghosh: 'Holistic Engineering and Hydro-Diplomacy in the Ganges-Brahmaputra-Meghna Basin', *Economic and Political Weekly,* Vol. 44, No. 45, Nov. 7-13, 2009 pp. 50-60.

Ramaswamy Iyer (2001): *Water: Perspectives, Issues and Concerns,* Sage, New Delhi.

Sinha Uttam Kumar, 'Water Security', in Satish Kumar (ed.), (2010): *India's National Security: 2010 Annual Review,* Routledge, New Delhi.

# 17

# *India's Energy Sector : Perils of Nuclear Power and Options of Alternative Energy*

*K.G. Thara*

India is the fourth largest energy consumer in the world after United States, China and Russia. The demand for electricity in the country has been growing at a rapid rate and is expected to grow further in the years to come. In order to meet the increasing requirement of electricity, massive addition to the installed generating capacity in the country is required. India's energy requirement is estimated based on the target of eradicating poverty and meeting the human development goals by sustaining economic growth of 9 per cent over the next 25 years. For fuelling this growth, the primary energy supply (including gathered non-commercial such as wood and dung) must increase at the rate of 5.8 per cent per annum. The Working Group Report of the Planning Commission (2012) estimated a capacity addition of about 76,000 MW during the 12th Plan to meet the demand projections of the country.

The Indian power sector is one of the most diversified in the world. We produce power from a range of commercial sources like coal, lignite, natural gas, oil, hydro electric and nuclear and non-conventional sources like wind, solar and agriculture and domestic waste. We are already importing seventy three per cent of our total requirement of oil. Over dependence on imported oil and the depreciation of Indian rupee make us quite vulnerable to global market price fluctionations of oil which also lead to trade deficit and general inflation.

As for natural gas, India is increasingly relying on imported LNG and is the sixth largest LNG importer as per 2011 statistics. Even with the expected increase in the supplies from new gas fields of ONGC and new LNG facilities, thirty two per cent of our demands remain unmet. Combustible renewables and waste constitute about 11 per cent of Indian energy use. This share includes traditional biomass sources which are used by more than 800 million Indian households for cooking. Other renewables such as wind, geothermal, solar, and hydroelectricity represent a thirty per cent share of the Indian fuel mix, while nuclear holds a paltry two per cent share.

Climate change issues of using coal, petroleum and other fossil fuels are being debated globally, particularly in the context of increasing growth rate in countries like India and China. They are also finite resources, and are considered to be non-renewable energy resources. What is important is that any capacity addition programme should be in conformity with the overall objective of sustainable development and should be cost effective also. This paper is an attempt to look into various aspects of the Indian energy scenario, with special reference to nuclear energy. Safety aspects and economic viability of nuclear energy are critically analyzed and the potential of alternative sources of energy is also explored.

**Indian Energy Scenario**

India's integrated energy policy is to "reliably meet the demand for energy services of all sectors including the lifeline energy needs of vulnerable households in all parts of the country with safe, clean and convenient energy at the least-cost"[1] Post-independent India has made significant strides in the energy sector. The per capita consumption of electricity in the country has increased from 15.6 units in 1950 to about 766 units during the year 2009-10. The National Electricity Policy of the Government of India (2005) stipulated that this is to be increased to over 1000 units per annum in 2012. Far from achieving this perspective, some 600 million Indians do not have access to electricity even now and about 700 million Indians still use biomass as their primary energy resource for cooking. In other words, the goal of the energy policy to provide energy security to all still remains a distant dream.

In a global perspective, China's current energy consumption is 1100-1200 Mtoe and USA's current consumption is 2400-2500 Mtoe. India on a per capita basis, currently consumes 6 per cent less than what the US consumes and about 41 per cent of what China consumes. India's per capita energy even with a projected population of 1.47 billion in 2031-32, will only be marginally above China's current per capita consumption. Moreover, contrary to other developed and developing countries, total primary commercial energy requirement in India has been falling with respect to the growth in GDP.

**Our Energy Sources and Reserves**

The Indian power sector is largely coal based. As per June 2011 statistics, coal occupies 55 per cent (99,503 MW), gas takes up 10 per cent (17,706 MW ), while diesel generating capacity is 1200 MW (1 per cent), hydro power is 38,206 MW (21 per cent), nuclear 4,780 MW (2 per cent) and renewable generation capacity is 20,162 MW (11 per cent). It is interesting to note that a major share of the installed capacity from renewable sources (16,936 MW) is in the private sector while the state sector constitutes only 3,226 MW.

As per 2013 satistics[2] India is the fourth largest consumer and also the fourth largest importer of oil and petroleum products in the world after United States, China and Japan. In 2011, India imported oil worth $75 billion. Continuing dependence on imported oil makes us vulnerable to global oil price fluctuations. An increase of $10 per barrel is likely to slow the GDP growth by 0.2 per cent and may inflate the current account deficit by 0.4 per cent[3].

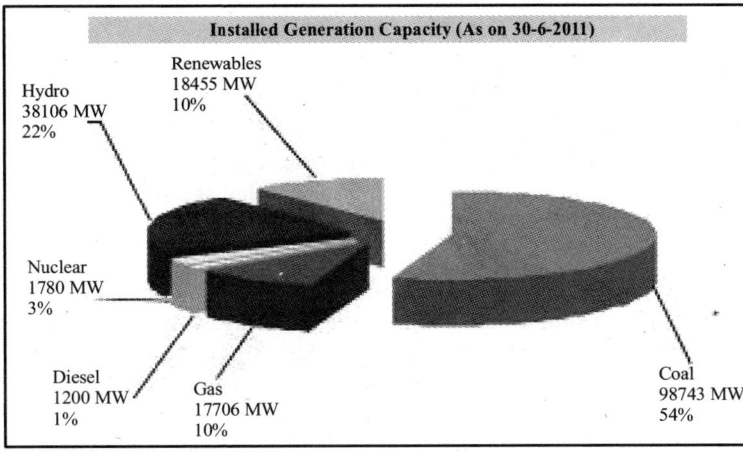


(*Source:* India Energy Book 2012, World Energy Council).

Presently, the country imports about 85 million tons of coal and the gap between supply and demand is ever increasing. The adverse impact of increased $CO_2$ emissions from increasing use of coal in thermal power stations and other industries is also well known. As on April 2011, India's inventory of coal resource was 284 Billion Tons (BT). Though the estimates for global peak coal extraction vary wildly, many experts suggest the peak coal (the point in time after which the rate of production will drastically decline) to occur in just about 50 years.

India has a total reserve of 760 million metric tones of crude oil and 1330 billion cubic metres of natural gas as on 1.4.2012. However, due to huge demand-supply gap in oil and gas in India, it is already importing sixty per cent of its crude oil requirement. In addition to lack of sufficient natural gas resources, the fact that most of the gas production and liquified natural gas (LNG) terminals are located in the western part of the country, adversely impact the availability of gas in the rest of the country.

India has an installed capacity of 84000 MW and ranks 5th in terms of exploitable hydro-potential on global scenario. It is the most widely used form of renewable energy and compared to other forms of energy, it has the added advantage that the generation cost is not much affected by price inflation over longer period of time. However, the share of hydropower has declined from 44 per cent in 1970 to 25 per cent in 2010, mainly because of the negative impact of most of these projects on the fragile, local ecosystem and the associated environmental, rehabilitation and pubic interest litigation issues. Impact of climate change on the flow of rivers in the next two to three decades also raises doubts about the long-term sustainability of hydroelectric power generation.

It is in this backdrop that the Indian government's outlook of mooting nuclear energy as the 'cheapest' and the 'best' source of zero carbon emission need to be critically evaluated.

**Is Nuclear Energy Really Cheap?**

One of the major arguments cited in its favour nuclear power generation is that it is one source which has zero carbon emission. Much of the debate on nuclear power therefore has been on its safety and its defectiveness. The third dimension is whether nuclear power can actually deliver the cheap power it promises, especially in time to help stop climate change.

The argument in favour of nuclear power is that at present, solar energy costs about Rs. 20/kWh, wind energy may cost Rs. 10/kWh, whereas our nuclear power stations are selling energy at Rs. 1/kWh at Tarapur, Rs. 3/kWh at Kaiga and Koodankulam will also be sold below Rs. 3/kWh. Wind energy has the additional constraint that it can be tapped only when the wind blows, limiting its tapability to 20 or 25 per cent of the time. Well known anti-nuclear activists have pointed out that, the 'apparent' low cost of nuclear energy is because of the huge subsidies the government offers to the nuclear power industry in the form of heavy water subsidy, fuel fabrication subsidy, insurance and liability subsidy, security subsidy, research subsidy, waste management subsidy, and many other hidden and unknown subsidies[4]. Without these subsidies, nuclear power will no doubt be the costliest form of energy. Statistics about nuclear energy being cheap therefore is wrong.

Experts estimate that to maintain the present share of nuclear energy in the world energy production, once the first 80 new plants have been built, another 200 plants are to be built between 2018 and 2028. Apart from being an unrealistic prospect, the fact that the industry has already witnessed a cost escalation of 33 to 45 per cent, also need to be noted. Introduction of additional safety features post Fukushima will naturally mean more time lag and further escalation of cost. For example, two fatal accidents and safety analyses in the Flamanville plant in France has resulted in a cost escalation of £2.7 bn and the plant installation is at least four years behind schedule. Initial cost of the Areva plant, the only other new nuclear plant being built by a state controlled French company in Europe, at Olkiluoto in Finland, is a staggering £ 516 bn, which is £ 2.6 bn over budget and power generation is already delayed by four years. In the world's ever worsening energy/environmental crises and escalating costs, this time lag itself can be crucial.

Another factor that affects the economics of nuclear power is the cost of dealing with the spent nuclear fuel, which can be either reprocessed or directly disposed of. Reprocessing as a waste management technique is far more expensive than direct disposal. Nuclear energy is considered as a cheap source because the cost of reprocessing the radioactive waste and the cost of insurance liability against is not accounted for.

The Department of Energy (DAE) claims that the international cost norms are not applicable to Indian nuclear Power industry as the types of reactors and scale of operations are different. However, no economic analysis has been done to substantiate this claim. The imported power reactors also need heavy investment to the tune of Rs. 250,000 crore and downstream commercial and industrial entities which rely on this power possibly would be worth an additional Rs. 800,000 crore. They will also need Rs. 12 lakh crore capital investment and Rs 3 lakh crore for setting up the electricity related industries in the vicinity[5]. Moreover, as far as India is concerned, imported reactors fueled by plutonium are not cost competitive as uranium is available in plenty, which can be used directly in reactors.

It is interesting to note that most of the nuclear power plants are designed, built and managed by private corporations. But, despite billions of rupees government subsidies, wherever nuclear power plants have been set up, the private sector has backed off from capital investment in this sector and the liability of paying compensation in the event of a disaster, is always vested with the government. Most of the US reactors were built by state-based utilities, incorporating the capital cost into their rate base. This means that the consumers bore the risk and paid for the capital cost. In India too, the state may have to bear the brunt of an escalated cost of fuel or of an accident.

Nuclear industry is not as cheap, energy efficient, sustainable, environmentally friendly or as safe as claimed, especially when the government cost, impact of uranium mining and the issue of long-term nuclear waste storage are factored in. A detailed study conducted by the Massachusetts Institute of Technology estimates a real levelised cost of 6.7 cents/kWh for nuclear power, 4.2 cents/kWh for pulverised coal and 3.8-5.6 cents/kWh for gas. In contrast, the renewable energy installations are emerging as the cheapest, low carbon source and most of the technologies are coming down in price.

**Prospects of Nuclear Energy**

No overall nuclear power policy exists in India but, in 2006, India declared its intention to add 26 GW (26,000,000,000 watts) of nuclear power to its energy supply by importing 40,000 MWe worth LWR (Light Weight Reactors) reactors within a span of twenty years. At present, nuclear power caters to just two per cent of our energy requirement and thus ranks fourth after thermal, hydroelectric and renewable sources of energy in catering to our demand. At a modest estimate of 20 crore/MWe, this capacity addition would cost the tax payer an amount of Rs. 8,00,000 crore[6].

India has only around 1-2 per cent of the global uranium reserves[7], while the thorium reserves constitute 30 per cent (660,000 tonnes) of Thorium of the total world thorium reserves[8]. India is generally considered as the leader of thorium based research in the world. India's original, three-staged nuclear programme initiated by Homi J. Bhabha in the 1950s envisages production of electricity using our vast resources of thorium to extract nuclear fuel[9].

Interestingly, while India is trying to import uranium technology from the US, forsaking the age-old thorium fuel cycle technology which has been in place since the Homi J. Bhabha days, experts world over have started to advocate thorium as a nuclear fuel in place of uranium to create nuclear power.

India is the only country in the world with a detailed, funded, government-approved plan to focus on thorium-based nuclear power. Another possibility is the use of thorium in a reactor especially designed for thorium (rather than mixing in thorium with uranium and plutonium (i.e. in existing reactors). Used thorium fuel remains a few hundreds of years radioactive, instead of tens of thousands of years[10].

As of now, India has 20 nuclear reactors in operation in 6 nuclear power plants, generating 4780 MW. Five other plants are under construction which is expected to generate an additional 2720 MW. By 2032, India aims at increasing the nuclear power output to 64000 MW.

The important question is to critically evaluate whether our nuclear infrastructure is capable of managing such an expansion and handle safety issues that may ensue. In fact, our nuclear power policy should re-emphasize the indigenous three-stage Bhabha Plan of the past, by giving priority support to the Pressurised Heavy Water Reactor, advanced heavy water reactor and Fast Breeder Reactor programmes which can utilize our vast thorium resources. Expert committee report of the Planning Commission[11] also endorsed the view that India can become truly energy independent beyond 2050 by tapping its thorium resources through the three-stage development process.

**Political Implications of the Indo-US Nuclear Deal**

The Indo-US nuclear deal was signed on 18 July, 2005. Under this pact, India plans to import 40,000 MWe of Light Water Reactors between 2012 and 2020 from US and agreed to separate its civil and military nuclear facilities and place all its civil nuclear facilities under Atomic Energy Agency (IAEA) safeguards. In exchange, the United States assured nuclear cooperation with our country.

Apart from the fact that this deal would mean over dependence on imported uranium and technology, it also endangers the indigenous thorium based power generation technology which India had painstakingly developed since the times of Homi J. Bhabha. The astronomical cost is also a major concern. An additional 30,000 MW of nuclear power from the proposed (by the Indo-US nuclear deal) imported reactors would roughly cost us 45 billion dollars.

Hyde Act 2006 and US Atomic Energy Act 1954 (Section 106) gives complete freedom to America to cease the nuclear cooperation, if India conducted a nuclear test. Hyde Act 103(a) 6 specifically gives unilateral right to the US president right to stop supply of fuel to India by any of the NSG (Nuclear Supply Group) countries also. Apart from that no life time supply of fuel by the US is guaranteed by any of these acts and agreements, India is also put to and additional constrain that we have to abide by the NPT (Nuclear Non-proliferation Treaty) for any transfer of ENR (enrichment and reprocessing) technologies. Under the Indo-US pact, while we still have the right to reprocess and recycle used fuel, the doors are shut to commerce related to enrichment and reprocessing technologies. India was hoping to set up plants for reprocessing used fuels arising from reactors, under IAEA (International Atomic Energy Agency) safeguards and also plants for enriching imported uranium under IAEA safeguards to feed our ongoing programme.

India can buy technology only from the US and considering the previous experience where the US breached the assurance of a lifetime supply of fuel to Tarapur plant, there is little reason to believe that the present Indo-US nuclear deal would ensure the supply of fuel needed to make good for the shortage of 40,000 MW. While reprocessing and recycling of used fuel from nuclear reactors particularly in fast reactors might address the challenge of climate change and ensure sustainable $CO_2$-free global energy supply, the safety concerns and proliferation concerns are too serious to be ignored.

**Specialities of Some Nuclear Plants in India and Safety Issues**

India has 20 nuclear reactors in operation in six nuclear power plants, which include Kaiga in Karnataka, Kakrapar in Gujarat, Kalpakkkam in Tamil Nadu, Narora in Uttar Pradesh, Rawatbhata in Rajasthan and Tarapur in Maharashtra[12]. Except the one in Kalpakkam and Kudankulam, all others are PHWR (Pressurised Heavy Water reactors). NPCIL (Nuclear Power Corporation of India Limited, a Public Sector Enterprise under the administrative control of the Department of Atomic Energy) is the main operator, with the exception of Kalpakkam, which is operated by Bhavini (Bharathiya Nabhikiya Vidyut Nigam Limited, a Government of India enterprise). They have a combined capacity to generate 4780 MW capacity. Five other plants are under construction. These are expected to generate an additional 2720 MW.

India's proposed (9900 MW) nuclear power plant on the west coast, in Ratnagiri District at Jaitapur is the largest under the ownership of the Nuclear Power Corporation of India Ltd (NPCIL), a public sector undertaking of the Department of Atomic Energy (DAE). This project is envisaged to have 6 European Pressurized Reactors (EPR), each of 1650 MW capacity. The fuel and critical equipment of these reactors are to be supplied by the French state-owned company Areva.

Preference of EPR over the Light Water Reactor is not sufficiently justified as the European Pressurized Reactors (EPR) has never been built or tested anywhere. Light Water Reactor has an established operational experience. The EPRs will be tested for the first time in India and likelihood of nuclear accidents in brand new, untested reactors could be high. Should we offer a testing ground for the untested European Pressurised Reactors, risking the lives of millions of people? Moreover, while pressurised Heavy Water Reactors (PHWR) cost no more than Rs 8 crore/MW, EPR will cost Rs 20 crore/Mw in terms of 2010 value[13].

Geologically, Jaitapur lies in the same stress regime as that of Latur (MW = 6.3) and the MW = 6.4 Koyna earthquake, this raises concerns about the probability of similar earthquakes directly under the power plant[14].

Jaitapur has no record of local seismicity in the past century but has frequently experienced intensity VII shaking from earthquakes in the vicinity. It also lies at a distance of 110 km from the location of Koyna earthquake of 1967. Earthquake tremors of magnitude between three and five in regions near to Jaitapur also indicate stress accumulation in these regions.

The plant at Kudankulam, Tamil Nadu, has two units of 1,000 MW Light Water VVER Reactors, designed to use light water both as coolant and moderator. The plant is being built by the state-owned Nuclear Power Corporation of India in conjunction with Russia's Rosatom. Russia has provided all the equipments including the reactor pressure vessel, steam generators and turbines, and will also be supplying the fuel for the entire life of the reactors.

The plant got only a vague environmental clearance in 1989 when the site was not decided and no EIA report or an Environmental Management Plan has been put in place. The public is opposed to the building of the plant since no Environment Impact Assessment was done and no public hearing, mandatory under law, has so far been conducted. Atomic Energy Regulatory Board has recently admitted that the safety recommendations of its own review committee have not been implemented at Koodankulam. The authorities claim that the reactors now being installed have enhanced safety and seismic features like the molten-core catcher to take care of beyond-design-basis accident but, the local people have not been taken into confidence.

The 500 MWe Fast Breeder Reactor prototypes at Kalpakkam, Tamil Nadu need only natural or even depleted uranium feedstock as input to its fuel cycle after its initial charge of plutonium. This plant has the added advantage that it can use the vast thorium fuel in India which is the world's second largest thorium reserves.

However, breeder reactors are considered to be prone to accidents and are more expensive than normal (non-breeder) reactors and most countries have given up on them[15]. The plant was originally designed to be commissioned in 2010 and is now expected to be operational by September 2014. Total costs, originally estimated at Rs. 3500 crore (35 billion) are now estimated at Rs. 5,677 crore (56 billion). The additional safety concern is that liquid sodium used as the coolant has the risk of exploding if it comes into contact with water and burns when in contact with air.

Tarapur Atomic Power Station (TAPS) in Maharastra is the largest nuclear power plant in India, with a total capacity of 1400 MW. The facility is operated by the Nuclear Power Corporation of India Limited (NPCIL). Original capacity of the two boiling water reactor (BWR) was reduced to 160 MWe due to technical difficulties.

The boiling water reactors at Tarapur one and two units are similar to but, much older than the reactors involved in the Fukushima I nuclear accidents. The two units were originally designed for 23 and 24 years (as of March 2012) and they already have been in operation for 16 years. The reactor's age and old design have raised serious safety concerns. In 2007, Atomic Energy Regulatory Board (AERB) evaluated seismic safety features at Tarapur one and two and reported many shortfalls, following which NPCIL installed seismic sensors at the site. Presence of three central schools and the local beach at Chinchani which is only seven kilometers from the colony, raises concern about the safety aspects.

The Kakrapar Atomic Power Station (KAPS) in the state of Gujarat consists of two 220 MW Pressurised Heavy Water Reactors (PHWR). Safety issues reported include closure of the plant for 66 days in the year 1998 due to a leakage in the cooling loop and the exposure of four labourers to low levels of tritium in May 2011[16]. On 10 March 2004 also, the reactor had to be shut off due to an irreparable damage which occurred during maintenance work in the supply for the control rods.

The Kaiga nuclear power plant in Karnataka has four units of 220 MW capacity fueled by indigenous uranium which has been in operation since March 2000. This plant is expected to supply electricity to Karnataka, Andhra Pradesh, Kerala, Tamil Nadu and Puducherry. The plant experienced some major accidents during its life time. The Nuclear Power Board categorized an area within five km of the plant as a 'sterilised' zone in 1986. Displaced communities have been struggling demanding reasonable compensation for their land and a job to each of the displaced families[17]. On 13 May 1994, the under-surface of the pre-stressed concrete dome of the reactor unit one collapsed during the final stage of construction, injuring 14 persons. This incident delayed the completion of the first two units, which was to be operational by June 1996. In November 2009, workers of the Kaiga plant suffered contamination from radioactive water (tritium poisoning) from the plant. Direct impact of these accidents was the delay which escalated the cost of the project from 750 crore (US$ 140 million) to 2275 crore (US$ 420 million).

**Potential Hazards of Nuclear Energy**

All energy technologies have risks and impacts, but nuclear power is exceptional in its potential to produce catastrophic accidents that can affect thousands or even millions of people and have profound human, environmental and economic consequences. Fortunately, such accidents have been rare in nuclear power's brief history. But this is no excuse for complacency. There are 443 nuclear power reactors operating in 31 countries in the world. The age, size and design type of all of these reactors varies considerably, but it is safe to say that all of them have very serious inherent safety flaws which cannot be eliminated by safety upgrading.

Apart from the risk of an accident, radioactive materials are regularly being discharged into the air and water even during normal operations. During the fission of radioactive elements, a large amount of energy ( . 200 million electron volts) is released, which can pose serious health problems to human beings. A 400-500 rem radiation is considered to be lethal. Plutonium, a by-product of nuclear power has a very long life (half life of 24,000 years) and can cross the placenta and get stored in male testicles.

The threats posed during mining, transportation and enrichment of radioactive materials, radioactive dumps at factories, and nuclear fuel facilities are also very high. Daily contamination caused by radioactive effluents and gases discharged, legally and illegally, into rivers and coastal waters or into the air often are also not taken into account in assessing the overall impact of nuclear energy.

Serious accidents have occurred in nuclear plants world over, due to human mistakes, faulty design and inadequate safety precautions (as in Chernobyl, Three Mile Island, Sellafield reprocessing plants in the U.K, Monju breeder reactor and reprocessing plant in Tokoimura, in Japan and many others), natural disasters such as Tsunami, earthquakes and floods — as in Fukushima. Potential threat from sabotage and terrorist attacks also cannot be ruled out.

Increased risk of lung-cancer in uranium miners due to inhalation of radon has also been indicated by a study conducted by the Indian Doctors for Peace and Development (IDPD) on the health status of the inhabitants of the villages around the Jaduguda mines in Singhbhum, Jharkand[18]. The study indicated three types of exposure such as inhalation of dust and gas produced by uranium mining and milling operations of radioisotopes (radon), surface water contaminated by discharges from the mine and gamma-ray exposure from mine-tailings.

Other clinical results show progressive or irreversible renal (kidney) damage, very high percentage of congenital deformities (9.25 per cent) in the new born babies, prevalence of spontaneous abortion among married women and chronic lung diseases etc. Couples living near the mining site were also found to be 1.58 times more vulnerable to primary sterility and the percentage of deaths before attaining 62 years were reported to be around 68.33 per cent[19].

A study on health impact of release of radioactive elements from Rajasthan Atomic Power Station (RAPS) located at Rawatbhata near Kota in central India also came up with similar findings regarding increased rate of congenital deformities and cancer deaths in villages near the plant[20]. Nuclear power therefore, is a reproductive rights issue as well as an environmental justice issue. Locating reactors in developing countries and also where poor African-American rural communities live, as in Georgia, also should be viewed as a human rights violation.

**Problem of Nuclear Waste**

Both short-term as well as long-term radioactive wastes are produced during production of nuclear power, most important of which is the spent nuclear fuel. Treatment of nuclear wastes need sophisticated techniques. The wastes also have extremely long periods of life (10,000 to millions of years). Some of the by-products of nuclear industry such as Technetium — 99 have a half-life of 220,000 years, Iodine-129, a half-life of 15.7 million years, Neptunium-237 a half -life of two million years and Plutonium-239 a half life of 24,000 years. In no unequivocal terms, the threat and the risk posed by these by-products which remain active for a very long time is huge[21].

At present, there are about 430 locations around the world, where nuclear wastes are being stored. Practices such as deep burial in geologic repositories and reprocessing of the spent nuclear fuel are also riddled with huge environmental problems as they produce highly radioactive wastes. Reprocessing involves the chemical processing of the spent fuel to separate out the plutonium (which is used as a fuel in nuclear reactors) and the depleted uranium. Interestingly, reprocessing is not allowed in the US and the country prefers to ship it to other nations. Reprocessing of civilian fuel from power reactors is currently done in Britain, France and (formerly) Russia and China and India are increasingly being looked at as emerging sites for potential reprocessing and waste disposal. There are also reports of toxic and radioactive waste being illegally sunk in the ocean[22]. Some are also illegally shipped to places such as Somalia, Kenya, Zaire and other developing countries. These toxic wastes containing radioactive waste cargoes are either sunk with the ship or buried on land. A study by the United Nations Environment Programme (UNEP) on Somalia indicate that the 2004 tsunami, might have been responsible for raking up the nuclear wastes illegally dumped off the coasts of Somalia, which could trigger serious health hazards in the region[23].

The nuclear industry also produces a large volume of low-level radioactive waste in the form of contaminated items like clothing, hand tools, water purifier resins etc. Disposal of the materials upon decommissioning of the nuclear reactor also poses a major problem.

The U.S. Department of Atomic Energy (DOE) has recently put up a proposal to get rid of 14,000 metric tons of its radioactive scrap metal which it has accumulated over the years from various nuclear tesing and wartime activities by recycling it into consumer products like belt buckles, zippers, eyeglass frames, jewelry, watches, silverware, toys, pet bowls and leashes, automobiles, city buses, coffee makers, toasters, braces for teeth and even surgical devices used by medical personnel on ill patients[24].

**Other Safety Concerns**

The Fukushima disaster in March 2011 was a wake-up call for nuclear power in the US and elsewhere. Prime Minister Manmohan Singh also promptly ordered a review of the safety status of all nuclear power units, both in operation and construction. The Nuclear Power Corporation of India (NPCIL) and the Atomic Energy Regulatory Board (AERB) also set up a number of task forces to review the safety features of the reactors. Scope of the review included risks posed by earthquakes, tsunami, floods, failure of electrical grid system and other unusual situations.

The results of these reviews surprisingly ruled out the possibility of any situation similar to that in Japan in our installations and claimed that due to adoption of conservative design features and above all absence of the severe intensity earthquakes, a Fukushima type of disaster can never occur in India[25]. However, the location map of nuclear plants in India, existing, proposed, or under construction, show that all of them fall in seismic probable areas[26].

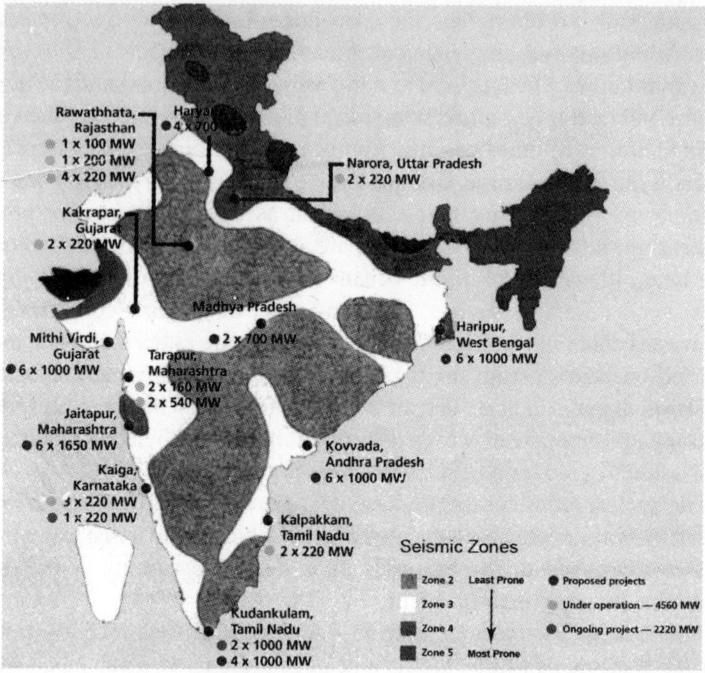


**MAP.I. Seismic Probability Map and Nuclear Power Plant Location**

(*Source:* India Meteorological Department, Nuclear Power Corporation of India).

AERB's report also suggested 17 safety regulations such as provision for portable air-cooled diesel generator sets to supply power to essential services without fail, ensuring adequate amount of fresh water available for cooling of the nuclear fuel, etc., which are intended to be complied and carried out in a phased manner by the nuclear plants. AERB's findings have however brought to light that so far the plants were working without even these minimum safety measures and the assurances the government has been giving about the safety of the plants were false. The review committee's observations that the Koodankulam nuclear power units are safer as they belong to the third generation of design evolution indirectly imply that safety of plants such as Tarapur, which belong to the older generation, is at stake.

**Nuclear Accidents**

Ageing of nuclear reactors and the additional safety factors necessitated by the Fukushima disaster have not only escalated the cost of nuclear reactors, but also has compelled the nuclear operator's world over, to reduce costs by compromising on the safety aspects. The risk factors involved in the industrial nuclear accidents have already been highlighted by incidents at Chernobyl, Ukraineon April 1986, Three Mile Island accident on March 28, 1979, Kyshtym accident in USSR on 29 September 1957 and accidents at Sellafield, UK on 10 October 1957, Emergency Response Centre, France in 2003, David-Besse reactor , USA in 2002, Mihama Reactor, Japan in 2004, Tokai-mura nuclear fuel plant in 1999 and Fukushima Daiichi Nuclear Disaster on March 11, 2011.

Major and minor accidents have happened in India also, the nature, causes and financial costs of which have not been researched upon in a detailed manner. This has resulted in a false notion of security in the Nuclear power industry. Indian nuclear scientists also have worked isolated from the international community, with little separation between military and civilian nuclear programmes, resulting in a culture of intense secrecy. The shroud of secrecy has no doubt left the general public by and large unaware of the dangers of the nuclear energy. Researchers at the American universities calculated that at least 124 'hazardous incidents' occurred at nuclear plants in India between 1993 and 1995, which include the refueling accident at Kalpakkam Fast breeder Test reactor on 4th May 1987 leading to the rupture of the reactor core and a two year shutdown, leakage of Iodine (700 times more than the normal levels) on 10th September, 1989, which took more than one year to repair and malfunctioning of the tube leading to leakage of 12 curies of radioactive materials into the atmosphere on 13 May, 1992, in the same plant. Report also dwell on incidences of fire break out at the Narora Atomic Power station in Bulandshahr (UP) on 31st of March 1993, leakage of radioactive helium and heavy water from the reactor at Kota, Rajasthan into the Ranapratap Sagar dam, forcing a two year shut down on 2 February, 1995 and leakage of hundred kilogram of radioactive sodium into the purification cabin of the same plant on 22 October, 2002, etc.

It is also frightening that it took nine months for the Japanese government to officially announce that the Fukushima plant has been brought to a state of cold shut down. The fact that the operator of the Fukushima plant (Tokyo Electric Power Company or TEPCO) hoped and aimed to stabilize the reactors only by the end of the year, also underlines the potential threat the delay poses to public health and safety.

The Japanese government has also conceded that no clear road map has been set for decommissioning and workers will not be able to start removing the molten fuel from the three worst-hit reactors for another 10 years. Removal of spent fuel from the four storage pools might also take two years. If Japanese government, which has long years of experience and expertise in the field could not avert the disaster, it brings home how precarious the situation can be for India.

**Post Fukushima Energy Policy Vis-à-vis India**

In the wake of Fukushima disaster, a strong shift to renewable energy sources is being observed world over. As of January 2012, 138 civilian nuclear power reactors had been shut down in 19 countries, including 28 in the United States, 27 in the United Kingdom, 27 in Germany, 12 in France, 9 in Japan and 5 in the Russian Federation (IAEA 2012a). There are plans to close up to 80 civilian nuclear power reactors in the next ten years. European Union ministry have agreed to launch a safety assessment of Europe's 143 nuclear power reactors and USA decided to slow down nuclear development and Germany closed down seven of its nuclear plants. Switzerland cancelled permission to buy new plants. China has also put an end to its process of establishing 27 new nuclear atomic plants. While many of these reactors are likely to have their operating licenses extended, they will eventually be decommissioned.

Though USA is the world's largest producer of nuclear power, accounting for more than 30 per cent of worldwide nuclear generation of electricity, it constitutes only 19 per cent of the domestic energy share. Coal is still projected to retain the largest share of the electricity generation mix to 2035, though by 2020 about 49 GWe of coal-fired capacity is expected to be retired, due to environmental constrains and low efficiency. As for the European Union, in marked contrast to its status as the world's leading importer of oil and gas, a shift to low-carbon technologies is observed now. Despite significant variation in national targets, an average of 12 per cent of electricity generation by renewbles by 2010 also is proposed. Focus on large wind turbines, solar power and bio energy, etc., is expected to cut green gas emissions at least by 20 per cent by 2020.

China had 15 nuclear power units generating 11 GW, accounting for 1.9 per cent of the total energy production but now, they too are investing heavily in the renewable energy field. It announced a new overall target of capacity addition of 49 gigawatts of renewable energy, of which 18 gigawatts will be from wind. It is also the largest producer of wind turbines and solar panels and they are expected to reach approximately 150 GW of wind capacity by 2015, most of which is already in various stages of the development pipeline.

Japan was depending heavily on imported fossil fuels to meet its energy demand and before the Fukushima disaster, nuclear power made up more than 30 per cent of the country's power profile. The country had planned to boost nuclear generation to more than 50 per cent of its supply by 2030. Post Fukushima, a clear shift to renewable energy options is witnessed with widespread expansion of solar, wind, hydroelectricity, and wind and biomass energy.

Quite contrary to the global trend, India's energy policy aims at developing both the renewable as well as nuclear energy resources. While acknowledging the potential of wind power and future plans to add about 20 GW of solar power capacity by 2022, India also envisages increasing the contribution of nuclear power to overall electric generation capacity from 4.2 to nine per cent, within the next 25 years. The country has five nuclear reactors under construction (third highest in the world) and plans to construct 18 additional nuclear reactors (second highest in the world) by 2025.

**Road Ahead**

Though India was the first country to set up a ministry for new and renewable energy (MNRE) to promote renewable energy technologies and to enhance its share in the total energy mix, the desired growth has not been achieved so far. Development of Renewable Energy Sources is being accorded emphasis in view of their inherent advantages. At present, it constitutes only 11 per cent of the total energy production but, ideally, a target of at least 20 per cent renewable energy by year 2020 should be set. As per the Government of India publication (2010), critical barriers are market-oriented, perception related, technology-biased and political in nature.

The solar radiation received over the Indian land area is estimated to be about 5,000 trillion kWh/year that offers a huge potential. India gets about 300 clear sunny days in a year in most parts of the country and the average solar radiation incident over India varies from four kWh/day to seven kWh/day. India's ambitious long-term plan is to attain an installed solar power generation capacity of 20,000 megawatts (MW) by the year 2020, 100,000 MW by the year 2030, and 200,000 MW by the year 2050.

Various technologies, both solar thermal and photovoltaic, have been pursued since the sixties to harness the abundant source of energy from the sun. However, in the early period, the development was focused more on low temperature solar thermal devices such as solar cookers and later water heaters. In the area of solar photovoltaics, the focus is on development of devices for off-grid and decentralised applications. The Jawaharlal Nehru National Solar Mission ( JNNSM) has a target of 20,000 MW grid solar power including 2000 MW of Off-grid capacity comprising of solar lighting systems and 20 million sq.m. solar thermal collector area by 2022.

The National Action Plan on Climate Change also has solar power generation as a major theme. For all these initiatives, an investment of $2.54 billion to $3.18 billion will be required during the Twelfth Five-Year Plan, 2012-2017. However, many of the announced targets (National Solar Mission, 2010) such as mandatory deployment of onsite or roof top PV applications in buildings and establishments owned by the government and public sector undertakings to achieve a target of 100 MW by 2012 remain to be achieved.

India's solar thermal developers are also facing a shortage of the fluid that receives the sun's heat to generate the steam. Solar thermal power plants use mirrors to concentrate sunlight for producing steam, which then drives a turbine and generator to make electricity. Heavy dust also is a problem for Indian solar thermal projects, as it seriously disrupts the direct sunlight that maximizes the solar electricity production.

The current potential for power generation from surplus agro and agro industrial residues or wastes is estimated at 17000 MWe. The Biomass Power and Bagasse Cogeneration Programme of Government of India aims at utilising biomass like agro-waste in the form of straws, stalks, stems and fines; agro-industrial processing residues such as shells, husks, deoiled cakes, wood from dedicated energy plantations and bagasse from sugar mills for power generation using combustion technology. With modernisation of techniques and technologies, this power potential can be increased to 22,000 MW. Initiatives are now limited to states of Tamil Nadu, Uttar Pradesh, Karnataka, Andhra Pradesh, Maharashtra, Chhattisgarh, Punjab and Rajasthan.

India has a potential of around 48,500 MW of wind energy, and with a capacity addition of 12,800 MW can contribute to 75 per cent of the grid-connected renewable energy power. Compared to other forms of energy, it is the fastest growing energy programme but, majority of these however, are set up through private sector investments. Wind power capacity of the states of Tamil Nadu, Gujarat, Maharashtra, Karnataka and Rajasthan have been utilized while states like Kerala which has immense potential, has not been effectively utilised.

The estimated potential for power generation in India from micro/ mini/ small hydropower plants is about 5.7.3.1 15,000 MW from 5718 identified sites. The Ministry has the mandate for developing up to 25 MW station capacities. So far, over 760 small hydro power projects aggregating to 2,803 MW have been set up in various parts of the country and 285 projects of about 940 MW are in various stages of implementation. At present, a capacity addition of about 300 MW per year is being achieved, of which about 70 per cent is coming through private sector participation for commercial projects and decentralized micro hydel for remote village electrification.

**Conclusion**

Energy is needed for economic growth, for improving the quality of life and for increasing opportunities for development. India aims to add 26GW of nuclear power to its energy supply over the next eight years, a prospect that has companies such as GE, Bechtel and Westing house of the US, Russia's Rosatom and Japan's Toshiba, Hitachi and Mitsubishi all looking towards New Delhi. It's crystal clear however, that any attempt to rely on foreign, imported technology for solving our energy crises, without boosting our traditional, non-conventional energy sources will be suicidal.

It is worth remembering that India does not have the 2000 -year historic record of moderate earthquakes as Japan, China and parts of Europe and the Middle East and any additional safety factors we might bring to nuclear plants in the light of Fukushima disaster, therefore, may not necessarily be full proof in that sense. The recent events in Japan also remind us that while the likelihood of a nuclear power plant accident is low, its potential consequences are grave. An equipment malfunction, fire, human error, natural disaster or terrorist attack could-separately or in combination can lead to a nuclear crisis and an accident like Fukushima could happen here.

Additional disadvantages of nuclear energy is that it has a high cost and capital intensive nature , takes a long time to commission and is acknowledged as a highly polluting source of power due to radioactivity released into the environment at almost every stage of the nuclear fuel cycle. Not only that there is no satisfactory solution to the radioactive waste problem, but also the risks posed to human health is of serious nature. The grave environmental concerns raised by the leakage of about 45 tonnes of highly radioactive water during the process of cooling the molten fuel in the plant's damaged reactors in Fukushima and the contamination of marine life due to the contamination of an estimated 90,000 tonnes of sea water during the cooling process also confirms this contention. It also has the potential to risk the security and peace of the nation.

River Network, a U.S. conservation group has recently come up with a report that coal, nuclear and natural gas power plants use more fresh water than any other economic sector, including agriculture. The most serious concern of nuclear energy options however are the time consuming, expensive procedure and the exorbitant cost involved in decommissioning, in case of a disaster. This is well exemplified by the fact that a plant at Sellafield, United Kingdom which was shut down in 1981 could be decommissioned only in 2011 and the Japanese Government expects at least 40 years to decommission the plant at Fukushima. The cost of decommissioning of Fukushima Daiichi Nuclear Plant also is an astronomical figure of 1.15 to 4 trillion yen.

India has to actively promote technologies that maximise energy efficiency; demand side management, conservation and energy security and this must be done by encouraging domestic research into such technologies and free access to suitable energy related technologies available abroad. It is worth noticing that India currently has a PV-module manufacturing capacity of 700 MW. However, there is no indigenous manufacturing capability for solar thermal power plants and the government is yet to chalk out a clear Action Plan. The present indigenous capacity to manufacture silicon material is also very low. As many of the declared targets in the National Solar Mission such as setting up of a National Centre for Photo Voltaic Research and Education at IIT, Mumbai, development of specialised courses in Solar Energy with financial assistance from Government and involvement of IITs and premier Engineering Colleges and instituting a government Fellowship programme to train 100 selected engineers / technologies and scientists in Solar Energy in world class institutions abroad, etc., remain to be achieved even in 2012, a white paper on the status of renewable energy, also need to be brought out by the government.

While considering alternative options, advantages of signing the proposed IPI Gas pipeline treaty with Iran cannot be missed as this would ensure cheaper supply of natural gas from Iran. Washington has been pushing very hard for the Turbekhistan-Afghanistan-Pakistan-India (TAPI) Gas pipeline and putting great pressure on India and China to cut dependence on the Iranian oil to avoid sanctions by the Trans-Atlantic alliance of the US and some of the western European countries. But, this pipe line is riddled with grave security issues as the pipe line has to pass through Afghanistan.

Energy-efficiency can also be promoted by enforcing energy standards effectively. Technical and commercial losses in transmission and distribution utilities also need to be brought down. Incentives for promoting renewables should be linked to outcomes (energy generated) and not just outlays (capacity installed). A National Energy Fund (NEF) also needs to be established to finance Reasearch and Development (R&D) in Energy sector.

The best option for India is to conserve electricity and energy use in general and to set up systems to ensure a nationally organised programme to cater to this objective. We may also ensure energy security by lowering the requirement of energy and expanding the domestic energy resource base. Electricity theft is one of the main reasons for power loss in India. Theft of electricity in India is estimated to amount to a nationwide loss of $4.5 billion. A technical roadmap needs to be initiated for integration of ICT technologies in power grid to reduce Transmission and Distribution (T& D) loss. Stringent and mandatory energy efficiency standard legislation on industrial and commercial usage, starting with the heavy industry also needs to be imposed.

The thrust of government policy is that renewable energy should not be perceived in the context of grid related power but, as a replacement of kerosene in rural lighting, cooking gas by biogas or solar plant, diesel or furnace oil by solar PV. Its ability to generate power in a decentralised, distributive mode and production at consumption points also is emphasised as the future prospect.

A decentralized model of energy system based on renewable energy, with energy access to all could be ideal for our nation. PSUs operating in the energy sector must also be able to operate with autonomy and also should be full accountable to ensure incentives for adequate investment through their own resources and improvements in efficiency in energy production and distribution. In US, citizen Groups in the neighborhood have legal powers on nuclear safety. Similarly, panchayats should be given democratic control on safety of plants in respective areas.

To conclude, Fukushima has raised concerns about the safety of nuclear power and wind, tidal and solar energy are emerging as the cleaner and sustainable options when compared with fossil fuels. The money spent on nuclear development should ideally flow into the development of safe renewable energy and conservation. Violent protests in Jaitapur, where France's Areva is hoping to build a 3,300 MW nuclear power station and the resistance of the

Tamilians against the Koodankulam power plant reiterates that future energy options of the country cannot be decided by a few bureaucrats and technocrats. Pros and cons of each energy options should be put to public debate and a white paper on the economy, safety and sustainability aspects of each energy option by the government will be the first step towards evolving a sustainable energy policy for our country.

**Notes**

1. Government of India, Ministry of Power, *Report of the Working Group on Power for 12th Plan* ( 2012-17), New Delhi, January 2012.
2. US Energy Information Administration, *Independent Statistics and Analysis,* 2013.
3. Ministry of Petroleum and Natural Gas, *Basic Statistics on Indian Petroleum and Natural Gas,* 2011-12.
4. DiaNuke.org , October, 2011.
5. Gopalakrishnan, A., *'The Asian Age'*, August 7, 2007.
6. Gopalakrishnan, A., *DNA Correspondent,* February 16, 2013.
7. Government of India, Press Information Bureau, *'Availability of Thorium',* 10 August, 2011.
8. Jayaram, K.M.V., 'An Overview of World Thorium Resources: Incentives for Further Exploration and Forecasts for Thorium Requirements in the Near Future', *IAEA Report,* 26 March, 2012.
9. 'Thorium Fuel Cycle-Potential Benefits and Challenges', IAEA, 2005, p. 45.
10. Report to the U.S Secretary of Energy, '*Blue Ribbon Commission on America's Nuclear Future',* 2012.
11. Government of India, *Planning Commission,* New Delhi. August 2006.
12. Gopalakrishnan, A., 'The Nuclear Cover-Up', *India Today,* February 4, 2011.
13. Gopalakrishnan, A., 'Abandon the Import of Nuclear Reactors': http://www.dnaindia.com/india/analysis_abandon-the-import-of-nuclear-reactors-dr-a-gopalakrishnan_1527965-all.
14. Roger Bilham and Vinod K. Gaur, 'Historical and Future Seismicity Near Jaitapur, India', *Current Science* (Vol. 101, No. 10), November 25, 2011.
15. Von Hippel, Frank, and Suzanne Jones, 'The Slow Death of the Fast Breeder', *Bulletin of the Atomic Scientists,* Vol. 53, No. 5, September/October, 1997.
16. 'Power Plant Workers Exposed to Tritium Leaks', *The Hindu,* July 25, 2012.
17. 'A Shot in the Arm of Kadiga Protesters', *The Hindu,* February, 12, 2012.
18. 'Black Magic of Uranium at Jadugoda', Study of Health Status of Indigenous People Around Jadugoda Uranium Mines in India, *Report by KOIDE of Kyoto* University, Japan, 2007.

19. Ajay Kumar Gupta, Effects of Low-Dose Ionizing Radiation Among the Employees at the 'Narora Atomic Power Station: A Cross-Sectional Study', 1999.
20. 'Study on the Health Status of Indigenous People', *Report by KOIDE of Kyoto* University, Japan, 2004.
21. World Nuclear Association, *'Nuclear Waste Management',* February, 2012.
22. 'Radioactive Waste Recycled Silverware', Naturalnews.com, February 07, 2013.
23. Nick Squires, 'Mafia Accused of Sinking Ship Full of Radioactive Waste off Italy', *The Telegraph,* September 16, 2009.
24. United Nations Environment Programme, 'After the Tsunami; Rapid Environmental Assessment', February 17, 2005.
25. *National Report* (Actions taken for Indian NPPs subsequent to Fukushiına Nuclear Accident) to the Convention on Nuclear Safety, May 2012.
26. 'How Vulnerable are India's Nuclear Power Plants to Disaster', *Down to Earth,* March, 2011.

# 18

# *India's Energy Scenario: From Centralised to Decentralised Model*

*Manendra Kumar Sahu*

India is one the most energy starved nations in the world. It imports over three-fourths portion of energy requirements from across the world. Is this energy dependence by default or is it by choice? At present this is an appropriate question, as energy imports is resulting into worsening of economy. India's current account deficit has reached record high of 6.7 per cent of GDP primarily because of surging energy imports. This is an unsustainable level for the Indian economy. In the light of surging energy imports, has India taken steps to explore its domestic resources? India has not taken sufficient efforts to explore its domestic resources. India resorted to energy import, neglecting domestic resources, because it was an easy option. On the one hand, the development of domestic resources required tough decisions, like resettlement of people for coal production. On the other, government, for long time, could afford to rely on import of energy and provide subsidised energy because the international prices of oil and gas as well as coal were low. However, the 'era of cheap energy' is over, current international prices are much higher and that is the primary reason for high current account deficit and slow growth in Indian economy.

Can energy scenario be changed? Dedicated effort to utilise more and more domestic resources could be viable option. In the present scenario two important events are taking place simultaneously. One, the high cost of oil and gas is allowing many local energy resources to become economically attractive. Second, rapid change in technology is taking place which favours decentralised energy production and distribution. The present paper argues that early incorporation of local resources and decentralised energy would provide better energy security than imported energy. It will also provide hosts of other benefits. It is estimated that even if India could reduce two per cent of its energy import and invest back in the economy it will result in 0.5 per cent growth in overall economy.[1]

**India's Energy Scenario**

India's energy demand can be divided into different sources of energy, viz. coal, oil and gas and renewable. Coal is the mainstay of the Indian energy sector which contributes 52.8 per cent of primary energy demand. It is followed by oil and gas which contribute 38.8 per cent and the rest is supplied by renewable.[2] Due to insufficient domestic production in both, coal as well as in oil and gas India is increasingly turning towards energy imports. India's coal production, as assessed by the Planning Commission of India for 2011-12, is 696.03 Million Tonnes (Mt) whereas supply is at 559 Mt. The gap of 137.03 Mt of coal would be met through imported coal in large quantity. This gap is ever widening, as a result India's coal import is rising at a five year CAGR of 16.2 %.

**India's Primary Energy Consumption[3]**
**(Million tones oil equivalent)**

| *Fuel* | *Oil* | *Gas* | *Coal* | *Nuclear* | *Hydro* | *Renewable* | *Total* |
|---|---|---|---|---|---|---|---|
| | 162.3 | 55 | 295.6 | 7.3 | 29.8 | 9.2 | 559.1 |
| Per cent | 29 | 9.8 | 52.8 | 1.3 | 5.3 | 1.64 | |

[*Source:* British Petroleum, BP Statistical Review of World Energy June 2012 (London: British Petroleum p.l.c., 2012)].

Similarly, in the case of oil and gas, dependence on imported oil is extremely high. India has proven oil resource of 5.5 billion barrels and its oil production is less than one million barrels. The domestic production is near stagnant for last several years growing by only a per cent per year since 1990. The demand is however much high, pegged at over 3.3 million barrels per day and its growing fast, as a result India imports over three fourth of its oil requirement from abroad. It has become the fourth largest oil importer in the world after the US, China and Japan. The situation is slightly better in the sector of natural gas where the domestic demand is around 2.3 Trillion cubic feet (Tcf) of gas and domestic production is around 1.8 Tcf. To meet the shortfall in demand India imports gas and has become sixth largest Liquidity Natural Gas (LNG) importer in the world consuming around five per cent of global trade.[4]

To maintain uninterrupted oil and gas supply from abroad, India has adopted a multi-pronged strategy. India regularly buys crude oil from spot markets, it has long term supply contracts with a few energy producing nations. Another strategy India has adopted is to invest in oil assets abroad. The ONGC Videsh Limited (OVL) is the leading public sector company of the government in acquiring oil assets abroad. It has assets located across the globe. In Russia, OVL has acquired the Imperial Energy Corporation Plc with oil assets located in Tomsk region of Western Siberia. The other important oil asset in Russia is Sakhalin-1. In Kazakhstan, OVL has invested in Satpayev project. In the Middle East, the company has investments in oil assets in Iraq and Syria. It has diverse investments in Africa. Sudan was the first oil asset investment by OVL which is now divided into two groups, Sudan and South Sudan. OVL has oil assets in Nigeria as well as in Libya. In Latin America, OVL holds assets in Brazil, Venezuela, Cuba and Columbia. The company also has oil asset in Vietnam and Myanmar.[5]

The experience in coal sector is not different. The demand when could not be met with domestic production, India turned to coal import. Today India imports coal from across the world ranging from Australia, Indonesia, Mozambique, South Africa, etc. There is sharp rise in coal imports in the last decade, coal imports has increased by nearly five times. In 2002-03 coal import was worth Rs. 2586 million which was increased to Rs. 12641 million in 2010-11. The sharp increase is observed mainly in type of coal used in power generation called as non-Coking coal which increased from Rs. 2274 million in 2002-03 to Rs. 12376 million in 2010-11.[6] There is also significant investment in coal assets made abroad. Australia attracted the largest chunk of coal investment from India. Adani Enterprise (AEL) has acquired the coal mines of Australia's Linc Energy. The International Coal Venture Ltd. (ICVL), a special purpose vehicle of five state owned public sector companies have coal reserve in Queensland, Australia.[7] LancoInfratech acquired Griffin Energy Group and Carpenter Mine Holdings with the aim to produce 15 mtpa of coal in near term. GVK Power and Infrastructure reached agreement to purchase the Alpha and Kevin's Corner projects.

In Indonesia, Tata Power purchased two coal mines of Bumi Resources in 2007 and the company further acquired PT Baramulti Suksessarana in 2012. The Essar Group has signed an agreement to purchase Aries Coal Mines in Indonesia. Jindal group has acquired coal block in Mozambique through its subsidiary Jindal Resources (Mozambique). Coal India Limited has awarded two coal acreages in Maotize region in Mozambique having an estimated reserve of one billion tonne of coal. JSW Energy Ltd. of India signed a Memorandum of Understanding (MoU) to acquire stake in Indian Ocean Mining Ltd., in South Africa. Investments have been made in the United States. Essar group has acquired Trinity Coal Partners LLC in US for its mines in Kentucky and West Virginia. JSW Steel has acquired coal asset in Western Virginia in US.[8]

**Cost of Energy Import**

However, India's increasing reliance on imported energy has created severe problems. The import of energy builds heavy costs on the nation. Between the financial year 2010-11 and 2011-12 India's annual average cost of imported crude oil increased by $ 27 dollars per barrel, making India's oil import bill rise from $ 100 billion to $ 140 billion dollars. This led to higher domestic inflation, increased input costs, and increase in the budget deficit which resulted in higher interest rate and slowdown in the economic growth. Higher oil prices raised the cost of fertilizers and hence the cost of food which hit hard the poorest of economies. The country experienced deterioration in the balance of payments, putting downward pressure on exchange rates as a result, imports became more expensive and exports less valuable, leading to a drop in real national income. Since the government could not pass on the full impact of high international oil prices, it had to shell out subsidies to consumers amounting to $25 billion.

It is estimated that a sustained 10 dollar increase in oil prices lead to a 1.5 per cent reduction in the GDP of developing countries which is clearly visible in India. Its GDP grew at 6.9 per cent during the last financial year down from the 8 per cent plus growth rate experienced in the past few years.[9] Furthermore, supply and demand projections for the Twelfth five-Year Plan indicate that imports will further grow to about 366 million tones oil equivalent (mtoe) in 2016-17. The growth in import of energy is taking place at high rate of ten per cent per annum and energy imports would nearly triple in just over a decade. It may result in much higher fiscal deficit which may further slowdown GDP growth.[10]

***Is it Tenable?***

India has paid billions of dollars to acquire oil assets across the globe but majority of them are located in volatile regions. These investments face acute fall in production during turmoil in the region thus posing question of reliability on such sources for energy security. India's investment in Sudan is a good case study. OVL invested $2.56 billion in undivided Sudan in 2003. For many years it was a secured investment but problems started in 2011 when the Republic of South Sudan was carved out of Sudan and the oilfield where investment was made became a contested territory between the two countries. In April 2012, South Sudan forcibly occupied the areas surrounding the oil asset and the heavy bombing affected oil production.[11] Oil production fell significantly due to conflict and the company suffered major losses. The OVL suffered similar losses in Libya, Iraq and Syria.

The other problem with investment abroad for energy is the behaviour of the host state. Their postures could change without notice. India's biggest oil and gas investment is made in Russia. As stated earlier, its two investments in Russia are Sakhalin-1 and Imperial Energy. When Sakhalin has been paying good results, Imperial Energy was not paying and as a result the asset was merged with Sistema, a diversified Russian public sector company. Sistema has also made investment in Indian telecom with a local Indian partner. In the alleged telecom scandal of A. Raja, Sistema faced cancellation of license. Russians became very upset with this event and expected the Government of India to resolve the issue. Meanwhile the Russian diplomat stated that Russia will not allow its public money (Sistema investment) to go down the drain and cautioned that Indian investment in oil and gas in Russia might face difficulty. Thus Russian and Sudanese experiences show that oil and gas assets abroad can face serious problems. Such problems could arise without notice, seriously affecting our energy security.

The coal import too faces several problems. As per the present growth in demand in coal, it is expected by analysts that by 2017, India's coal import would touch 300 million tonnes. This is equal to the total exports of Australia or of Indonesia, South Africa and Canada put together. Would India be able to secure such a huge coal supply?[12] There are other challenges in exporting countries like infrastructure, political stability, tax regime and law and regulatory framework. It is observed in the past that cost suddenly escalates if these factors change. In 2011, when Indonesian government changed the mining laws its coal became four times costlier. The major concerns in coal import for India from exporting countries are as follows;

***Australia***

- Coal mining operations are very costly in Australia and are a major contributor to increased coal price volatility.
- The vast distance to Indian coastal port is not very attractive as the voyage time is long and shipping costs are high especially from Eastern Australia ports.
- In Western Australia, getting access to the railway infrastructure which is managed by private companies is difficult. These companies sometimes resist new miners gaining access to their railway networks.
- Another important aspect is weather related problems, especially between December and May which limit rail speed and port handling.
- There are major issues related to the legal and regulatory framework. The federal government wants to impose new mining tax through the Carbon Tax and Mineral Resource Rent Tax.

***Indonesia***

- Indonesia's reliability as a supplier is not guaranteed as there exists doubts about the accuracy of its coal reserves. The quantity and quality of coal resources it possesses is a matter of concern.
- Indonesia's legal and regulatory framework is not very conducive, and the Government of Indonesia frequently changes the country's mining laws.
- The implementation of a 25 per cent export tax on coal with a further increase to 50 per cent is a major stumbling block.
- Another major hurdle is the Domestic Market Obligation (DMO) where every miner has to set aside a certain percentage of the coal production for domestic requirements.

***South Africa***

- There is policy ambiguity involving black economic empowerment programme in the country. Over the years coal companies will have to incorporate indigenous people, who were historically disadvantaged. How the government promotes this policy in future will be crucial for our interests.

- Most of reserves are located in the Central region which is already over exploited, its future potential is uncertain.
- Watersberg is a rich coal reserve for future exploitation but major hurdle is poor infrastructure for coal transportation. It is not yet directly connected to the Richard Bay export terminal, the country's major coal handling facility.
- Other well-endowed region like Vereeniging, South Rand and others have export restrictions based on the size of the company shareholdings in Richard Bay Coal Terminal.

***Mozambique***

- Mozambique's exact coal reserves are not known accurately as explorations are still going on in different provinces.
- The government is under continuous pressure to review its existing deals and thus there is uncertainty over what shape it will take in future. The government has also imposed a levy on the transfer of mining licenses.
- Infrastructure to transport coal to the ports is inadequate.[13]

Thus, it is safe to conclude that as investment in energy assets does not fully guarantee energy security, development of domestic resources are important in achieving energy security. Have we given enough attention to develop local resources?

**Domestic Energy Scenario**

It is noteworthy that when India is investing in oil asset abroad it has yet to explore its sedimentary basin fully. It is estimated that to fully explore its own sedimentary basins fully it will take another fifteen years. As a step to explore its sedimentary basin, India launched New Exploration Licensing Policy (NELP) in 1999. Till that point only eleven per cent of sedimentary basin was explored. Thus, to encourage more exploration NELP opened exploration for private sector including foreign oil companies. Prior to 1999, oil and gas sector, including explorations, was restricted to the government oil and gas companies[14].

The result was not so encouraging. NELP failed to bring any major change in the oil and gas sector. At the end of nine NELP rounds till 2012, there were around 60 large and small discoveries. The major discoveries were Mangala, Aishwariya, Raageshwari and Saraswati (MARS) in Rajasthan by Cairn Energy. However, NELP failed to attract the major international investors as our policies and regulatory frameworks were full of inconsistencies. A good example is the termination of Eni's exploration contract in Rajasthan block in 2012. Eni, an Italian oil company got exploration licence in 2005 NELP bid. The company could not complete exploration of the allotted block because half of it falls in the national park where drilling is forbidden. The company expected complete clearance at the time of block allocation, but the officials in the

Ministry took the position that getting clearance is the responsibility of the respective companies. As a result exploration of the block was abandoned.[15]

In addition to explorations, India has not been able to fully utilise the discoveries which have been made. In the last decade out of around 60 discoveries, 51 were gas discoveries. However out of all gas discoveries made in the country only two of them have got into production and they too are largely under producing. The gas discovery in D-6 block in the Krishna Godavari basin in 2002 received much attention not only because it was our biggest natural gas reserve ever but also it was the world's largest gas discovery of 2002. The Reliance Industry, the operator of the block estimated around 10 Tcf of gas in the block. Though the production from this block started in 2009, the production from KG-D6 is continuously falling. At its peak the field provided 69.43 million standard cubic meters per day (mmscmd). KG-D6 became the single largest source of domestic gas which accounted for about 44 per cent of total gas production and provided almost 35 per cent of the total gas consumption in India. However over the time gas production from KG-D6 significantly declined and today the production stands reduced to 17.3 mmscmd. It has resulted in increasingly relying on imported energy sources.

India also lacks adequate technological capabilities to explore its complete sedimentary block and overcome the geological challenges. Offshore oil and gas reserve is the largest part of reserves in India and today around 56 per cent of production of crude oil comes from offshore locations. India still relies on the technological capability of other countries for deepwater drillings where it requires drilling upto 10,000 meter below the sea level. Similarly to exploit oil and gas trapped in the Deccan region special technology is required because it has the world's thickest layer of lava and volcanic rocks.[16] Newer forms of hydrocarbon resources like shell gas and gas hydrates are coming up. India too has sizeable share of these newer forms of energy but lacks technological capability to exploit them. The government is yet to take concrete steps to develop technological capability within the country.

The mess in coal sector starts right from the clearance stage. It takes much longer to get even the clearance to start exploration of coal block. There are 70 environment clearances to be sought along with 120 forest clearances for starting the work. As a result, there are several proposals lying with the government awaiting clearance, and governmental agencies are taking their own time to clear them. The process of allocations sometimes are mindless and faulty. The government allocated Coal Bed Methane (CBM) contracts but on the same blocks coal mines contracts too were allocated. A clash of interest took place between both the awardees and they could not come to terms to start exploration which resulted in an embarrassing situation. Out of the 33 CBM blocks awarded not one has started production.[17] Theimportant problems in the coal sector in India is listed below.

1. *Environment Restrictions*: The delay in getting environment clearances leads to implementation of projects as mentioned earlier. There is a stipulated time frame for getting regulatory approvals but it is rarely followed. Without these clearances the mine developers do not get the mining lease grant.

2. *Social*: In several cases to run mines, land acquisition is necessary. However, land acquisition is a major hurdle, owners of land are not willing to part with land. The people are very skeptical of government's rehabilitation and resettlement plan. In several cases affected people feel that adequate compensation is not paid to then land owners. These factors make land acquisition a herculean task and results in indefinite delays.

3. *Transport:* Transport infrastructure to carry coal from mines to power stations is inadequate. Rail network play a crucial role in coal transportation and carries about fifty per cent of coal. These railway routes are overly saturated. Railway network across four metropolis, i.e., Delhi-Mumbai-Chennai and Howrah constitute only sixteen per cent of rail networks in the country but carries sixty five per cent of freight including coal. It takes longer to carry coal in such saturated networks. Indian railway runs passenger and freight on the same track and difference in speed of two types of trains erodes capacity utilisation.[18]

Technological issues in coal sector too are important. Coal is primarily utilized as a fuel in thermal power stations, where it is burnt to produce heat but there are several other innovative technologies to utilise coal. Coal-to-oil is a mature technology and is in use for several years. It is particularly useful for India where low grade coal is in abundance. It is not economical to carry them to far off power stations. Another innovative use of coal is In-situ Gasification when coal is gasified in underground mines and only gas is taken out and used as a fuel for turbines to produce electricity. In-situ Gasification is an environment friendly technology. Such innovative use of coal would require investments in technological development. Thus, investing in energy technology along with complete exploration of sedimentary basin and effective utilisation of domestic resources would provide better energy security than relying on imported energy.

**Decentralized Energy Model**

It is important not to overlook locally available sources of energy. A big mistake in India has been that the energy scenario has been painted with one brush overlooking various locally available resources. It has a centralised model in which, electricity mainly from coal for household need and oil for transportation has become the dominant source of supply for a large part of the country. Why was the centralised model adopted? The centralised model was a choice of policy planners for two important reasons. One, the cost of energy from coal and oil was affordable for a very long time. The prices of oil has escalated by several times in the last decade, the cost of a barrel of oil hovered around only $ 20 which hit a peak of $ 147 in June 2008. It has been hovering around $ 100 per barrel in the last few years. It is because of the escalating prices that today we have accepted the fact that the 'era of cheap oil is over'. The coal prices too have seen similar surge in prices. Can the centralised model be practiced in the context of the prevailing high energy prices?

The higher energy prices have wide repercussion on the Indian energy scenario. The government regulated prices of both electricity and oil in the country and provided subsidised energy through budgetary provisions. The government could subsidise energy under reasonable coal and oil prices but in the background of the saving international energy prices, the government finds itself in a conundrum. On the one hand it could not increase domestic energy price because of popular pressure and on the other, budget deficit due to subsidy, as stated earlier, started directly hurting the overall growth of our economy. What is the way out? A long term strategy to develop local energy resources and a gradual shift from the centralised model could help develop a viable energy model. This would be in accordance with earlier statement that if India could reduce two per cent of its energy import and invest back in the economy it will result in 0.5 per cent growth in the overall economy.

A successful strategy to overcome centralised model is to locate the source of energy close to the customer and utilise more and more local sources of energy. This in fact is the decentralised energy model. It employs small to medium scale facilities to provide multiple energy services. Decentralised energy model is closely related with energy security as it uses all locally available resources which are renewable like biomass, sunlight, wind etc. As a result, dependence on energy import progressively comes down. It further enhances security as it shifts focus from finite source of hydrocarbons to infinite source of energy. Decentralised model along with energy security also offer hosts of other benefits like local development, customised design according to region and community and allow for active involvement of participants. A comparison of centralized vs. decentralised model is presented in the following table. Electricity supply through the grids taken as a centralised model in the table, however it is equally applicable to petroleum products.

**Centralised Model**

| *State of art/Approach* | *Characteristics* | *Consequences* |
|---|---|---|
| **Technical** | | |
| • National Grid Extension | • Centralised | • Very slow electrification rate |
| • 2-3 wire high voltage transmission | • Complex technique& require expert knowledge | • Excludes majority of people |
| • Large-scale centralized Electricity production | • Long distance distribution network | • No local resources used, hardly local job |

| **Political** | | |
|---|---|---|
| • Top down approach | • Lack of democratic decision making | • High prices through corruption |
| • Centralised 'Master-plan' | • Strong links between govt. and weak regulation favours corruption and nepotism. | • Disenchantments with politics |
| **Social** | | |
| • Large part no electricity | • Use of other sources lack basic appliance (mobiles, fan, radio) | • Hazardous and dangerous<br>• Expensive (diesel/kerosene)<br>• Education and health constrains<br>• Rural exodus/brain drain<br>• No broad participation |
| **Economical** | | |
| • Government controlled | • Lack of private sector | • Fewer jobs, mostly in urban area |
| • Reliance on foreign donors and foreign loans | • Centralised planned market | • No business opportunity<br>• Exclusion of rural population |
| • State owned utility companies | • Increase of foreign debt | |
| | • No competition | • The gap of income and development is wider |

## Decentralised Model

| *Technical* | *Characteristics* | *Consequences* |
|---|---|---|
| • Micro-grids | • Infinite renewable energy Resources | • Effective electrification |
| • Solar Home System Convention and SWER | • Small scale Implementation<br>• Decentralised production and Distribution<br>• Cost effective, simple design Technique<br>• 'Low skilled' maintenance<br>• Bigger voltage fluctuation | • Customises solutions |
| **Political** | | |
| • Bottom up approach | • Local decision process, increased transparency | • Active involvement in plan<br>• Self-determined. |
| • NGO involvement | | |
| **Social** | | |
| • Effective and prompt Electrification, compared | • Provision of small DC appliance (SHS) like radio | • Increased inventive to live areas |

| | | |
|---|---|---|
| to conventional approach | • Provision of advanced AC appliances like cooling Street light, machinery<br>• Strengthening of community life | • Access to modern energy and its benefit.<br>• Ease rural life |
| **Economical** | | |
| • Create new energy market | • Increase off-grid demand Competition | • Private business opportunity |
| • Private economic approach | • Reduce foreign dependency | • New finance and lending Opportunity. |
| • Reformation of existing structure | • Cost effective and efficient Rural electrification<br>• Tax generation<br>• Increased transparency<br>• Value added chain | • job creation in rural areas in many fields.<br>• Economic Development<br>• Increase in wealth |
| **Environmental** | | |
| • Small scale renewable Energy Supply<br>• Local emission free energy Generation | • No emission during electricity production<br>• No dependence on fossil fuel<br>• Climate friendly | • No local environmental impact |

(Table adopted from Jacob Graf (et.al.), *'Comparative Analysis between Grid Extension and Decentralised Solutions for Electrification- Case study: Sofala Province in Mozambique'*, in Martin Schafer, Noara Kebir, Daniel Philipp (ed.), *Micro Perspective for Decentralised Energy Supply: Proceedings of the International Conference,* Technische Universitat Berlin, 7th-8th April 2011.)

As shown above, locally available resources are positively associated not only with energy security but also with overall development of the region. In planning energy need of a region, locally available sources should be preferred. In coal bearing region more and more electricity driven vehicles can be used where as in sugar producing regions ethanol as a motor fuel can be used. This will help not only in reducing dependence on external sources of energy but also lead to more and more investment within the region. There are several experiments already in use which shows that localised model is sustainable. The 'Husk Power System' (HPS) is an attempt to generate electricity with locally available rice husk and aims at distribution in the neighbouring villages.[19] HPS is run in villages in north-eastern Bihar. Rice Husk is a by– product in this rice producing region. The husk generated electricity is supplied on a monthly fee which is affordable to the rural community. People are willing to pay because it is cheaper than kerosene lamp which they otherwise use for lighting. Electricity is supplied to around 2,00,000 pcople. It is a unique model of decentralised electricity generation and distribution using local resources. It is also a good example of rural empowerment enterprise.

The Indian Solar Loan Programme conducted by United Nations Environment Programme (UNEP) provided yet another example of decentralised model of energy generation. The programme was conducted in states of Karnataka and Kerala in which credit facility was provided to rural households to purchase Solar Home System (SHS). Two large nationalised banks Canara Bank and Syndicate bank along with several regional Rural banks, were associated with the project to distribute loan through their branch offices. The rural households were mostly without electricity grid or erratic grid supply. The SHS emerged as an attractive ling term option because it provided guaranteed good quality power totally independent from the grid. It is also relatively simple, reliable and quickly constructed. Once installed, solar energy provided the basic need of rural household lighting and relative new use of mobile charging. The project provided an excellent example of self-sustaining decentralised model of energy in rural households and won the prestigious Energy Globe award.[20] Yet another significant leap in providing alternate source of transport is Flexi Fuel Vehicles (FFV).

**Missing Flexi - Fuel Revolution**

There is a silent revolution taking place in the vehicle fuel. The world is not only concerned about depleting fossil fuel but also about gyration in the international oil prices. Relying solely on fossil fuel is risky. As a response to the uncertainty associated with fossil fuel, hybrid technologies have been developed which are flexible and cost competitive. Flexi Fuel Vehicle (FFV) is a similar hybrid technology. It is a multi-fuel vehicle which is capable of running on any combination of ethanol and gasoline. This vehicle is fitted with special sensors which can automatically tune engine to run on any combination of fuel. They are able to beat the gyration in the international crude oil prices. Ethanol works as balancer of the two fuels. If gasoline prices are affordable then the consumer uses a suitable mix of gasoline and ethanol. If gasoline price is very expensive the consumer would like to fill larger part of ethanol. As a result, higher gasoline prices does not cause higher financial burden.

In many ways FFV is considered better than a vehicle run on gasoline. Apart from flexibility of fuel they are considered efficient. It has a motor octane number of 98 which exceeds that of gasoline. Since it has a motor octane number higher than gasoline, it can be used in engines with a higher compression ratio (12-to-1, compared with 8-to-1 ratio typically found in gasoline-fueled engines). As a result, ethanol fueled engines are approximately 15 per cent more efficient than motors using gasoline. Additionally, ethanol flammability in air is also lower than that of gasoline which reduces the number and severity of vehicle fire. FFV also has a lower vapor pressure than gasoline, which results in lower evaporative emissions. Exhaust emission associated with ethanol are less toxic than those associated with gasoline and have lower atmospheric reactivity. This makes FFV less polluting vehicle.[21]

There are sound reasons to introduce FFV in India. India is the second largest sugar producer, after Brazil, in the world. The oil shock of 1973 hit both the countries hard. However, Brazil after the shock, with consistent research and development could become world leader in ethanol production as well as in FFV. Brazil has world's largest number of FFV. Brazil could achieve energy security with its ethanol programme. India has no such major ethanol programme and still is struggling to introduce 15 per cent ethanol blending with gasoline. With proper support increasing the ethanol production is not difficult in India. The task of introduction of FFV is easy for India as the leading FFV manufacturer like General Motors, Fiat, Renault have their vehicle manufacturing hubs in India. 'Made in India' FFV is much easier.

FFV is not only able to solve problem of reliance on imported energy but also cater to rural development. Vibrant ethanol sector is closely related to rural development and for India it is much more pertinent. In Brazil, it is observed that when ethanol was doubled it resulted in bringing out one percentage of the population out of poverty.[22] Similar cases could be repeated in many other countries where a large section of population is involved in agriculture. Ethanol creates a huge chain of production ranging from sugar cane cultivation to fuel retailing. It creates large number of employment. This is extremely necessary in countries like India where agriculture sector faces severe problems. Agriculture involves a large number of population but at the bottom of value chain. Farmers fail to get higher economic returns, and they are not able to come out of poverty.

## Conclusion

Are the decentralized models all about replacing the existing energy system? It is not possible to reduce India's energy dependence very soon, but progressive introduction of decentralised model would reduce dependence on imported energy. The reduction in dependence would also reduce undue economic pressure built on the Indian economy. Both, current account deficit as well as high inflation could be brought to reasonable levels. Furthermore, decentralized model of energy would provide hosts of other benefits. It will bring community development. As energy would be produced close to the consumption centre the community could be actively involved. It will not only create local jobs but also would allow for investment within the community. As the focus would be more towards renewable energy, where technology upgradations are bringing costs consistently down, it would reduce environment problems associated with fossil fuel. Above all, as the fuel for energy would be locally generated, it will bring down dependence on imported energy thus providing true energy security to the nation.

## Notes

1. Ashok Sreenivas and Shantanu Dixit: 'Are We Serious About Our Energy Security?' *Economic and Political Weekly* (Mumbai), Volume XLVII, No. 20, May 19, 2012.

2. British Petroleum, B.P., *Statistical Review of World Energy,* June 2012, London: British Petroleum p.l.c., 2012.
3. Coal Controller's Organisation, *Provisional Coal Statistics 2011-2012*, Ministry of Coal, Government of India, Kolkata June, 2012.
4. U.S. Energy Information Administration provides comprehensive Indian energy profile. India page can be obtained from http://www.eia.doe.gov/emeu/cabs/India/background.html
5. OVL maintains a detail list of investment on its website www.ongcvidesh.com
6. Australian coal was mainly used in steel industry due to its higher quality whereas coal from South Africa and Indonesia is used in power and cement sector due to both less in cost and quality. op.cit., f.n. 3.
7. The participating companies are Steel Authority of India Limited (SAIL), Coal India Ltd. (CIL), National Mineral Development Corporation (NMDC), National Thermal Power Corporation (NTPC) and Rashtriya Ispat Nigam Ltd.
8. List of overseas investment in coal mines is given by the Ministry of Mines in their Annual Report. Ministry of Mines, Annual Report 2010-11, Government of India, New Delhi.
9. The address of Mr. Jaipal Reddy, Minister of Petroleum and Natural Gas, at the 5th OPEC International Seminar at Vienna, on 13-14 June 2012. The copy of Address, published by the Press Information Bureau, Government of India, New Delhi.
10. *Op.cit.* f.no. 1.
11. 'Sudan and South Sudan: Giving Divorce a Bad Name', *The Economist*, April 14th-20th, 2012.
12. 'Energy in India: The Future is Black', *The Economist,* January 21st-27th, 2012.
13. Ashish Gupta, 'The Dynamics of Importing Coal: Lessons for India', *ORF Issue Brief*, Observer Research Foundation, New Delhi, Issue Brief #44, October, 2012.
14. The Ministry of Petroleum and Natural Gas maintains a section on New Exploration Licensing Policy (NELP) at www.petroleum.nic.in
15. 'Oilmin Cancels Italian Co Eni's Exploration Deal in Rajasthan', *The Economic Times* (Mumbai), 30 August, 2012.
16. 'Navigating through the Energy Crisis', *The Economic Times* (Mumbai), 15 June, 2012.
17. *Ibid.*
18. Ashish Gupta, *India's Coal Supply Security: Pushing Imports at the Expense of Domestic Reforms*? Observer Research Foundation, New Delhi.
19. Andrew C. Revkin, 'Husk Power for India', *The New York Times*, December 24, 2008.

20. United Nations Environment Programme (UNEP), I*ndian Solar Loan Programme: Programme Overview and Performance Report,* UNEP RISO Centre, February 2005.
21. Jose Goldemberg, 'Brazilian Biofuel Industry, Biotechnology for Biofuels', Volume 1, No. 6, May 2008.
22. Lee R. Lynd, Jeremy Woods, 'A New Hope for Africa', *Nature,* Volume 474, 23 June 2011.

# 19

# *Ethics of Journalism*

*K. Govindan Kutty*

I don't care to know what that celebrated young cricketer's private passions are, if he has any. Yet, thankfully, we know it now. In an act of supreme generosity or professionalism, our media told us about those private matters. We lapped it up with pathological relish. They fed us feverishly.

Why did they give us what we did not quite need or want, what was a mad foray into an irrelevant privacy? Well, they told us for no grosser reason than that no one took exception to it, at any rate, not in so many words. Media told us because policemen told them. Policemen told them because they thought anything was good enough to berate a bad boy.

No mind master from Freud downwards has told us about any connection between cricket and preventative devices. Yes, some people like Krishna of Gita have seen a cause-effect relation between kama and krodha. But there is nothing yet to link sex with spot-fixing. Why did then our cops spread the word? They thought they could get away with it for once. Why did our media purvey the safe-sex scoop? They thought nothing of trotting out some bit of scandal, breaking basic norms of ethics.

**World's Giggle**

And, scandal is good news. Not quite so ethics. It will be naïve to run away from this reality of human nature. Nor do we need be overly worried about it. There is an old Malayalam poem by N. V. Krishna Warrier that defines news with a certain creative cynicism. A compulsive reader picks up the morning paper and devours the "world's giggle and pettifoggery". He finds it a "clatter of absurd bits of unconnected tidings," something that turns his "mind into a fish mart". Like all truisms, it is a hyperbole. But we have learnt to live with somewhat of a "fish market inside", with a little bit of scandal and pettifoggery, and, of course, nonsense.

We started off with Sreesanth's private passions which were once, though briefly, an engaging subject for media coverage. Forget Sreesanth. I don't presume to try or defend him. I know no cricket. I bring this up only to assert that media conduct can run counter to ethics with no premeditation, no external motivation, pecuniary or psychological. Not only Sreesanth's, anyone's life we may intrude with abandon even if it has no connection with his public conduct or, if you like, misconduct. The other way of saying it is that we are not always bogged down by ethical considerations when we dish out the day's news.

Those who violate ethics often do not know that they are doing it. Most of them are more like those tarred with the infamous banality of crime in Hitler's Germany and less like Jesus's tormentors. Ethics of journalism is broken by ordinary reporters and editors, simple people like the German folk who helped their Jewish neighbors be dragged to the gas chamber, in a fit of guileless uncreative enthusiasm or helplessness, not as an act of evil. It may be unfair to dub them as inveterate killers of truth and sanctity. It must be asserted, at the same time, that the very casualness of the violation makes it ever more sinister.

**Satyam Brooyad**

What is ethical journalism? It may be simplistic, and yet close to truth, to suggest that good journalism is all about speaking the truth. Satyam brooyad. The next line of the adage, priyam brooyad, speak well, may not hold good in this sphere. Trot out any tepid stuff, even truth, and it will not be relished. There is so much of sour and bitter matter that awaits exposure.

And, exposure subserves social good. In fact, journalism may not be worth it if it exposes and disturbs no crook. If it stops short of doing that, it will be failing in its basic function. That is being unethical. It is not only telling a lie, suggestio falsi, that is unethical but also hiding a fact, suppressio veri.

One unethical practice for which journalists are often pilloried is for not speaking the whole truth. Sometimes, not always, it is an unfair charge. The journalist is a quintessential witness. What he witnesses may not be a total view, and what he views may be from one limited angle or another wrong angle. With the best of his attempts at self-regulation, objectivity may remain an inaccessible ideal. This is indeed quite different from occasional journalistic essays in blatant falsification or presenting chosen facts to suit a pre-determined design. Such conscious falsification is criminal, and merits no discussion as professional failing.

Talking about truth, it may be a tall order to ask for total truth from journalists. No one, a journalist still less, really has a way to see the complete face of truth which is proverbially covered by a golden lid. Kierkegard went so far as to say that truth is subjectivity. That extremist motto may be counterproductive in journalism but its other extreme will stifle all inquiry, depriving journalism of its relevance.

**Plurality of Truth**

What is most unethical is to claim ultimate certitude or monopoly of truth. Any piece of sensitive information that comes one's way may be presented as a possible reflection of reality, but no more. And what comes one's way will necessarily be fragmented fact. Journalists are only channels, not sources. They will be true only to the extent to which their sources are true. Sources themselves may be ill-informed or may manipulate their discharge with their own motives. Successful sources vend their acerbic ware with such finesse that even skilled scribes can end up as unsuspecting tools in a grand game other wily men play.

It is often so tempting to lap up the bits of news revealed to one as gospel, just as it is difficult to disabuse oneself of the tendency to hold on to one's original presentation even when it increasingly turns out to be untenable. There is the existentialist view, "there is no truth, there are only truths." That should be a guide to journalists too. For journalism is a constant inquiry, never arrival at a final destination. When one's own version becomes incorrigible, leaving no scope for amendment, fascism sets in. Fascism, in journalism or other pursuits, is the negation of ethics.

We have to live with the fact that journalists, in their journalistic role, are not privy to any information. They seek it or are given it by someone else. The giver may be a genuine do-gooder or one with an axe to grind. Often you go along with him as a matter of professional compulsion-as long as what is sold and bought is not patent falsehood. Plain lies are hard to spread. My view of human nature, and journalistic conduct, is not so dark as to assume that everyone is a liar and everyone an inveterate purveyor of lies.

**Suitcase Saga**

I will discuss two old stories to illustrate how tough it is to determine the ethicality of an approach. First, there was that nation-shaking report of a suitcase of one crore of rupees being gifted to the prime minister. The story was crudely manufactured in Mumbai and exported to New Delhi for appropriate presentation. It was politically useful to some people who seized it with alacrity. It was too embarrassing to others to attempt an instant inquiry into the truth of the story. So it did the rounds for a while, a week or two, entertaining everyone but possibly the imagined giver and the alleged donor, and the readers and the writers went on to open or close other suitcases.

A whole nation was taken for a stupid ride. What could be more unethical? Was it done in the full knowledge that it was untrue and unethical? Was it only the manufacturer who knew it was untrue or did the distributor also knew it? What difference will such prior knowledge make to the havoc the story plays on people or to the venality of the manufacturer and the distributor? Will a wrong story foolishly purveyed absolve the reporter or the editor of a gross charge of venality?

It could be argued that a faux pas is not an ethical lapse. It may be possible to dismiss it as a professional lapse, almost like an error of a surgeon's judgment in a moment of medical crisis or a fatal mistake a driver makes while negotiating a treacherous, unfamiliar, curve. But it is only 'almost like', not fully.

**Life is Beautiful**

Life is so beautiful—not quite the way Trotsky saw it just before his assassination—for journalists that it affords opportunities to assess and avoid mistakes before or during or after their commission. There can be two reasons why they do not do so.

One, they avoid avoiding, or stick to, their mistakes because of obsessive self-righteousness. They assume they know, when they don't. They hold on to their original position, and resort to cheap sophistry, when nearly proved wrong, claiming, as they say in Malayalam, their rabbit has two horns.

Two, they have a gain to make out of the persisting falsehood in which they play a key role. Shame or moral restraint or etiquette is no inhibiting factor. The second reason is criminal, not professional. It presents a total lie and a total lie may not be seen as journalism in decay. It is just that, total lie.

The second story I discuss is not as well-known as the saga of the suitcase. This is about a politico-religious issue involving some monks and sleuths. Some monks were suspected to be shady. A senior official who was watching them studiously and steadily passed on a whole lot of information, complete with documents to quote when needed, to a friendly reporter.

The reporter knew it was a plant. No one really suffers from such strong civic sense as to pursue a reporter or editor with a story risking his job or reputation unless of course he has a valid self-interest or, at best, what he may regard as a larger community interest. The reporter in question also knew that the story was coming to him as part of an organised plan for leak, not a do-gooding exercise. There should have been a compelling reason for the leak: its content may be being contested stiffly within the official machinery or its disclosure may foil some clandestine plans well under way.

Such cloak-and-dagger operation is risky—for the reporter, not the source, in this case. He may well be being taken for a ridiculous ride. He is apt to be mocked at as a police agent. An agent—police, political or foreign—is no honorable man when exposed. And agents are usually known to be paid for their services. Accepting remuneration, lump sum or deferred, is sin when discovered. So it involved some hard-headed consideration whether the story should be swallowed or spit out. It involved a hard-nosed assessment of the motives and the methods of the source.

The story was run. It had, I take it, the desired effect. There was no remuneration except a lunch or two and a car ride during the long-winded discussions on the twists and turns of the story. There was no political goal to reach. I can vouch for it because I was the reporter concerned. I had no qualms about it though it was a story based on a single source.

The case of the suitcase story, with which I was associated in some capacity too, was morally different. For one thing, it turned out to be a plant, and an unsustainable one at that. For another, it had been planned in furtherance of an unabashed political game. For all I know, no monies were disbursed in the process of the creation or circulation of the story. But money need not be paid or received to make a story sale unethical.

In a total breach of ethics, journalists lap up a lie and spread it around frenetically not because someone pays them underhand in cash or kind. They do so more because of a callous approach to truth and what is known in the world of journalism as plant. Venality is not entirely ruled out.

Yet it should be recognised that one reporter or editor or a team of them will not be able to sell a lie with success on a regular basis. Even the most adroit of them are apt to get caught and weeded out sooner or later. So it is my assertion that breach of ethics, including sale of lies and reckless probe into privacies, happens as a matter of professional incompetence or gullibility.

**One Correction**

One important correction is by way of addition. It may also be because of professional conceit. Journalism flourishes in the rain shadow region of power. It deals with power, and comes to wield some power. To be taken seriously, journalists need to be able to get things done through the powers-that-be, ringing up a revenue divisional officer to delay some recovery proceeding by a day or getting a government flat allotted to himself on paltry terms or recommending to the party president or the chief minister a good friend's case for a berth in the Council. Journalists can move hills, if faith can move mountains. If they don't, we consign them to political monasteries.

Three years ago we were shaken up by reports of conversations between the redoubtable fixer-public relations wizard, Neera Radia, and high-profile journalists. The conversations had been tapped by taxmen and criminal investigators. The conversations found their way to newspaper columns and television screens. God be praised! And, with him, astute news planters!

They were talking about making some ministers, tainted or not, and dropping some others or getting desired judgments. They were all good journalists, scoop masters and sharp shooters. With such intimate links with those who turn the levers of power, they could not have been less than they were.

They thought better of themselves. They had access to the top people; they were even friendly to the wielders of power and makers of decisions, to whom they were obliged and who to them sometimes. They thought it was well within the parameters of propriety to try to get some berth for someone or deny it to someone else, just as someone had probably helped themselves to rise in the echelons of career.

There is some saving grace in this murky exercise of professional power: it can now and then be exposed, and its participants discredited, as happened in this episode involving Raja and Radia. Mind you, discredit, yes, but no total eclipse. They have more than managed to retain their media relevance. Which is a measure of the community's view of media mascots' para-professional adventures.

As a revelation, that was at once shocking and relieving but not what really went on between ace journalists and power players. Political journalists cannot but remain close to politicians in power or aspiring to win it tomorrow. Being close means being trusted. Being trusted means doing nothing that would go against the perceived interests of those whose trust is held. This has gone on always, everywhere. Perhaps it was not so blatant or unashamed;

perhaps it was for a larger community cause. It is unlikely to be otherwise in times to come. It cannot be banned by law. Homilies, in this world or elsewhere, hardly work.

Phil Graham of the Washington Post suggested that journalists avoid getting too close to the people in power. That would ensure a degree of independence and veracity. That is but like asking someone to get out of his magnificent obsession, his fundamental function. Which editor or manager will keep in position in the capital a political reporter who cannot whisper some mumbo-jumbo in the chief minister's bursting ears?

**Culture of Balance**

What we can do is to try to imbibe a culture of balance and detachment, much like Krishna for whom nothing remains undone, nothing to be attained, yet he kept doing his calling. A golden rule may be: keep your contacts but limit the level of their intimacy. Assume that no one is a saint, and everyone not a sinner.

Thank heavens, there is also our dear CBI which will, when it so chooses, expose an ebullient wheeler dealer in the fourth estate. The Press Council can duly dish out an admonition. Editors will be constrained to clip the psychedelic wings of their delinquent reporters. In their living rooms, readers and viewers will say ha-ha for a day, or, be generous, two. That it happens is reassuring.

Editors themselves may have to go out as happened even in the celebrated New York Times. It was not long ago that a highly decorated reporter was found to have been concocting his wave-making interviews and features. He had no blue eyes to be a blue-eyed boy because he was an African American. He had been chosen and groomed by the editor. Eventually both had to go before it became a serial story on failing journalism.

Closer home, there were editors who quietly packed up when their bylines appeared under articles originally written and published by others. After the sack, some of them went to lecture on ethics—like the anti-hero of a 1970s film, The Front Page, who quit as managing editor to teach good journalism after he employed his share of dirty tricks.

**News for Payment**

Ethics of journalism is often discussed in the context of what has come to be called paid news. A friendly, even a rather unfriendly, news source may try to please a scribe and manage to have an agreeable picture drawn. But who will purvey patent nonsense even if it carries a hefty reward? And who will believe it? What is not believable goes out the window the day after tomorrow, if not tomorrow.

I had an editor who was genuinely concerned about paid news flooding the paper. He was a good man who wanted everyone else to be good, absolutely good, yielding to nothing that may detract from goodness. In a word, he was taking a puritanical approach to bribes, inducements and gifts. He saw no difference between them. Anything given/taken was a bribe in his view. He was much like another editor of mine who was unable to distinguish between someone who takes a drink and a drunkard. Alcohol, in his view, is taken only by boozers.

The newly joined editor's corrective measure was to insist that every reporter should give at the end of his report a list of the gifts he had received from the source of the news. The reader should be able to see through the slant that may have crept into the report written by someone who had received a gift, a hand radio for instance in olden days, something significantly costlier today.

It was not perhaps appreciated that no one who was honest enough to make a clean breast of his illicit receipts would act as a vehicle for proven disinformation. There was a popular white-clad and full-sleeved leader in the capital who would gift umbrellas, besides sumptuous lunch and liquor, to journalists who covered his organisation's annual conference. Those who could not make it to the event would have their gifts home-delivered. They were grateful; but none could say nice words about him always, even while his umbrellas saved them from inclement rains.

**Something Funny**

There is something funny about ethics in journalism. There is not one, repeat, one, journalist or consumer of his concoction, or self-designated moralists who does not debunk unethical practices. All of them say in a chorus loka: samasta: sukhino bhavantu. May the whole world be happy! May everyone speak the truth, the whole truth. No one is a votary of lack of ethics. Everyone wants everyone else to be ethical. The damn thing, lack of ethics, still persists.

It may be boring to quote authorities and laymen on the evil of unethical journalism. Everyone berates it. To give the flavour of unanimity, a paragraph from the report of a Press Council subcommittee on ethics may be reproduced:

> "The phenomenon of paid news has attracted the critical attention of many individuals and sections of Indian society. For instance, the Vice President of India and Chairman of the Rajya Sabha, Shri Abdul Hamid Ansari, Union Ministers such as Information and Broadcasting Minister Smt. Ambika Soni and Human Resources Development Minister Shri Kapil Sibal, spokesperson of the Indian National Congress Shri Manish Tewari, senior leader of the Bharatiya Janata Party (BJP) and Member of Parliament (MP) Shri L.K. Advani, the Leader of the Opposition in the Lok Sabha and BJP MP Smt. Sushma Swaraj, the leader of the Opposition in the Rajya Sabha and BJP MP from the Rajya Sabha Shri Arun Jaitley, the General Secretary of the Communist Party of India (Marxist) Shri Prakash Karat, the Chief Minister of Andhra Pradesh Shri K. Rosaiah, noted actor Shri Amitabh Bachchan, among many others, have all expressed their concern about the paid news phenomenon in the country. A number of seminars and conferences on the issue have taken place."

That the issue still rages, and increasingly so, shows two possibilities. First, all are not equally concerned or sincere in their concern about the evil. They can live with or down the evil over time. Secondly, the evil is so ingrained in human nature that it refuses to go away even when vociferously, universally, commanded to do so.

The Press Council and other media watchdogs, not to speak of oracles among commentators, have held forth at length on politicians buying publicity for a price during elections. Give money and have what you like written. The proposition is as simple as that. Now is such purchased publicity really worth it? Do candidates get elected on the strength of the agreeable reports published in half a dozen newspapers for a price? How many serious scribes are available to produce and publish desired reports for a prescribed fee? Can the scribe ensure publication of his script as a rule?

**Praise as News**

Any serious player in politics and media knows that favourable coverage can come for nothing. Any candidate who is seen as remotely relevant gets written about even without his trying for it. An inescapable election feature is about "a day in the life of a candidate."

A reporter travels with a candidate and comes back in the evening to produce constituency copy studded with encomiums. I am yet to read a report that says that the candidate with whom the reporter went round is a fool whom the people are going to dump in the bin of history. This kind of constituency or candidate coverage is invariably pleasant copy ranging from alliterative description of landscape to plain sycophancy. It costs the candidate nothing. Those who pay for it can really use some brains, theirs or others'.

Paid news is bad for two reasons. One, it is untruth in varying degrees. Two, it is trotted out for an undeclared fee. Raise the fee and release anything you like, calling it anything but news, we have no quarrel. A column of free news about a potion that may help hair grow on a barren pate is easily dubbed as unethical; a full page advertisement on the efficacy of that legendary elixir from the ocean of milk brings to the media much-needed revenue. Perhaps it is the assumption that an advertisement need not be right but news has to be wholesome truth. Standards vary. The brain is split, as American psychologist Michael Gazzaniga repeatedly tells us.

Time was when we did not take seriously cynics who said news was what was printed between two ads. But those cynics got impromptu endorsement through newspapers which had no news on front pages. Front pages were reserved for useful ads which, though, did not generate their cost of production. I have not seen such newspapers in my time. It is for historians of journalistic ethics to examine when the shift started in favour of news and, in a manner of speaking, against advertisements.

**Ads and News**

In the course of the great shift, ads were proscribed on front pages, except possibly as ear panels, a precarious proportion between news and ads were prescribed, and newsmen and admen seemed adversaries. Admen cajoled their clients by offering to have some complimentary news published along with the ads; newsmen suspected, and spiked, anything that was proffered by admen, even in pure, if unlikely, public interest.

Intransigent editors insisted on ad-free front pages, besides giving overweening primacy to news and views over advertisements. When financial enlightenment dawned on owners, and editors too, a modicum of ads started appearing on editorially approved front page space. A quarter page below the fold, at best: that was the unalterable limit fixed by the editor.

The perceptions changed, and with them, practices. The whole front page was allowed to be filled with ads, the newspaper becoming, shall we say, the ads paper. A new trouble soon emerged. As an absurd mathematical limit, there could be only one front page in one day's newspaper, page one never being more than one. Space men and newsmen of newspapers had a stroke of genius when they brought out their ware with two page ones, not one. We should hope to see page ones becoming three and four and more as long as wants remain unlimited and resources limited as good old Adam Smith put it.

The advertisement manager's job depended on the revenue he brought through ads; the editor's stature rose when he could limit the advertisements and expand the news segment. In the early eighties, I remember a new editor telling us in his inaugural address that it would be his endeavour to limit the news: advertisement ratio to 55:45. So it was done whenever there were no more ads.

The editor's role changed, shall we say, expanded in a curious way, before long. The Times of India, respectfully called the Old Lady of Bori Bunder, is still derided by journalists for what it did with the editor and ads. One editor of it had claimed that his job was the second most important in the country after the prime minister's. He lost it soon. The editor's print line was made unintelligibly small. The resident editors of various editions were put in charge of their respective "markets", not regions.

Space marketing became a creative exercise. Scoops of news remained important but not more than money-yielding ads. Advertisers got a new deal. They could pay for a whole section of the newspaper and fill it with whatever they wanted. And, they could print it making it look like news. The old imperious editorial practice of labeling specifically as 'advertisement' anything that resembled news in lay-out or text consciously abandoned. The era of advertisements began.

**Marketing Editor**

There was no more condescending attitude from editors to admen. The latter brought money. Money was what kept the paper going. No one rejected the offer of the editor's job. Jockeying for it continued, more or less like before. But the new editor had a "market" to supervise, not a cloistered newsroom. The editor or the managing editor was becoming virtually the marketing editor. Hark back with hilarity to the era when even newsroom had not come under the editor's close or regular scrutiny.

Grand old editors lavished their attention on the edit page where erudite opinion on everything under the sun appeared. The day's news was left to be laid out by chief sub-editors. From them to the editors who participate in space marketing is a far cry, a fall, old-timers would say.

In point of fact, it need not be dreaded as an ethical collapse. It is simply that the vital importance of money in running a paper is recognized. In the process, there has come about a certain change in the relationship between news and ads. The editor and the adman betray themselves when they start mistaking ads for news or the other way round. Advertisement is, besides a revenue-earner, an essential announcement of certain products and services and commercial propositions. A classical definition is that advertisement induces in the user a want for what he does not need.

That is harmless. That seeks to influence the user's choice, no more. That precludes paid-for publicity for any product or service that is patently fake. In ancient times, even avaricious admen would not touch anything that appeared to be a hollow claim, not a hard, plausible announcement.

There was this advertiser of a wonder drug for AIDS, a munificent patron of every newspaper in the state, whose help we sought for a frugal supplement we had planned. Not only did he agree to help us but kept increasing the space he wanted to buy.

Such generosity, or business acumen, was embarrassing, suspicious. It was not exactly my business to read the ad copy but I did and decided that it should not go. But our admen would not budge. Their reason to carry the ad was not only that it brought good money but also that it was being carried for long by other sister publications. Nonsense circulated by someone else makes sense for us too.

Another ad I tried to veto in my weekly and failed was about the benefits of black magic. An intellectual journal such as ours should not stoop so low as to pick up a few thousand bucks from such a stupid ad, which was my argument. Our admen's argument was that they were not able to generate many ads on their own for our esteemed journal and I should not foil this limited plan of theirs. They won, naturally.

Admen should know what they will not buy. Just as newsmen should be able to determine what they will not circulate as news. That involves a hard ethical consideration. That is possible only when the man who funds the paper decides not to do anything to make money. Ads are useful when they do not turn out to be proven nonsense. Too many ads are as dangerous as too few of them. A paper printing any ad for money makes a deception of its trade. A no-ad paper must have a vast and probably remote source with more than money on its mind. Fun lasts until it is divulged.

Like life, with all its imperfections, journalism moves on with occasional forays into dirty alleys. There is no ground for breast beating. Everyone is not a liar. The very fact that the liar is not yet hailed as the messiah is an insurance against proliferation of lies. Now and then liars are exposed, sometimes expelled. Let us celebrate that possibility.

Ethics in journalism is, simply, speaking the truth, avoiding taking an inviolable opinion. Institutional safeguards can be helpful. Yet it is ever more useful to spread an awareness of C.P. Scott's century-old dictum: "Facts are sacred, comment is free".

# 20

# *Commercialisation of Education and Professions*

*C.P. Narayanan*

The objective of imparting education in a modern society is to equip new generations to grow as good citizens and contribute to productive growth. In India the additional objective is to instill the lofty ideals of democracy, secularism and social justice in future generations. That is why it was envisaged in the constitution to impart elementary education to all children of the age group 6-14. Though the constitution envisaged in bringing all children of this age group to school within 10 years of adopting it, it took more than 50 years to amend the constitution to this effect and pass the Right to Education Act. Even now the central and state governments together have not been able to start enough schools within the reach of students in various parts of the country and provide enough class rooms, trained teachers and other facilities to impart quality education to all of them.

According to government statistics out of 8,23,162 primary schools 62.85 per cent are government owned, 22.96 per cent are owned by local bodies, 6.57 per cent are private aided where education is free. Only 7.62 per cent schools are in private unaided group. In the secondary sector about 80 per cent children attend government or aided schools. The rest of them study in unaided sector. But in the case of pre-primary schools private unaided category has 21.43 per cent.

A recent newspaper report regarding pre-school brings out ground realities:

> Six months ago, Yogaraj Patel and Akshay Gupta, two young II Tians, decided to map the potential of the segment and set up a chain of pre-schools in Central India.
>
> "Schools are supposed to be non-profit organisations by law and we could not find any investor. That is when the idea of starting a pre-school came as it requires far less investment and is a lucrative business opportunity" says Patel. As part of their due diligence he and Gupta visited schools in Mumbai, Surat, Allahabad, Indore and Bhopal. 'Countryside', the first pre-school in their chain is set to open in Indore this month.

> According to industry estimates, the pre-school market in India is pegged at $770 million (about Rs. 4460 crore). It is expected to be worth Rs. 13,300 crore by 2015-16, according to a Crisil research report (Business Line, Jan. 4, 2013).

The report says this estimate pertains to 2.5 per cent of the urban school going population in India. The above quoted government data shows that actually children attending unaided pre-schools is eight times of the urban students estimated by Crisil which means that the "pre-school business" in India is worth at least Rs. 30,000 crore even now. If this is the magnitude of money paid for infant education to the education businessmen of the country, one can attempt to estimate the mind boggling amount that "free education" in India offers as income to its masters.

Incidentally, one may note that even at a young age these two IIT'ians are trained to look for "lucrative business opportunities" in which they do not leave out even pre-school education. It provides sufficient insight into the ideals and value they had imbibed from their course and alma mater. During the last two decades the very purpose of education has been changed from public good to private good, a point which even the Supreme Court had upheld in its (now well known) judgement in the TMA Pai Foundation case. This shift in the perspective of education is not an overnight change, but one that had begun from the days of internal emergency in 1970s.

The first Commission on education appointed in independent India was University Education Commission appointed in 1948 with Dr. S. Radhakrishnan, who was later elected as the second President of India, as Chairman. That Commission was asked to submit a report on how to develop university education in India. It said that the aim of university education should be to produce able citizens who can take up national responsibilities successfully in various fields. The university has to produce leadership in various walks of life in the best interests of the nation. Quoting the preamble of Draft Constitution of India, the report says: "We are engaged in a quest for democracy through the realisation of justice, liberty, equality and fraternity".

Another education Commission which had gone into the entire gamut of education was headed by Dr. D.S. Kothari during 1964-66. It was Kothari Commission which suggested 10+2+3 year structure, which one has to undergo to secure a university degree, combining numerous paths to a degree existing till then. Kothari Commission underlines importance of education as far as a developing country like India is concerned when it emphasises that "education determines the level of prosperity, welfare and security of the people". While the Radhakrishnan Commission has suggested notionally that education has to be allocated six per cent of the GDP, Kothari Commission does so after a detailed analysis. While both Commissions welcome private investment in education, they underline that the state must make a much larger share in order to ensure the larger goals of the nation, viz., liberty, equality, justice and fraternity.

Kothari Commission had made a detailed study of school-education as a whole which greatly influenced the National Policy on Education (NPE) in 1968 and 1986. As in the case of Radhakrishnan Commission recommendations, Kothari Commission recommendations also were highly praised in words, but mostly discarded in practice.

This was one main reason for the pre-independence educational conceptions to continue actively in force. Without a set of conceptions educational edifice cannot continue functioning. What both these Commissions seriously attempted to do was to make educational system in India and its ideology firmly rooted in democracy, secularism and social justice. But the powers that be rejected it. Hence pre-capitalist ideas, relations and practices rule over the education scene in India even now, perhaps more vigorously than before.

It is the absence of democracy, critical thinking and people's (which means student's, teacher's and parent's) participation which helped private interests to gain more and more control over education. The very same conditions have, during the past two decades, promoted neo-liberal forces in the field of education in the country.

In Radhakrishnan and Kothari Commission reports and in the National Policies on Education, adopted in 1968 and 1986, the emphasis was that government should take the leadership in expanding education and improving its quality while individuals and agencies who are socially committed might join this effort by making educational institutions without any profit motive. But by 1980s various groups in different parts of the country had initiated a new trend mainly with profit motive.

This trend is clearly reflected in judgements of two Constitution Benches of the Supreme Court. One is the Unnikrishnan case in which the Supreme Court in early 1990s directed the self-financing professional colleges to admit 50 per cent of students, with high merit, at government college fee rates and charge higher fees on the other 50 per cent of students having lesser merit. This judgement was declared unconstitutional by an 11 member bench of Supreme Court in 2002. That judgement interpreted Article. 19(1) (g) of the Constitution which bestow on any citizen the right "to practice any profession or to carry out any occupation, trade or business", in conjunction with Article 26 and Article 30, extended to any citizen the right to establish and maintain educational institutions. Article 19 of the Constitution pertains to the fundamental rights of citizens. The court was thus arrogating "the right to establish and maintain educational institutions" which was provided particularly to minority communities (religious or linguistic) in Article 30(1) of the Constitution to any citizen belonging to any community, whether majority or minority. After this judgement Article 30(1) in effect becomes infructuous since any citizen belonging to any community can resort to this right without any reference to his community status; majority or minority.

Also this judgement classifies education as a private good whereas even now Western countries which are championing neo-liberal policies characterise education as a public good. All along the period since the advent of the capitalist society-it was then that the present educational system came into being-education was considered as a public good. It is to prepare individuals to carry out tasks for the well-being and advance of the society, which incidentally will ensure betterment of individual's status, that education is imparted. This underlines that education has a social outlook.

But neo-liberal forces which wanted to include education and health, in general the service sector, into the framework of GATT (General Agreement on Trade and Tariff), tried to depict a different perspective of education. It was they who tried to characterise education as a private good instead of public good. This ipso facto means that the onus of educating the people is not vested in society but on each individual or her family. It was based on the guidance given by this line of argument that World Bank in early 1990s directed governments not to take up responsibility of educating the society. It said that government may at the most, fund primary education, not any higher layer of education.

By the beginning of this century it was estimated that education at global level is a business worth a trillion (one lakh crore) dollars involving one billion people. It was identified that mainly governments were handling this operation and involvement of private sector was for much less than one hundred billion (10,000 crore) dollars. Multinationals wanted to have a much bigger share in education and to make a lot of profit from it.

As far as school education is concerned, smaller states like South Korea, Singapore, in Asia, and some small states in Central Europe top the list in PISA (Programme for International Student Assessment), a study conducted by Organisation for Economic Co-operation and Development (OECD) among 15 year old school students in various countries. It assesses the activity of students in Mathematics, Science and reading. Almost all G-7 states are much below these countries in the rank list. PISA has brought out the fact that for progress in education it is not private school charging hefty fees, but active interest taken by, and participation of, teachers, parents and local authorities in schools run by LSGs that is critical. Which means that in school education what is crucial is the local government's active involvement and support to government run schools.

Though various disciplines handled by universities and research institutions are common to developed, developing and under-developed countries, what is taught will usually take local, regional and national requirements into consideration. Many of the students from developing countries like India and China who go to developed countries for higher education prefer to get employed in such countries since the education they get there make them more fit for employment there itself rather than in their own countries. Also they are able to lead a better standard of living in those countries.

Some brilliant students from any developing country may attempt to get admission to a university department or research institute in which a Nobel laureate or an outstanding professor is teaching/doing research. Such a practice may be promoted in order to develop a group of outstanding teachers/ researchers in some universities/research institutions in India. It is not possible or feasible to send a large number of students to a developed country.

For over a century US has been promoting a large number of outstanding students from other countries to do higher studies in universities/ research institutions and join them in order to ensure that they have the best brains in the world to work for them. This was one of their policies in transforming US into a world power. Britain also was pursuing such a policy when it was an empire over which the sun never set.

But in recent times, from the days when Mrs. Margaret Thatcher was Prime Minister, Britain was pursuing a policy of attracting overseas students to do higher studies there. They were admitted to new institutions without basic facilities and competent teachers in order to mobilise a substantial amount as fees from them. This practice converted education which was considered a public good till then into a private good. Private good for both these universities and the students who were prepared to pay much higher fees compared to those charged by some well-known universities and colleges in Britain.

In recent years we find that those who indulge in educational business in Western countries are not satisfied by attracting some students from developing countries like India. They want to have a bigger piece of the education cake in India for which they are interested to open branches or franchisies of their universities in the West. None of the well-known universities like Oxford, Cambridge, Harvard, Stanford, etc., are participating in this venture. Those universities which are in the fray consider this more as a fund mobilising exercise than as an educational or research activity. It is in this background one has to view the move of our government to allow foreign universities to start their centers here.

The verdict of the 11 member Constitution Bench of the Supreme Court, delivered on Oct 31, 2002, was a watershed as far as education in India is concerned. Concepts like education, its role in creating opportunities for vertical growth of individuals, which was lauded as a unique feature of democracy, keeping religion out of activities of the state, supremacy of interests of polity as against those of an individual-were given a goby in this judgement. During the decade after this judgement various other judgements and decisions of government have in practice established that in this country education is of the rich by the rich and for the rich. This is a great departure from the path followed by the nation during the first five decades after independence. Going through some paragraphs of the 2002 Supreme Court judgement will help the reader to appreciate the point.

> 26. The right to establish and maintain educational institutions may also be sourced to Article 26(a), which grants, in positive terms, the right to every religious denomination, or any section thereof to establish and maintain institutions for religious and charitable purposes, subject to public order, morality and health. Education is a recognised head of charity. Therefore religious denominations or sections thereof, which do not fall within the special categories carved out in the Article. 29(1) and 30(1), have the right to establish and maintain religious and educational institutions. This would allow members belonging to any religious denomination including the majority religious community, to set up an educational institution. Given this, the phrase 'private educational institution' as used in the judgement would include not only those educational institutions set up by the secular persons or bodies, but also educational institutions set up by the religious denominations; the word 'private' is used in contradistinction to government institutions.

What this paragraph tries to do is to establish that all rights extended to minority religious institutions are enjoyed by the majority religious institutions as well as far as education is concerned. The Constitution brackets minority linguistic and religious institutions together. To be fair to the Constitution and Constitution makers the verdict must have bracketed linguistic and religious educational institutions. Here what it has done is to establish that majority religious educational institutions enjoy all the rights enjoyed by the minority religious educational institutions. In a way this verdict impinges on the secular character of the Constitution.

> 36. The private unaided educational institutions impart education, and that cannot be the reason to take away their choice in matter inter alia of selection of students and fixation of fees. Affiliation and recognition has to be available to every institution that fulfills the condition for grant of such affiliation and recognition. The private institutions are right in submitting that it is not open to the court to insist that statutory authorities should impose the terms of the scheme as a condition for grant of affiliation or recognition; this completely destroys the institutional autonomy and the very object of establishment of this institution.

One perceives in this paragraph of court judgement the stamp of the neo-liberal times. It has umpteen times been stated by anybody interpreting the constitution, including the courts, that no right granted by the Constitution is absolute. It has its checks and balances. Can an educational institution have an autonomy which does not give any consideration to the rights of students, teachers and other employees? The court has forgotten that all private institutions in fields other than education are liable to observe statutory restrictions on them. Here this paragraph reflects the neo-liberal philosophy that the Rich by themselves are a separate state governed by laws which they themselves dictate.

> 48. Private education is one of the most dynamic and fastest growing segments of post-secondary education at this turn of twenty first century. A combination of unprecedented demand for access to higher education and the inability or unwillingness of government to provide the necessary support has brought private higher education to the forefront. Private institutions, with a long history in many countries, are expanding in scope and number, and are becoming increasingly important in parts of the world that relied almost entirely on the public sector.

Even in countries which champion the case of neo-liberalism, higher education is still available and affordable to all bright - even poor - students. Private institutions there, other than the very famous ones, cater to those who have performed comparatively poorly in qualifying examinations and wanted to get enrolled into specific courses of their choice. Expansion of higher education of quality is not at a very fast rate as the court contends. Enough statistical proof is available to confirm it. The above paragraph clearly brings out the fact that the court sitting in a metropolis states that the situation available there is true for the whole country.

> 49. Not only has demand overwhelmed the ability of the government to provide education, there has also been a significant change in the way that higher education is perceived. The academic degree as a "private good" that benefits the individual rather than a "public good" for society is now widely accepted. The logic of today's economics and an ideology of privatisation have contributed to the resurgence of private higher education, and the establishing of private institutions where none or very few existed before.

Here what one can conclude on reading the above paragraph from the judgement is that the Supreme Court judges, many people in the government and private managers as also their lawyers think differently from the general public in India. Even in US, Britain and other European countries the concept that education is a public good is more prevalent even now than that it is a private good. It is among the neo-liberal minded people that the opposite line of thinking is strong. Their views get much better publicity in media than the opposite view which is shared by more people. Since the strident campaign for privatisation of higher education in Supreme Court by unaided private managements was high pitched and since the opposite view was not effectively put across by the government, the prevailing view during the hearing of the case was in favour of neo-liberalism. From early 1990s discussions and reporting in media on education were mainly focused on higher education, particularly, professional education. The following paragraph of TMA Pai case judgement underlines this point.

> 54. The right to establish an educational institution can be regulated, but such regulatory measures must, in general be to ensure the maintenance of proper academic standards, atmosphere and infrastructure (including quality staff) and prevention of mal-administration by those in charge of management. The fixing of a rigid fee structure, dictating the formation and composition of a management body, compulsory nomination of teachers and staff for appointment or nominating students for admission would be unacceptable restrictions.

In all these and many other paragraphs in the judgement the focal argument is the right of the private person or body to establish and maintain an educational institution which is arrogated into a fundamental right. When the Supreme Court was issuing the judgement in TMA Pai Foundation case, even the Constitution amendment to make education upto 14 years of age a right was not passed by the Parliament. That amendment was adopted by Parliament in December 2002 whereas Right to Education Act was adopted only in 2009 and became operational from 2010 onwards. Managements were awarded their right much earlier!

Now, the right to education is that of the student, the person who wants to know and learn about the world and herself. The International Commission on Education for the 21st Century appointed by the UNESCO (of which Dr. Karan Singh was a member) has highlighted four pillars of education as (1) learning to know, (2) learning to do, (3) learning to live together and (4) learning to be, which also underlines the above point. These four points clearly point out that education is a collective activity which then necessarily has to be formulated, systematised, transacted and synthesised collectively. Since this is a social process, in modern societies government has a major role to play in imparting education. Universal, compulsory education to be imparted free to all children of the age group 6-14 can be visualised, planned, implemented and financed only by the government for the society. This is the basic fact about education in India, not only of elementary education but also of secondary and higher education since vast majority of people cannot afford to meet the expenses of private education.

But the ruling class, particularly the section which leads them create a camouflage and try to convey the impression that it is the unaided educational private institution which extend educational opportunities to majority of students (This notion is reflected in the above judgement also). This is not true. In India only 27 per cent of school going children are enrolled in private schools, according to latest figures. Though there is a higher percentage of children in private secondary schools, that comes only to 33. In universities and colleges there were about 170 lakhs students in 2011-12. But here too those who attend government and aided colleges and universities substantially outnumber those attending the unaided private colleges and universities. It is only in the case of professional colleges, unaided private institutions have a larger share of students. This is because unaided institutions without necessary infrastructural facilities, laboratories, libraries and qualified and experienced staff are being given permission and affiliation in the light of TMA Pai Foundation case judgement.

Unfortunately, even a great institution such as Supreme Court was carried away perhaps by the success stories of unaided institutions in urban areas narrated by their lawyers. That is why in various judgements from early 1990s it has consistently argued for the unfettered freedom for unaided educational institutions. The justification is that whether school or college, an unaided institution has a far better standard compared to a government educational institution. In Para (61) it is stated that:

> There is no compulsion on students to attend private schools. The rush for admission is occasioned by the standards maintained in such schools, and recognition of the fact that the state run schools do not provide the same standards of education.... It is in the interests of the general public that more good quality schools are established; autonomy and non-regulation of school administration in the right of appointment, admission of students and the fees to be charged will ensure that more such institutions are established.

It is common knowledge that unaided schools charge exorbitant fees on students, and teachers are paid less salary, compared to government run schools, which is the real reason for "more such schools are established". What this 11 member Constitution Bench did was to keep doors wide open for the unaided schools and colleges in which right of appointment, admission of students and fees to be charged are left unfettered.

It is through drawing strength from this neo-liberal interpretation of the Constitution and Acts of Parliament that governments and courts vie with one another to allow everyone who apply to start new schools and colleges. This is at a time when Right to Education Act motivates all poor children of the age group 6-14 to attend schools while most of the new schools opened are unaided. Most of these new entrants are admitted in government LP schools where there are only one or two teachers. None of the unaided schools is interested in admitting them. In urban areas and states like Kerala starting of hundreds or thousands of such private unaided schools makes many government run schools redundant. This results in jeopardising the educational prospects of a number of students from poor families.

The hallmark of neo-liberalisation is that it does not sympathetically react to any of the problems of the mass of people. It is concerned only with reforms and measures which substantially enrich the uppermost layer of the rich. Thus an initiative to universalise education in India and to offer every bright girl and boy opportunity to get training in skills or higher education, which would have helped India for a great leap forward, has been transformed into a big enterprise worth hundreds of billions of dollars. It is to reap a substantial share of it that overseas education entrepreneurs are making a bee-line to India.

Now, such entrepreneurs are mainly interested in starting new professional colleges. While there are about two crore youth undergoing university education, those engaged in professional education will be less than 10 per cent of that. The major contingent among professional students is from engineering faculty which has an enrolment of about 12 lakhs. Next contingent is from management who constitute 3.8 lakhs followed by pharmacy of 1.21 lakh. Enrollment of students for MBBS is about 42,000. For B.Sc nursing is 12,500. There are similar professional courses and degrees which attract lesser number of students.

Why do professional courses which admit only about 10 per cent of those who join all university courses get more importance and publicity in media, discussions at government level, community level and among people at large including parents?. Not all such courses attract the attention and imagination of the public as Medicine, Engineering and Management do. It is because professionals in these fields get comparatively much higher income - de jure or de facto. One reason is that their number is much less than what is needed.

Now we have one doctor for 1700 people on an average - which means that there are over seven lakhs doctors working in India. But the world average is one doctor for every 1000 people which requires over 12 lakhs doctors. So over five lakhs doctors more are needed, mostly to work in rural areas. Medical students who join self-financing medical colleges, and spend Rs. 50 lakhs and more, will not be interested to work in rural areas. Hence more medical colleges, in government sector is the need of the hour. As far as nurses are concerned, there is a gap of three lakhs persons between demand and supply.

Over the last so many decades a philosophy has been developed in the country that a medical practitioner has to work at all times of the day for which she/he will be remunerated by every patient over and above the salary paid to her/him. Private hospitals charge the patient exorbitantly in order to pay the doctor a thick salary packet. This situation can be rectified only by making more doctors available.

Engineering works are executed by contractors, where it is for government or private purpose. Engineers in the government departments/private companies expect contractors to pay him a retainer over and above the salary he is paid. Engineers in the IT field are paid salary on a scale higher than the general salary scale of an engineer in India.

Management experts are supposed to bring big profit for the company for which she/he is working. So management experts are also in a high wage island.

It is such disproportionate salaries and perks paid to the professionals which resulted in many a parent dreaming such a covetable job for their child/

children. It is this expectation of one section of parents which has created a safe and competition free market for different professional courses. Since a section of parents being professionals are in high income bracket, they do not mind the fees that are charged on their child/children. There are similar sections like various kinds of businessmen, NRIs and others who are in a position to pay big amounts as fees. Adding to that rich families in the country like landlords and such other sections. As it is, enrolment to professional courses now is less than 20 lakhs. Over and above the sections mentioned here, one section of middle class also aspire to send their children to professional colleges. This is what provides a fertile breeding ground to the self -financing professional colleges.

Already enrolment in private unaided professional institutions outnumbers enrolment in government and aided institutions. This trend is going to be strengthened in coming years as is clear from statements of ministers like Kapil Sibal and organisations of private entrepreneurs like FICCI. The motive force behind these organisations is profit, to maximise which they resort to all techniques of business including black marketing and corruption. Already the black market has landed in professional educational institutions in the form of capitation fees. This trend will compel future professionals like engineers, doctors, lawyers, management experts, etc., to resort to corruption in a big way. Already such influence is clearly visible in dealings at all levels of government and government run institutions and agencies.

The only way to avoid it is to restrict education to government controlled institutions. To improve their physical infrastructure and teaching/research quality substantially, government will have to spend much more on higher education and research. That is the only way to ensure quality service in all spheres of life to people and improve their quality of life continuously. They may have to pay more taxes for this purpose. But they can rest assured that corruption and other social evils do not tarnish the body politic and social justice is maintained. What neo-liberalism has offered as a panacea to all their problems is not a solution to any of their problems, but a sure ticket to a crisis ridden life.

The Government of India are goading both students and vendors of education to increase enrolment in higher education to 30 per cent of the 18-24 age group population by 2020 as was announced by Kapil Sibal, Central minister. In 2000 the gross enrolment ratio (GER) was 10 per cent which rose to 13.8 per cent in 2010. At present there are 600 universities, 31,000 higher education institutions, in India with 1.49 crore students enrolled. The number of higher education institutions in India is highest in the world while in student strength India ranks third after China (2.67 crore) and USA (1.83 crore). The 12th Plan document envisages to raise student strength to 3.59 crore or GER to 25.2 per cent by 2017.

During 2001-11 private sector in India has become the major player in higher education. The number of private institutions rose from 43 per cent to 63 per cent while enrolment in them increased from 33 per cent to 52 per cent. In engineering private sector has a share of 91 per cent, in architecture 67 per cent, in teacher education 68 per cent and in medicine 50 per cent. With population in the age group 18-24 in 2011 at 23.3 crore in India, 22.4 crore in China and 4.4 crore in USA, private sector sees the largest market for higher education in India and China. And that is the great danger looming ahead. In 2020 if GER is 30 per cent additional seats required will be 2.54 crore in number.

Now the situation is more alarming than what is reflected by numbers. These universities and colleges can be provided with sufficient physical infrastructure if government and private managements mobilize all resources at their behest. But to produce enough teaching faculty with good quality and experience is something which a government cannot produce with higher budgetary allocations and enacting laws. This mushrooming of colleges and universities has resulted in a large number of them having poorly equipped faculty who are not capable to teach students to become above normal graduates, not to speak of first rate scientists, social scientists, technologists and other professionals. The growing number of students is good fodder for the grinding mill of unaided professional colleges and their owners who wants to make profit through them at a very fast rate.

Here one has to review what has been done during the past two decades and the transformation undergone by the national institutions like Medical Council of India (MCI), All India Council for Technical Education (AICTE), National Council for Teacher Education (NCTE), etc., set up by the Government of India (GOI) to oversee various sectors of professional education and ensure uniform quality and standards all over India and to improve them continuously.

In the realm of higher education in India for more than 50 years the hierarchy is as follows: at the national level stands the University Grants Commission (UGC) which is not only the centre from which grants to the universities and other institutions in various states are distributed; it also supervises the academic activities of universities. A nominee of UGC is a member of the committee constituted by the concerned state government to scout for a proper candidate to become new Vice Chancellor of a university. UGC committees regularly inspect various departments of universities and suggested improvements in working. It is the University Syndicate which sends committees to visit places where new colleges are to be established.

When demand for approval of private professional colleges became acute, the authority to sanction them and give final approval, as also to send committees to inspect colleges to ensure their academic quality - many of these functionaries are usurped by all India professional apex institutions like MCI, AICTE, NCTE, etc. Within a few years these institutions came under severe pressure to sanction approval to colleges which did not have even minimum physical and academic facilities according to the prescribed norms. Most of these unaided professional colleges were instituted by either politically influenced groups or business or caste/religious organisations which brought intense pressure on the governing bodies of these professional apex institutions.

The result was that the governing bodies and committees they deployed to inspect the new colleges were coaxed or threatened in various ways to submit favourable reports. The net result was that almost all these apex professional institutions became so corrupt that government was forced to take stringent action against them including dismissal. Those people who were nominated or appointed to these governing bodies were mostly well known names in the respective professions. Soon an impression was created among the people that even very respected professionals are corrupt or nepotic or amenable to various forms of enticements or pressure. But the biggest victim during this process happens to be the respectability of these professions which was established through selfless toil of numerous professionals. It was sacrificed at the altar of avarice of private vendors of professional education, at the altar of neo-liberalism.

Government of India should have maintained all India professional institutions like MCI, AICTE, etc as watch towers over respective professions to point out any wrong tendency among them, to suggest regular amendment of approved norms over a period of time or whenever it is warranted and to act as trouble shooters if situation anywhere so warranted. Instead, GOI tried to centralize most of the powers regarding medical colleges in MCI, powers regarding technical institutions in AICTE, and so on. This led to the confirmation of the old dictum "Absolute power corrupts absolutely". Also it has thrown the practices in the university, its authority over affiliated colleges and time bound regular work of the university to the winds.

It is true that the old British model of affiliating universities is no longer valid in a situation where there are hundreds of colleges affiliated to a university. It has been found from experience that autonomous college or deemed university is not the alternative to it. Other models are to be developed through practice. It is not advisable to have dual powers over colleges like university and MCI, etc. In many countries academic committees at the college, department levels are given wide powers. It may be tried instead of allowing private managements to have all powers.

Here one finds a tendency on the part of GOI which has become very pronounced during the last two decades when neo-liberalism spread into almost all spheres of governmental activity. In 1950 when the Constitution came into being there was a clear delineation of power among central and state governments. The 42nd amendment of the Constitution led to shifting some of the powers in the state list to the concurrent list. One of such power transferred was education. In any item of the concurrent list if union government legislates a law, then the law of any state has to be subservient to it. This has led to dual power in higher education. In the case of medicine and engineering the central Acts relating to MCI and AICTE often penetrate into the state acts relating to universities in the state. Recently the Supreme Court issued a verdict stating that AICTE cannot interfere into the powers of a university over its affiliated engineering colleges. GOI is trying to overcome it by amending AICTE Act. But the real issue is intervention of central authorities into the powers of state level institutions denying both democracy and decentralisation.

One can understand such issues cropping up in a vast country like ours where there are 29 states. But the salient issue here is this : why AICTE should enter into nitty-gritty of routine functioning of an engineering college under a university. In a situation where there are over 3500 engineering colleges and more than 15 lakhs students in the country with every possibility that these may increase over the years, GOI and AICTE should realise that centralising all powers regarding engineering colleges in AICTE is impractical. What GOI and institutions like AICTE and MCI have to realise is that there has to be clear division of power between the centre and states and also between MCI/ AICTE, etc, and respective universities and colleges. There has to be decentralisation of power and democratic functioning up to the level of colleges. GOI and MCI/AICTE, etc., must not play to the tunes of private professional colleges and their managers.

As mentioned earlier, Supreme Court verdict on TMA Pai Foundation case has in practice shifted the right to establish and maintain an educational institution from the state/community to an individual citizen. The Court has averred that Article 19(1)(g) bestows the right to establish and maintain an educational institution on any person and the state has to give sanction to it if norms for such an educational institution are satisfied, without any enquiry whether people of a locality require such an educational institution or not. This means that an educational institution can be started at a place just like a provision/stationery or any other shop. Whether starting a new educational institution at that place will affect already existing institutions need not be taken into consideration, the verdict declares. This insistence of the court appears to be violative of Article 19. (6) of the Constitution which states:

> Nothing in sub clause of the said clause shall affect the operation of any existing law in so far as it implies or prevents the state from making any law imposing, in the interests of the general public, reasonable restriction on the exercise of the right conferred by the said sub clause and, in particular nothing in the said sub clause shall affect the operation of any existing law in so far as it relates to, or prevents the state from making any law related to:
>
> (i) the professional or technical qualifications necessary for practising any profession or carrying on any practice, trade or business, or
>
> (ii) the carrying on by the state or by a corporation owned or controlled by the state, of any trade, business, industry or service

whether to the exclusion, complete or partial, of citizens or otherwise.

Nobody raised such loopholes in the TMA Pai Foundation case verdict though a number of cases came up before the Supreme Court after 2002 on the issue of privatisation of professional education. Private sector used this favourable environment to bring majority of colleges and seats under their control. From the professional colleges alone the annual turnover of private sector will be more than Rs. one lakh crore. 64 per cent of higher education institutions and 59 per cent of enrolment are in the private sector now. Federation of Indian Chamber of Commerce and Industry (FICCI) has made elaborate plans to further expand private share in higher education. With their entry a lot of control and restrictions have become necessary in higher education. This is borne out by the fact that about 15 bills on higher education are pending before the Parliament. This is because various things practiced by the government colleges and universities as a tradition are being openly violated by the private sector, necessitating legislation on every one of those areas of operation.

USA used to be the country with highest number of university students. This is due to two reasons. That it is a developed country with a population of about 30 crore is the first reason. The second reason is that bright students from all countries throng to US for higher studies. According to recent data about 4 lakhs students from India go to other countries for higher education at the expense of $12 billion (1,200 crore dollars).

Now that situation is fast changing since China and India with populations more than four times the size of US population are advancing in higher education. Hence during the next decade China and India will overtake US in the number of students getting higher education. Already there are signals that the flow of students to western countries for higher education is decreasing for a number of reasons.

Actually the big campaign to substantially increase the enrolment of students for higher education in India is not at all planned. Even government authorities agree that about 50 per cent of the faculty in universities and colleges are not properly equipped to transact their job. Some studies show that 75 per cent of successful engineering graduates (they were seven lakhs in 2011) are unemployable while 85 per cent of all university graduates are in the same boat. The move of GOI to raise GER to 30 per cent by 2020 will only worsen this state of affairs.

GOI or state governments do not have a clear man-power planning. Actually in all spheres of employment a much larger number of technicians and skilled workmen than available today are needed compared to graduates/post graduates in professional and science/arts subjects. Hence there has to be more courses in developments of various skills for those who have completed higher secondary education and do not want to go for higher education.

This is needed for another reason as well. There is high percentage of wastage (failure in examination) at university level. In 2011 there were more than 15 lakh students for engineering out of which only less than 50 per cent have passed. For those who fail in examinations it is not easy to pass and get decently employed. Even among those who pass the examinations, only a small percentage gets employed. This is a reflection on the courses and the way they are transacted in colleges. This is true of not only professional courses, but all other higher education courses.

What any sensible person will expect of the government is to ensure universal school education and provide sufficient courses of good quality for development of various skills and necessary number of university level courses in all sciences, arts and professional subjects so that the youth are equipped to earn a living and the society has enough workmen in different fields of production and other activities.

For decades the government paid scant attention to this aspect. Now, goaded by neo-liberal forces it wants education expanded at a fast rate, without ensuring quality, equity and the needs of the society, but guaranteeing enormous profit for peddlers of education. This is most conspicuous in the case of professional education. It is also at the expense of the development of basic disciplines which is fundamental as far as future growth of the nation is concerned.

**References**


- *The Report of the University Education Commission* (Dec. 1948 - Aug. 1949), Ministry of Education, Government of India, 1950.
- TMA Pai Foundation and Ors vs State of Karnataka and Ors, 31 October, 2002, *Supreme Court Judgement.*
- *Education and National Development – Report of the Education Commission,* 1964-66, Chairman : Dr. D.S. Kothari, National Council of Educational Research and Training, 1970.
- *Report of UNESCO* of the International Commission on Education for the Twenty First Century: Learning the Treasure Within – UNESCO Publishing, 1996.
- *Constitution of India.*

# 21

# *Criminalisation of Politics*

*R.K. Suresh Kumar*

## Introduction

Criminalisation of politics cannot be singled out for a debate independently of the ongoing discourse on the quality of democracy. This necessitates a look into the content of democracy and related issues as criminalisation of politics negates the very content of that ideology by denying its fruits to the people. It can be discerned from Aristotle's 'Politics' that the subject of politics which is a branch of ethics is studied within the framework of a city state. Obviously the idea of good citizen gets closely associated with the account of the good man. To the Athenians 'Democracy' ensured a 'virtuous form of government' conducive to the well-being of the society at large. The Greek concept of citizenship viewed political authority as distinctive because it was the authority of office holder exercised over citizens according to constitutional law. Citizenship was impossible to any one without sufficient leisure to understand political issues. The demise of direct democracy and the city states saw the advent of representative democracy and the nation state. But the new version failed to sustain the spirit of direct democracy based on 'active public trust'. The nature of 'public trust' today is qualitatively different from that prevailed in the 'polis'. A representative democracy is intended to be a "regime based on the principle of popular sovereignty, usually institutionalized through periodic multi-party elections" (Francis Fukuyama, 2001:201). But criminalisation of politics alienates large sections of society from the political process pushing them to the periphery.

In theory every government represents but in actual practice representation is impossible. The Magna Carta ensured the rights of the few; the Bill of Rights, the rights of the many; and Parliamentary Democracy and Parliamentary Government, the rights of the majority. The impossibility of representation is stretched by Political thinkers to include every type of representative government which, in a sense, builds up oppressive political, social or economic systems that damage people living under them. To the Elite theorists like Pareto, Mosca and Michels the representation that was guaranteed under democracy was nothing more than a circulation of elites. The neo-elitist critique of democracy shows concern about how easily money, property and power can manipulate representative institutions to the benefit of the elites (Bachrach : 167).

The debate over the representativeness of modern democratic governments has also shifted from political questions to socio-economic issues. All these raise the question which ought to govern us in a just polity? Should we be subjected to the racketeers who run politics? The answer is a definite 'no' because it is not only the negation of the virtues of representative government passed on to us from the period of the ancient Greeks but also a going back to the rights of the 'few' only. Democratic politics should consider whether it is safe to keep power in the hands of a few criminals and their accomplices or to spread it more widely among the populace.

**Ushering in a Just Polity: The Indian Legal Framework**

India has a comprehensive structure of laws to administer and conduct its elections. The formal legal framework can be found in certain provisions of the constitution, the Representation of the People Act 1950, the Representation of the People Act 1951, the Presidential and Vice-Presidential Elections Act 1952, the Delimitation Act 1972 and the various rules and regulations framed and orders issued under these statutes. In addition, certain provisions of the Indian Penal Code and a few other Acts are relied upon to provide for punishment as well as disqualification of candidates and members of various houses. The constitution in Article 326 provides for universal adult suffrage for election of representatives of the people to the House of the People and to the Legislative Assemblies of States. India is a party to many international covenants recognising the electoral rights of citizens like the Universal Declaration of Human Rights (UDHR). The election laws constitute a code by itself which has been further strengthened by the various pronouncements of the Judiciary from time to time.

The Election Commission of India is one of the pillars of the Indian democracy. The Constitution makers attached highest significance to the presence of an independent electoral machinery for the conduct of elections by giving wide ranging powers to the Election Commission under Article 324 of the Constitution. For Dr. B.R. Ambedkar "Article 324 proposed to centralise the election machinery in the hands of a single Commission, to be assisted by regional Commissioners working under the supervision, direction and control of the Election Commission". The centralisation of the electoral system was done to prevent injustice being done by the provincial governments to sections of people other than those who belonged to the provinces racially, linguistically and culturally.

The Election Commission consists of the Chief Election Commissioner and such members or other Election Commissioners, if any, as the President may from time to time fix and the appointment shall, subject to the provisions of any law made on that behalf by Parliament, be made by the President. This shows that the Constitution did not want the matter to be left to the discretion of the executive. So far no law has been enacted under clause (2) of Article 324 to regulate the power of appointment.

**Role of the Regulators**

It is important that the organisation and management of elections are not only fair and free but also appear to be so. The constitutional status or the special law enacted for the conduct of elections need not necessarily lead to the independence of the Election Commission from the power of the Executive. Moreover, many suggestions for reforming the electoral law was ignored by successive governments, forcing the Election Commission to come up with a 'Model Code of Conduct' for election campaigning, which in the hands of a strong Election Commissioner proved to be an effective instrument to uphold the purity and fairness of elections. The Code eventually assumed the force of law. The powerful role played by T. N. Seshan as Election Commissioner in 1990s is worth mentioning in this regard. To give teeth to his expansive interpretation of the model code of conduct, he issued orders claiming authority to de-recognize any party that blatantly violated the code under the terms of the 1968 Election Symbols Ordinance.[1]

The first-past-the-post system adopted by our Constitution, instead of proportional representation, enables a candidate to win an election when he gets more votes than his strongest single competitor, but has not necessarily polled a higher total than the combined opposition. Thus in the general election of 1952, 1957 and 1962 the Indian National Congress got 75 per cent of seats in the People's House with 45 per cent, 48 per cent and 45 per cent of votes respectively. In 1967 and 1971 it won with 54 per cent and 68 per cent of seats with 40 per cent and 44 per cent of vote share. Even during its best performance, i.e., in 1984, when it got 77 per cent of the seats in Lok Sabha it had a vote share of only 48 per cent[2]. The fact is that no political party could strike a balance between the seats it got and the votes it polled. As this practice does not ensure the representation of the political and social minorities, this raises a question mark on the representativeness of Indian Parliamentary democracy. How representative are the candidates, with 30 per cent of the entire electorate, does not require much imagination. The possibility to win elections with the support of low vote share provides for the play of money and muscle power in elections[3].

A former Secretary-General of the Lok Sabha, P.D.T. Achary, made a significant observation regarding elected representatives with criminal records. He observed:

> Legislators with criminal records adorning the benches in the Legislature are not a very happy sight. Legislators being brought to the House straight from jails to attend the sessions of Assemblies or Parliament, under police escort, are not a rare sight in India. There was a member in the 13th and 14th Lok Sabha who was involved in as many as 33 criminal cases involving murder, dacoity and rape. That member was defeated in the 15th Lok Sabha but the member who defeated him is seeking security cover from the government because he fears that he will be killed by that man. There may be

> many such cases in the Assemblies. Statistics show that the percentage of legislators with criminal record is increasing. Criminals becoming law makers are an entirely Indian phenomenon which throws up many disturbing questions, about the credibility of our democratic system.... In a fight between a decent man and a criminal, the criminal will most probably get elected. The political class has not looked at this problem with the seriousness that it deserves (Achary, P.D.T., : 2013 : 62-63).

In August 1997 the then Election Commissioner G.V.G. Krishnamurthy released a press note entitled 'Sample Profile of Criminalisation of Politics' in which he "disclosed that nearly 1,500 of the 13,000 candidates who contested the preceding election had a criminal record of either murder or dacoity or rape-history sheeters in police language![4]. "One Prime Minister (I.K. Gujral) even lamented the fact that in Parliament we are rubbing our shoulders with persons with whom we would be ashamed to be seen outside" (Madhava Menon, N.R.,: 2013: 53).

In many instances the people have realized that the electoral system does not help them to get a clean Parliament. The Election Commission's decision to reject the nomination papers of candidates convicted of the many offences, listed in Section 8(1) and (2) and Sub-section (3) of the Representation of People Act, was aggressively confronted in the Parliament and in the Supreme Court and the law was diluted to such an extent that criminals continued to flourish in electoral politics (Madhava Menon N R : 2013 : 53-54). All these prove that the system cannot rely on the chance of getting pro-active and committed persons in top posts. As changes in the election law have been slow and few, the debate on electoral reforms continues endlessly.

It is in the above background that we should consider whether the electoral system has succeeded in ensuring a "true and meaningful democracy with hope for the future" as the ancient Greeks had attempted for a "virtuous form of government conducive to the well-being of the society at large".

**The Depth and Reach of Criminality in Indian Politics**

Despite the lack of any constitutional sanction for the perpetration of criminal activities it continues unabatedly in our polity. Criminalisation of politics is trivialised in our country by the political leadership. They forget that crime is the anti-thesis of democratic politics. Politics involves activities leading to consensus or near consensus in society resulting in the creation of public trust which is the force behind the institutions of governance and politics. Condoning crime, inspite of incriminating evidences to the contrary, amounts to erosion of public trust.

The bold ones among the civil servants, taking on the offenders of law, soon shrink back with fear when they see their bosses behaving in a servile manner making politics and governance a freeway for the criminals. The lonc rangers who wage battles soon find it hard to carry on singularly as the whole system succumbs to the criminality of those masquerading as politicians. If we wink at the outrageous act of criminal — politician nexus we would be pushing back politics to the dark ages.

Criminalisation of politics is unfortunate but often seen as a necessary means to secure political ends in India. Political parties are audacious enough to foray into unchartered territory. They easily overtake the whistle blowers with swift, smart and clever moves. It is not an exaggeration to say that it has become almost impossible to fix the depth and reach of criminality in Indian politics. Politics has become coterminous with crime or unlawful activity in general. When politicians and criminals come together, criminalisation of politics and politicisation of crime takes place. Politicisation of crime involves the increased use of anti-social forces for fund collection, rigging of election, blackmailing, and implementation of party programmes and for creating fear among the people. On the other hand criminalisation of politics points to the direct entry of criminals in to political parties and representative institutions including the Parliament. It also means the use of criminal methods and tactics to influence political processes and procedures. Violence is resorted to by criminals to inflict psychological as well as physical harm. Thus criminalisation of politics creates an inhospitable climate for democracy to sustain thereby refuting the liberal democrats like Friedrich Hayek and Milton Freedman who have highlighted the role of liberty and free choice in the success of modern democracy (David Muller (ed.) 1999:119) and C.B. Macpherson who focused on the role of equality and social justice (Macpherson, C.B., : 1973).

To the post-Nehruvian political leadership in India, a free media that exposes the misdemeanors of the rich and powerful indulging in graft, greed and corruption became an anathema. The Emergency of 1975-77 placed serious curbs on the freedom of press, and the aim was to tame it to subjugation facilitating the entry of criminals in to politics for the continuity of the dynastic rule. The tendency to gag the press and media, and the present day media's focus on entertainment, in place of serious information dissemination, due to competition has hastened the process of criminalisation of politics. No wonder, paid news is becoming the regular feature of the media industry.

Classical economists and later Marxists have pointed out the intimate connection between class rule and governance patterns. The last few decades have seen the emergence of a "corporate-led growth" in India. "The state power is interested only in the allocation of natural resources like land, minerals, water and airways to private players. Economic illegality, fraud and corrupt practices have ballooned in recent times forcing most citizens to suffer while a few are rapidly enriched" (Satish Misra : 2012). Such governance pattern offers enough space for criminalisation of our political system. The Parliament finds itself disabled in the discharge of its essential functions as criminals enter the Legislatures and Parliament. The expulsion of some Members of Parliament (MPs) in 2005 in the cash-for-query-scam, the allegations against some members about their alleged role in human trafficking and a Minister of state in Uttar Pradesh being declared an absconder in a cow smuggling case (New Indian Express 5 February 2013) all point to the eroding character of parliamentarians.

As far back as in 1949 Dr. Rajẹndra Prasad stressed the importance of character and said that India needs nothing more than a set of honest men who will have the interest of the country before them. He also opined that "however good a Constitution may be, it is sure to turn out bad because those who are called to work it happen to be a bad lot" (Ravi, N., 2007: 4). We should be able to combat the forces and elements that are trying to vitiate our socio-political fabric and undermine our institutions of democracy so that people do not lose faith in the system. Unless we are able to do so no force, no army can help save the system (Somnath Chatterjee : 2007:4). Just as a government is accountable to Parliament, in turn Parliament as the highest legislative institution of India owes its accountability to the people of India.

Over time, election that started as gentlemanly contests turned into ugly fights due to the attractions of office. The popular will as expressed through the ballot box was sought to be distorted by different means like capturing of booths, rigging through enrolment of bogus voters and voting, offering bribe to voters and extravagant spending for campaign. All these required the active help of criminal elements. Worried about the situation, the Government of India appointed a Committee under the Chairmanship of N.N. Vohra, then Home Secretary, to look into the activities of crime syndicates/mafia organisations which had developed links with, and were being protected by, government functionaries and political personalities. The Vohra report said:

> An organised crime syndicate/mafia commences its activities by indulging in petty crime at the local level, mostly relating to illicit distillation / gambling/organised satta and prostitution in the large towns... In the big cities the main source of income relates to the real estate... Over time, the money power thus acquired is used for building up contacts with bureaucrats and politicians... The money power is used to develop a network of muscle power which is also used by the politician during the election (Vohra Committee Report).

In certain states like Bihar, Haryana and UP these gangs enjoy the patronage of government functionaries. Some political leaders become the leader of these gangs/armed senas and, over the years, get themselves elected to local bodies, State Assemblies and National Parliament. "Resultantly such elements have acquired considerable political clout, seriously jeopardising the smooth functioning of the administration. The network of mafia is virtually running a parallel government pushing the state apparatus into irrelevance.... The cost of contesting election has thrown the politicians in to the lap of these elements...." (Vohra Committee Report).

The essence of the Vohra Committee Report indicates that crime syndicates flourish under political patronage and the politician-criminal nexus was assuming alarming proportions, pushing the state to irrelevance. Initially politicians hired criminals to help them win the ballot through foul means. Today the notorious criminals manage to get party nomination, win election and enter the Parliament and even the cabinet. "In the 14th Lok Sabha of the 542 members, there were no less than 100 MPs who have been charge sheeted in criminals cases, ranging from misdemeanors like 'disturbing peace' to the ominibus charges of 'rioting' to serious offences like murder, rape and loot.... A dozen have murder charges against them, another 10 have been charged with attempted murder. Around 11 of them are, in public perception, known as dons. And at the state level nearly 700 members of the State Legislative Assemblies are involved in criminal cases and trials are pending against them" (Ahmad Shamshad and Ansari, N.A., : 2008 : 874).

**Combating Criminalisation: Efforts and Hurdles**

The Vohra report and events thereafter, however, led to a soul searching by the Election Commission and the Judiciary. They emerged as the two unlikely heroes to ensure that law breakers cannot be allowed to be law makers. To protect the Constitution, the Election Commission and Judiciary had to resort to Constitutional vigilantism of sorts in extending their power beyond the original mandate. It was T.N. Seshan, appointed the Election Commissioner in 1990, who changed the role of the Commission from a passivist one to an activist one. In doing so he did not hesitate to overreach, since he wanted to shake up the sleeping giant. He disciplined officials under the state and central administration, deputed for poll, and ensured that voter rolls were in order, that polling took place according to the rule book, that the candidates did not indulge in spending beyond limits, and that persons in authority did not misuse their official positions to gain undue advantage.

The process has continued since then but on a low key. Article 324 vests in the Commission the "superintendence, direction and control" of elections and it has been greatly aided in its task by the Supreme Court's interpretation of this Article as a power house that would enable it to fill the missing links in the law to ensure fair elections.

The Commission thus brought a Model Code of Conduct for ministers and other candidates that were considered as binding, to order the transfer of partisan officials, requiring candidates to disclose details of their educational qualification, property and criminal record, asking political parties and candidates to submit audited accounts, and set detailed norms for electioneering. The impartiality and integrity of the elections received an added boost with the introduction of Electronic Voting Machines (EVM) and computerised rolls.

The Judiciary on its part systematically tried to ensure that rule of law prevailed under all circumstances and that political office could not shield the guilty from criminal charges. The November, 2000 judgment of the Delhi High

Court, in the petition filed by the Association for Democratic Reforms, directing the Election Commission to secure for the voters information about the antecedents of the candidates was one benchmark. It was followed up by an appeal filed by the Union of India in 2001 challenging the above direction, the May 2002 decision of the Supreme Court upholding the Delhi High Courts' judgement, and the Election Commission notification of June 2002, prescribing the format of the affidavit by candidates. Under the new rules all candidates seeking elections to the Lok Sabha or the State Legislative Assemblies are required to furnish an affidavit, along with the nomination papers, information with regards to whether the candidate is convicted/acquitted/discharged of any criminal offence in the past, if any, whether he is punished with imprisonment or fine prior to six months of filing of nomination, whether the candidate is accused in any pending case, of any offence punishable with imprisonment for two years or more, and in which charge is framed or cognizance is taken by the court of law. Further, the contesting candidate has to declare the assets of the spouse and the dependents' liabilities, if any, and disclose his educational qualifications. This was contested by the Union Government which had the tacit support of all political parties. The draft bill of July 2002 was aimed at limiting the information to details of offences of 'heinous crimes'. Later, even these were withdrawn.

The Representation of the People Ordinance (later Act) 2002 eliminated the duty to give information on assets, liabilities and education of a candidate from the voters rights so that criminal charges and convictions had to be revealed to a lesser extent. The Supreme Court struck down parliament's attempts to nullify the voter's right to know the details of their candidates and restored the original decision in the Democratic Reforms Case - II (2003). The criminals in Parliament continue under the plea that they have not been convicted because their long drawn trials were continuing. As the Supreme Court cannot increase the disqualification known to the law, it is certain that information and voters alone can expose the criminals and bar their entry into the People's House.

The Representation of the People Act itself contains a list of 16 offences under the Indian Penal Code, and there are other Acts under which conviction would disqualify a candidate. In a separate amendment, also titled R.P. (Second Amendment) Act, 2002, a person is disqualified if convicted and fined for offences relating to sati, corruption and POTA and for a period of six years from the date of release, if jailed (Sivaramakrishnan, K.C., : 2002). But the government did not consider disclosure of financial assets and liabilities at the time of contesting elections. Only the elected were required to furnish the information to the Lok Sabha Speaker.

The Election Commission and Courts have fought the battle with practical proof. But the current position appears to be not well constructed since many ambiguities exist. If they are not corrected in a systematic and timely manner criminalisation of politics has the potential to wipe out democracy itself. When representatives charged with serious offences, like murder and dacoity, contest and win from prison cells or when those convicted of crime continue to be our representatives, people will start questioning the legitimacy of the political process itself.

The Supreme Court in a recent landmark judgement, that augurs well for Indian democracy, ruled that if any sitting member of Parliament or of state legislatures is convicted, they shall stand disqualified.[5] But the Bench made clear that this disqualification would not apply to convicted MPs and MLAs who have filed their appeals in the higher courts before this verdict (New Indian Express, 14 July 2013).

Only if political parties sincerely retract from steps that will demean our constitutional bodies, can we put an end to the strangle hold of criminals in politics. The strength of the criminal class is that it has become indistinguishable from the political class. The 'muscle power' and the 'finances' that they mobilize are in-fact the lifeblood for political parties which will look for ways to frustrate the law and cheat the voters again (George, T.J.S., 2013).

The verdict is a major move towards de-criminalisation of union and state legislatures. It will be a pity if those in governance are averse to course correction and happily decide to sink further in the quicksand of wily politics.

The task is complicated because of the presumption of innocence of any person charged with a crime before his conviction and the danger of cases being foisted on political opponents through misuse of political positions. To overcome this, the task of prosecution should be placed beyond the influence of the political executive and the criminal justice system should be pruned up to deliver speedy justice.

**Need for Enforcing Ethical Standards**

In America you find a prudent 'filter' like the Presidential Electoral College or a Senate representing states rather than citizens and an indirectly appointed Federal Court system to weed out unwanted elements. In India this job is to be performed by the political parties and their leaderships. They should block persons with criminal background from contesting elections. Our elections should be freed from the dominance of money power. The use of unaccounted money in elections has become a fact of life. The big business and industrial houses finance political parties during elections. If legitimate money is not made available through state funding of elections this practice cannot be ended.

Prescribing minimum educational qualification for the representatives can also be considered for the better functioning of our parliament and for de-criminalising elections. The Election Commission should provide the details regarding the candidate so that the voters can evaluate their candidate. Though the Model Code of Conduct has been in existence for many decades, it still lacks statutory backing. Public opinion is the moral sanction for its enforcement. Legal measures should be taken to see that it is being observed in its true spirit.

Ordinary citizens and the civil society have a major role in the political process. There should be conscious effort by the government and the media to involve the illiterate and literate masses in the political process. The Women's Reservation Bill, which seeks to reserve 30 per cent of all seats in the Lok Sabha and State Legislative Assemblies for women, is a right step in this regard. In view of the vastness of the country and huge electorate, the EC has also made a proposal for the appointment of regional Commissions in different zones to reduce its work load. The implementation of this proposal will bring in more efficiency in its functioning.

Though parties are bound by law to maintain accounts regularly and file return of Income every year, election expenditures lacks transparency. Goswami Committee did not include spending by independent supporters in the election expenditure limit but made such unauthorised spending a penal offence. It also advocated a ban on company donations to political parties. The Goswami Committee (1990) and the Indrajit Gupta Committee (1998) suggested limited state funding. If the legitimate money is difficult to collect, political parties may find illegitimate sources of money leading to criminalisation of politics. This requires urgent measures to make election contributions and expenditures transparent. The political parties should also be made to adhere to their constitution regarding the holding of organisational elections at all levels. The Election Commission should be given the powers to de-recognise a political party in case it violates the law. These measures can help to reduce the entry of criminals, and pave the way for clean candidates who find it difficult to enter the election fray due to lack of resources.

The entry of criminals in to Parliament has also contributed to the erosion of democratic and moral values in our parliamentary life. Even a single member can disturb the proceedings of the House and can hold it to ransom (Surya Prasad, K.,: 2013 : 186 - 187)[6]. In this context, it is better to lay down certain statutory disqualifications by giving a definition to the term 'pernicious behaviour', i.e., what does and what does not constitute pernicious behaviour of parliamentarians (*Ibid* : 106). Members violating the rule should be asked to leave the House for the day and if they refuse they should be suspended for the session. A second suspension should entail disqualification and termination of membership and the member should be debarred from contesting the election for a specific period (*Ibid* :197).

In short, participation of criminals is the soft underbelly of our political system. Flagrant violation of laws, poor quality of services and the corruption in them, protection for law breakers on political, group, classes, communal or caste grounds, partisan interference in the investigation of crime and poor prosecution of cases, inordinate delays lasting over years, and high costs in the judicial process, mass withdrawal of cases, indiscriminate grant of parole, etc., are the more important of the causes. The opportunity to influence crime investigators and to convert the policemen from being potential adversaries to allies is the irresistible magnet drawing criminals to politics. The elected position and the substantial protection that it can give, helps him either to further and expand his activities or to evolve into an entity with higher political ambitions. As for political parties, such individuals bring into the electoral process their ability to secure votes through use of money and muscle power. This is a short term win - win situation for all, except for public good and good governance (Ramachandran, V. : 2012).

**Conclusion**

The contribution of parliamentary democracy as such to the creation of modern India was immense. It transformed the traditional society, undermined untouchability, promoted the concept of social democracy, assured fundamental rights and made the voter the ultimate sovereign at the political level. As for its limitations, it failed to recognize that parliamentary democracy or the Westminster model, as transplanted from Britain, had to work in a different culture and environment.

The democratic experiment in India has succeeded in establishing institutions of politics and governance. But the success of democracy depends on a number of interconnected activities such as free and fair elections, social and economic equality, an active civil society, an independent and unbiased media and good governance. The Indian democracy is yet to comprehend the dynamics of a democratic polity based on universal adult suffrage. Indian elections have demonstrated the fact that ideology, policies and programme can no longer ensure enough supporters for political parties to win an election. Thus money and muscle power entered the scene leading to criminalisation of politics and the emergence of parallel governments and parallel economies. For confronting the growing criminalisation of politics several initiatives began and the government responded to such demands through the constitution of Committees for reforming the electoral system in a half-hearted manner. The recommendations were neither radical nor fool proof. The problem remains too complex to be addressed by such recommendations and conventional amendments.

The Nehruvian project for introduction of the British model was at odds with indigenous values. We have not learned how to participate in elections as rights — bearing individuals and are yet to come to grip with the concerns of civil society and respect for the rule of law. Instead of approaching the formal structures of politics, the people at large seek protection from god fathers' who dispense it unlawfully (Stuart Corbridge: 2010, 259 - 60). In India the elections are also an arena of struggles for social identity and dignity (Yogendra Yadav: 2010, 352). Parliamentary democracy in India has drifted to a mere number game.

Nehru earnestly believed that the congress party will provide the necessary oil to work the system with utmost responsibility. But it failed to blend the indigenous values with the model that was replicated. Gandhi, it seems, had the foresight to see such a development considering his view that political life was basically an arena for working out personal, moral and existential problems and that mere replication of western liberal institutions without consideration of space and time will not succeed.

In India today, only figuratively do legislatures represent the people; in real terms they represent the wily political class seeking to frustrate any move from the whistle blowers to clean the system. This stark reality is evident from the combined move by the ruling as well as opposition parties to amend the Right to Information Act so that political parties will remain outside its purview. Today in India the law makers have turned law breakers. They are recklessly manipulating the spirit of free and fair elections that constitute the bedrock of our liberal democracy.

A change in the existing state of affairs cannot be expected soon. The real problem that India faces is not the absence of strong laws or a favourable public opinion but the absence of will power to move against the perpetrators of crime. Electoral politics has provided a fertile ground for criminalisation of politics in India. It also provides scope for active citizen participation. The only hope lies in the voters using their wisdom through the ballot. They should strive for de-criminalisation of politics, political party reforms, law to prevent misuse of religion for electoral gains, punishment for electoral offences, action against false affidavit by the candidates and the provision for negative vote.

**Notes**

1. "T.N. Seshan in a confrontation with government and politicians marked the delineation of the 'electoral period' during which the Commission's Model Code would be in effect, which began with the official announcement of the date of elections. Ultimately this agreement had to be accepted despite resistance. In all these challenges to its authority, the Election Commission used the courts to ventilate the constitutional foundation of its special powers during 'electoral time'. The Model Code was put to good use by employing immediate punishments against violators. Government largesse of any sort, which could be interpreted as an attempt to sway votes was open to close scrutiny during election campaigns." (Madhava Menon. N.R. (2013) : 'Electoral System : Massive Experiment in Democracy', in Raman Pillai, K., et.al, (ed.), *Electoral Reforms,* Kalpaz Publications, Delhi.
2. In the 2004 general elections 16 candidates who were elected to the Lok Sabha polled below 30% of the total votes polled. As many as 322 out of 539 newly elected MPs were returned with less than 50 per cent of the votes. [Election Commission of India - General Elections, 2004, (14th Lok Sabha)].
3. At present the Lok Sabha has more than 379 Members of Parliament hailing from multi millionaire's families or are themselves multi-

millionaires. The election expenses are very high forcing the candidates to spend 15 - 30 times higher than the limit prescribed by the electoral laws. Money is spent on intermediaries to buy votes, distribute liquor, hiring criminals of the locality, bribing officials, and to indulge in booth capturing and rigging. The high cost of election has made political parties and candidates to heavily depend on black money, big business and, the wealthy. This leads to corruption in governance. In the 2009 general election to Lok Sabha, the Congress Party officially spend Rs. 1500 crore, BJP 1000 crore, BSP and NCP Rs. 700 crore each; DMK Rs. 400 crore and AIADMK Rs. 300 crore.

4. In the current Lok Sabha nearly the one-fifth of the members of various political parties have criminal records. RJD leads with 43.5 per cent and Biju Janata Dal has the smallest proportion of MPs with criminal cases. In respect of criminal cases with severe penalties (i.e., five or more years of imprisonment), RJD leads with 34.8 per cent MPs, BSP with 27.8 per cent and Samajwadi party with 19.4 per cent. The proportion of Congress MPs who fall in to this category account for 7.6 per cent of their total number and BJP MPs account for 10.9 per cent [Sangita, S.N. (2013): 'Electoral Process and Inclusive Governance', in K. Raman Pillai, et.al. (eds.), *Electoral Reforms,* Kalpaz Publications, Delhi, p. 76].
5. The Bench consisting of Justice A.K. Patnaik and Justice S.J. Mukhopadhyaya struck down Sub-section (4) of Section 8 of The Peoples Representation Act, 1951 as ultravires of the Constitution. This particular Section says that disqualification of the convicted legislator will not take effect if an appeal against conviction is filed or pending in a higher court.
6. Pernicious behaviour of our elected representatives has transformed the Parliament in to a non-entity, incapable of performing even its primary function. The damage or losses caused to the nation due to this unruly behaviour is really shocking. In the XIV Lok Sabha 26 per cent of precious parliamentary time was lost due to interruption and adjournments. During 2007 the Lok Sabha lost 133 hours and the figures for 2006 and 2005 were 98 and 75hrs respectively. During the XIIIth Lok Sabha 356 hrs have been wasted without transacting any business. Moreover, during 2002-2003, budget allocation worth Rs. 7,68,836 crore have been passed without any debate because of interruption. (For details see Surya Prasad, K : 2013).

## References

Achary, P.D.T (2013) : 'Revisiting Electoral System in India', in Raman Pillai, K., Suresh Kumar, R.K. and Sukumaran Nair, P. (Eds.), *Electoral Reforms,* Kalpaz Publications, Delhi.

Ahmad Shamshed and Nafees Ahmed Ansari (2008): 'Corruption, Criminalisation of Politics and Development', *Indian Journal of Public Administration* (Vol. LIV. No. 4), October- December, 2008.

Bachrach, Peter (1967): *The Theory of Elitism,* Boston, Little, Brown.

David Miller (Ed.), (1994): *The Blackwell Encyclopedia of Political Thought,* Oxford, UK.

Francis Fukuyama, (2001): 'The Limits of Liberal Democracy', in Joel Krieger (Ed.) (2001) : *The Oxford Companion to Politics of the World* (Second Edition), OUP, New York.

George, T.J.S., 'Will the Criminals and Their Patrons Heed Judicial Ruling?' *New Indian Express,* 14.07.2013.

Madhava Menon, N. R. (2013) : 'Electoral System : Massive Experiment in Democracy', in Raman Pillai, K., Suresh Kumar, R.K. and Sukumaran Nair, P. (Eds), *Electoral Reforms*, Kalpaz Publications, Delhi.

Macpherson, C.B., (1973): *Democratic Theory,* Oxford, Clarendon Press.

*New Indian Express,* 5.02.2012.

*New Indian Express,* 14.07.2013.

Ramachandran, V., (2012): 'Ethics in Governance', *Social Science in Perspective* (Vol. 4) July - Sept. & Oct. - Dec. 2012

Ravi, N.,: 'Two Unlikely Heroes : The Election Commission and Judiciary', *The Hindu Supplement*: Independent India at 60', 15 Aug. 2007.

Satish Misra : (2012) : 'Congress After Indira Gandhi' (Spl. Issue : Fearless Journalism), *New Indian Express*, 5 February.

Sivaramakrishnan, K.C.,'Disclosure by Candidates', *The Hindu,* 27, June 2002.

Somnath Chatterjee :'Six Decades of Parliamentary Democracy', *The Hindu Supplement: Independent India at 60'*, 15 August 2007.

Stuart Corbridge (2010): 'Politics and Culture' in Niraja Gopal Jayal and Mehtha P.B. (Eds.), *The Oxford Companion to Politics in India,* OUP, New York.

Surya Prasad, K., (2013): 'Pernicious Behaviour of Elected Representatives — An Unresolved Challenge to Indian Democracy' in Raman Pillai, K., Suresh Kumar, R.K. and Sukumaran Nair, P. (Eds.), *Electoral Reforms,* Kalpaz Publications, Delhi.

'Vohra Committee Report', *The Indian Journal of Public Administration* (Spl. number), July-Sept.: 1995.

YogendraYadav (2010): 'Representation' in Niraja Gopal Jayal, et.al., (Eds), T*he Oxford Companion to Politics in India*, OUP, New York.

# 22

# *A Bull in the China Shop: MNCs/FDI in the Indian Market*

*P. Suresh Kumar*

In India, economic development is a major concern in its socio-economic and political discourses. Since its independence in August 1947, it had experienced different phases in its quest for finding solutions to its pressing socio-economic problems. In fact, even under the domination of the British rule, it had dreamt of its own independent development path in various formulations such as the Bombay Plan or the Peoples plan engaged in by different groups of people and national leaders. All these perceptions settled finally in the formation of the Planning Commission in 1950 as the ultimate agency determining the development path of India. The National Planning Commission has undertaken its task of building the economic foundation of the nation through its Five Year Plan programme. These Plans were broadly fitted into the nationalistic vision envisaged in the Constitution of India. The execution of all the Five Year Plans, including the present 12th Plan, though has not deviated away from the constitutional purview, a thought on the present Indian economic development policies, pattern and process reminiscence one of much more than a bull in the China shop.

In India, it was a mixed economic framework that was formulated as an economic frame to initiate the process of economic development. However, the political framework was one with socialist leanings, and it favoured socialist orientation in its economic policies. The dominant strategy under this milieu was that in the development process the 'commanding heights' vested in the public sector. A strong public sector, with an emphasis on inward looking strategy of national growth, has also provided a comfortable space to the private capital as supportive, and subservient, to the major goals and motives of the national plan. This strategy, by and large, had produced not so less a growth rate of 3.5 per cent on an average from early 1950s to early 1980s. Of course, it was less than the targets set in each of the five year plans. However, it was not a poor achievement. Still, this growth rate was not sufficient to make a positive change on the living standards of the people. The continuance of millions of people below the poverty line and an extensive level of unemployment and the structural problems that emanated from the growth process and strategy for all these period of more than three decades necessitate an urge for change in the development discourse.

The development strategy did change in 1990s with the onset of new economic policy. It was a total 'U' turn. However, the change in discourse was more influenced by events and forces which are of more technical and parochial. The balance of payments position, concern for foreign exchange, stock reform measures for stimulating growth, etc., became the determining factors overarching the constitutional goal of establishing a socialistic pattern of society which was not achieved in the previous development phase. Of course, growth rate has more than doubled on an average since 1991 and upto a period of 2007-08. This higher growth, however, has not created any remarkable improvement in the quality of life of the common mass, leaving growth of economy and living condition of the common mass of people as unrelated variables. In this shift of the Indian growth process and in the non-deliverance of higher growth to common benefit necessarily require a focus on private capital and more on private foreign capital.

**Development Lessons**

A stock taking of these experiences gives us some explicit lessons. Primarily it relates to the role accorded to private capital within the constitutional schemes of the Indian economy. Capital is the primary means of production and it should be channeled productively to meet the needs of the society is a view well entrenched in the Indian planning process. The mixed economic framework well accommodated this view. However the regulatory system involved in the 'Licence Raj' led to chocking of the productive powers of the economy. A demand led and a supply constraint model, in which the private capital worked, assured them a return beyond a normal level without any compulsive or incentives for technological or managerial improvement or upgradation. The sheltered profit led to formation of large monopoly houses that were engaged in producing goods often only catering the needs of an emerging middle class. The private monopoly capital in India thus never structured, or oriented, to a production system serving the requirements of the general mass. The role of public capital too was not much different from that of the private capital. It absorbed primarily the role of an industrial catalyst creating an incentive base so that more private capital is emerging to augment the production base of the economy. Thus the Indian capital as a whole strengthened an industrial base which was more in the nature of monopolistic character rather than competitive one. The monopolistic element and the absence of competition prevented the Indian industrial sector transforming as a mass based production system. To put it more technically, the spread effects and backwash effects, the dominant growth stimulants were not sprouted. An all-round industrial progress was simply evaded from the development process in India. While this was a conclusive outcome occurred in the pre-liberalised period, the liberalised era shows a still more strengthening of this trend.

An attempt of an organic and an auto-centric development involved by and large in the Indian planning goals, which were further given credence by the Constitutional provisions, were simply missed during the liberalised period in India. The development failures and non-deliverance of the benefits of economic progress to common people and an absence of a mass oriented development forced for an alternative path of development. Anchoring the arguments on the premises of conventional economic orthodoxy, the official India, led by technocratic and bureaucratic perceptions, emphasised on the fundamental scarcities facing the nation which, they believed, could be addressed through a global integration. It was believed that such an approach would address Indian policy deficits and will lead to higher growth and better sharing and deliverance. Indeed this wisdom spread by global capital through different mechanisms, subscribed in India, as elsewhere. The global capital, had discovered its own channels of inflows and outflows of capital around the world, particularly in economies where scarcity can be picked up as the structural limitation of development. The special purpose vehicles the global capital has developed to push in developing economies include among other development theories and ideas, the FDI, the SEZs and the operations of MNCs.

**The Global Capital**

To understand and assess the role of FDI, MNCs and other forms of capital inflows into developing economies one should be familiar with the nature and character of the global capital. Global capital is an entity which has transformed into many shades on the basis of the evolutionary process of capitalism. It was the product of extensive colonial exploitation in the beginning. The source of this capital was both direct vertical and horizontal transfers from the primary production. Principally, this capital became instrumental in the initiation, development, strengthening of industrialisation in Britain and many parts of western economies. During this phase of industrial expansion capital inflows and outflows were limited to mainly in Britain, other parts of Europe and America. The global capital underwent a transformation during the phase of industrialisation of the West. Growing source of capital was now more based on manufacturing process. It was the profit that extracted from labour process which constituted the main source of global capital. The lure for more profit caused the diffusion of global capital beyond the developed economies mainly into the Third World. Though, global capital emerged from the profit possibilities of trade and manufacture, the global transactions necessitated financial intermediation which, in course of time, became by itself the major part of global capital named as finance capital. Capitalist practices with the finance capital has grown in such a way that at present it became an entity decoupled with production base of the economy. The implications of the growth and transformation of the global capital on the Third World economies are much complicated in the context of development efforts of the developing economies.

### India and the Global Capital

As one of the major economies that have embarked on development efforts, India has experienced with the flow of this global capital in different phases of its development history. Inadequacy of capital was a perennial problem faced by India in its early phase of development. In theoretical development model, it has been pointed out as saving - investment gap. This sizeable gap was attempted to be filled in with foreign aid and grants which were available mainly as government to government level transfers the flows of which were mostly related with international political circumstances and strategies rather than objective development goals. True that it helped to build in a national industrial base, though in itself was insufficient for a mass based industrialisation of the country. However, the development philosophy of 'commanding heights' with the public sector along with an inwardly oriented development strategy became not conducive for an inflow of private capital. Thus on the whole it was a restricted flow of private foreign capital which in no meaningful way helped the general public in the country.

It is in the liberated era that the flow of global capital started hectically flowing into India in different forms such as incoming of MNCs, setting up of SEZs and inflow of FDI.

### Implications on Indian Economy

We may analyse the implications of global capital inflows in terms of different perceptions. In the development views of non-industrialised economies, it is widely accepted that FDI, MNCs and SEZ are the most powerful economic entities with which a country can cross its perpetual underdevelopment. This view is derived from the conventional economic theory that shortage of capital exerts a limit on the development potential of an economy. The Indian development experience shows that this theorisation has a sound validity in both phases of policy shifts. In the previous phase while a powerful industrial base has constructed with global capital under public sector, in the latter phase the global capital helped to build private empires in India. However, an important issue to reckon with these flows is that it was not helped to the mass industrialisation of the country. This fact indicates that though global capital is helpful for growth, growth per se need not produce mass development. Only if capital became people centered is that we can say the capital development interaction as a positive real relation benefitting all.

This failure of capital in the Indian context takes us to another important perception of capital as an exploitative one. Strictly speaking it is a Marxist perception based on Marxian theory of exploitation. The difference between value of labour and value created by labour is the source of capitalist surplus. Though Marx was right in his analysis, the believers should not forget that surplus is a social entity which is inevitable for progress of any civilisation. A 'reformed' surplus can have a positive and dynamic role particularly in poor economies.

No doubt in each of these theoretical views there is an element of truth though they try to overstate their own positions. However, there is a unanimous feel that capital is inevitable for growth. Given the fact that there is an entity called global capital, it is essential to see that the capital is used productively for growth and for improving the living standards of millions of people around the world who are mired in poverty and destitution. But how to ensure that the flow of capital move is in the right direction for the benefit of common mass?

It is unlikely to happen in any spontaneous form. Let us take the MNCs. MNCs are the products of the capitalist transformation. Intrinsically, the insatiable quest for profit by capitalists spin the technical power in the production process leading to concentration and centralisation of capital. This process necessitates search for avenues of profitable investment in all areas around the globe which led to the emergence and spread of MNCs. In many Third World economies which were battered precariously under colonial domination formulated an inward looking development pattern since the cessation of colonial subjugation. However, the international capital has created a development philosophy justifying the free capital flows. Thus, we find the intrusion of MNCs in to the Third World economies replicating the capitalistic production process. In the saving-investment gap model, the role of foreign capital was intrinsically modulated. Moreover, the new forces of development, such as technology and capitalistic organisational practices, were theorized as inevitable models. All these factors eulogized the MNCs' role in poor economies. Historical experience of many economies showed that such inflows have not restructured the mass production base of the Third World. Further, it also increased the wedge in the socio-economic milieu of developing economies in the form of different kinds of dualism.

It was after the spread of globalisation that MNCs have intensified their operations in developing economies. In the earlier phase capital flowed in to domestic economies and engaged in physical production. However, this phase subsequently transformed in to an exploitative one by insisting for various concessions from the developing economies. Also, the transfer pricing mechanism has been extensively used to plunder the resource from these economies. Thus MNCs became a mechanism of draining away of resources though, it initially pretended to enhance the productive powers of the recipient economies. There are several ways by which the multinationals exploit the poor economies. Monopolisation of natural resources is a dominant mechanism by which the MNCs extend their exploitation network over labor and resources. In India this strategy is widely pursued with the connivance of a corrupt political class. Access to vast tracts of land and other mineral resources in different parts of the country were given to MNCs by various state governments and also by the central government. The increasing struggles in almost all these instances reflect the inconsistency of development with people's needs and requirement. An oft repeated economic argument is that the secondary effects of MNCs productive activities in the recipient economies will lead to creation of forward and backward linkages stimulating local industrial progress. However, the modern production strategy of MNCs is that its outsourcing requirement need not be linked with domestic economic environment. There is no guarantee that the monopoly over the natural resources in a domestic economy will lead to limiting production in the areas of its extraction. Also, the local economic condition need not be inevitable for the organisation of MNCs. This delinking deprives the possibility of growth which conventional economic theory has emphasized as occurring by appropriating scale advantages.

It is a fact that in the Indian context the operation of MNCs has not produced any secondary process of industrialisation in the country. Two other areas where MNCs are preferred in developing economies are related to its employment generation potential and the technological diffusion. It may be remembered that on these two counts MNCs' contribution were limited in India. The local labour is underpriced substantially on international comparisons, depriving the local labour. The possibility of technological diffusion is remote in the context of multi-level outsourcing done by MNCs from around the world. A crucial concern for an economy like India is the ecological damages caused by the operation of the multinationals. The 'comedy' of the Bhopal gas tragedy is an indication of the MNCs and official India's approach to such disasters. It is a powerful example that indicates how influential the MNCs are and how they are capable of altering and prolonging decisions in their favour depriving the genuine compensation the affected people deserve, by any means. The market principles and the sophisticated norms, such as let the polluter pays, are simply vanishing as basic tenets of decision making in such circumstance.

The conversion of vast tracts of agriculture land for the benefit of MNCs directly hit millions of poor people of their livelihood and source of employment. This sort of deprivation of the petty producers increases their vulnerability beyond any kind of restoration even if compensation has been fairly disbursed to them.

It is difficult to expect that the FDI, MNCs, and SEZs will come and settle where it is most needed and in most suitable productive sectors. The capital will never become human in that way and, moreover, it only inclined to reap more profit and exploitation. It is at this juncture that we have to think about alternative mechanisms to ordain capital in the right direction. This urge of using capital in the most socially desirable way would amount to putting conventional economics in the backyards. It is not productivity and profit that should be reckoned as points of optimisation. Rather, we should devise optimisation in terms of how we can create and sustain the livelihood activities of millions of people. In other words, optimisation in terms of productivity and profit cause poverty and destitution whereas optimisation in terms of sustainable livelihood activities leads to use of capital more humane and more socially desirable way.

In this context a pertinent question is that how it is possible to tame the global capital on humanistic lines. It depends more on the characteristics of the population and the structure of the economy. In the Indian context we have to agree that capital flowed more to the requirement of its big business and to the rich. Some capital might have percolated but limited to the needs of upper middle or the middle class consumption pattern. Ninety per cent of the working population is engaged in unorganised sector is the most visible evidence that convinces the biased inflow of capital. The profit clamour of the finance capital and the bureaucratic—technocratic domination of Indian economy prevent the global capital flowing towards socially desirable channels. Rather in the name of policy shifts, development initiatives, privatisation and globalisation, the dominant political powers competing each other in accommodating the vested interest of the capitalists both inland and foreign—colluded through different networks in plucking and looting the natural resources and labour power pushing the general mass into extensive poverty and destitution. In a country like India, where there are numerous and tremendous diversity exist in its social, economic, religious, geographic and cultural spheres, fragmentation is easy to create giving leeway to capitalistic games. Rule of law, transparency and ethical codes and practices which are essential norms of democracy is systematically weakened through machinations at different levels. This huge deficit in democracy transformed people powerless to a large extent. Unscrupulous political class of regional and national variety, in their own competitive power struggle to capture and maintain political power, often align with vested capital interests. Such alliances are compelled to formulate policy framework suiting to the requirements of capitalist interests. The use and flow of capital is occurring in Indian economy under these circumstances. This will prevent capital flowing into sectors and activities beneficial to common mass. The much discussed issues on FDI is a classic example in this regard.

As usual, the role of FDI for intensifying the speed of economic growth was put forward as a justification for formulating domestic policies in favour of FDI inflows in retail trade. It is strange to understand and accept the points raised by the Planning Commission Deputy Chairman Montek Singh Ahluwalia on the official stand for the ratification of FDI on retail. His first thesis was that FDI in retail was implemented in China some 20 years back. He said, "to say that India can't open up 20 years after China did suggests a total lack of confidence in our ability". He further argues that the present system is highly inefficient, with multiple chains of intermediaries, with no integrated logistic infrastructure like refrigeration and transport facilities. There is huge wastage and the losers are the farmers who get a low price and the consumers who have to pay more. He had also suggested distinguishing broadly the modernisation of retail from introduction of FDI in modern retail, offering favourable policy frame work inviting FDI in modern retail. All these arguments are economically tenable. But who cares about the predicament of millions of poor farmers, people and workers who depend on retail trade for their existence. It was pointed out that out of 71 million jobs in services in the urban areas, around 36 per cent are in the retail and whole-sale trade and repair services. They are not getting a fair return from their activities. They linger precariously in these activities simply because this sector constitutes the employer of last resort, as there is no employment opportunities in agriculture and manufacturing. By any stretch of imagination, it is unlikely that this massive number of people will get absorbed by the inflow of new FDI in retail sector. The capitalistic hunger for profit never desist them from employing vulgar practices in any society. The disastrous financial frauds committed by the capitalist class in the US and its resonance as a recession in the global economy is something which is always itching the collective wisdom of humanity. Given this intrinsic behaviour of capital, the produces and consumers will ultimately benefit from FDI inflow will remain only as a myth. May be in the beginning the retail price may come down from the scale operations of the FDI entrants. But the scale itself results in monopoly practices sometimes later, often leading to rise in price of commodities. At this point, consumers are at a receiving end. The petty producers scattered over a wide area are increasingly forced to get in to contact with representative middleman of FDI. Once the FDI succeeds in disciplining the producers, they start dictating price and product specifications, depriving the producers and consumers both economically and from enjoying heterogeneous products and nurturing diversity in production.

In India, the capital inflow in its different forms such as formation of special economic zones, setting up of MNCs and other forms of capital inflows have not produced a systematic and mass based development. Rather, it has produced more social confrontation and economic inequalities. The upper hand the capital is getting over the natural resources of India such as land, water, minerals and forests, in fact, led to estrange people from their primary livelihood sources. Their displacement has created, cheap commodification of their labour power to be released, and used menially in the service sectors. In services also the foreign capital has established its domination in a number of ways. This looting of resources and labour, in collaboration with local elites, has enormously strengthened the global capital and weakened the general mass.

The traditional economic theorisation that more inflow of capital filling the resource gap thus leading to higher growth and welfare of the people remain as an illusion in Indian context. Also the argument that it fills the current account deficit enabling the economy to sustain its economic development remains as a questionable proposition. In fact, the outflow of resource in the form of profit repatriation and other forms of payments and fees only leads to a perpetual dependency on foreign capital in the country. The inflow of foreign capital need not necessarily end up in a structural transformation of the economy benefiting its majority of the farmers, petty producers, unorganised workers and the common man. Policy reforms for more growth entails only a single model with the present political class in the form of globalisation and integration. However, they are willfully forgetting that integration can occur in numerous other ways than the presently dominating capitalist discourse. An organic and humanistic perception of development can emanate only from local needs, local people and local culture. What we require is an indigenous model of development, based on democracy, decentralisation and humanism. The role of foreign capital in its variety of forms such as FDI, MNC, FII and SEZs should only to be allowed to occur within these parameters.

## References


Adam, G. (1975) : 'Multinational Corporations and Worldwide Sourcing', in Hugo Radice (ed.) *International Firms and Modern Imperialism,* Penguin Books.

Amin, S. (1974) : *Accumulation on a World Scale.* New York, Monthly Review Press.

Baran, P. (1957) : *The Political Economy of Growth.* New York, Monthly Review Press.

Baran, P. and Sweezy, P. (1966): *Monopoly Capitalism,* Baltimore, Penguin.

Caves, R.E. (1982): *Multinational Enterprice and Economic Analysis.* Cambridge, Cambridge University Press.

Chakravarty, S. (1998): *Development Planning : The Indian Experience;* OUP, Delhi

Frank, A.G. (1969): *Capitalism and Underdevelopment in Latin America,* New York, Monthly Review Press.

Jalee, P. (1968) : *The Pillions of the Third World,* Trans. Mary Clopper, New York, Monthly Review Press.

Kurien, C.T. (1994): *Global Capitalism and the Indian Economy,* Orient Long man.

Magdof, H. (1969): *The Age of Imperialism,* New York, Monthly Review Press.

Sweezy, P.M. (1972): *Modern Capitalism and Other Essays*, New York, Monthly Review Press.

# 23

# *Mounting Corruption and Political Indecisiveness*

*P. Sukumaran Nair*

## Introduction

Lord Acton's oft quoted statement "Power corrupts; absolute power corrupts absolutely" seems more significant in the contemporary world. Corruption has been a part of human society from times immemorial. It is found in almost all countries, although its nature, volume, dimensions, etc., vary from government to government and from one environment to another. 'Corruption is anti-national, anti-economic and anti-poor'. It causes impediments to good governance and development. It adversely affects the quality of life, destroy cultural heritage, violates generally accepted standards of behaviour, erodes greater transparency in governance and causes road block to national prosperity. The Supreme Court in a judgement (State of Madhya Pradesh V. Jagdish Prasad Gupta, AIR 2000, SC 870) has observed: "Corruption in a civilised society is like cancer, which if not detected in time is sure to malignise the polity of the country, leading to disastrous consequences. It is... not only contagious... and spreads like fire in a jungle.... Unless nipped in the bud at the earliest, it is likely to cause turbulence, shaking of the socio-economic political system...."[1]

*Times of India* poll on 7th May, 2002 showed that corruption is the biggest problem—the number one problem—in the country. It is not merely bureaucrats and top public sector executives, who are accused of corruption. Fingers are even pointed at senior Cabinet Ministers. It is shocking to see that some of the top and hitherto unsullied captains of the industry are involved in corrupting the system[2]. The 15th Lok Sabha has been disrupted many times due to corruption scandals[3]. The former Central Vigilance Commissioner (CVC) N. Vittal, saw a vicious circle of corruption involving four major players, viz Neta (politician), Babu (bureaucrat), Lala (businessman) and Dada (criminal)[4]. Even though the country has adequate legal and institutional devices to deal with corruption, it thrives mainly due to the indecisiveness of the political executive in addressing the root cause of corruption and ensuring speedy and timely justice.

## Understanding Corruption

The word corruption is derived from the Latin word 'Rumpere' meaning 'to break'[5]. It implies that something is broken; it might be a moral code, a social code of conduct or an administrative rule and the predominant motive behind this break is generally personal gain or benefits. International Encyclopedia of Social Science defines corruption as the misuse of public power for personal gains. It refers to decisions that politicians and public bureaucrats make based on authority delegated to them by the populace[6]. The term corruption also connotes bribery, finance abuse, clientelism, cronyism, fraud, embezzlement, extortion, graft, kickbacks, machine politics, misappropriation, misconduct, nepotism, patronage, rent-seeking, scandal, side payments, special interest politics, theft and venality[7]. Corruption is a deliberate and intentional exploitation of one's position, status or resources directly or indirectly for personal aggrandizement. In short, it is an act by a public official violating legal or social norms for private or particular gain. It is a form in which people try to increase their income at the cost of others.

Corruption exists in two broad forms—administrative and Political. Administrative corruption refers to acts of bribery, kickbacks or grease money in which public officials extract a payment for implementing an existing decision. Political corruption takes place when political leaders either allocate national budgets or introduce legislation to facilitate projects from which either they themselves or their close associates will benefit.

**Corruption in India Today**

The first generation of political leaders of free India, who came through the National Movement, had a clear vision of a corrupt-free India. Dr S. Radhakrishnan reminded that "unless we destroy corruption in high places, root out every trace of nepotism, love of power, profiteering and black marketing, which have spoiled the good name of our country, we will not be able to raise the standard of efficiency in administration as well as in production and distribution of necessary goods in life".[8] What we see today is mounting corruption in all spheres of activity. India's position is 94th among corrupt countries, according to Corruption Perception Index.

It is pertinent to recall the findings of a study conducted in June 2008 under the joint auspices of the Transparency International, India, and the Centre for Media Centre on Corruption.[9] The Study team selected 19 Indian states for the purpose of study and classified (the 19 states) them into four categories–most corrupt, very highly corrupt, highly corrupt and moderately corrupt. According to them, Jammu and Kashmir, Madhya Pradesh and Uttar Pradesh are the most corrupt states, while Rajastan, Karnataka and Tamil Nadu belonged to the very highly corrupt category. Six states, viz., Gujarat, Chhattisgarh, Delhi, Jharkhand, Kerala and Odisha, were categorised as highly corrupt states. Moderately corrupt states included Maharashtra, Andhra Pradesh, Haryana, Punjab, Himachal Pradesh, West Bengal and Uttarakhand. The survey also found that among the corrupt departments, the Police Department ranked first on corruption, followed by the Forest Department, Land Records, Registration and Housing respectively. The other corrupt services included the Electricity, Banking, Education, Water Supply, and NREGE.[10]

The most inevitable function any state ought to perform is the maintenance of law and order. Without a strong and effective police force this task is absolutely unattainable in any system of governance. The police should perform their duty with integrity, responsibility, courage, prudence and trust. But the performance of the police department is much below our expectation. There is illegal use of police power for personal gain.

In terms of public trust for law enforcement, only 56 per cent of people rated the police as having a high or very high ethical standards, as against 86 per cent for nurses.[11] Forms of corruption involving the police personnel include: misuse of authority, kickbacks, opportunistic thefts, bribe, giving protection for those involved in illegal activities in return for payments, fix, indulging in direct criminal activities such as robbery and false registering of FIR, etc.[12]

National Crime Records Bureau brings the gravity of the police corruption in India.[13] According to NCRB survey, Delhi Police is the most corrupt police force, followed by Uttar Pradesh and Madhya Pradesh. Out of 61765 complaints filed against the force across India, 22 per cent were registered in Delhi, 19.4 per cent in UP and 17.3 per cent in MP. Further, the report of NCRB indicates that only 47 complaints registered ended up in conviction. In short, the performance of the police personnel directly or indirectly set the stage for corruption.

Post-Independent India also witnessed a series of scams and scandals involving huge corruption. The genesis of scams and scandals can be traced to the Provisional Parliament in 1951, with Mudgal case in which H.G. Mudgal, MP was alleged of corruption.[14] Some of the important scams and scandals that rocked the Indian Polity included Geep Scandal (1948), Mundhra Scandal (1957), Bofors Guns Deal (1987), Securities Scam (1992), Sugar Import Scandal (1994), JMM Bribes Scandal (1995), Fodder Scam (1996), Urea Deal (1996), CRB Scam (1997) Plantation Companies Scam (1999), Stock Market Scam (2005), Taj Corridor Scam (2006), Hassan Ali Khan Tax Evasion Case (2008), Army Ration Pilferage Case (2008), Rice Export Scam (2009), Orissa Mines Scam (2009) Koda Mining Scam (2000)[15], 2G Spectrum Scam (2010), and Coal Block Allocation Scam (2013). In a recent study, T.S.N. Shastry has pointed out that the total amount involved in all scams and scandals since independence has come to more than Rs. 910, 603, 234, 300, 000 which is equal to US dollars 20.23 trillion[16].

Thus, it is obvious that every Department is plagued with corruption. Here, it is pertinent to examine the role of legislature and judiciary in bridling the mounting corruption that destroys the very vitals of our democratic polity.

An over view of the functioning of our Parliament since the first Lok Sabha reveals some disturbing facts. Earlier our Parliament could legitimately boast of having some very outstanding and accomplished parliamentarians who could do honour to any Parliament of the world[17]. In terms of character of the legislature, the level of participation, the number of days on which the

House met and the time devoted for discussion and its quality, the People's House (Lok Sabha) occupied a pre-eminent position. People liked to listen to leaders of Parliament initiating debates on national and international issues. Today, the House witnesses indecorous behaviour and indiscipline, resulting in devaluation of Parliamentary authority, deterioration in the quality of members and poor levels of participation. The character of Parliament has considerably changed consequent to changes in the membership composition. Unlike members of the earlier Houses, now a good number of members, belonging to all parties, are selfish, power-hungry, greedy, dishonest and power brokers, with the result that welfare of the people is at the bottom of their priorities. In order to retain and remain in power, they are prepared to make any compromise with offenders of law.

There is an increase of members with criminal background in our Parliamentary system. They are present in substantial numbers exercising their undue influence on policies, decision making and governance. The numbers of representatives facing criminal charges and with criminal records are increasing at an alarming proportion. According to a survey conducted by the Association of Democratic Rights, a Delhi based NGO, 162 out of 545 MPs of the 15th Lok Sabha and 1258 out of 4032 sitting MLAs have criminal cases pending against them[18]. This number was 156 in the previous Lok Sabha. Similarly the number of *crorepatis* at present is 360 as against 128 in the 14th Lok Sabha. Entry of elected representatives with criminal records in our democratic polity is a threat to democratic process. Accepting the influence of money power, muscle power and mafia power from the gangsters, these representatives maintain an unholy nexus with them which in turn induce them to be more corrupt. In the J.M.M. MPs case 10 MPs were bribed for votes on the floor of the House (in 1995). Similarly in the Hawala case a number of prominent leaders stood accused for receiving money from a business man and his associates.

Even in the allocation of MP Local Area Development Schemes (MPLADS) also there is enough potential for massive corruption. The Comptroller and Auditor General (CAG) in the latest report pointed out that there are violations of guidelines and irregularities in the implementation of MPLAD scheme from 2004-05 to 2008-09. In the report it is also alleged that the MPLAD funds are used for private purposes. Moreover, the corporate industrialist lobby always tries to influence the representatives through corrupt deeds. In this context, it may be observed that steady decline in Parliamentary behaviour, deterioration in the conduct, changes in the composition of members, poor level participation in the debates, craze for amassing more wealth and the unholy relationship at political and bureaucratic levels have gravely affected Parliament's capacity to address the issue of corruption.

The role of the Judiciary is also seems to be dwindling when it comes to cases of corruption involving the wealthy and the mighty. Its integrity too has been questioned and people have started losing their confidence in its performance. The Law Commission in its report in 1958 viewed that corruption among the staff of courts was substantial and had existed for a longtime[19]. Santhanam Committee's recommendation in this regard also deserves special mention."...we were informed by responsible persons including Vigilance and Special Police Establishment Officers that corruption exists in lower ranks of the judiciary all over India, and in some places it has spread to the higher ranks also."[20]

The Judiciary suffers from an unbecoming misbehaviour syndrome as serious charges have been made against the judges in different parts of the country including at the Apex Court. The highest level of judiciary has been accused of corruption to the extent that in the Apex Court an affidavit has been submitted stating that at least six former judges of the Supreme Court were corrupt.[21]

It cannot but be stated that a number of judges have involved in corruption related cases for obtaining material benefits. To illustrate a few, in 1995 the Chief Justice of Bombay High Court was forced to resign as it was found that he had received Rs. 70 lakhs as book advance from a publishing company, known to have links with the underworld.[22] A judge from the Calcutta High Court was arrested in 1996 for FERA violation after retirement as he has made it a routine to issue exparte-ad-interim stay orders on anticipatory bail pleas for smugglers, having links with the Mumbai underworld. In 2000, former Chief Justice of India, A.S. Anand was accused of using his position to get the subordinate judiciary to rule in favour of his wife and mother-in-law in a suit that had been barred by limitations for two decades.

In November 2002, Sunita Malviya, a Jodhpur based doctor, alleged that a deputy Registrar of Rajasthan High Court sought sexual favours for himself and for justice Arun Madan to fix a case in her favour. Three judges of the Punjab and Haryana High Court (M.L. Singh, Mehtab Singh Gill and Amarbir Singh) sought the help of disgraced Punjab Public Service Commission (PPSC) Chief R.P. Sindhu to ensure that their kith and kin topped examinations conducted by the Commission. Former Chief Justice of India, K.G. Balakrishnan has also been accused of corruption with the revelation that his brother and two-sons-in-law were in possession of unaccounted wealth. He also faced mounting pressure to quit his post as chairman of National Human Rights Commission.

From the above, it is obvious that judiciary is not functioning in an impartial manner as it ought to be in our judicial system. Administration of Justice, the prime duty of any judicial system, has become inordinately delayed, costly and inaccessible. An authoritative source indicate that there are over three crore cases pending in courts, many of these lying undecided for decades.[23] The conviction rates in Indian courts is only 6 per cent. The average time taken for the disposal of cases range between 10 and 20 years. Ninety per cent of cases which are brought before the courts get acquitted. According to Transparency International India's study on corruption, 79 per cent of respondents of the survey said that there was corruption in judiciary. Of those who had paid bribes, 59 per cent had paid money to a lawyer, 30 per cent to court officials five per cent to judges, 14 per cent to middle men and eight per cent to public prosecutor to get their work done.[24]

It may be stated that all judges are not corrupt nor the judicial system is meant for corrupt practices. But the moral deterioration that has crept into the judicial system due to corrupt tendencies, of at least some judges, has resulted in the soft pedaling of many cases involving massive corruption and loot.

**Addressing Corruption: Committees, Institutions and Legal Framework**

All countries have enacted laws to curb corruption. Government of India has initiated steps to bridle corruption as it was realised that corruption would be an impediment to nation's prosperity. The Indian Penal Code (1860) and the Prevention of Corruption Act provided scope and legal definition of corruption. In 1946 the anti-corruption police organisation known as Delhi Special Police Establishment (DSPE) was setup, which later merged with The Central Bureau of Investigation (CBI) when it was instituted in 1963[25]. In 1947, the Prevention of Corruption Act was passed, with the intention of eradicating corruption, which was later modified in 1988. Another attempt in this regard was the creation of 'Commissions of Enquiries' under the Commission of Enquiries Act 1952. In the early 1960s Government of India had created a legal framework and an investigative structure to deal with corruption among the public servants.

In 1962, when the issue of corruption assumed frightening proportions, Lal Bahadur Shastri appointed a Committee, popularly known as 'Santhanam Committee', with K. Santhanam as Chairman and a few other members including top civil servants, to study and report with recommendations on corruption.[26] The Committee submitted its final report on March 31, 1964 before which an interim report was also submitted. The Report contained as many as 137 recommendations on various aspects on corruption. The Committee, among other things, suggested the constitution of the Central Vigilance Commission (CVC). The M.J. Desai Committee (1966-69) on Administrative Reforms recommended the constitution of an 'Ombudsman type' high level independent body, to enquire into allegations of misconduct and corruption against ministers and other public personnel. Appointment of the 'Shah Commission' was yet another step adopted by the Janata Government to deal with corruption. The Veerappa Moily Commission, appointed by the UPA Government, has also submitted its report on corruption. The Public Interest Litigation, Anti-defection Law and Foreign Exchange Regulation Act (FERA) also constitute important innovations to fight corruption.

The Government, at the central and state levels, has initiated several measures to address corruption from time to time like the Central Vigilance Commission (CVC), the Central Bureau of Investigation (CBI), the Anti-Corruption Bureau (ACB), the State Vigilance Commission (SVC) institutions like the Lok Pal and Lok Ayukta. But it may be noted that these institutions have not succeeded in carrying out its functions successfully. Moreover, these organisations are part of the executive and it is very difficult to investigate the corruption charges against them.

**Factors Sponsoring Corruption**

According to CSDS Poll Survey, corruption has increased in India over the last four years. The perception of increased corruption rose from 39% in 2011 to 69 per cent at present[27]. Many people irrespective of their rank or social status are indulging in it overtly or covertly. It seems that the basic value system of the society is eroding when it comes to corruption. Corruption at higher levels has undermined people's faith and credibility in the government. No wonder, India is rated as one of the most corrupt countries of the world. Why this perilous situation? Doesn't India have sufficient legal means to redress this? The factors promoting corruption include the following.

**Lack of Political Will**

The Preamble of the Constitution of India resolved "to secure to all its citizens Justice, Social, Economic and Political". The basic philosophy of the Constitution exhorts to provide good governance to the people of India irrespective of religion, caste, colour, sex, place of birth or any of them. During the first two decades since the promulgation of the constitution, the country's administration was more or less in the right path. But things changed subsequently. In the beginning the concept of 'Politics-Administration dichotomy' worked well, according to which politics laid down policies and the task of administration was to carry out these policies as economically and efficiently as possible. Political neutrality has been in existence. The civil service of independent India had a creditable record in matters of political neutrality. The members of Indian Civil Service succeeded in adapting themselves to the changing socio-political milieu of the country and they were eager to undertake new challenges to promote the welfare of the people in a non-partisan manner.

Gradually the traditional concept of neutrality of civil service eroded, deteriorated resulting in the decline of the spirit of service to the nation. Since then corruption has grown exponentially. In such a scenario both the political and permanent executive lost their credibility. They also lost their sense of justice and fair play. The sanctity associated with public funds and their utilisation eroded, making our polity and its governance insensitive to the sufferings of the people. Entry of criminals in to politics and the undue influence exerted by them by virtue of money power and muscle power resulted in the misuse of authority for their personal and private gain. The government of the day gradually lost the political will to set things right.

**Incapability of Institutions**

The institutions, which are empowered to formulate and implement laws, have also become vulnerable to corruption. Apart from formal organs of government, the anti-corruption departments like CBI, CVC, etc., also seems to be lethargic in their functioning. The Central Vigilance Commission, which is supposed to dismiss the corrupt officers, is only an advisory body. The Government is not always interested to implement the advice of CVC to dismiss the corrupt officers. Similarly, it is also a known fact that there is corruption within the CBI and the Vigilance Department. Recently in an infamous scandal - Coal Block Allocation Scam - Justice R.M. Lodha of the Supreme Court said: "The CBI is like a caged parrot speaking his master's voice. It is a sordid saga that there are many masters and one parrot. The CBI's job is not to interact with government officials but to interrogate to find the truth".[28] Thus the institutional failures promote corruption.

**Incapability of Political Parties**

There is no alternative to party government, save dictatorship, in any modern state. They are inevitable in a democracy as they are indispensable for the smooth functioning of a democratic government. In India the party system originated in the colonial era. We have multiple party systems at national and state levels comprising national parties, regional parties, localised parties and parties dominated by caste and communal forces. Even though parties are expected to function properly for the orderly functioning of democratic polity, the actual functioning of Indian parties is far from this. With the decline of one party's dominance at the centre and in states and with the simultaneous emergence of coalition politics, regional political parties came to play a predominant role in the politics of the country. The regional parties maintain electoral alliance with national parties in many states to capture power and form the government. Often, the national parties have to accommodate the demands of the regional parties to share power. Parties need huge unaccounted money for political activity, to build and strengthen the organisation, to train party cadres and fight elections. No doubt, such endeavours will persuade them to accept corrupt deeds like generating black money and promoting parallel economy.

Political parties do not maintain accounts and are not subjected to any independent audit. Recently when the National Information Commission requested all political parties to submit the audited accounts before the Commission under the RTI Act for maintaining transparency in governance, all parties protested and the Union Cabinet is going for a law to exclude political parties from the ambit of RTI. How far the political parties go in protecting the vested interests of the party men is evident from the following observation made by a former cabinet minister, regarding the allotment of public funds during floods wherein he said: "What principles of probity are you talking about? I shall tell you what is real politics. In my constituency", he said "every year there are floods. Unfortunately there was none this year. All my workers are angry".[29] No wonder, our political parties have become active sponsors of corruption.

**Politician-Bureaucrat - Criminal Nexus**

A coterie consisting of politician, civil servants and criminals constitute the core of a corrupt system. No major corruption is possible without the mutual consent of the political boss and the civil servant. The minister cannot execute his nefarious designs without the support of civil servants.

During the period of internal emergency (1975-77), the concept of committed civil service emerged and it caused a permanent damage to the fabric of the services. The civil servant, afraid of losing his job, position and respect, voluntarily surrendered before the powerful politician. Accordingly, a new breed of civil servants was born who were prepared to crawl when asked to bend and were prepared to do the bidding of their political masters often by guessing their wishes.[30] Transfer and postings were made by the Prime Minister's household and private office, and accordingly the type of civil service subordination gave birth to an unholy nexus between politicians and administrators. The post-emergency period witnessed division of civil service in to two hostile groups - those who were aligned with political masters and those who were ignored. Business people exercised an un-denying role in the transfer and posting of civil servants, and they were expected to be at the beck and call of their political masters.[31] Subsequently, neutrality concept eroded and also, with it, the system of checks and balances which prevailed in the system of governance. Politicians with intense desire to remain in, and retain power, collaborated with career bureaucrats for engaging in just or unjust, legal or illegal, moral and immoral things.

This unholy nexus that developed out of the relation between these two groups eventually led to criminalisation of politics in the sense that politicians needed criminals and vice-versa. For the sustenance and survival of power, politician needed the support of mafia gangs on the one side, and criminals needed the undue support of the politician for their protection against the process of law. In these circumstances corruption is the inevitable concomitant. As Justice V.R. Krishna Iyer rightly pointed out, "the moneyocracy has infiltrated into the political system through crypto-criminal methodology and a new dependencia syndrome had come to stay, the result of which is criminalisation of politics and politicisation of criminals".[32]

**Escalating Election Cost**

Elections are the alchemy of politics. Democracy and elections go hand in hand and one cannot exist without the other. In democracy power is exercised by the political elites who have to be elected to enable them to exercise power. Party's thirst for power and the actual measures employed by them to attain the same make the electoral system corrupt, dishonest and exploitative. Added to that, the impact of money power, muscle power, mafia power, etc., and the entry of representatives with criminal background in Indian elections make the system more corrupt. Elections have become a costly affair in India and it makes the entire system corrupt. According to one estimate there are about

1600 political parties registered with the Election Commission of India, and a considerable number of them never contested elections.[33] Despite some innovative changes in the electoral system, the system still, in several ways, is conducive to corruption and malpractice. Reliable sources indicate that a party man requires crores of rupees to fight and win elections. Recently, a senior Congress leader and Rajya Sabha MP from Haryana (Chaudhary Birender Singh) said that an undisclosed Rajya Sabha MP has claimed to have spent Rs. 80 crores for a ticket.[34] Even in the local body elections, the expenditure has increased at an alarming rate. In a local body election in a village called Dacheppali, in Guntur district in A.P., the Panchayat Sarpanch spent four crores of rupees in a Panchayat election.[35]

Thus, it is obvious that the election cost and the ways through which parties try to amass the same result in corruption.

**Black Money**

Black money is the fuel for corruption. Black money implies money generated by illegal means. Democracy needs elections, and elections need a lot of money, and that too in cash. This money is mostly black money. Illegal means of securing black money involve corruption. According to the study conducted by the National Institute of Public Finance and Policy, (NIPFP) the black money to the extent of 21 per cent of the GNP was in circulation in the Indian Economy.[36] N. Vittal (former CVC) stated that 40 per cent of India's economy is black money. It is said that Indians have 1456 billion dollars in Swiss banks, the amount which is 13 times larger than the country's foreign debt[37]. This money is utilized for bribing and buying top politicians for promoting illegal and terrorist activities. Black money is very dominant in areas like real estate, politics / film world, etc. Every corrupt public servant hoards black money. It flourishes in our system, hindering national security and healthy growth of democratic institutions.

**Measures to Combat Corruption**

Corruption is so much widespread and ingrained in our polity that for many people it has become a way of life. It respects no borders, knows no economic distinctions and infects all forms of government. In the long run, no country can afford the social and economic costs that corruption entails. Therefore the fight against corruption has become a significant agenda for all countries of the world - developed and developing. Considering the grievous nature of corruption, the Organisation for Economic Co-operation and Development (OECD), under the leadership of the United States, has signed the anti-bribery convention which came into force from February 1999. In the first Global Corruption Conference, 90 countries, including India, participated, and 142 countries took part in the Second Conference held in The Hague, hosted by The Netherlands. OECD ministerial meeting, held in Paris in May 2002, discussed among other things, the modus operandi to fight for a corruption - free world.

Being one of the most corrupt countries of the world, it is obligatory on the part of India too to take effective steps to deter this hydra-headed monster. A well-designed, multi-faceted strategy is required to address the vital issue of corruption in India. Growth of corruption is basically due to the system's weakness and the element of greed in some people and the mania in them to get-rich-quickly.

The following remedial measures should form part of any programme to combat corruption in India.

**Axing the Politician - Bureaucrat Nexus**

Excessive discretionary powers enjoyed by the ministers in matters of allotment of plots of land, homes, shops, agencies of various public sector undertakings, etc., give them abundant opportunities to indulge in corrupt activities. Moreover, the privilege possessed by the political executive in matters like promotion, transfer, posting, etc., places the permanent executive at their beck and call. This type of discretionary powers enables them to misuse their positions and become corrupt. Therefore, such discretionary powers, enjoyed by the political executive and other bureaucratic personnel, should be done away with. Key posts in government must be insulated from outside interferences so as to remain free from political influences. All sensitive posts should be filled by a process of appointment based on panels recommended by a neutral and objective Commission. Administrative corruption can be curbed through a three pronged action plan, viz., preventive, detective and punitive measures. It is seen that corrupt political elements use their good offices to corrupt bureaucrats. In order to prevent this, the corrupt politician should be publicly identified and isolated. Strict laws and policies need to be framed and implemented so that there is no room for discretion for politicians and bureaucrats.

**Reforming Outdated Laws**

Reforming obsolete laws should form an integral part of a well-defined strategy to fight corruption. Rules and regulations must be simplified, as they are most complicated at present. Greater number of laws cause red-tapism, and also greater scope for red-tapism tempts corruption. Outdated laws and regulations provide the opportunity to the bureaucrat to harass citizens whom they are supposed to serve. In order to promote a corruption free environment, a systematic campaign should be launched to remove obsolete laws from the statute book.

**Strengthening the Institutional Framework**

Institutional deficiencies should be addressed immediately. Institutions like the CBI should be vested with legal powers to investigate corruption cases involving top politicians and officials without the prior consent of the government. Similarly Central Vigilance Commission should be strengthened by giving it the power and status of an independent autonomous authority to conduct investigation, considering the increasing number of cases. Even though CVC has autonomy, it does not possess its own investigative machinery. This has been provided by the CBI which itself functions under the executive. Added to that, the power of the state Vigilance Department, Lok Ayukta and the anti-corruption branch of the government need to be strengthened to enable them to initiate and pursue investigations effectively, independent of government directions. The existing offices of Lok Ayuktas in many states have to be strengthened and depoliticised. The Lok Pal must have the authority to look into complaints of corruption against the Prime Minister, the Judiciary and Members of Parliament.

**Electoral Reforms**

Elections should be made least expensive than at present. Criminals form a sizeable section of the country's political executive, and unless it is checked the existing system will become a mockery of democracy. Systematic political reforms are necessary in the functioning of political parties as well. Parties should not be allowed to contest elections unless and until they submit the annual accounts, duly audited by an auditor. A Person who has been accused of an offence involving moral turpitude, as per the decree of the Election Commission, should be banned from fighting election so as to prevent the entry of criminals in elected bodies. State funding of elections should also be considered, as is done in UK, Australia, New Zealand and Canada. Electoral reforms suggested by the Election Commission from time to time must also be implemented.

**Representatives with Integrity - The Need of the Hour**

The concept of integrity implies soundness of moral principles, character of uncorrupted virtue, uprightness, honesty and sincerity. Lack of integrity promotes corruption by using unfair means. It is quite appropriate to recall the observation made by the Santhanam Committee on Corruption that members of Parliament and State Legislatures should behave with integrity so as to create a favourable social climate against corruption.

**Enactment of More Stringent Laws**

A feeling persists that even if one is caught, he can come out of it by hiring the best legal brains through the money acquired illegally. The loophole in the law comes to the help of the corrupt often. Therefore, it is quite appropriate to enact a law to confiscate property. Each state should be asked to pass the Corrupt Public Servants (Seizure of Property) Act 1999, as recommended by the Law Commission. This will ensure that illegal wealth of the corrupt is confiscated and is not enjoyed by them. So far the Bill has not been enacted. Similarly, the corrupt public servants hide their ill-gotten wealth by depositing them in bank accounts and property in another's name, known as benami transaction. The Government of India passed the Benami Transaction Prohibition Act 1988, according to which benami properties can be confiscated. The rules have not been framed so far. So appropriate agencies should be asked to frame rules and procedures for enforcement of the Act.

**Implementing the Transparency and RTI Act in its True Spirit**

Administration, in the traditional sense, functions on the principle of secrecy. If it is secretive in letting out information to the people whom they serve, that system will no doubt lead to corruption. Lack of transparency is one of the important elements promoting corruption. Therefore, we must use information technology to bring transparency. The efforts made by governments of Andhra Pradesh and Tamil Nadu in bringing out transparency like SMART, (Simple, Moral, Accountable, Response and Transparent) and STAR (Simplified and Transparent Administration Registration) found some success in those states. Moreover transparency in policy making, decision making, and implementation is also required.

The Legislation guaranteeing the Right to Information, which came into vogue in June 2005, is a major step towards ensuring a participatory developmental process in the country, which in turn ensures transparency in governance. But, this doesn't mean that this Act has been free from flaws. The Act envisages to make available to the general public the information they require, barring some confidential information concerning national and international security. The present provisions of the Act should be strengthened by all means to remove the loopholes, pendency and delay in appeals. Strong actions have to be taken against erring officials who refused to comply with the Act.

**Ensuring Accountability**

Accountability is an important factor in ensuring honesty in administration, as it can create favourable climate for establishing a corrupt-free administration. It implies a sense of duty and commitment to social values and system. When corruption issues take the central stage, a lot of noise is created to identify the real culprit. It is not easy to fix the responsibility. The usual version of bureaucracy is that no one is identified. This should be overcome by stressing on clarity in assigning responsibilities.

**Making the Criminal Justice System Effective**

There is urgent need to make our criminal justice system more effective to combat the menace of corruption so as to ensure quick dispensation of justice. These protracted legal processes should be replaced with simplification of legal procedures. The expensive justice delivery system should be reformed to make it cheap and affordable to the poor defenders. There is also need to initiate reforms in our criminal justice system so as to ensure conviction and punishment. Necessary steps should be taken to improve the quality of our criminal justice system so that rate of conviction in criminal offences is significantly enhanced. The recommendations of the National Police Commission (1977-80), Justice Malimath Committee on Reforms of Criminal Justice System (2002-03) and other Committees and Commissions appointed by the Central and State governments need to be implemented to raise the quality of criminal justice system. Proper co-ordination between the investigating and prosecuting agencies on a regular basis is also an important step to ensure the successful conduct of prosecutions in the court. Every judge should deliver the judgement as quickly as possible to ensure judicial accountability. Judiciary has to ensure the surety of punishment to the offenders. There is a need to strengthen the special courts with judicial officers having exclusive responsibility.

**Reforming the Policing System**

Like many governmental departments, corruption has crept into the police department also due to obvious reasons. Hence effective reforms have to be adopted to curb the menace of corruption. In this respect, the report and recommendations of various Committees and Commissions like the National Police Commission, Justice Malimath Committee, etc., including the seven directions given by the Court in Prakash Singh's case (2007) regarding Police Reform, needs to be implemented. The seven directions include: (i) Setting up of State Security Commissions; (ii) Selection and minimum tenure of Directors-General of Police; (iii) Minimum tenure of Inspectors-General and other officers, (iv) Separation of investigation from law and order duties, (v) Setting up of a Police Establishment Board (vi) Setting up of a Police Complaints Authority and (vii) Setting up of a National Security Commission.[38]

**Curbing Black Money**

Black money is a serious threat as it adds fuel to the engine of corruption. Stringent measures should be employed to get rid of black money for which government should come forward with a clear cut strategy and will power. The government should firstly adopt legal measures to deter the generation of black money. Then amnesty should be provided to all holders of black money to come out and declare the black money. Stringent action should then be taken to book those who do not fall in line.

**Promoting the Positive Role of the Media**

The media has been playing a very crucial role in exposing various scams and scandals in India. Both the print and electronic media perform the role of educating the public about the corrupt deeds and build public opinion. The fourth estate is being increasingly questioned by the government in this regard. It is essential that the media should perform its positive role by informing the people, keeping an eye on the functioning of various organs of government and bringing to book the corrupt.

**Promoting Civil Society Initiatives**

The civil society has been active in seeking judicial remedies in case of violation of law, seeking transparency and accountability in administration. A few civil society organisations are active in dealing with corruption. It was the civil society campaign that culminated in the enactment of the Right to Information Act. The civil society movement led by Anna Hazare has been instrumental in the establishment of a more effective - Lokpal. Prominent civil society groups like the Mazdoor and Kissan Sangharsh Samiti (MKSS) are focusing on the right to information. Association for Democratic Reform (ADR) has taken up electoral reforms, Commonwealth Human Rights Initiative (CHRI) is engaged in Police Reform, and the Campaign for Judicial Accountability and Reform (CJAR) is concerned with improving the judiciary. For combating corruption, these civil society organisations are engaged in searching and seeking the truth, sponsoring the agenda for action, securing commitment from authorities, sensitising bureaucracy and strengthening the citizenry. No doubt this type of initiative will help to eradicate corruption and more and more civil society initiatives have to come forward in various parts of the country to fight against corruption. Therefore, it is necessary on the part of all concerned to strengthen the civil society initiative to address corruption.

**Conclusion**

Corruption in India has resulted in the decline of moral values. It has exposed the political indecisiveness in dealing with the menace. The half-hearted measures attempted by the government to curb corruption are not producing any result. Naturally, the problems cannot be solved by the same level of thinking that created them. Corruption in India has to be combated with a revolutionary fervour like never before.

India needs a value-based leadership, which is lacking today. There is need to inculcate ethical and moral values — a culture of integrity to all people, especially to the youngsters right from their school days. The Family, as a unit, and the NGOs have an important role to play in curbing corruption. The citizens should also resist corruption by not giving bribe to anybody. Social ostracism of the corrupt should be more effective.

In this connection, it will be quite appropriate to reiterate the Gandhian values to address this evil. It will be worth remembering the seven social sins which Gandhiji referred to in '*Young India*', viz., politics without principles, wealth without work, pleasure without conscience, knowledge without character, commerce without morality, science without humanity and worship without sacrifice. Gandhiji also referred to the issue of corruption in a prayer meeting in Delhi by saying that "corruption will go when the large number of persons given to the unworthy practice realise that the nation does not exist for them, but that they do for the nation. It requires a high code of morals, extreme vigilance on the part of those who are free from the corrupt practice and also influence over corrupt servants. Indifference in such matters is criminal".

It is true that corruption cannot be eradicated easily from this society as it is deeply immersed in the body politic of the country. But, with due restraint, it can be curbed. It will be well and good if the politicians, bureaucrats, policy makers, and the general public remember that "the war against corruption is the mother of all the wars". What is needed is a change in the mindset of the people.

## Notes


1. Sathya Narayan Misra, 'Corruption and Crisis of Governability in India', *Journal of Indian Institute of Public Administration,* (Bhuvaneswar), Regional Branch, Odisha, Vol. XVIV, 2011-12, p. 45.
2. C.P. Chandrasekhar, 'Age of graft', *Front Line* (Madras), May 31, 2013. p. 10.
3. T.N. Dhar, 'Corruption Eruption: Paths of Redemption', *Indian Journal of Public Administration* (New Delhi), (Special Issue) Vol. LVII, July - September, 2011, p. 402.
4. N. Vittal, (2003): 'Corruption in India', Academic Foundation, New Delhi.
5. Sibranjan Misra, (2009): 'Governance, Corruption and Development - The Indian Case' in Kanak Kanti Bagchi (ed.), *Good Governance and Development - An Indian Perspective*, p. 7.
6. *International Encyclopedia of Social Sciences,* (2008): 2nd Edition, p. 143.
7. John Germin and S.C.Thader, 'Political Institution and Corruption; the Role of Unitarianism and Parliamentarism', *British Journal of Political Science,* 34, 295/30-2004 (U.K), p. 300.
8. Subhash C. Kashyap, 'Revisiting Corruption: Need for Systemic Reforms to Strengthen Democratic Structures', *Indian Journal of Public Administration,* Vol. LVII, July-Sept. 2011, p. 448.
9. Subramaniam Swamy, (2009): *Corruption and Corporate Governance in India,* New Delhi, Har Anand Publication, p.18.
10. *Ibid.,* p. 20.
11. Rich Martin, M.S., 'Police Corruption - An Analytical Look into Police Ethics' ht,pp:IIw.w.w.gallup. Enll poll/122264/nurses shine while bankers slump ethics' (Assessed April 16, 2010).
12. Rangaswamy, D. and Nanjunda, 'Police Corruption and Administration of Criminal Justice India: Some Unrevealed Truth', *Social Science in Perspective*, (Trivandrum) Vol. 4, Nos., 3-4, p. 316.
13. PTI, October 29, 2012.
14. S.S. Aswathy, (2008): *Indian Government and Politics*, New Delhi, Har Anand Publications, p. 160.
15. Subhash C. Kashyap 'Revisiting Corruption : Need for Systemic Reforms to Strengthen Democratic Structures' *Indian Journal of Public Administration*, Vol. LVII, July-September 2011, p. 453.
16. *Ibid*.
17. Subhash C. Kashyap, (2008): *Our Parliament,* New Delhi, National Book Trust, India, p. X.
18. *The Hindu* (Trivandrum), June 22, 2013.
19. R.K. Bharadwaj, (1978): *Indian Police Administration,* New Delhi, National Books, p. 128.

20. R.K. Bharadwaj, (1978): *Indian Police Administration,* New Delhi, National Books, p. 128.
21. *Indian Journal of Public Administration,* Vol. LVII, July - September, 2011. p. XII.
22. 'History of Corruption in Indian Judiciary since Independence : 1947 - 2003' (www.indian corruptjudges.com/plot4plot/A 108 htm.
23. T.N. Dhar, op. cit., p. 408.
24. Kamaleshwar Nath, "Judicial Ombudsman for Subordinate Judiciary in India", *Indian Journal of Public Administration*, LVII, July-September 2011, p. 495.
25. M.P. Shahi, (2000): *Crime and Corruption in Digital Age*, New Delhi, Author's Press Under the Auspices of Crime Against Man, p. 18.
26. S.R. Maheswari, (2005): *Public Administration in India, the Higher Civil Service,* New Delhi, Oxford, p. 224.
27. *The Hindu,* July 24, 2013.
28. *The Hindu,* May 9, 2013.
29. Subhash C. Kashyap, op.cit, p. 451.
30. Madhav God Bole, 'Bureaucracy at Cross-Roads', in U.C. Aggarwal (ed.), *Public Administration, Vision and Reality*, IIPA, Golden Jubilee Publications, New Delhi, p. 450.
31. *Ibid.*
32. V.R. Krishna Iyer, 'Ethical Entropy in Public Life', in *Public Administration, Vision and Reality*, op.cit, p. 492.
33. T.N. Dhar, op. cit, p. 404.
34. *The Hindu*, July 30, 2004.
35. Jayaprakash Narayan (2013):, 'Electoral Reforms - How It Can Be Done'?, in *Electoral Reforms*, K. Raman Pillai, R.K. Suresh Kumar, P. Sukumaran Nair (eds.), New Delhi, Kalpaz Publications, p. 313.
36. Ahmad Shamshad, 'Corruption : A Social Evil in India', *Indian Journal of Public Administration*, op.cit., p. 811.
37. *Ibid.,* p. 811.
38. Riju Ramachandran, 'Time to let the Caged Bird Sing,' *The Hindu*, May, 11, 2013.

# 24

# *Do We Have the Will to Fight Corruption?*

*K. Narayana Kurup*

It is easy to criticise and condemn corruption. But, it is difficult to eliminate it from human society and much more difficult to avoid being tempted into it when our own turn comes.... We can hope to root out corruption from the world only if we are able to root the rot out of our own hearts and minds.

**Ramifications of Corruption**

It is no exaggeration to say that in every walk of life corruption has become rampant. We know that one-stumbling block to progress in our country is the existence of all-round corruption. This malady has assumed the proportion of an epidemic, sufficient enough to devour the entire nation. 'Corruption is a tree, whose branches are of an unmeasurable length, they spread everywhere, and the dew that drops from thence, hath infected some chairs and stools of authority.' (Francis Beaumont and John Fletcher, *The Honest Man's Fortune*). Corruption knows no geographical boundary, nor does it know any institutional boundary. We find corruption in capitalist countries, authoritarian countries and democratic countries. We find corruption everywhere. It is as old as the hills, as blind as a bat and as common as dirt. The root cause of corruption, one could say, is lust for money, and greed. This is more so in democratic countries, where, politicians and political parties try to garner huge funds to fight election battles that will anoint them with enormous and everlasting power. This money has to be raised by hook, or by crook. Be it in the U.S.A., England, India or Philippines, it is a well-known fact that politicians and political parties shell out huge sums of money on political activity. It is common knowledge that the money thus spent is hardly ever collected from individuals in the form of voluntary contribution. This money comes from a number of sources, most of them illegal and unethical; commissions received on purchases made, and contracts given on behalf of the State, grant of largesse, favours and licenses, manipulation of prices, supply of quota of scarce raw materials and the like. These unethical and sometimes anti-national activities are resorted to by political parties and politicians in almost every country in the world. Individual corruption is fuelled by man's individual greed and lust for money. This phenomenon is common throughout the world. It is known by different names in different countries.

In Italy, 'pay off' to individuals is known by the term 'Bustarelle'. A small envelope containing currency bills are left on the desk of the Government official. This practice also prevails in the United States where it is operated through the device of 'black account'. Under this system money kept in a foreign locker (deposit box) is doled out as the need arises. There are no receipts, no official records, nothing. Usually, 'black account' has small amounts in it, but, it is not unusual to find large sum of money pumped into it. Money running into millions is operated through numbered Swiss bank accounts which the agents themselves open for the beneficiaries.

Corruption at high places is usually looked down with disdain and contempt. The Thais call it 'gin muong' - nation eating, implying that corrupt men erode the economy of the nation. Chinese regard corruption as a greedy impurity or 'tan wu' and in Japan, it is called 'oshoke'-dirty job. Despite public disapproval and condemnation of corruption, the malady has spread its tentacles in every nook and corner of the world. In Thailand, Government officials accept bribes openly and unabashedly. Businessmen let a well filled wallet slip to the floor exclaiming the amount they have stuffed into it, which is a communication to the official concerned regarding the quantum of bribe brought by the man. Thai officials, at times, surprise the businessman offering the bribe by telling him: "Oh, no, I dropped my wallet with $10,000 in it", indicating the amount he would accept in order to grant him the desired favour.

**Corrupting Influence of MNCs**

Various nations have adopted crafty devices to combat corruption, but without success. Laos once established an agency to investigate economic offences and corruption. Soon, its members began demanding money from the very people they were supposed to investigate. No branch of government or security organisation is free from the influence of corruption. Even NATO is not an exception. It has come out that American companies have been bribing high officials of NATO nations to obtain favourable orders for their aircrafts. This involves top brass of NATO, including European Generals, whose decision could be influenced in future by the threat of revealing their acceptance of bribes. After the Japanese top leadership was accused of taking bribe from Lockheed Aircraft Corporation of America, the Japanese Prime Minister, Fukuda, is reported to have said that the Japanese people are not tired of living in a free society, nor are they inclined towards socialism or communism, but they have become disenchanted with the growing impression that politics is run by money. Fukuda was right in his assessment of the people's mood. In fact, all over the world, people have begun to feel that politics is power and the basis of that power is money. Lockheed pay-off revelations caused tremors in several countries of the world. In Japan, a Prime Minister was found guilty of accepting bribes. In Italy, the Defence Minister was charged with corruption and in the Netherlands, Prince Bernhard, husband of the reigning Queen Juliana was found guilty of accepting $1.1 million as bribe from Lockheed. Lockheed was not the only multi-national to have made pay-offs, more than 25 multi-national companies have admitted to have made pay-offs in more than three dozen countries of the world.

In transactions involving oil purchases, millions of dollars change hands. In most cases bribe giver and receiver hardly ever meet, they deal through middlemen or agents. Among the middlemen, hardly anyone rates higher than Khashogi, a fabulously wealthy Saudi Arbian, who has at one time or other, represented among others, Lockheed, Northrop, Chrysler, and so on. There is not even a single British company selling capital equipment and military hardware to areas like the Middle East and Latin America that has not made payments of special commissions. The commission ranges from 2.5 to 10 per cent of the purchase price. In fact, bribes have become a part of international business. It has posed a serious problem in various industries. Companies refusing to pay bribe have lost much of its business. Therefore, most of the multinational businessmen believe that it will be foolish not to offer bribes, if it is expected.

**Fate of Kick-back Recipients**

The primary object of floating a company is to earn profits, and company executives are therefore duty bound to boost business in every possible manner. This is another argument in favour of bribe giving. According to the deposed Chairman of Lockheed Company, he increased profits and sales for the shareholders and employees, and therefore, he cannot be faulted. Just as individuals react differently to any given situation, corrupt officials also respond divergently upon exposing their evil deeds. Corrupt men in various parts of the world when convicted and sentenced for their misdeeds find it hard to bear the shame. As public officials, they enjoy a position of trust. Their fall from grace shatters their ego. These dignified and respectable offenders feel unbearably disgraced and unable to live with shame. Take the case of White House National Security Advisor, Robert McFarlane. He was implicated in the Iran-Contra affair in 1987. He unsuccessfully attempted suicide by taking an overdose of tranquilizers. Donald Manes, the powerful Borough President and Democratic Party boss of Queens, New York, was in his prime when he came under suspicion of taking kick-backs from the city's Parking Violations Bureau. Manes injured his wrist and ankle by slashing them against a car.

Though he survived, he had a bout of depression. Two months later, while talking to his psychiatrist on telephone, he plunged a kitchen knife into his heart and killed himself. See the fate of Pennsylvania's state treasurer Budd Dwyer. He was convicted of masterminding a kick-back scheme. He called a press conference and gave the reporters a lengthy statement airing his ire against his tormentors and his persecution. At the end of the conference, when the T.V. crew started packing, he pulled a pistol from an envelope, put the barrel into his mouth and pulled the trigger, ending his life. His conviction had made him a criminal in the eyes of his family and the public. The shame became unbearable to him, his self- esteem was shattered to pieces.

Bess Myerson was a popular former Miss America. She was tried along with another for the offence of trying to influence a Judge in a divorce case. She found the shame intolerable. She was not yet convicted and sentenced, when she, in order to run away from her family and friends, devised a plan to get arrested and sent to prison. She shoplifted in a Pennsylvania Department Store, upon which, she was immediately arrested, and sent to jail. Allen Rosin, the Chicago Circuit Judge, expecting an indictment the next day on charges of accepting bribe, entered a downtown health club, sat on a stool and shot himself with a revolver.

He preferred a public suicide thinking that this was a dignified way to handle dishonour and disgrace. Public officials accepting bribes know in their heart of hearts that what they are doing is shameful and disgraceful. They, therefore, on being apprehended and indicted of a crime, feel stigmatised socially, which prompts them to commit suicide as an easy escape from public censor. This applies equally to bribe givers. United Brands Corporation Chairman, Eli Black was given to understand that soon there was going to be a disclosure about his company's payment of a $ 1 million bribe in the State of Honduras. The sense of shame became so strong and pressing upon his mind that he left his seat in his office on the 44th floor of New York's Pan Am building, headed towards the window and leaped to his death.

At the other extreme, there are individuals whose belief in their essential innocence may persist well after they are caught. One gentleman, by name, Anthony Daniele of St. Louis Police Department, had been sentenced to 8 years for committing mail fraud, extortion and conspiracy. According to him, he was innocent and he had done nothing wrong. On the next day of his conviction, Daniele held the police Commissioner at gunpoint for 25 hours, apparently because the Commissioner's testimony had resulted in his conviction. In Philippines, President Marcos and his wife Imelda Marcos have been known for corruption, and fleecing their national exchequer of exorbitant sums. On their ouster, the people of Philippines elected Corazon Aquino (Cory) to be their President on the clear understanding that she would give her nation a clean and corruption-free Government. But the expectation of the people of Philippines turned out to be a mirage, an illusion, since she utterly failed in her mission. In the case of Cory, she herself had not been accused of corruption, but her close relatives and associates have been incriminated. But she did a good thing in appointing a Presidential Commission on Good Governance (PCGG). But the irony is that the Presidential Commission on Good Governance had itself become the subject of corruption charges, which led to the resignation of its Chairman followed by an arrest order issued against another Commissioner.

**Corruption Scenario in China**

It will be interesting to have a look at the Chinese scenario in this context. Children of highly-placed Chinese party officials and Government servants enjoy privileged life. They are known as 'Taizi Pai' or the 'Princely Class'. They attend the best schools and get the best jobs, live in luxury apartments and drive Mercedes-Benz or Toyota to shop in special stores and get haircut in choicest saloons. There is a network of nepotism that binds senior Chinese leaders and perpetuates their influence through their privileged off-springs. Sons, daughters and close relatives of the leadership occupy upper ranks of the party, military, state-run business and other areas of power. Children of higher-rank cadres had risen like helicopters, vertically and dramatically. Another form of corruption in China is 'guando' or 'official profiteering'. Leaders at all levels routinely use their position to obtain free restaurant meals or theatre tickets. They buy things at subsidised prices and sell them in the open market for handsome profits. The Chinese who cultivate personal relationship with officials are very much in demand in the society. They charge their fees and assist people in getting hospital beds, scarce medicines, doctors' appointments, etc. 'Maotai', China's fiery liquor has become an all-purpose tool for cultivating personal relationship, namely, bribing bureaucrats. Just about every major event in a person's life in China requires a bribe of good liquor. If you have liquor, even in a difficult situation, problems are solved as the bottles are handed over and glasses are raised in toast. If you don't, there are many things you will never accomplish. Entering nursery school, beginning a career, changing jobs, helping a loved one to a hospital, even sending a dead body to a crematorium requires some good liquor as grease. Cultivation of personal relationship is called 'guanxi' in Chinese. Without connections, one will always find it rather impossible to possess even a bi-cycle, not to speak of a residential flat. Right 'guanxi' or right connection at the crematorium is a must to secure placement of the urn bearing ashes of a beloved one on an eye-level shelf for the convenience of relatives. As a result, a new class of middlemen has grown up in China using backdoor channels to acquire for their clients everything from cigarettes and imported clothing to refrigerators, and other commodities.

**The Indian Scenario**

In the Indian context, during the last one decade several cases of corruption involving crores of rupees have come to public notice due to a vigilant press and pro-active judiciary. The various scams which surfaced in India are only the tip of the iceberg. Apart from scams there are cases of corruption in the collection of revenue, income tax arrears, etc. Another area of revenue loss relates to non-recovery of bank loans from industrialists, amounting to a whopping Rs. 50,000 crore. In my opinion, default on bank loans should be made a penal offence with additional provision for attachment of property. Yet another field is corruption and money laundering in the banking sector. The security scam alone involved Rs. 1,28,534 crore, according to the

Joint Parliamentary Committee (J.P.C.). Corruption in public life and administration is fatal to economic growth.

Corruption also erodes the authority of the State, promotes crime and violence, and undermines rule of law and the very foundation of democratic polity. Unchecked corruption exists in medical and health services, in the agencies in-charge of controlling pollution and implementation of the Drugs and Cosmetics Act endangering public health and safety. Since poor public revenue result in inadequate defence out-lay, national defence will be jeopardised. It also has adverse effect on foreign investment and funding from the International Monetary Fund and the World Bank who have warned that future aid to underdeveloped/developing countries may be subject to the requisite steps being taken to eradicate corruption, which prevents international aid from reaching those for whom it is meant. Increase in corruption has led to investigative journalism which is of value to a free society. The need to highlight corruption in public life through the medium of Public Interest Litigation (PIL) invoking judicial review is quite frequent in India. Suppose the investigating agency which is charged with the responsibility to bring wrong doers to book drags its feet or develops cold feet? The result will be undermining the rule of law. In such a situation, the courts will be duty bound to protect the rule of law.

An important ingredient of the rule of law is equality. If the rich and the important get away, while the poor and those without resources and right connections are hauled up, equality is dealt a death-blow. The courts cannot countenance this. We find there is a growing tendency on the part of the government of the day to spend time catching the financial sprats, while the big sharks swim freely in the ocean. There have been many instances wherein the punishment of minor offences, in inferior persons, has been made the means of screening crimes of a high order, and in men of high description. (Edmund Burke, *Impeachment of Warren Hastings*)

**The Havala Case**

Reverting to the original theme of investigating agencies developing cold feet, let us see what happened in the 'Havala' case. A diary was seized in the course of raids at the premises of a terrorist. It seemed to be a record of payments. Against figures specifying the amount appeared initials, that were said to match the names of politicians and civil servants. The C.B.I. did not investigate the contents with any diligence. The matter was taken to the Supreme Court. The court directed the C.B.I. to investigate the case swiftly and thoroughly. More importantly, the Court directed the C.B.I. to regularly inform it about the progress of the case. The court thought it fit to keep track of the investigation to such an extent that many criticized it, for in effect, supervising the investigation. However, it pressed ahead.

It went beyond the specifics of the 'havala' case. As the ailment seemed to be systemic, the court set out the entire scheme. It gave detailed instructions about how the Chief Vigilance Commissioner and the Head of the C.B.I should be selected. It directed that until Parliament enacts legislations on the matter, the Executive should adhere to the scheme the Court had spelt out. It also declared that there is an urgent need for State Governments to set up credible mechanisms for selecting Chiefs of Police as well as lower level officials of the Police. It also directed the Central Government to pursue the matter with the States.

**St. Kitts Forgery Case and Supreme Court's Equivocation**

The very court and indeed the very Judge, who was so zealous in the havala case, had an opportunity of a similar kind in the St. Kitts case. There, N.K. Singh, a distinguished Police Officer was appointed as the Head of the Special Investigation Team (S.I.T.) that had been constituted to nail the facts in a series of cases involving not just corruption, but the use of state machinery for perpetrating a massive forgery to fix a certain political opponent. A fictitious bank account had been created in St. Kitts in the name of Ajay Singh, son of V.P. Singh, former Prime Minister. By March 1991, the investigation into St. Kitts forgery was as good as complete. The Deputy Director of Enforcement A.P. Nandy confessed the truth. Persons extremely close to Chandraswami had also come out with the truth. It was at that point of time that pressure was brought to bear on N.K. Singh to drop the investigation. When he did not relent, the then Prime Minister who also held charge of the Home Ministry, transferred N.K. Singh out of C.B.I. That ended the investigation. The officer appealed to the Central Administrative Tribunal against the order of transfer. The Tribunal shut its eyes to the string of events the officer had narrated about the links of the authorities to the suspect, of the pressure they had brought to bear on the officer, etc. It found a curious but dangerous reason to dismiss the appeal. According to the Tribunal, the issue is whether the Government has the authority in law to transfer an officer. The Tribunal felt that there was no need even to call for a counter-affidavit from the then Prime Minister and Law Minister. Here, by transferring the officer out, the authorities had in effect stultified the investigation. According to the Tribunal, it is for the Government to consider as to whether a case which has been taken up for investigation should be processed or how it was to be processed. This is in the realm of executive policy which is to be decided by the Minister concerned and not by the civil servant working under him. Civil servant, however highly placed, is bound to implement the policy decisions and directives given by the Minister concerned.

According to the Tribunal, the Minister and the civil servant under him cannot pull in opposite directions in the conduct of Government business. No Government department, including the C.B.I., can function as an island of power or as an independent agency. In case the Minister takes a decision or gives a direction which is not to the liking of an officer, the officer cannot ignore the same and make it a grievance or cause of action in legal proceedings concerning his service matters, alleging malafides on the part of the Minister. Whether the public interest will be prejudicially affected by the transfer of the officer, according to the Tribunal, is primarily a matter for the executive. The executive is the best Judge of what constitutes public interest in a given situation. A civil servant cannot take the position that he is the best person to perform the duties and responsibilities of a particular office and that removing him from the scene in mid-stream when investigations commenced by him are half-way through, amounts to mala fides. The concept of indispensability of an individual officer, however upright, honest and efficient he may be, is unknown to good governance under any legal system. A civil servant trying to uphold the public policy and public interest against the decisions and directions of his own Minister or Ministers who are his political masters, is also alien to the legal system, the Tribunal said. On appeal, the Supreme Court turned round and held against him. According to the Supreme Court, the officer belongs to a disciplined post and as a senior officer, would be making several transfers himself.

Quite likely, many of his men, like him, may be genuinely aggrieved by the transfer. If, even a few of them follow his example, and challenge the transfer in Court, the Officer would be spending his time defending his actions, instead of doing the work for which he held the post. Challenging transfers in court when the career prospects remain unaffected, and when there is no detriment to the Government servant must be eschewed and interference by the court should be rather only when the judicially manageable and permissible grounds are made out. The Court opined that the litigation is ill-advised. The result, therefore, was that the Supreme Court endorsed the Tribunal's doctrine: an officer even when charged with investigating such a serious criminal case should leave to the Ministers the decision regarding how the investigation should be pursued and when it was to be dropped; he should confine his crusader's zeal to carrying out whatever directions the Ministers give; and even when the directions are manifestly intended to kill the investigation, he must act as a member of a disciplined force and not take upon himself the task of safeguarding public interest. Both the Tribunal and the Supreme Court held that no officer is indispensable. I feel the view adopted by the Supreme Court is not in tune with the high morality it preached in the 'havala' case. It is not a question whether a particular officer is indispensable, on the contrary, the question is whether his transfer has been effected with the oblique motive to 'kill' the investigation into an important case.

**No Political Will to Fight Corruption**

There is no dearth of legislation in India to combat corruption. After India gained independence, the Parliament passed the Criminal Law Amendment Act, which conferred power on the State Governments to appoint Special Judges to try cases of corruption speedily. The Special Judge can take cognisance of an offence either on a private complaint or on a police report or suomotu. In 1952, the Commissions of Inquiry Act was passed and several Commissions of Inquiry headed by Supreme Court and High Court Judges were appointed since then, to enquire into charges of corruption against certain Chief Ministers and Union Ministers. The findings of the Commissions lead to Public Men quitting their offices. Criminal Law Amendment Act of 1958 enlarged the list of 'public servants' and pursuant to Santhanam Committee report, a new offence of possession of disproportionate assets to one's known source of income was incorporated in the Prevention of Corruption Act, 1988. An M.L.A. has been held to be a 'public servant' within the meaning of clause (viii) of Sub section (c) of Section 2 of the Prevention of Corruption Act 1988, since an M.L.A. holds public office and performs public duty. The law as it stands now, in a prosecution under the Prevention of Corruption Act, once the prosecution proves facts giving rise to a presumption of guilt, the burden shifts to the accused and he has to rebut the presumption by proving his case on preponderance of probabilities. The Central Vigilance Commission was also setup in 1964. Pursuant to the recommendations of the Administrative Reforms Commission headed by Morarji Desai, it was proposed to set up the institution of Lok Pal and Lok Ayukta to fight corruption in administrative and public life. In addition to all these, any citizen can file a Public Interest Litigation in the High Court / Supreme Court alleging commission of corruption by Public Men. Though these authorities have power to inculpate the person whose conduct is under enquiry, their findings are not enforceable. Quitting public office is left to the standards of public morality of the office holder. In spite of the existence of various fora to expose corruption, the path is not yet an easy one. It requires enormous guts, energy and money from an ordinary citizen, however public spirited one may be to take on the political big-wigs. The question ultimately crystalises whether we have the will to fight corruption or are we serious in tackling corruption? In my opinion, the political will to combat corruption is dismally lacking for which we are paying a heavy price. Otherwise, what is the explanation for not enacting into law the Lok Pal legislation, whose aim is to root out corruption in high places and which has been on the anvil for the last four decades?

**Judiciary and Corruption**

Similarly, we are yet to enact a legislation that empowers confiscation of properties of public servants adjudged guilty of corruption. The result: there is no legal sanction against corruption in high places and corruption and nepotism have become the "most infallible symptom of constitutional liberty" (Edward Gibbon, *The Decline and Fall of the Roman Empire*). Though corruption in the higher echelons of judiciary is rare, the disquieting fact, as reported by men of high authority, is that it is very much there. Judicial decadence and debauching are fraught with lethal consequences, for judiciary as an institution is the bulwark and sentinel on the *qui vive* of the rights and liberties of citizens. Judicial corruption damages not only the image of the individual judge involved, but the institution of the judiciary as a whole, because honour is indivisible. "Thieves for their robbery have authority, but what happens when judges steal themselves". (William Shakespeare, *Measure for Measure*). It will be a formidable blow to the flawless reputation of the fraternity of judges. "Take all the robes of all the good judges that have ever lived on the face of the earth, and they would not be large enough to cover the iniquity of one corrupt judge" (Henry Ward Beecher, *Proverbs from Plymouth Pulpit*).

**Ineffectiveness of Prevention of Corruption Act**

Now, let us have a look at the actual working of the Prevention of Corruption Act. There are several constraints in the administration of the Prevention of Corruption Act. The first constraint is that the heads of Central Bureau of Investigation (C.B.I.)/Anti -Corruption Bureau (A.C.B) are appointed by the Prime Minister or the Chief Minister as the case may be. There is no functional autonomy, much less financial autonomy, which is absolutely essential for effective functioning. The organisation is understaffed. There is limited talent in the investigation team. A major portion of officers are drawn on deputation from the police force of the State, which cannot cover even 10 per cent of the prevalent corruption. There are serious limitations in proceeding against the big fish before the Courts. No head of the C.B.I. / A.C.B. will dare enough to proceed against the Prime Minister or the Chief Minister except under Court orders. The C.B.I. cannot enquire against the Chief Minister of a State or a member of his cabinet, even if the Prime Minister wishes to do it. Under Section 6 of the Delhi Special Police Establishment Act, 1946, prior consent of the State concerned is necessary if the C.B.I. wants to step in and exercise its jurisdiction. Without this consent, there will be no enquiry. However, a Commission of Inquiry can be appointed by the Prime Minister on any matter of public importance, including corruption charges against the Chief Minister or a Minister under the Commissions of Inquiry Act. But the findings of such Commission may not lead to prosecution and conviction by a Court of Law. Since the appointment of such a Commission of Inquiry and the dismissal of the State Governments are selective, they are not of much help in arresting corruption at high levels.

Senior officers have protective umbrella or armour. Both at the Centre and in the States, executive instructions exist requiring the C.B.I./ A.C.B. to take prior permission of the Government if they want to enquire against a certain level of senior officials. So much so, no serious enquiry is possible against these creamy layers of bureaucrats. This strikes at the very root of the matter. Though the preamble of the Prevention of Corruption Act proclaims that the avowed object of the legislation is to eradicate corruption, the executive instructions defeat its very purpose.

**The Quid Pro Quo**

In this connection, it will be of interest to know the reasons behind these executive instructions. It leads to a straight conclusion that the Heads of Government will protect senior officers from enquiries by the C.B.I./A.C.B. and they, in turn, will cover up the dishonest acts of the political executive while building the files in a way that gives no scope for the political executive to write an embarrassing order/decision. Therefore, it is a matter of 'quid pro quo'. The officer is protected and in consideration, the political executives are also protected by the manipulation of files by the officers. This arrangement keeps both of them safe and sound above the reach of law. This is there as on why we find that so many cases against politicians have been discharged without even framing of charges, not to speak of conviction. As the law aimed at stamping out corruption becomes more innovative, so also the ingenuity of its violators.

Besides, the enquiry reports have to be approved by the Government for the registration of an F.I.R. and further investigation and in addition, the Government has the final authority in taking decisions on the investigation reports of the C.B.I. /A.C.B. Here, the Government can modify a recommendation to prosecute either as departmental action or even drop further action. To cap it all, the Government has the power to withdraw from prosecution even if it is in the final stages of hearing in a court of law on grounds of public interest. In fact, the provision authorising the Government to withdraw from prosecution has been upheld by the Supreme Court. As a result, hundreds of cases are withdrawn thereby stifling prosecution which has reached the final stage. What is the public interest?

# 25

## *For Ensuring Food Security in Future*

*R. Hali*

India today has a place of pride and honour in the global agriculture map as a green power capable to provide, with magnanimity, large quantities of food grains to the needy nations, as loans and as donations. These accomplishments made by India especially in the grain and food production sectors are really a model to all developing nations. The nation has now crossed the two hundred and fifty million tone mark in the grain production front and hundred and twenty million tone mark in the milk sector. The achievement of India in the production of rubber, sugar, cotton, spices, beverage crops and vegetables are also really commendable. No country in the world will dare to term India as a begging bowl, as was done in the fifties, sixties and mid-seventies. India is now recognised as a strong exporter and dependable trader in the global market especially in the farm commodities trade centres.

**Heroes are Farmers**

The real heroes of this achievement are the farmers of the country. They continue to be the centre of our strength for building up a sustainable achievement that will provide great might to the nation. Truly speaking, they are the real source of strength for India to give shape to the food security bill which provides food as a right to over eighty crores of people. The nation's stature has grown by leaps and bounds all over the world, by giving shape to such a gigantic effort at a cost of 1.4 lakh crore of rupees per year. This has also enhanced our prestige among the countries which depend on large scale grain imports.

Assuring food to over hundred and twenty crores of people without fail need a lot of preparation. Two aspects which need serious attention in this regard are regular and continuous production of food grains and an efficient distribution network. Production of food grains and agricultural commodities are facing many serious challenges due to climatic changes, changing life styles, paucity of agriculture labour, and poor profitability to the farmers, and the lack of enthusiasm of the younger generations to accept farming as a challenging entrepreneurship. Agriculture especially production of food crops, milk, egg, etc., are not generating stable and adequate income. Some of the surveys done by the official agencies reveal that 40 per cent of the farming population in India are ready to leave the profession, if better opportunities are provided to them, without any hesitation. Many incidents taking place in different parts of the country confirm this view. Several states are launching gigantic development programmes for inducing farmers to switch over to more profit generating cash crops. In the North, Punjab is encouraging farmers to take up citrus crop, while in the South, Andhra Pradesh and Karnataka are vigourously encouraging horticulture and floriculture for enhancing the returns of the farmers. In a rice rich state like Andhra Pradesh, lakhs of acres of paddy are left barren since farmers and farm labour feel that the crop is incapable of giving them a fair income to carry on a decent living. Farmers' organisations termed these phenomena as a holiday given to rice cultivation. In the state of Kerala the rice area has come down from nine lakhs hectors to less than three lakh hectors. Kerala's paddy fields are left barren and are exposed for large scale conversion to garden lands for building housing complexes, entertainment centres, and playgrounds and for other uses. This is resulting in the elimination of hills and hillocks and water sources, resulting in acute drinking water shortage and several ecological imbalances.

**Agriculture–The Biggest Provider**

In India, agriculture is the biggest provider of livelihood security to our masses. At the time of independence, 75 per cent of the people was dependent on agriculture, and today it has come down to 50 per cent as per available statistics. Acritical look at the agricultural scenario will bring out hidden truths and governmental responsibilities. The country's population which stood at 35 crores has now crossed the 120 crore mark. In short, 60 crores of people are accommodated in the farming sector now where as it was only 20 crores at the dawn of independence. So the responsibility of the nation to produce food has enhanced several times. The fast changing lifestyles of the people have increased the demand for more quality items like fruits, milk, vegetables, egg, meat and ready to use processed food materials. All these show that the challenges facing the farm front are really becoming more and more tough that needs much more attention by the nation.

**India's Potential**

India has adequate potential to make it a sustainable producer of any crop and livestock–seen in any part of the world, due to its unique agro-climatic gifts. Our nation is the largest producer of milk and the second largest producer of wheat, rice, sugarcane, cotton, fruits, vegetables and tea. India's livestock too is equally big as it has more buffaloes than any other country in the world. In activities like poultry production and goat rearing also we have the second position. The greatest advantage in this sector is that our farmers have rich traditional knowledge on the production of crops and rearing of livestocks, and if these could be combined with the excellent research and extension network built up in the country, it will produce great results. We have at present forty three state agriculture universities, forty four central research institutions, thirty two national research centres, fifty nine all India co-ordinate research projects and twenty three network research projects under the Indian

Council of Agriculture Research. Apart from this, each state has got its own departments of agriculture, horticulture, animal husbandry and diary and several boards and corporations covering the entire country. It is also well known that the research, extension, input and supply agencies have reached every nook and corner of the country. This offers enormous opportunities both for knowledge generation and its timely dissemination.

**A Home of Malnourished People**

In this context, we must also remember that India is the home for more than 27 per cent of the world's under nourished population and 79.2 per cent of our children under the age of three, 56.2 per cent of women and 24.3 per cent of men are malnourished and anemic. We should also remember that India has the largest number of hungry people than any other country, and that 2.1 million of its children die every year before reaching five years of age, and about 30 per cent of our babies are born underweight. World Food Programme Report: 2008 reveals several drawbacks that we should address with proper care, and they could be eliminated only by enhanced agricultural production and by offering better life to the people in the rural areas. We have at present enough technologies even for doubling the agricultural production, but equipping the hundred million farm families to take up the job in their holdings is indeed a very formidable task.

**Farming: Not Profitable**

Farming is not providing enough profit to meet their growing demands like education of children, medical care, and entertainment needs. Infact, the farming community continue to produce more quality goods, but they are deprived of good profit while the consumers are paying very high price at the terminal centres. The highest procurement price of paddy in the country is seventeen rupees per kilograms, but the price of rice at the consumer point is between 60 and 90. So the real profit the farmer gets comes to less than Rs. five per kilogram, whereas the trade absorbs a huge chunk. The tragedy is that the entire loss, if any, occurs is also to be borne by the farmer and not by any trade agencies since they are handling the finished products. This makes the farmer poorer and poorer and the trader richer and richer. Unless and until a system is devised to create an Actio Apportum (a new method), under which the farmer gets a legal right of share of profits, generated out of his farm produce, things will not change. This process will enable the farmer to get a profit generated from the ultimate centre, where the consumer collects the materials produced by him. Government should undertake the collection of a cess from the terminal market, which could form a fund for distributing the Actio Apportum, in the light of the great responsibility of making food available as a right, to over 80 crores of people. The farmers must be encouraged not only to produce more but also the youngsters should be motivated to come forward and take up farming as a profitable enterprise. As the government is the largest buyer and distributer of food grains, it is easy to maintain the records of the food grain procured from each farmer, and offer a handsome amount as Actio Apportum. The principle behind this system is that everyone, irrespective of caste, colour and creed, should be prepared to acknowledge the service of the farmer who produces food for the entire community. Thus the entire community becomes a participant in the food production process. This will assure India to produce enough food materials not only for our own needs but also for export. This will be the best insurance to make and enable the farmer to produce more from the farms and fields of the country. We must not forget that India needs over two hundred million tons of food grains and hundred and twenty million tons of milk every year. Even if we have money, no country will be able to supply us even half of our requirements. So it goes without saying that India's food security, as well as rural prosperity, depends on the hard working farmer population and their secure life. It is high time, we realise that farmer welfare and food security are two sides of the same coin.

# 26

# *A Welfare State Remedy*

*B. Vivekanandan*

## I

Bertrand Russell, the British philosopher, in his famous book, *Violence, Monkeys and Men*, made an analysis of the causes of violence and brutality in societies. Taking into account of the psychic factors, he found that violence occurs when there is lack of food and room. Similar analysis could also be made on other negative expressions of human behaviour, which promotes stealthy conduct, manifested in many forms, in administration and elsewhere, to apply suitable correctives to them as well. However, it is important for the statesmen of the world to keep these fundamental elements of human behaviour in mind when they endeavour to build good societies for the humanity to live.

### Welfare State System-Most Successful

Of all the socio-economic systems democratic polities have experimented during the last hundred years, the most successful one has been the welfare state system, based on human solidarity, which has promoted the goodness in man. Therefore, the welfare state system merits serious consideration of political leaderships of all countries, which aspire to build a good, transparent, humane, responsible, responsive, and corruption-free polity for future. This is mainly because the programme which the welfare state system provides carries the assurance of a fairly good quality of life for everybody in society, on the basis of equality, distributive justice, and solidarity, under the direct supervision of a transparent democratic state. The state assumes the responsibility for raising the resources for it, and for providing the benefits under it by applying the principle of universality. It is a system by which a benign democratic state promotes the collective well-being of all its inhabitants, and assures an acceptable living standard for everybody by balancing growth and distributive justice. It is a system in which nobody is at the mercy of another person, and everybody, transcending nationalities, cultures and continents, is provided with more or less equal facility to lead a life with dignity, and free from fear and want. That will be the harbinger of a civilised non-violent society. It will entirely change the living environment and behaviour pattern of humans, which will result in the vanishing of many hitherto intractable ills in our societies.

A welfare state system entails a state set up in which a benign democratic state increasingly assumes direct responsibility for matters like the provision of gainful employment, social security, health and medical care, education, housing, social services, unemployment provisions, pensions, family allowances, and so on, for the entire population. The funds required for undertaking these responsibilities by the state would be raised largely through universal taxation. Indeed, adoption of a welfare state system by any state would mean the recognition of everyone's social right to have an equal share of the fruits of growth in society. It would also provide an incentive to promote a sense of solidarity, and a mentality of sharing the fruits of one's own labour without any heartburn. It is a higher form of social engineering for building a new, more civilised, society in the world.

**Foundations**

Ideologically, the welfare state system is anchored in the basic tenets of democratic socialism. Equality, freedom, solidarity and distributive justice are its guiding principles. But, historically, the origin of the term Welfare State goes to the credit of an anti-socialist German Chancellor, Otto von Bismarck, who coined the term in 1840, and used it as an incentive to reduce the emigration of German workers to the United States, where there was high wages, but no welfare provisions. Simultaneously, he used it to win the workers' support for his empire, and also to arrest the growth of the German Social Democratic Party (SPD).

With these multiple objectives in mind, Bismarck introduced old-age pensions, accident insurance to workers and medical care for them. But, ironically, the SPD was attracted by the new methodology of the state taking the direct responsibility of welfare measures, and adopted the welfare state as SPD's own future programme. But the SPD could not give much practical content to it since it was away from power and since Germany was ruled largely by dictatorial regimes.

**Democratic Socialists and Welfare State**

However, the present construct of a welfare state system is a social democratic or democratic socialist construct of the 20th century. Social democratic parties of Scandinavian countries like Sweden, Denmark, Norway and Finland have championed and piloted it from 1930s.

The impetus for it came from the Great Depression of 1928-1931 in Europe, and the solutions political leaderships had put forth for meeting the economic crisis. The Great Depression had resulted in the closure of hundreds and thousands of factories all over Europe and made millions of people unemployed. Different political ideas were advanced by various political parties regarding how to combat Depression at that time. In Sweden, the Swedish Social Democratic Party (SDP) came out with a programme of a full-employment policy and the construction of a welfare state to meet the situation. On the basis of this programme, the SDP was elected to power in the elections held in 1932. The SDP formed the government in Sweden and stayed in power continuously for 44 years since then. It was during this period that Sweden had built up the most advanced and benign welfare state system in the world, and took that country to the top in the human development index in the world. That system is now known as the cradle-to-the-grave welfare state system. Other social democratic parties of Scandinavia also followed the Swedish lead and established the welfare state systems in their countries too, taking all of them among the first top five of the human development index in the world. Significantly, they are not only at the top in the human development index, but also in the list of the least corrupt, or most honest, societies in the world, which indicate the positive impact the welfare state system has made on the psyche and the general behaviour of the people in the whole region.

**Promotion of Equality**

The welfare state system is attuned to promote equality in society. It is programmed to widen the state's responsibility for people's well-being. Its governing principles are equality, solidarity and distributive justice, and aimed to ensure an acceptable standard of living for everyone universally, irrespective of a person's socio-economic background. Many famous democratic socialist economists like J.M. Keynes, Gunnar Myrdal, Ernst Wiggfors, William Beveridge, etc., had worked hard to refine the welfare state system. Following them, there emerged a new stream of welfare economists in the world. Dr. K.N. Raj, Dr. Amarthya Sen, Prof. John Kenneth Galbraith, etc., belonged to this stream of welfare economists.

**Texture of Welfare States**

Under the welfare state system people are entitled to various kinds of social security support, which provides direct financial assistance to individuals and families in the forms of old-age pension, family allowances, etc., from the central government, and receive social welfare assistance from local governments directly.

These supports are organised generally under certain broad categories like families, children, women, elderly, unemployed, disabled, and so on. And, the responsibility of running all these programmes is vested either in the central government or in local governments. While launching the programme of building up welfare states, the social democrats have argued that the government's fiscal and monetary policies should be used to regulate the economy in a socially beneficial manner. The tax policy, growth policy, employment policy, wage policy, income policy, etc., can be synchronised to achieve greater equality in society.

Welfare state system implies the government responsibility for the provision of social security, free health and medical care, free education, housing, social services, unemployment provisions, family allowances, pensions, provisions for elderly care, etc. It is an explicit recognition of the social right of every inhabitant to have a fair share of fruits of growth in society. It insulates distributive justice from the vagaries of market forces, and ensures that all citizens have a stake in society and that each individual has a responsibility to contribute to the common weal. It promotes solidarity among the people and ensures equality before law and equality of opportunity. It provides a security cover for everyone to enable him to carry on his normal activities in life, and provides for his basic needs, for bringing up his family, and for leading a satisfactory retired life under the welfare state's protective umbrella.

The system rests on the fact that there is an element of altruism latent in all human beings, and that the state and society should be organised in such a way that they provide adequate incentives to promote altruism and goodness embedded in them, so that their basic approach is not dominated by crass selfishness, greed and unabashed acquisitiveness, which stimulate violence in thinking and action. Therefore, the welfare state system is the most stable, and the most enduring peace structure in the world, which can create a new outlook which would constantly stimulate peace, accommodation, non-violence, non-aggressiveness, and a sharing mentality among the people in a broad frame work of human solidarity.

It is, indeed, a superior approach to build a peaceful, civilised and stress-free society, and constitutes the most effective democratic and peaceful solution to inequality in the world.

**Needs a Strong and Resourceful State**

The welfare state system pre-supposes the existence of a strong, democratic and benign central state, which would function both as a regulator and also a provider. It should have the power, capacity and resourcefulness to effectively intervene in economy and social life, since social transfers play a major role in the construction of the welfare state system. It underlines, as a primary task, that nothing should be done to weaken the democratic state's authority and its resource base.

Therefore, attempts of the conservative and neo-liberal forces to hollow out or weaken the state through globalisation, liberalisation and privatisation will have to be opposed and defeated. The state should always have the power and resources at its command to effectively intervene at any time in favour of the needy people in society. A firm state control over the national economy and finance is imperative for carrying out welfare state responsibilities.

## II

**A Model Welfare State: Sweden**

In order to understand the texture of a model welfare state, we have to see how the 'cradle-to-the-grave' welfare state system works in a Scandinavian country like Sweden. The key national policies which were attuned to build up a welfare state system in Sweden are a full employment policy, a steeply progressive taxation policy linked to egalitarianism, free health and medical care, free education for all, child allowances, old age and disability pensions, unemployment allowances, insurance against accidents, etc. The central government has passed the enabling legislations, and the local municipalities are made responsible for the dispersal of benefits to the people. Through such measures, everyone in the country has been brought under the social security cover provided by the state. The Swedish Social Democratic Party and the Left, and the Labour Movement were the vanguard of this historic transformation.

**Cradle-to-the-Grave Welfare State System**

In Sweden, the State's assistance to a child begins when the mother of a new-born received a sealed packet, containing baby clothes and other baby items for the use of the new-born child, from the government with an official stamp of the government affixed on it. From then onwards the State's attention and responsibility for the child's well-being continues all through its life. The State provides free medical support for the delivery of the child. After that, the parents receive a child allowance, until the child reaches 17 years old, for the child's nourishment.

The child's education is free. When the child completes studies, the State is constitutionally responsible to find a gainful employment for him/her, failing which the State will have to give him/her unemployment allowance, which compels the government to follow an employment-friendly policy. When the person gets a gainful employment, he becomes a tax-payer, thereby a fund provider for the upkeep of the welfare state system. Thus he becomes a benefactor of the welfare state, while remaining its beneficiary too. When a person retires he receives about two-thirds of his pay as pension, which enables him/her to maintain, more or less the same standard of living after the retirement also.

All old people receive an old-age pension. Health care in old age is also totally free. When a person breathes his/her last, his/her funeral expenditure is also met by the State. That is how the cradle-to-the-grave welfare state system is organised in Sweden. As a result, people are freed from all kinds of worries and dependencies.

**Social Security**

Social security in Sweden encompasses the right to work, right to education, a decent place to live, and so on. Under the system, the entire population is insured against sickness. Everyone gets equal educational opportunities in top quality educational institutions run by the state. Housewives are entitled for vacation annually anywhere in Sweden at the government cost. The system protects all employees from work related accidents and sickness.

All employees are granted five-weeks paid annual holidays. All employees are entitled to compensation for industrial injuries. All mothers receive maternity grants. Under a family law, either father or the mother is entitled to seven months leave from work, with full pay, after the birth of a child to look after the baby.

**Pensions**

Sweden has a highly developed pension scheme. The old-age pension scheme entitles all old people to a pension. Similarly, all disabled people, after the age of 16, are entitled to a pension. If a person is fully disabled, he/she would get a full disability pension, which is equal to the old-age pension. Similarly, parents of disabled children are entitled to child care allowances, if they themselves nurse their disabled children.

**Free Medical Care**

In Sweden, medical care is free, except a nominal prescription fee. Under the Sickness Benefit Insurance System, those who suffer from income loss due to illness, injury or disability, are entitled to compensation. The sickness benefit is 90 per cent of the person's pay prior to his/her illness, injury or disability. The cost of health insurance is shared between the State, employers and self-employed people.

**Promotion of Equality**

The welfare state system in Sweden is attuned to promote egalitarianism in the Swedish society. The steeply progressive income-tax system and the solidarity wage structuring have substantially reduced the income disparity between the take-home pay of the high paid and low paid employees.

I went to Sweden in 1985 to study the changes the welfare state system has brought about in that country. At that time, Prime Minister Olof Palme's Economic Advisor, Dr Klaus Eklund, showed me some charts, which he prepared for the Prime Minister. First he showed me a chart pertaining to the gross salaries of wage-earners in Sweden, which showed a big difference between the salaries of the lowest paid, and the highest paid employees in the country.

Then he showed me another chart which showed the take-home pays of all those wage-earners, after the application of the steeply progressive income-tax. In that chart, the income ratio between the lowest paid and the highest paid employees in the country was brought down to 1:4. Then he showed me another chart, showing the comparative position of incomes between the lowest and the highest income family units in Sweden. The income difference between family units in the country was astonishingly low - the ratio between the low income and the high income families in Sweden was only 1:2. No other country in the world has achieved such a high level of income equality. Significantly, this has been achieved democratically, through parliamentary means. It blurred the class distinctions in Sweden. Now in recent years, under the impact of globalisation and liberalisation, and due to the activities of the multi-national companies, some marginal changes in this ratio have taken place.

Though the initial objective of the construction of welfare state in Sweden was alleviation of poverty, in due course, it has gone far beyond that agenda, and infused in it larger objectives like the reduction of inequality, promotion of distributive justice and human solidarity, besides schemes like social insurance and services to the needy people. The agenda of distributive justice has been pursued both vertically and horizontally—vertically from rich to the poor through a steeply progressive taxation system, and horizontally, through the establishment of a cradle-to-the-grave welfare state system for the entire population, without exception.

**A Stress-free Society**

The Swedish experience has shown that the welfare state system is good economics, good politics and good sociology. It is a splendid example of how public spending on welfare creates general conditions for the economic growth, and how preventive policies reduce potential social problems, and influence the development of a healthy, stress-free society. It has brought a remarkable change in the psyche and ethos of the Swedish society. It has virtually freed people from worrying about their own security or about the future security of their children and grandchildren, as they are sure that the system will take care of all of them when time comes. Therefore, the Swedish people are, by and large, free from stress-based diseases, which are increasingly a phenomenon in most of the non-welfare state societies. The system has freed the country from corruption. Indeed, people have no incentive or compulsions to become corrupt. The solidarity approach has radically changed the psyche of the people. It has enhanced people's respect for each other, which is manifest in their interactions with one another.

**Scandinavia Emulates the Swedish Model**

All other Scandinavian countries—Denmark, Norway and Finland–have emulated the Swedish welfare state system and impart similar benefits of their people. As a result the security of everyone, including children, the elderly and the disabled, irrespective of their family circumstances, is ensured everywhere in Scandinavia.

Even a communist leader like Mikhail Gorbachev of the Soviet Union got tremendously impressed by the welfare state system of the Scandinavian social democracies that he had sent a team of top Soviet economists to Stockholm and Helsinki to make an in-depth study of the texture and working of the welfare state system in Finland and Sweden. Indeed, Gorbachev had expressed a strong desire to pattern the Soviet system after the Scandinavian welfare state system. This he said publicly to a BBC Correspondent, in the midst of the 'Putsch' in the Soviet Union, in 1989.

**Expansion of Social Rights**

A notable outcome of the establishment of the welfare state system in Scandinavian countries is the significant expansion of the citizen's social rights, like social security, education, healthcare, employment, etc., which are assured through various insurance schemes, state funding, and through contributions from the employers and the employees. And these benefits are extended to everyone in the land without discrimination. There is no narrowly based 'targeted' group charity approach, which are still followed in non-social democratic, non-welfare state systems. These benefits are reinforced by a co-determination process in the industrial establishments, collective bargain, and contractually binding wage agreements between the employers and the employees in the region. Significantly, over the years, there registered a big leap in the social budget too. From a virtually non-existent social budget in 1930s, the welfare expenditure of Scandinavian countries today account for 27 to 37 per cent of the national budgets–Sweden spends 37 per cent–against India's four per cent!

**Impact on People's Behaviour**

A striking feature of an outcome of the welfare state system in Scandinavia is the positive change it stimulated in the general behaviour of the inhabitants of this region. The fact that the welfare state system has brought about equality and distributive justice among the whole population in a peaceful manner, through their democratically elected parliaments, the people have realised that each one of them is uniformly assured of a just share of the social product in the state, and that the wealth of the community is used transparently for the benefit of the whole population, and not of a section or of a few sections in the rural or urban areas.

It has left little room for bickering or for general complaints. When universalism has been adopted as the principle in running the programme, under which everyone participates in it both as a contributor and a beneficiary, and that too under the framework of equality and solidarity, it has created a general atmosphere of cooperation, peace, honesty, and mutual respect, displacing aggressiveness, and self-aggrandisement. The contemptuous and arrogant behaviour in human interactions, which, to a great extent, springs from extreme inequalities in society, is a thing of the past in Scandinavia, as, in a broad sense, everyone there leads a comparable quality of life. Through the welfare state system, they have overcome most of the pressing socio-economic problems and divisive issues. When equality, solidarity and distributive justice have got fused in social engineering, it has created a new outlook and approach among the people. It may be recalled that Scandinavia, where democratic socialists are able to establish welfare state systems, was historically the home of the legendary Vikings who were known for their aggressivencss, and who were nightmares of many powerful countries like

England, France, Germany and Russia. Between 9th and 11th centuries they were notorious for their ruthless plundering expeditions. But, following the spectacular change in their living environment, as a result of the establishment of the welfare state systems in their countries, they now present the picture of the most peaceful and civilized people in the world. It is extremely difficult to see a violent response, or hear an uncivil abuse, from them even in tense situations.

Civilised non-violent behaviour has become their natural way. There is a strong element of mutual respect ingrained in their general behaviour. Politically, it has promoted consensus building, with greater emphasis on co-operation and conciliation. Cumulatively, it has made Scandinavia the most peaceful region in the world. Therefore, this political design, developed by democratic socialists, deserves emulation in all countries of the world for the benefit of the humanity. Its realisation requires a political will, and a commitment to human solidarity, both can be achieved through the establishment of strong democratic socialist parties, at national levels, everywhere. That is the way a new world society, based on peace, democracy, equality, prosperity, distributive justice and solidarity, can be built up.

Welfare state systems in Scandinavia have not only eliminated poverty in the classical sense, and drastically reduced inequalities in the region, but also have achieved distributive justice to a level which few countries can match. They have provided generous benefits to all categories of people universally. They have promoted equitable income distribution and ensured individual security, which have virtually freed people from worrying about the future security of their children and grandchildren. They have also made adequate provisions for education, health care, child care, and care for the aged and infants, which no market system in the world can match. Above all, they have achieved social cohesion and solidarity, which could not be shaken even by the recent two serious economic crises—one of the early 1990s, and the other which is ongoing since 2008.

## III

### The Indian Imperative

#### *Constitutional Provisions*

Where does India's political will stand on the agenda of the country's transformation into a welfare state? In the Indian Constitution there are many provisions in favour of establishing a welfare state system in India. The 'Preamble', the 'Fundamental Rights', and the 'Directive Principles of State Policy' make it clear that our Constitution makers wanted India to become a welfare state.

The 'Preamble' speaks about "justice social, economic and political" for all people, and wants the state to work for the well-being of all. It wants India to become a society based on equality and justice. In tune with that many provisions have been made in chapters on Fundamental Rights and the Directive Principles of State Policy. Equality of opportunity, right to freedom, right against exploitation, are all parts of it. More distinctly, the Directive Principles of State Policy has pointed the way how India should develop itself into a welfare state. Article 38 says that "the State shall strive to promote the welfare of the people by securing and protecting as effectively as it may a social order in which justice, social, economic and political shall inform all the institutions of the material life." Similarly, Article 39 speaks about the right of all people for adequate means of livelihood, equal pay for equal work, healthy work environment, protection of children against exploitation and material abandonment, and made it incumbent on the state to ensure that "the ownership and control of the material resources of the community are so distributed as best to sub-serve the common good". Article 41 makes the state responsible to make "effective provision for securing the right to work, to education and to public assistance in case of unemployment, old age, sickness and disablement, and in other cases of undeserved want." Similarly, Articles 42 and 43 have made the state responsible for provision of maternity relief, and for securing all workers jobs, "a living wage, conditions of work ensuring a decent standard of life and full enjoyment of leisure and social and cultural opportunities".

Article 45 provides for free and compulsory education for all children upto 14 years of age. Similarly, there are also provisions which stipulate that children should be provided with opportunities and facilities to grow and develop in a healthy manner and in conditions of freedom and dignity.

***Lukewarm Approach***

Sixty-three years have passed after these welfare state provisions have been incorporated in the Indian Constitution. Since most of these provisions are in the Directive Principles of State Policy, and therefore are non-justiciable, their implementation depends on the political will, priority and design, besides a passionate commitment towards the objectives of these provisions, of the political party in power. Though the Congress Party was in power in the Centre continuously for 30 years after independence, it has followed a lukewarm approach towards the welfare state programmes and took only some token measures in that context, like limited expansion of free public education and free public health care services, adoption of labour intensive industrial policy and approach, and so on. However, essentially they were all half-hearted measures.

The ruling Congress governments, both in the centre and the states, have made a facade of it and followed this lack-luster approach mainly because, unlike the Socialist Party, the Congress Party was not ideologically equipped or committed to vigorously pursue thc welfare state agenda. Indeed, they could not comprehend the dynamism of a welfare state system, nor could take a holistic view of it, and therefore took only some piece-meal superficial measures, ostensibly to help the poor people on matters like health care, education, and so on, and spent a small proportion of the budget for the purpose. Tokenism and expediency characterised their basic approach. In any case, the Congress Party has neither tried to make the welfare state as India's national vision, nor to build a political consensus around it. That was basically the position during the prime minister tenures of Jawaharlal Nehru and Indira Gandhi.

***Anti-Welfare State Measures of Dr. Manmohan Singh***

Whatever little initiatives Jawaharlal Nehru and Indira Gandhi had made to lead India towards the path of a welfare state; they have been systematically undone by the Indian votaries of liberalisation, privatisation and marketisation, like Dr. Manmohan Singh and his henchmen, stealthily during the last two decades. By continuously holding important backroom advisory positions in the Central government, or as a member of the Planning Commission, or as a Minister or Prime Minister, Manmohan Singh has deftly strained every nerve to hollow out the Indian state and to curtail its participation in the domain of public welfare.

He has made stealthy, and sometimes overt, moves to progressively get the public welfare responsibility of the state shifted out to the private market, and to get market principles applied in important sectors like health care, education, and so on. To hasten the process, the government hospitals have been systematically starved of funds, so that they are in bedlam, and appeared shabby, ill-equipped and understaffed, willfully to compel people to turn towards private hospitals for treatment, even at unaffordable costs. Similarly, the government schools and other educational institutions have also been systematically starved of funds, staff and equipment, to compel students and parents to increasingly seek admissions in private educational institutions, which take capitation fees or huge donations for admissions, or in the despicable new breed of extortionist self-financing educational institutions for education, even after loading themselves with huge sums of loans from banks. Education, which is a public good in a welfare state system, is being systematically transformed into a private good in India by Manmohan Singh and the Congress governments in the Centre and States. What ethical standards the products of such education shops would uphold when they occupy the seats of power in the country is anybody's guess. No doubt, such educational institutions are the breeding grounds of potentially unabashed corrupt persons of the country.

***Serving the Rich***

However, in pursuing the task of cutting down the welfare state responsibilities of the government, Manmohan Singh's determination has surpassed even the determination displayed by its progenitors like Margaret Thatcher and Ronald Reagan. Indeed, it appears that Manmohan Singh has become prime minister with a clandestine agenda to stealthily hollow out the Indian state, in as many areas of activities as possible, from within, and roll back the role of the state from the arena of public welfare, and transfer the task to market forces, and thereby to scuttle the establishment of a welfare state system in India in future. It requires a lot of brazen qualities for a person to willfully get into the government to undermine it from within, through all kinds of crafty methods—a blend of domestic measures, including executive decisions, and international agreements—which smacks tremendous intellectual dishonesty. However, there is no doubt that for a public service oriented welfare state system in India, people's best bet is a strong, democratic and resourceful Indian state that can effectively function both as the regulator and a provider.

But, unfortunately, that is what is being systematically hollowed out by Manmohan Singh at the behest of the IMF and the World Bank. He has shown contempt for Gandhiji's advice to the ministers which says: "Whenever you are in doubt or when the self becomes too much with you, apply the following test: Recall the face of the poorest and the weakest man whom you may have seen and ask yourself if the step you contemplate is going to be any use to him. Will he gain anything by it? Will it restore him to a control over his own life and destiny? Will it lead to Swaraj for the hungry and spiritually starving millions? Then you will find your doubts and your self-melting away". But what Manmohan Singh does is the opposite. Instead of recalling the face of the poorest man in the country, he recalls only the face of the sleazy richest man in the country, like Ambanis and others. The consequences of such a mind-set governing the country, will be disastrous for the poor people in India.

***Impact on the Poor People***

The poor people in India however, are increasingly denied even the slender welfare state support which the government has hitherto provided to them. Indeed, during the last two decades serious erosion of the welfare state content in India's public policies has been engineered by Manmohan Singh and his cronies in government. As a result, labour welfare, child welfare, education, healthcare, and so on, have become less and less a state responsibility.

Increasingly, the market forces and the private providers have been tightening their hold over the public welfare sector. If this process is not reversed soon, the Indian State will lose its centrality in organising and regulating public welfare for the benefit of the whole population. That will be detrimental to the poorer people, as they simply cannot afford to buy services from the unscrupulous private market.

***Value of the Centrality of the State***

Therefore, the centrality of the state in the provision of high quality welfare services to people, through public institutions, should be preserved and promoted at all costs. Its resource base should also be kept strong and sound. We have to remember the fact that richer the democratic state, better will be the living conditions of the poorer people, and vice versa. Therefore, it is imperative that the Indian state should be kept strong, resourceful and sovereign. Leaders who strive to undermine its resource base are not only anti-poor, but anti-welfare state as well, and, therefore, should be flushed out from the government.

***India Wasted 65 Years***

In terms of human development, India has wasted sixty-five years of its independence without developing a national welfare state vision. Of these 65 years, the Congress Party was in power in the centre for more than 50 years. Therefore, for the drift India has experienced all these years in this regard, the responsibility goes squarely to the Congress Party and its leaderships. However, it is high time that India too moves ahead with a national welfare state vision, and an agenda for a uniform elevation of the quality of life of all its inhabitants, based on principles of equality, justice and solidarity. According to Bhikhu Parikh, what India needs is a "social democratic state, not a neo-liberal state that we are bent on becoming, carefully monitored global integration, and close attention to the quality of life available to all our citizens, especially the poor. The state must guarantee basic welfare and education to all its citizens as of right, develop their capacities to take charge of their lives, give them a stake in country's development and legislate against their increasing exploitation and vulnerability". In brief, what Bhikhu Parikh prescribes is that India should become a welfare state.

***Elements of Indian Welfare State***

What should be the elements of an Indian welfare state? First India should adopt a full-employment policy and recognise the centrality of having a gainful job in a person's welfare. The state should be responsible for the maintenance of full employment, so that all socio-economic, financial and technology policies in India remain employment friendly. All employable persons should be provided with opportunities to produce something useful to society. Undoubtedly, a full employment policy and the drive for achieving it, holds the key to India's prosperity, greatness and social peace in the 21st century. In addition to a full-employment policy, India should adopt a steeply progressive income-tax system.

Such a tax system would not only ensure a steady flow of resources required for the upkeep of the welfare state system but also would reduce the income disparity between people, and between households, and promote egalitarianism and mutual respect in people's behaviour–a first sure step for the development of a new pacifist culture. It can free people from greed, exhibitionism and hyper-acquisitiveness, and eliminate corruption at various levels. Indeed, a welfare state system can significantly change people's perception, attitude, and behaviour pattern, and create a new, healthy and harmonious environment in India. It can also free the country from many divisive issues like demands for job reservations based on caste, community and economic considerations, which plague our political life and social harmony, and which vitiates people's attitudes towards fellow human beings. It will effectively destroy incentives to do crime and corruption and will promote peace and harmony in society, which is essential for building a new India, a new culture and a new civilisation befitting the spirit of this age. It will provide effective remedies, mainly through preventive measures, to many problems India is faced with today.

***Equality, Distributive Justice and Universalism***

India's welfare state system should be based on principles of equality and distributive justice. It should be directed towards ending of poverty and ushering in an egalitarian society. The approach should be universal and non-discriminatory, so that everybody becomes a contributor and a beneficiary of the system, which can also ensure the widest public support for it. Its broad framework should be human solidarity. All inhabitants in India should be entitled to social benefits as a matter of social right. The general objective should be to steadily level up the living standard of the lower strata of the society.

There should be special efforts to strengthen the public sector, especially in areas like finance, key and strategic industries, public services, and pharmaceuticals, and roll back the government's agenda of their privatisation. As public utilities are very much an integral part of the welfare state system, they should be totally delinked from the narrow profit motive. The cooperative sector should also be strengthened in a big way to effectively contain middlemen's exploitation in several sectors.

***Welfare State Should be India's National Vision***

India should make development of a welfare state system in the country as its national vision. But, as A.P.J. Abdul Kalam has said, having a national vision alone is not enough. We should strive to make the whole people of the country to share that vision, and work together for its realisation. As a preparatory to it, there should be a nationwide discussion regarding the long-term benefits of the welfare state system for the present and future generations. As already noted, politically, welfare state system is a democratic socialist design for the future. Ideally, its effective implementation needs a political party which has an abiding faith in it, and a deep commitment to do it. Obviously, past experiences show that the Congress Party does not have that required faith or commitment. Therefore, the best way to pursue this vision is through the re-establishment of a strong, and credible all-India Socialist/Social Democratic Party, by bringing together the like-minded people and political organisations sharing the same vision, to give leadership to the realisation of this vision, as done in Sweden and other Scandinavian countries. In India today, most of the major political parties are functioning as entities engaged mainly in playing various tricks to hoodwink the masses and perch on to the seats of power.

Clearly, they are not driven by any national vision, whatsoever, to enhance the quality of life of the whole population. Therefore, the way forward is to make the construction of a welfare state system as India's national vision, and build up consensus and political alliances for its realisation in the coming decades. It is an attainable goal even for a big democracy like India. What is required is the political will, which can be built up by conscious efforts.

# Index

## C

## D

## E



## F



## G

## H



## I

## O



## P

## Q



## R

## S